This long-awaited book by Mwita Akiri is a triumph of interdisciplinary scholarship. Making use of cultural studies, history, ethnography, and sometimes theology, he reaches some important and illuminating conclusions. For instance, the tensions between mission Christianity and the African cultural heritage could sometimes be creative and enriching, but were often far otherwise. African church workers gave surprisingly effective and influential leadership, but it usually fell below the radar of colonial mission societies (and most historians). And the colonial administrations – first German, then British – had a decidedly double-edged impact on Christian churches and schools. In his very thorough research, not only has Dr Akiri worked through the manuscript record and historical publications, but he has also interviewed dozens of men and women who participated in this history or had significant knowledge to share. This book has implications far beyond central Tanganyika before 1933, for it can be read as a particularly telling case study of the mutual impact of foreign missions and indigenous cultures worldwide.

Alan L. Hayes, PhD
Bishops Frederick and Heber Wilkinson Professor of the History of Christianity,
Wycliffe College, University of Toronto, Canada

Mwita Akiri is to be highly commended for this book which is likely to prove indispensable in any historical review and understanding of the period under its purview in the establishment of the church in central Tanganyika. Whereas previous texts have focused almost exclusively on the role played by foreign agents and Western missionaries in Eastern Africa and in Africa generally, Bishop Akiri seeks to explore the inarguably pivotal and central roles played by indigenous agents of Christian mission in Ugogo and Ukaguru. This book is based and grounded on oral and hitherto untapped primary sources to provide a rich and fresh understanding of the roots and spread of the present church in this area.

Mwita Akiri's work is well written, persuasive and cogently argued. It immerses the reader in the world of the Gogo and Kaguru of Central Tanganyika in the second half of the nineteenth century, exploring their social worlds, culture and religions during this pre-Christian period and laying the ground for understanding the world that the pioneer missionaries encountered and sought to evangelize. It also discusses the threat of Islam which in a sense predated Christianity in the area.

Bishop Mwita Akiri knows this story well and tells it in a lively and convincing manner. His many years of work and residence in Dodoma, Central Tanzania, located in the heart of Ugogo and Ukaguru homelands, undoubtedly contributed to his deep understanding of this bygone era and space, and his sound reinterpretation and lively retelling of this rich and complex story. It will no doubt prove to be a rich resource for all interested in this story. I fully commend it. This work is a joy to read.

Aloo Osotsi Mojola, PhD
Professor, St Paul's University, Limuru, Kenya
Honorary Professor, Faculty of Theology,
Pretoria University, Pretoria, South Africa

In the Church Missionary Society histories of Anglican mission in Tanzania, little space has been given to the initiatives, contributions and experiences of indigenous teachers. Rather the spotlight was cast on the western missionaries who made great sacrifices in service to God.

This socio-historical study seeks to redress that bias in mission historiography. Written from an Afro-centric rather than Western-centric tradition, it sheds much-needed light on the indispensable role of the indigenous agents during the early mission years, 1876–1933.

This work is also more than a historical analysis. Weaknesses in the CMS mission model, namely irrelevant and non-contextual leadership training, and a legalism devoid of connection to African culture, has continuing relevance for the Anglican Church of Tanzania today and its struggles with nominalism. History is a great teacher and there are strong and abiding lessons to be learned from this study for the ongoing ministry of CMS in Africa.

Rev Canon Peter Rodgers
International Director/CEO,
Church Missionary Society, Australia

Africa is, in numerical terms, now the most Christian continent on the globe. But the African church is still wrestling with the question of what it means to be at the same time authentically African and authentically Christian. Mwita Akiri's valuable in-depth study of the early years of the Anglican Church in Ugogo and Ukaguru (central Tanzania) reveals the problems left by misconceived missionary strategies of Christian education, but also the crucial role played by indigenous Christians – both male teachers and "Bible women" – in the shaping of modern Tanzanian Anglicanism.

Brian Stanley, PhD
Professor of World Christianity,
Director of the Centre for the Study of World Christianity,
University of Edinburgh, UK

Christianity in Central Tanzania

A Story of African Encounters and Initiatives in Ugogo and Ukaguru, 1876–1933

Mwita Akiri

ACADEMIC

© 2020 Mwita Akiri

Published 2020 by Langham Academic (Previously Langham Monographs)
An imprint of Langham Publishing
www.langhampublishing.org

Langham Publishing and its imprints are a ministry of Langham Partnership

Langham Partnership
PO Box 296, Carlisle, Cumbria, CA3 9WZ, UK
www.langham.org

ISBNs:
978-1-78368-778-7 Print
978-1-78368-802-9 ePub
978-1-78368-804-3 PDF

Mwita Akiri has asserted his right under the Copyright, Designs and Patents Act, 1988 to be identified as the Author of this work.

All rights reserved. No part of this publication may be reproduced, stored in a retrieval system or transmitted, in any form or by any means, electronic, mechanical, photocopying, recording or otherwise, without the prior written permission of the publisher or the Copyright Licensing Agency.

Requests to reuse content from Langham Publishing are processed through PLSclear. Please visit www.plsclear.com to complete your request.

Scripture quotations are from Revised Standard Version of the Bible, copyright © 1946, 1952, and 1971 National Council of the Churches of Christ in the United States of America. Used by permission. All rights reserved.

British Library Cataloguing-in-Publication Data
A catalogue record for this book is available from the British Library

ISBN: 978-1-78368-778-7

Cover & Book Design: projectluz.com

Langham Partnership actively supports theological dialogue and an author's right to publish but does not necessarily endorse the views and opinions set forth here or in works referenced within this publication, nor can we guarantee technical and grammatical correctness. Langham Partnership does not accept any responsibility or liability to persons or property as a consequence of the reading, use or interpretation of its published content.

To my parents,
Tata Edward Mwita Akiri and Mayo Silibia Mugure Akiri,
and my oral informants in Ugogo and Ukaguru.

Contents

Acknowledgements xv

Abstract xix

Abbreviations xxi

Notes on Names and Terminology xxiii
    Names xxiii
    Terminology xxv

Chapter 1 1
  Nature of Study, Scope, and Research Methodology
    1.1 Nature of Study 1
        1.1.1 Purpose 1
        1.1.2 Relation to Other Studies 2
        1.1.3 Significance 3
    1.2 Scope 4
        1.2.1 Date 4
        1.2.2 Geographical Area 5
        1.2.3 Omissions 6
    1.3 Research Methodology 7
        1.3.1 Method of Analysis and Presentation 7
        1.3.2 Methods of Data Collection 9
    1.4 A Complementary Role of Data Sources 20

Chapter 2 21
  Gogo and Kaguru Societies in the Late Ninteenth Century
    2.1 Geography of Ugogo and Ukaguru 22
        2.1.1 The Geography of Ugogo 22
        2.1.2 The Geography of Ukaguru 22
    2.2 The Formation of the Gogo and Kaguru Societies 23
    2.3 Political Organization 25
        2.3.1 Gogo Political System 25
        2.3.2 Kaguru Political System 28
    2.4 Social Structure 30
        2.4.1 Gogo Social Structure 30
        2.4.2 Kaguru Social Structure 31
    2.5 Aspects of Gogo and Kaguru Social Customs 31
        2.5.1 Circumcision and Puberty Rites 32

  2.5.2 Marriage 35
  2.5.3 Dance..38
 2.6 Aspects of Gogo and Kaguru Religions 39
  2.6.1 Aspects of Gogo Religion...40
  2.6.2 Aspects of Kaguru Religion..43
 2.7 Conclusion 45

Chapter 3 47
Christian Developments in Ugogo and Ukaguru 1876–1900
 3.1 King Mutesa of Buganda and Henry Stanley 47
 3.2 Mpwapwa: A Place of Significance 52
 3.3 Mpwapwa, Chamuhawi, and Mamboya: The Survivors 53
  3.3.1 Some Local Challenges to a Christian Cause 54
  3.3.2 First Baptisms at Mpwapwa and Chamuhawi 58
  3.3.3 Oral Tradition and Stagnation at Mpwapwa 59
  3.3.4 Missionary Methods: A Key to Success at Chamuhawi 59
  3.3.5 The Beginnings at Mamboya 64
  3.3.6 First Baptisms at Mamboya Hill Church............................66
  3.3.7 Difficulties of Communicating the Christian Message 67
  3.3.8 The Valley Church and Its First Fruits................................69
  3.3.9 The Dawn of the "Official" German Colonial
    Administration 69
 3.4 The End of Self-Preservation and the Birth of an Expansion Era ..71
 3.5 Conclusion 76

Chapter 4 77
The Initiatives of the Gogo and Kaguru Chiefs
 4.1 Chiefs as Indigenous Agents...78
 4.2 Chiefs and the Establishment of Mission Stations...................80
 4.3 Chiefs, Buildings and Literacy Classes..................................84
 4.4 Chiefs and German Colonial Education Policy 88
 4.5 The "Threat" of Islam...91
 4.6 Standing by the "Fence": Chiefs and Conversion 96
 4.7 Conclusion 100

Chapter 5 103
Educational Contributions of Indigenous Teachers
 5.1 Literacy Training as a Missionary Method..........................104
 5.2 The Out-School as Chief Agencies for Evangelization 105
 5.3 The Medium of Instruction in the German Colonial Era 109
 5.4 Teaching Methods at the Out-Schools 111
  5.4.1 The Cloth Sheet and *Ikangambwa*...................................111

    5.4.2 Traditional and "Modern" Songs..113
  5.5 Missionary Focus on Children 115
    5.5.1 Reasons for the Focus 115
    5.5.2 African Conversion and Motives of Child Converts..........118
  5.6 Competition with Roman Catholic Missions................................125
  5.7 African Conversion and Motives of Adult Converts 133
    5.7.1 Protection from Cruelty...134
    5.7.2 Employment Opportunities...137
    5.7.3 The Influence of Indigenous Teachers over
          Tax Collectors..137
  5.8 The Catechetical Process 139
    5.8.1 Categories of Baptism Candidates 139
    5.8.2 Duration of Instruction before Baptism.........................140
    5.8.3 Public Admission to the Catechumenate Status 141
    5.8.4 Catechumens and Pre-Christian Past 142
    5.8.5 The "Policing" of the Baptism Candidates 149
    5.8.6 The Inadequacy of the Catechesis 151
    5.8.7 The CMS Mission and Traditional Practices 157
    5.8.8 Female Circumcision: A Lost Battle? 161
  5.9 Conclusion 168

Chapter 6 171
Missionary Contributions of Indigenous Teachers
  6.1 The Nature of Appointments and Contributions 172
    6.1.1 The Appointment of the Indigenous Staff.....................172
    6.1.2 Indigenous Teachers as Pioneer Missionaries..................175
    6.1.3 Teachers' Wives as Co-Pioneers.......................................182
    6.1.4 The Contribution of Bible women 185
    6.1.5 Indigenous Teachers as Mission Strategists.....................187
    6.1.6 Indigenous Teachers as Local Church Leaders................191
  6.2 Biographical Notes of Some Indigenous Teachers and
      Missionaries 193
    6.2.1 Damari Sagatwa: "A Maidservant of God" 194
    6.2.2 Andrea Mwaka: A Trusted Leader and a Great Pastor....196
    6.2.3 Danieli Mbogo: Musician and Reliable Companion 204
    6.2.4 Yohana Malecela: A Rainmaker Turned Pioneer
          Missionary..209
    6.2.5 Andrea Lungwa: "One of the Very Best"..........................214
    6.2.6 Haruni Mbega: A Man of Principle 215
    6.2.7 Daudi Muhando: Writer, Preacher, and Pastor...............219

  6.2.8 Yeremia Senyagwa: "A Man with Insight into
    Scripture" 222
 6.3 Indigenous Initiatives During the First World War..............227
  6.3.1 Disruption in Ukaguru..229
  6.3.2 Wartime Indigenous Contributions in Ukaguru 230
  6.3.3 Disruptions in Ugogo 231
  6.3.4 Wartime Indigenous Contributions in Ugogo..................235
  6.3.5 Wartime Experiences of the Wives of the Indigenous
    Teachers 238
 6.4 Conclusion 241

Chapter 7 243
Secularization of Mission Education and Its Impact
 7.1 Background of the Philosophy of Adaptation 244
  7.1.1 The Phelps Stokes commissions 244
  7.1.2 British Government Policy on Education in Africa 246
  7.1.3 Le Zoute Conference and Adaptation 248
 7.2 British Educational Policy in Tanzania 252
  7.2.1 Educational Policy 1919–1924 252
  7.2.2 Educational Policy 1925 Onwards 253
  7.2.3 A Re-definition of the Role of Out-Schools and
    Indigenous Teachers 254
 7.3 Government Educational Policy: Conflicting Responses 259
  7.3.1 Frustrations of Missions...259
  7.3.2 Language Debate and Adaptation 266
  7.3.3 "Eagles Not Chickens": Aspirations of Indigenous
    Teachers...270
  7.3.4 Socioeconomic Benefits for Indigenous Teachers.............275
 7.4 Conclusion 282

Chapter 8 285
The Training and Development of Indigenous Teachers
 8.1 In-service Semi-residential Training...287
  8.1.1 The Nature of Weekly Courses...287
  8.1.2 Syllabus and Course Contents 288
  8.1.3 Some Weaknesses of In-service Semi-residential
    Training 291
 8.2 Residential Training 301
  8.2.1 Justification for the Need 301
  8.2.2 Lack of Resources, CMS Missionaries and
    Indigenous Spirit 303

8.2.3 Obstacles to Overseas Training 308
8.2.4 Ecumenical Possibilities 310
8.2.5 Kongwa Teachers' College 311
8.3 Women's Training 312
8.4 Ordination as a "Climax" of Leadership Development 314
    8.4.1 Earliest Prospect of Ordination of Africans 314
    8.4.2 The Duration of Testing Time 316
8.5 A Delayed Ordained Ministry: Some Factors 318
    8.5.1 Poor Educational Standards among Teachers 318
    8.5.2 The Threat of Withdrawal 321
8.6 A New Era for Indigenous Leadership Development? 326
8.7 Conclusion 329

Chapter 9 331
General Conclusion
9.1 Aims of Study and Chapters Revisited 331
9.2 Relevance for Mission of the Anglican Church of Tanzania 333
    9.2.1 Toward a Revised Catechesis and Catechism 333
    9.2.2 Some Modern Dangers of Post-Mission Christianity 336
9.3 Toward a Dialogue with African Traditional Heritage 338
9.4 The Study of Christianity in the Non-Western World 343
    9.4.1 Mission Christianity and African Culture in History 343
    9.4.2 Use of Archival and Oral Sources 346

Appendix 1 351
Dealing with CMS Statistics: Some Problems

Appendix 2 355
The CMS Mission and the Maji Maji Uprising

Appendix 3 359
Photographs of Some Indigenous Agents

Appendix 4 381
Maps

CMS Glossary 387

Bibliography 389
    Primary Sources 389
    Published Sources 391
    Oral (Personal) Interviews 406

List of Photographs

Photograph 1: The First Students of Kongwa College, 1914 359

Photograph 2: Andrea Mwakamubi Makanyaga, c. 1907 – First Pastor of Ugogo 360

Photograph 3: Mama Damari Sagatwa, c. 1960 – Bible Woman and Missionary 363

Photograph 4: Mama Mariamu Malogo, c. 1909 – One of the First Bible Women in Ugogo" 365

Photograph 5: Danieli Mbogo, c. 1909 – Musician and Reliable Companion" 366

Photograph 6: Madari Mulutu, c. 1910 – Bible Translator" 367

Photograph 7: Paulo Chidinda, c. 1911 – Quasi-pastor at Handali 368

Photograph 8: The First Indigenous Clergy – In Ugogo and Ukaguru 370

Photograph 9: Chief Mazengo Chalula – Paramount Chief of UgogoUgogo .. 371

List of Maps

Map 1: Location of Tanzania in Africa 381

Map 2: Caravan Routes Passing Through Central Tanzania (19th Century) ... 382

Map 3: CMS Mission Sphere 383

Map 4: Districts of the CMS Mission in Ugogo and Ukaguru (1913) 384

Map 5: Dioceses of the Anglican Church of Tanzania (1999) – Former CMS and UMCA Spheres 385

Acknowledgements

Several individuals and organizations have contributed to the successful completion of this study. The fact that I cannot list them all here does not mean lack of appreciation or recognition for the part they have played. I am grateful to my British sponsors: the Langham Trust, who took a larger share of responsibility for my studies; Crosslinks, who made significant financial contribution through Langham and also paid maintenance costs for my family during my field research in Tanzania; and All Saints Educational Trust for paying almost half my fees direct to the University of Edinburgh for three years.

My field research in Tanzania in 1997 was made possible through funding from the Research Enablement Program, a grant program for scholarship supported by The Pew Charitable Trusts, Philadelphia, Pennsylvania, USA, and administered by the Overseas Ministries Study Center, New Haven, Connecticut, USA. I should also thank the distinguished members of the Review and Selection Committee of the Research Enablement Program: Dr Gerald H. Anderson (Director of Overseas Ministries Study Center, USA), Professor Daniel H. Bays (University of Kansas, USA), Professor Robert Eric Frykenberg (University of Wisconsin, USA), Professor Paul G. Hiebert (Trinity International University, formerly Trinity Evangelical Divinity School, USA), Professor José Míguez Bonino (Instituto Superior Evangélico de Estudios Teológicos, Argentina), Mary Motte (Mission Resource Center, RI, USA), Professor Dana Robert (Boston University, USA), John S. Pobee (WCC, now bishop in Ghana), and the late Professor David A. Kerr (University of Edinburgh, UK). I thank them for counting my research worthy of such a highly acclaimed and competitive international award.

I benefited greatly from the constructive criticism and guidance from some of them who were assigned to my consultation group during the 1998 Colloquium Program in Nashville, USA – namely, Professor Bays, Professor

Frykenberg, and Professor Robert. I also thank another consultant assigned to my group, Professor Richard H. Elphick of Wesleyan University, USA, who took special interest in my research topic and gave valuable suggestions. The advice from Professor J. F. Ade Ajayi (University of Ibadan, Nigeria), Professor Andrew Walls (University of Edinburgh), and Dr Kevin Ward (University of Leeds, UK), who also attended the colloquium, was valuable and stimulating.

Yet this study would not have taken shape had it not been for the sustained guidance, criticism, and encouragement from my supervisor, the late Dr T. Jack Thompson, at the University of Edinburgh, to whom I am very grateful. I am also indebted to my fellow research students for their helpful criticisms of my work during the departmental "Work-in-Progress" seminars. I appreciated greatly the continued support I received from the staff at the Centre for Study of Christianity in the Non-Western World – Anne Fernon, Margaret Acton, and Elizabeth Leitch. I also valued the assistance I received from other members of the university staff, particularly the computing staff at the Faculty of Divinity and the Divinity Support Team at the main library. I should also mention Marie Cope, the lab supervisor at the Graphics Department, JCMB, Kings Buildings, and members of her team, for enhancing the quality of the photocopies of maps and photographs I had. Also, I would like to thank archivists at the Special Collections, (Birmingham University Library), Rhodes House Library (Oxford University), and Lambeth Palace Library (London) for the assistance I received during my visits to their libraries. The assistance received from the late Professor Josiah Mlahagwa and the librarian at the East African Collection, both at the University of Dar es Salaam, Tanzania, was greatly appreciated during my field research.

I wish to thank my colleague, Professor Thomas Power – Wycliffe College Adjunct Professor of Church History and Theological Librarian at the University of Toronto – for his valuable assistance with locating page numbers of some of the material in the bibliography that were not in my possession.

There are many outside the academic sphere that have supported and encouraged my family and I throughout our time in Scotland. I can only name a few. Our next-door neighbours at Portobello, Eva and Ian Brown, are some of the best friends we made in Scotland. The friendship of our landlords – James and Joyce Martin (Milton Road West), Marie Mackay (Musselburgh), and Stanley and Effie Warburton (Joppa, Portobello) – was valuable. In England,

Acknowledgements

I am grateful to members of St Hellen's, Grindleford (Sheffield), especially Christine Peake and her late husband Dr Harry Peake; Conniston Avenue Housegroup at Christ Church, Moldgreen (Huddersfield); and the Friends of the Clergy Corporation for their prayerful and practical support.

In Tanzania, I owe gratitude to Rt Rev Hilkiah Omindo Deya, former Bishop of the Anglican Diocese of Mara, and all Christians there for their prayerful support during my time in Britain. I am also grateful to the late Rt Rev Godfrey Mdimi Mhogolo, former Bishop of the Diocese of Central Tanganyika; Rt Rev Dr Simon Chiwanga, former Bishop of Mpwapwa; Rt Rev Dudley Mageni, former Bishop of Morogoro; and their staff, for the support I received during my field research in those dioceses. I should particularly thank Hon John S. Malecela (former Prime Minister of Tanzania). He made effort to arrange an interview with Canon Stephano D. Malecela in Dodoma and lent me a framed photograph of the first students of Kongwa college, including his own grandfather, the late Yohana Malecela.

Many family members and personal friends have supported us. But no one took more responsibility to manage my affairs, our house, and many important things during a long absence than my sister Philligona (Mama Nyamanche) and her husband, Hon Kisyeri Chambiri. I am grateful to them. It is a custom that one's own family is saluted last, but not least. No one has daily supported my work as faithfully – or would have coped as well throughout my time in Edinburgh – as my wife Mukami. No words would convey adequately my gratitude to her, and in a way, this study is hers as much as it is mine. I should thank my daughter, Mugure, too. On several occasions, she spotted something she knew I intended to take with me to college (for example, my lunch box) and brought it to me before I left home or as I reached the door on my way out. To all I have named, and those I haven't, I say *asante* (Kiswahili for "thank you").

Abstract

This study explores and assesses the initiatives and contributions of indigenous agents (men and women, converts and non-converts) in the growth of mission Christianity in Ugogo and Ukaguru, central Tanzania. To some extent, it is also an attempt to rewrite the story of the work of the Church Missionary Society (CMS) mission in that region. The thesis argues that like other missions in Africa in the nineteenth and early twentieth centuries, the CMS mission adopted strategies of Christianization mainly through literacy training, and preaching as well. The active involvement of the indigenous agents was indispensable to this process. The fact that their role has been largely ignored in the standard literature relating to the work of the CMS mission in Ugogo and Ukaguru exposes a bias in mission historiography. To redress this omission, this research explores and evaluates the actual contributions and experiences of indigenous agents in the growth of Christianity in Ugogo and Ukaguru.

The study uses a sociohistorical method and takes into account the context in which Christianity grew. It therefore considers the challenges posed by the resilience of the traditional Gogo and Kaguru social and religious practices to mission Christianity. The dynamics of operating under the German and British colonial governments; and the impact of the competition with Islam, and the Benedictine Roman Catholic mission upon the growth process are explored. A thematic presentation of the material begins with an analysis of some aspects of political, social, and religious life of the Wagogo and Wakaguru before and at the time of the arrival of the CMS mission. Aspects considered are those that the CMS mission regarded as controversial as mission work progressed. The initial work of the CMS from 1876 to 1900 is explored and assessed in the next chapter. It is argued that little growth took place in this first phase, yet, African initiatives and contributions began to emerge in this period.

The chapter that follows examines and assesses the contribution of the chiefs. It argues that though most of them maintained loyalty to their traditional political, social, and religious obligations, their initiatives were indispensable to the establishment of literacy and preaching centres nonetheless. With that foundation in place for the period 1900 onwards, the next chapter explores and evaluates the contribution of the indigenous teachers in the educational and catechetical front. Some factors that motivated the Wagogo and Wakaguru to associate themselves with mission Christianity are examined here. The next chapter analyses missionary contributions and initiatives other than educational work. Biographical notes of some of the teachers and indigenous missionaries are given. The notes incorporate the unique contributions of the individual teachers and missionaries concerned. The chapter concludes with an analysis of the impact of the First World War upon the indigenous contributions, as well as the experiences of the teachers and their wives during the war.

The introduction of the philosophy of adaptation during the early period of the British colonial government is examined in the next chapter. This chapter explores and evaluates the reinterpretation, if not the shake-up (through the philosophy of adaptation), of the traditional mission education in Tanzania and its implications for the role of the indigenous teachers. It suggests that the philosophy of adaptation was somehow a verdict on the suitability of the indigenous teachers as providers of education in schools beyond literacy training and catechesis. Yet, on the other hand, it brought new socioeconomic prospects for teachers. One of the impacts of the philosophy was the implicit creation of two categories of teachers – the secular mission teacher and the traditional teacher-catechist. The growth of Christianity depended more on the latter. Therefore, the chapter that follows examines and evaluates the nature of the training of the indigenous teachers, and their development as leaders in Ugogo and Ukaguru up to 1933.

The study concludes with a reflection on the implication of its findings for mission and mission historiography in the non-Western world, and for the understanding of the relationship of mission Christianity and African culture and worldviews.

Abbreviations

ACNE	Advisory Committee for Native Education (Tanganyika)
ACNETA	Advisory Committee on Native Education in Tropical Africa
ARCCMS	Annual Report of the Committee of CMS
BUL	Birmingham University Library
CC	Church Council of the Tanganyika Mission
CCC	Central Church Council
CMI	*Church Missionary Intelligencer*
CMIR	*Church Missionary Intelligencer and Record*
CMR	*Church Missionary Review*
CMS	Church Missionary Society (later Church Mission Society)
CMWM	Conference of Missionaries of the Western Mission
CSSH	Comparative Studies in Society and History
CTDL	*The Central Tanganyika Diocesan Letter*
CUP	Cambridge University Press
DC	Diocesan Council of the Diocese of Central Tanganyika
DCT	Diocese of Central Tanganyika
EC	Executive Committee of the CMS Mission
HGF	Holy Ghost Fathers
IMC	International Missionary Council
IRM	*International Review of Missions*
LPL	Lambeth Palace Library
MH	Mackay House Archives (Diocese of Central Tanganyika)
NEO	Native Education Ordinance
NLS	National Library of Scotland
OPDZ	Official Papers of the Diocese of Zanzibar

PCMS	*Proceedings of the Church Missionary Society for Africa and the East*
RC	Roman Catholic
RHL	Rhodes House Library
RUUM	Report/Review of the Usagara-Ugogo Mission/Ukaguru-Ugogo Mission
SCM	Student Christian Movement
SOAS	School of Oriental and African Studies
TNR	Tanganyika Notes and Records (later Tanzania Notes and Records)
UMCA	Universities' Mission to Central Africa
WCC	World Council of Churches
WMC	World Missionary Conference

Notes on Names and Terminology

Names

Names for Places
In this study, where possible, preference has been given to what might be referred to as "post-colonial" place names as they appear in most modern maps of Tanzania and Africa. Thus, the name "Tanzania" (which came into being in 1964 after the union of Tanganyika and Zanzibar and the Pemba isles) is used, and not "German East Africa" or "Tanganyika." The exception to this rule is when quoting from both archival and printed sources or when a colonial name is in use to-date.

In light of this, throughout this study, the place formerly known as Kisokwe (variant Kissokwe) is referred to by its modern name – Chamuhawi. Also, it should be noted that the Kigogo vernacular spelling of Mhamvwa was changed to "Mpapua" by the German authorities in 1903. It appeared that, for some reason, though the indigenous name disappeared (except when used occasionally in vernacular speech today), the name introduced by the Germans did not become popular either. The place is identified in modern Tanzanian maps as Mpwapwa, and it is this name that is used in the study.

The case of Ibwijili is the opposite. In 1903, the Germans changed the indigenous name "Ibwijili" to "Buigiri." For some reason, it is the latter that has been adopted by the local people and is spelled thus in this study. A note should also be made regarding Kigogo or Kikaguru vernacular words and names that have been italicized and defined, either immediately after the word in the text, or in the footnote. Whenever possible, the consonant "k" has been preferred to "ch" or "c" to reflect the modern usage. For example, Chigogo becomes Kigogo and Chisambo becomes "Kisambo." Also, with the exception of names printed on maps, where a place name has been preceded by a vowel – e.g. "i" – the vowel has been dropped to reflect modern pronunciation. For example, Gingi and Bokwa are used instead of Igingi and Ibokwa, respectively.

Names for People

Effort has been made to identify all teachers or chiefs by both their first and surnames. However, this has not been possible for all persons mentioned in the study – particularly Tanzanians, but occasionally, foreigners as well. In many cases, only single names of the indigenous agents appear in the CMS archives. Where the same first name is used to identify more than one person, confusion has been avoided either by noting the date of recruitment, or if possible, the location of recruitment, either Ugogo or Ukaguru. The problem of single names is found in oral data too. Some oral informants referred to the people they mentioned – for example, former colleagues at mission schools or churches – by a single name only. Apart from time gaps and loss of memory, another reason for this is that both teachers, pupil-teachers, and pupils went to school or out-schools from widely scattered villages. Remembering names more than six decades after leaving school has not been easy for many older informants.

Use of the Name "CMS Mission"

To avoid confusion, the name "CMS mission" shall be used throughout this study, except when quoting a source that called it by a different name. The reason for this is that the CMS mission in central Tanzania was identified by so many names at different stages of its development that it would be impossible to keep consistency. First, it was without a name, for it was covered under the Nyanza mission. A list of CMS archives at Birmingham University suggests that the name "Usagara mission" came into use in 1900. Yet, as early as the 1880s, the Tanzania section in the CMS periodicals and annual reports was headed "Usagara Mission."[1] During much of the 1880s, however, the name "Usagara and Unyamwezi" was used, with "Usagara and Usukuma" being used more often in the 1890s, until 1898 when the use of "Usagara

---

1. See *CMIR* 6 (September 1881): 554; *PCMS*, 1889, 46.

mission" became more permanent. This was used until 1903 to reflect the region (central Tanzania), which was then misunderstood to be "Usagara."

In 1904, the name "Usagara-Ugogo mission," or "Usagara and Ugogo" came into being to reflect the presence of the mission both in Ukaguru and Ugogo. This name was used interchangeably with "Ukaguru-Ugogo mission." It is also suggested that the name "German East Africa mission" came into use in 1911, but CMS annual reports were already using it even as early as 1908.[2] The use of the latest name – "Tanganyika mission" – started at the beginning of the British occupation of Tanzania in 1919, after which the Diocese of Central Tanganyika (DCT) was created in 1927. As may be seen, it is therefore better to use a single name, "the CMS mission," to maintain consistency.

Terminology

CMS Missionaries

The phrase "CMS missionaries" is used in this study, instead of "British missionaries" or "European missionaries," for two main reasons. First, the CMS often recruited some of its personnel from other countries and continents. Some recruits for East Africa came from Germany (for example, Ludwig Krapf, John Rebmann, and Jacob Erhardt). Those who served in Ugogo and Ukaguru are of interest here, and only some may be named. There was Charles Stokes and Elizabeth Forsythe from the Republic of Ireland (though, of course, before 1922 that part of Ireland was still under the United Kingdom). Others were from Canada and Australia. The Canadians were Thomas Buchanan Reginald Westgate, whose name often appears in documents as "T. B. R. Westgate," and one Mr Crawford. Australians who were recruited before the take-over by the Australian CMS in 1927 include Ernest Doulton (1894), Katie Miller (1905), Effie Jackson (1909), Emily Good (later Mrs Emily Ernest Doulton, 1912), Elsie Veal (1918), Amy Gelding (1919), and Annie Barling (later Mrs Annie John Briggs, 1919). However, it will be noted that the word "European" appears in the oral interview excerpts. Most informants used the Kiswahili term *mzungu* in their narratives, by which they meant a "European" as opposed to an "African."

---

2. See *PCMS*, 1909, 56.

The second reason why the term "CMS missionaries" is preferred is that it distinguishes foreign missionaries from indigenous Tanzanian missionaries. It is interesting to note that the CMS annual financial statistical tables, dating as far back as the nineteenth century, distinguished between "European Agency" and "Native Missionaries."

Indigenous Missionaries and Indigenous Teachers

Despite the distinction made between foreign and indigenous missionaries, two cautionary notes are necessary. First, while technically all foreign personnel were missionaries involved in cross-cultural mission, only a number of indigenous personnel in Ugogo and Ukaguru fell into that category and spent part or all of their career serving among people of ethnic groups other than their own. Second, these two broad categories – "indigenous teachers" and "indigenous missionaries" are not mutually exclusive. The term teachers or indigenous teachers is used to refer to both those whose primary responsibility was in preaching and teaching converts (catechists) and school teachers, whose main task was to teach children in the classrooms. The distinction of these roles became more obvious perhaps after the First World War. However, it must be stressed that even after the war, the CMS mission still expected school teachers (even those employed in government schools) to be involved in religious instruction. That is why, in this study, the term "indigenous teacher" is preferred to "catechist" or "evangelist."

CHAPTER 1

Nature of Study, Scope, and Research Methodology

1.1 Nature of Study

1.1.1 Purpose

This study explores and assesses the initiatives and contributions of the indigenous agents (both men and women, converts and non-converts) in the growth of mission Christianity in Ugogo and Ukaguru, central Tanzania, in what was the Church Missionary Society (CMS) sphere, from 1876 to 1933. In other words, it is an attempt to look at the topic from an Afro-centric, rather than the traditional Euro-centric, perspective. The study argues that, like other missions throughout Africa during the nineteenth century, and much of the twentieth century, the CMS mission adopted strategies of Christianization through literacy training in schools. Such a Christianization programme was carried out mainly through the so-called "bush" schools, but to some extent, through preaching too. It follows that the active involvement of indigenous agents was indispensable to this process. The fact that their role has been largely ignored in the standard literature is a methodological omission that exposes a bias in much mission historiography, whether by Western or African scholars. To redress the consequent omission in existing scholarship, this research explores the actual indigenous contributions and experiences in the growth of Christianity in Ugogo and Ukaguru, central Tanzania.

1.1.2 Relation to Other Studies

CMS institutional histories pay no attention to the initiatives, contributions, and experiences of indigenous agents. Indeed, in most of them, the CMS mission in Ugogo and Ukaguru gets very little space. Such studies include those by Eugene Stock,[1] Gordon Hewitt,[2] and Keith Cole.[3] Studies that focus primarily on Ugogo and Ukaguru include those by George Chambers,[4] Nancy de Sibtain, and Elisabeth Knox.[5] Unlike Chambers and Sibtain, Knox's *Signal on the Mountain: The Gospel in Africa's Uplands before the First World War* mentions the names of some indigenous agents, and at times, their roles, and is sometimes critical of the way the parent society handled its mission in Ugogo and Ukaguru.[6] However, the book focuses mainly on the life and the work of CMS missionaries.[7] Furthermore, it covers the period up to 1914 only. Carl-Erik Sahlberg's book, *From Krapf to Rugambwa – A Church History of Tanzania*, mentions (but only sporadically) Christian developments in all major denominations with historic links with missions and other groups such as Pentecostal churches. Sahlberg mentions some leading indigenous leaders. However, if his book has any priority, it is largely to document the activities of Western missionaries.

The anthropologist Thomas Beidelman is an author who has published extensively, either in relation to the CMS mission in Ugogo and Ukaguru or on the Kaguru as a people. One of his well-known books on central Tanzania is *Colonial Evangelism: A Social Historical Study of an East African Mission at the Grassroots*. In this book (as well as in other smaller works),[8] the author views missions as an extension of colonial domination of one people by another through a set of alien values, which, in his view, were nonetheless full

---

1. Stock, *History*, 4:77–80.
2. Hewitt, *Problems of Success*, 1:174–204.
3. Cole, *History of the Church*, 52–92.
4. Chambers, *Tanganyika's New Day*.
5. Sibtain, *Dare to Look Up*.
6. Knox, *Signal on the Mountain*, 149–154, 199.
7. This is indicated also in the design of the chapters, most of which begin with the story of the activity of a Westerner. See, for example, chapters 1, 2, 3, 4, 10, 11, 12, 13. Roland Oliver's work *The Missionary Factor in East Africa* is not particularly about the CMS mission in central Tanzania but has a similar perspective.
8. See, for example, Beidelman, "Social Theory," 235–249; Beidelman, "Contradiction," 73–95.

of contradictions. In light of this, Beidelman regards the contributions of indigenous teachers as a burden placed on their shoulders by their mission "rulers." The case is obviously overstated, and as some reviewers have noted, his methodology and understanding of the CMS mission and its work is rather misguided.[9]

Outside central Tanzania, there are a number of useful studies that focus, either substantially or in part, on the indigenous initiatives and contributions in East and Central Africa. Some of the best-known works in this category are as follows. Aylward Shorter and Eugene Kataza's *Missionaries to Yourselves: African Catechists Today* (1972) focuses on the role of the catechists in the Catholic church in East and Central Africa. Louise Pirouet's *Black Evangelists: The Spread of Christianity in Uganda 1891–1914* (1978) explores, substantially, Catholic and Anglican indigenous contributions in Uganda. Tom Tuma's *Building a Ugandan Church: African Participation in Church Growth and Expansion in Busoga 1891–1940* (1980) focuses on the CMS mission sphere in Busoga. John Karanja's unpublished doctoral thesis, "The Growth of the African Anglican Church in Central Kenya" (1993) locates the work undertaken under the CMS mission within the Kikuyu social and religious milieu in central Kenya. Jack Thompson's book, *Christianity in Northern Malawi: The Donald Fraser's Missionary Methods and Ngoni Culture* (1995), though focusing on the interaction of mission Christianity and the Ngoni society, nonetheless pays considerable attention to the role of the indigenous South African missionaries and local catechists in northern Malawi.[10] The list is hardly exhaustive. As may be observed from the list above, none of the studies explores the role of the indigenous agents in the CMS sphere in Ugogo and Ukaguru, central Tanzania. This makes the present study necessary.

1.1.3 Significance

The concern of this study, of redressing the literature's omission of the role of indigenous agents in Ugogo and Ukaguru, is in line with current trends in

---

9. Beidelman's failure to conduct oral interviews with CMS missionaries and African Christians to confirm his views for an ethnographic study is one of the weaknesses of *Colonial Evangelism*. See, for example, reviews of *Colonial Evangelism* by Pirouet (86–88) and Westerlund (161–163).

10. To this list might be added Adrian Hastings's *The Church in Africa 1450–1950*. This is broad and covers the whole continent.

mission historiography. As Brian Stanley puts it, the aim is no longer to write "for the edification of the faithful as an encyclopaedic catalogue of European achievements and institutional progress."[11] In such constituent studies, which Stanley refers to as "an exhausted and dying breed," Western missionaries have often been portrayed as saints, heroes, and humanitarians who made great sacrifices to offer service to Africa.[12] A shift is occurring in the study of the interaction of Western and non-Western cultures and societies and the indigenous initiatives in non-Western societies.[13] This study endeavours to achieve this shift and, in that sense, adds knowledge to the existing literature in this genre. It therefore hopes to make a contribution to the understanding of world Christianity.

1.2 Scope

1.2.1 Date

The role of indigenous agents and their experiences are analysed within the context of Tanzanian social-political history from 1876 to 1933. In terms of political evolution, this includes the pre-colonial period, especially the late nineteenth century, when the political structure of the Wagogo and Wakaguru centred on the chiefdoms ruled by the chiefs. The period of German colonial occupation (1876–1891), in which Tanzania was the only non-British colony in tropical Africa with an Anglican mission,[14] as well as the early period of British colonial occupation 1919–1933, are covered.[15]

As for Christian developments, the year 1876 is when the CMS mission commenced its operations in central Tanzania. The end date for this study – 1933 – is chosen because it is the year that, arguably, marked the end of a missionary phase begun in 1876 in Ugogo and Ukaguru. From 1933 onwards, the missionary focus shifted from central Tanzania to western and northwestern Tanzania, also part of the CMS sphere. Another reason is that, by 1933, most of the leading and long-serving indigenous teachers had been promoted to

---

11. Stanley, "Some Problems," 38.
12. Ekechi, "Studies on Missions in Africa," 147.
13. Stanley, "Some Problems," 40.
14. Hewitt, *Problems of Success*, 1:183.
15. The British colonial occupation ended in 1961.

higher leadership positions, especially after ordination. This study excludes the institutional development in the local church. However, it should be mentioned that 1933 was also the year when some major institutional changes were introduced in the CMS sphere. The changes included the promulgation of a constitution for the historical Diocese of Central Tanganyika (DCT) – the diocese carved out of the existing diocese of Mombasa in 1927. This led to the official abolition of the executive committee of the mission. Such changes allowed a greater symbolic participation of the laity in church governance.

1.2.2 Geographical Area

In terms of geographical scope, the study focuses on central Tanzania, namely the regions now known as Dodoma and Morogoro. The entire CMS mission sphere in Tanzania (as shown on map 3) bordered the sphere of the UMCA (outside the square on the same map).[16] It covered the provinces now known as Morogoro, Dodoma, Singida, Rukwa, Kigoma, Tabora, Mwanza, Shinyanga, Kagera Mara, and Arusha, as well as part of Iringa province. Three reasons have led to the decision to focus on Dodoma and Morogoro provinces. First, Wagogo and Wakaguru form the majority population in these provinces. Second, it is here that the work of the CMS mission survived beyond the nineteenth century. Third, until 1933 the CMS mission concentrated its efforts within these provinces.

Other stations that were started between 1878 and 1888 were either discontinued before the end of the nineteenth century or transferred to other missions early in the twentieth century. Such stations are Uyui (1879) in Tabora province,[17] as well as Msalala (1883), Usambiro (1888),[18] and Nasa (1888)[19] in Mwanza province south of Lake Victoria. Moshi (Kilimanjaro province, northern Tanzania) was commenced in 1885 but was transferred

---

16. See map 3, pg 383.

17. *CMIR* 6 (August 1881): 499. A mission house was built at Uyui in October 1878, but Alfred Copplestone resided there only from 15 October 1879 after his trip to Uganda. See also *PCMS*, 1880, 28. By the time of its closure in 1888, Uyui had at least twelve Christians who had been baptized in 1885. However, the majority if not all of them were Ganda, Sukuma, Yao, and Sumbwa immigrants. See *PCMS*, 1886, 44.

18. Usambiro is a wide area. The station itself was located at Mutereza. See *PCMS*, 1889, 50. Unfortunately, it is Usambiro, and not Mutereza that appears in most maps produced at the time.

19. *CMIR* 14 (March 1889): 167.

in 1893 to the Leipzig mission.[20] Early in the twentieth century, Nasa was handed over to Africa Inland Mission (AIM).[21] All of these fall out of the geographical scope of this study. The same applies also to other stations such as Bukoba (1929), Rubungo (1930),[22] and Ngara (Bugufi, 1932) in northwestern Tanzania.[23]

1.2.3 Omissions

It would have been interesting to include an examination of the indigenous missionary movement from Ugogo and Ukaguru to western and northwestern Tanzania in this study, and the growth of Christianity there from 1934 onwards. It would have highlighted the cross-cultural dynamics between Wagogo and Wakaguru on the one hand and Waha and Wahangaza on the other. Moreover, the people of western and northwestern Tanzania have more cultural affinity with the countries they border – namely, Rwanda, Burundi, and Uganda – than with central Tanzania or, indeed, the rest of Tanzania. An examination of the impact of the East African Revival Movement on this area would equally be important. However, given the geographical size of the area, and the importance of incorporating the indigenous perspectives (through oral research), it would have been too ambitious to try to accommodate those areas within the time allocated for fieldwork for this study. That inquiry should be a subject for other research.

Also, only limited references are made in this study, to the role of indigenous agents in the UMCA (Anglo-Catholic) sphere. But since this sphere is as large as the CMS sphere, it was impossible to carry out oral research

---

20. See *PCMS*, 1885, 45; Groves, *Planting of Christianity in Africa*, 3:80–81. The station was closed in October 1892. This was due to a misunderstanding between the German colonial government and the resident CMS missionaries. The German army was badly defeated by chief Meli of Uchaga on 10 June 1892. The officials then claimed that CMS missionaries supplied arms to Meli. On the other hand, Meli and his advisors became suspicious of the CMS missionaries, and almost withdrew their support to mission work. With a German "revenge" attack inevitable and imminent to restore lost prestige, CMS missionaries decided to withdraw to Taveta, Kenya. See *CMIR* 17 (August 1892): 627, and *CMIR* (September 1892): 693. The Leipzig mission proposed to occupy the vacated station. See *PCMS*, 1893, 44; Groves, *Planting of Christianity*, 3:81. Moshi reopened in 1928 under the DCT. This suggests that the takeover by the Leipzig was only temporary. See ARCCMS, 1929, xxix.

21. Nasa was transferred to the Africa Inland Mission in 1909. Before then it was part of the Uganda (Nyanza) mission. See *PCMS*, 1910, 73.

22. ARCCMS, 1930, xxix.

23. ARCCMS, 1933, xxix.

without which an adequate assessment of archival material would be difficult. Also, despite the fact that the two missions commenced their work in Tanzania hardly a decade apart, they also differed in theological outlook and church polity.

There is also the issue of the vernaculars, including the translation of the Bible, hymnbooks, prayer books, catechism, and other material, into the Kigogo and Kikaguru languages. Indications are that indigenous Christians and teachers, such as Madari Mulutu, played a role in the translation of such material.[24] Unfortunately, documentation on this in mission and church archives is only sporadic, and oral interviews did not yield sufficient data for the period under review in this study. The task of reconstructing the indigenous contributions in this area would certainly require an elaborate piece of research that would be best undertaken separately.[25]

1.3 Research Methodology

1.3.1 Method of Analysis and Presentation

The study adopts a sociohistorical method for the analysis of indigenous initiatives, contributions, and experiences and uses a thematic approach, rather than a chronological one, in the presentation of the material. A thematic presentation of material allows an adequate engagement with the socioreligious and sociopolitical factors or "forces" that shaped the context in which the CMS mission was operating. An implicit argument is that (as both Eric Sharpe, in his article "Reflections on Missionary Historiography," and J. F. Ade Ajayi and E. A. Ayandele, in their article *Writing African Church History*, have pointed out) a study of mission as well as church history should take

---

24. See notes below photograph 6 in appendix 3 for details on the contribution of Madari Mulutu in translation work in Ugogo. Several books of the Bible were translated in Kigogo as follows: Luke (1887), Matthew (1891), the Epistles (1899), Ruth (1893), John (1904), Exodus and Numbers (1910), and the whole New Testament was completed in 1911. See *CMR* 61 (1910): 488; *PCMS*, 1912, 45. As for Ukaguru, by 1891 translations of worship and hymn books, and parts of the New Testament – e.g. Luke's Gospel – had already been translated into the Kaguru language. See Minutes of the Executive Committee of the CMS Mission (EC), 18, 19, 21/12/1903, G3 A8/0/1904/12; Minutes, EC, 6/4/1900, G3 A8/0/1900/20; Rees to Baylis, 16 August 1900, G3 A8/0/1900/37; Minutes, EC, 6 & 7/6/1901, G3 A8/0/1901/25, BUL.

25. See, for example, Sanneh, *Translating the Message*; Sanneh, "Gospel and Culture"; Mbiti, "Biblical Basis for Trends"; Mbiti, *Bible and Theology*; Smalley, *Translation as Mission*; Barrett, *Schism and Renewal*; Bediako, "Understanding African Theology"; Kenyatta, *Facing Mount Kenya*.

into account both the internal and external contextual innovations and challenges of a particular locality.[26] This, as E. A. Ayandele has noted in his book *African Historical Studies*, is best done when African historical studies take the form of a sociohistorical analysis.[27]

For that reason, this study pays significant attention to the interaction of mission Christianity with the social and religious context of the Wagogo and Wakaguru. The aim is to highlight the resilience of the Gogo and Kaguru religions and social values. The writer intends to indicate that in many of the fiercely contested values of the Christian religion on the one hand, and the Gogo and Kaguru religions and practices on the other, it was mission Christianity that appeared to be in a disadvantaged position and lost many of the "battles." The study takes into account some sociopolitical factors too. These include slavery, some policies of the German colonial administration, the Maji Maji uprising and the First World War, and the British colonial government, particularly the introduction of a new educational policy in the mid-1920s and its impact on the mission schools and indigenous teachers. The influence of Islam and the competition with Roman Catholic missions are noted too. These factors are taken into account because, to varying degrees and at different times, they influenced the pace and nature of the indigenous initiatives, contributions, and experiences in Ugogo and Ukaguru.

Organizing material around themes has its insurmountable challenges, not least the difficulty of maintaining a sequence of events, both on the religious and sociopolitical front. Even so, an attempt is made to enable a sense of chronology to emerge. That has been the guiding factor in dealing first with Gogo and Kaguru societies before and during the arrival of the CMS mission, then the initial work up to 1900. The role of the chiefs is viewed as foundational and precedes the analysis of the role of indigenous teachers on the educational and catechetical front.

The analysis of the educational and catechetical contributions is followed by that of other contributions outside the schools and concludes with the experience of Christians and their teachers during the First World War. This

---

26. Sharpe, "Reflections on Missionary Historiography," 80. Ajayi and Ayandele, "Writing African Church History," 93, 94–95, 97; Sanneh, "Horizontal and the Vertical," 165. See also Sanneh, *Translating the Message*, 157–191.

27. Ayandele, *African Historical Studies*, 235.

ends the German colonial era, though subsequent chapters continue to make reference to that era. Politically, this was followed by the period of British colonial occupation. On this basis, the educational changes it introduced, especially from the mid-1920s, are considered next. Indigenous teachers did not escape the impact of those changes to educational policy as the British colonial government and missions sought to establish a common ground for cooperation in education. But the study highlights positive socioeconomic implications for African teachers that emerged here, including the quest for better training.

This writer regards this as a suitable prelude for considering the final chapter on training and the leadership development of the indigenous teachers in the CMS mission, which was inadequate in many respects. Also, the training and leadership development is dealt with last in order that the study may end on a "churchly" note. After all, in hindsight, the CMS mission hardly learned the lessons of the time – the need to offer better training to its lay and ordained ministers and take seriously their socioeconomic needs. The same could be said of the Anglican Church of Tanzania which replaced the CMS mission, so the last chapter becomes a better place to conclude the assessment of the role of the indigenous teachers who form the bulk of the indigenous agents considered in this study.

1.3.2 Methods of Data Collection

1.3.2.1 Archival sources

This study employs three major data sources: oral interviews, archival material, and secondary (documentary) material which is used mainly as a supplement. Archival research involved *mission archives* and *church archives*. Mission archives relating to the work of the CMS mission in Tanzania were studied at the Special Collections Department of the Birmingham University Library (BUL) in England. The focus was on letters written by individual CMS missionaries in Ugogo and Ukaguru, as well as official letters written by various secretaries of the mission, to the Society's headquarters in London. Minutes of the meetings and reports of the executive committee of the CMS mission in Ugogo and Ukaguru were examined too, as were various relevant manuscripts found in the boxes consulted.

Documents containing correspondence between various Anglican bishops of Mombasa, who had the oversight of Tanzania from 1899 until 1927, were consulted as well. A visit was also made to the archives of the Lambeth Palace Library (LPL) in London. Here, some documents relating to Anglican dioceses overseas, whose bishops were subject to the authority of the Archbishop of Canterbury, were studied. The archives of the Universities' Mission to Central Africa (UMCA) were also studied at Rhodes House Library (RHL) at Oxford University. All these sources have been listed in the bibliographic section of this study.

Some scholars have noted the value of the local church records or archives located in the non-Western world for mission studies, especially in their complementary role for the interpretation of the world Christian movement when used in conjunction with mission archives.[28] A study of church archives took place in Tanzania. Various locations were visited in order to examine the surviving church records. Records examined included the minute books (containing minutes of meetings), logbooks, registers of baptism and marriage, and a register of clergy. The majority of these are located at Mackay House (MH) – the headquarters of both the historical and the modern DCT in Dodoma town. A small amount of similar materials was found in the houses of clergy in rural parishes.

The writer was given unlimited access to these archives. However, the state in which they are kept, especially at MH, means that time was spent first doing the task of an archivist before researching. It can only be hoped that, in the future, resources might become available to the local diocese, and indeed other dioceses and churches in Tanzania, to enable a better organization and preservation of church archives. Local periodicals produced in the historical DCT were studied too. Personal diaries of some of the indigenous teachers and missionaries were also examined, especially those written in Kiswahili.[29] A list of these has been compiled in the bibliography.

---

28. See Walls, "Structural Problems," 151, 154; Walls, *Missionary Movement*, 143–159; Ranger, "New Approaches," 183; Ranger, Recommendations of History Committee, Appendix A, "Future Religious Research in Africa: Conclusions of Disciplinary Groups, Workshop in Religious Research, 1968," in Barrett, *African Initiatives in Religion*, 279–280; Oliver, *Missionary Factor*, xiii, xiv.

29. I am indebted to Bishop Mdimi Mhogolo for taking time to look for the diaries of some former indigenous teachers at short notice. Diaries written in Kigogo were not consulted due to limited time, as it would have needed working with a Kigogo translator.

The use of mission archives, and indeed, church archives that were produced largely by CMS missionaries, raises a methodological issue. The issue is whether sources written from a Western perspective are suitable at all for reconstructing the role of indigenous agents in the growth of Christianity in a non-Western context, such as in Ugogo and Ukaguru. For as J. F. Ade Ajayi and E. A. Ayandele observe, scholars have tended to use such sources "to chronicle exclusively the activities of the white missionaries who inevitably emerged as oversized 'heroes' planting the gospel seed and supervising its growth and nurture."[30] To this, one observation might be added: there is also the question of whether the material one finds is all that was produced in the first place or whether some documents, perhaps those containing information considered detrimental to the past image of a mission, have been left out or destroyed.[31]

But the broader issue is that of perspectives in historiography and how documents play a part in this. Edward Carr, in his book *What Is History?*, argues that "the facts of history do not come to us 'pure,' since they do not and cannot exist in a pure form: they are always refracted through the mind of the recorder."[32] Ogbu Kalu, in his article "Church Presence in Africa: A Historical Analysis of the Evangelisation Process," observes: "It is increasingly becoming obvious that historiography is basically ideology, that, in spite of a certain degree of scientific methodology, history has been constantly used to shape the future and to underprop preconceived goals."[33] In other words, historiography, whether secular or religious in nature, can be a vehicle for promoting or demoting status, whether of an individual or a nation. That is why B. Jewsiewicki and V. Y. Mudimbe, in their article "Africans' Memories and Contemporary History of Africa," have noted how, until the mid-1950s, European writers of African history (then the main source of information about the continent) painted a picture such that – if Africa had a past at all before the arrival of the Europeans – "its history does not exist."[34] Once this falsified image is successfully erected, all spectacular and puzzling African

---

30. Ajayi and Ayandele, "Writing African Church History," 91.
31. Walls, "Structural Problems," 151; Kalu, "African Church Historiography," 176.
32. Carr, *What Is History?*, 22.
33. Kalu, "Church Presence in Africa," 13.
34. Jewsiewicki and Mudimbe, "Africans' Memories," 1.

achievements, such as the Great Zimbabwe's walls and tower, are therefore considered to be the work of an external hand, "some highly civilized race" – a notion rightly refuted by Basil Davidson.[35]

That no such thing exists as "pure" historical facts and "pure objectivity" in historiography has long been recognized by scholars, including Carr. This is so because, as Jan Vansina puts it, "we cannot arrive at a full understanding of the past because the past is something outside our experience, something that is other."[36] Moreover, as David Bebbington notes in *Patterns in History: A Christian Perspective on Historical Thought*, "facts take place once and for all and cannot be recovered afterwards in their full integrity." He adds, "objectivity in the sense of detachment in beyond the historian's power."[37]

It follows inevitably that historiography involves the task of selecting data and interpreting what happened from a particular perspective. This writer has therefore selected and interpreted the archival material that supported the case for the role of indigenous agents and their experiences. Effort has been made to respect the evidence found and to present a picture as accurate as could possibly be achieved.[38] A declared bias in perspective and selectivity of the archival material has not therefore meant a compromise of scholarly integrity.

1.3.2.2 Oral sources

Though effort has been made to select and use written sources that advance the case for the role of the indigenous agents and their experiences from a Tanzanian perspective, these alone, without oral research, would undoubtedly be inadequate for the task proposed in this study. A greater part of fieldwork in Tanzania was therefore devoted to oral research. Oral interviews were conducted with at least thirty-seven men and women. Some were interviewed more than once, and the total number of interviews reached forty-two. Oral interviews have been used in this study for several purposes. First, to provide the indispensable insight necessary to review and interpret the mission and church archival material from an indigenous Tanzanian perspective. Second,

---

35. Davidson, *Africa in Modern History*, 35; Davidson, *African History*, 147–148.
36. Vansina, *Oral Tradition*, 185.
37. Bebbington, *Patterns in History*, 11, 16; cf. Bradley and Muller, *Church History*, 33–62.
38. Carr, *What Is History?*, 28.

as a tool for empowering the local church in general, and, in particular, those who participated in the interviews.

These points are reiterated by Donald Moore and Richard Roberts in their article "Listening for Silences" when they say, "Historians and anthropologists rely on formal and informal interviews, surveys, questionnaires, and participant observations in order to generate data and to privilege an African perspective on society, culture and change. Fieldwork serves both as a political statement empowering African voices and as a rite of passage for Africans."[39] As far as this study is concerned, the empowerment of the Wagogo and Wakaguru during the oral interviews was enacted (1) by the use of an open-ended informal questioning method, (2) by the way locations were selected, and (3) by the method of identifying suitable informants. This process of empowerment has culminated in this study by allowing the informants' voices to be heard through their own words – hence the extensive interview quotes that will be found in the subsequent chapters.

The three methods of empowerment may be elaborated as follows. The writer devised key guiding questions on the basis of the themes of the study and the unanswered questions that arose from archival research. But, as stated, informal interviews gave the informants the freedom to share their perspectives on the issues raised but also the freedom to be *silent* and even to be *deliberately forgetful*. This was therefore a kind of dialogue in which both this writer and the informants took part in producing the testimony. Moore and Richards stress that "selective memories as well as forgetting," or an informant's choice of what he or she wants to reveal, is part of the dialogue and part of empowerment.[40] It means, as Richard Roberts states in his article "Reversible Social Processes, Historical Memory, and the Production of History," that oral interviews perform another task – that of enabling informants to reconstruct their histories. This is a kind of rite of passage – "even if it means that I [the researcher] can no longer control the process of the production of knowledge."[41]

---

39. Moore and Roberts, "Listening for Silences," 319.

40. Moore and Roberts, 321.

41. Roberts, "Reversible Social Processes," 348. See also Townsend, "Out of Silence," 351–358. Townsend makes a similar point in relation to fieldwork research on women's experiences.

The enthusiasm with which most, if not all, informants shared the information and expressed their gratefulness that at last someone was interested in their personal histories, as well as local church histories (or the contributions of their relatives), indicated that they felt they were being empowered.

On the choice of locations, it should be stated that the locations were scattered over a wide area in Ugogo and Ukaguru (see map 4). Jan Vansina, in his classic on oral tradition, *Oral Tradition: A Study in Historical Methodology*, points out that where informants are scattered over a large area, "the first places on the list will be those where historic events have taken place, for the informants there usually know more about them than is the case elsewhere."[42] In the context of the oral research conducted for this study, the locations visited were the original mission stations of the CMS mission – namely, Mvumi, Buigiri, Mpwapwa, Chamuhawi (formerly Kisokwe), and Kongwa in Ugogo; and Mamboya and Berega in Ukaguru. Given the time limit, and the problems of public transport, Itumba and Nyangala were not visited. However, older Kaguru informants who had either been born and grown up there or had lived and worked there during the era of the CMS mission were sought and interviewed. Oral material that has been used in this study is therefore a "local product."

The identification of informants was done with the assistance of senior church leaders in each of the three Anglican dioceses visited – Central Tanganyika, Mpwapwa, and Morogoro (see map 6) – and by the help of the local pastors in rural areas. Informants whose parents or relatives participated in the expansion of Christianity in Ugogo and Ukaguru were also visited in the places where they lived. The informants were comprised of confident enthusiasts and the less confident who often suggested that the writer should consult written documents on local history. Informants in the first category included Yusufu Masingisa in Ukaguru and Lazaro Ndajilo, Cleopa Mwaka and Elimerik Mlahagwa in Ugogo. It will become evident in the subsequent chapters that extensive use has been made of the data supplied by such informants. But even those in the second category were amazed at the end of interviews that they knew and remembered more than they first thought. In this sense, too, oral research became an empowerment process.

---

42. Vansina, *Oral Tradition*, 196.

Selection of representative individuals for interviewing is what Catherine Marshall and Gretchen Rossman, in their book *Designing Qualitative Research*, refer to as "élite interviewing."[43] It is "elitist" because, as the authors say, it involves individuals considered to have influence and prominence, who are well informed and possess expertise in relation to one or more aspects of research. For Marshall and Rossman, the term "élite" also means "intelligent and quick-thinking people, at home in the realm of ideas, policies, and generalizations."[44] This implies that they can be people who may tell stories that are not based on actual life situations, either their own or others'.

However, in view of the oral research conducted by this writer, the term "élite" has to be qualified. The informants in Ugogo and Ukaguru were interviewed either because of the historical knowledge they possessed or because they were themselves actors in the growth of Christianity. Even those interviewed in towns (including retired professionals) provided information mainly in relation to their relatives or rural locations where a parent or relative served. It is in that sense that they were prominent and influential in society and not in the sense in which Marshall and Rossman use the term "élite."

Most of the interviews were on a one-to-one basis, and only on two occasions did a group interview occur. Interviews were conducted in Kiswahili, the national language of Tanzania. With the exception of one case in Ukaguru, where an elderly woman wasn't fluent in the language, all interviews were conducted without an interpreter. Interview data was preserved through note-taking and tape recordings. All notes and tape recordings have been reviewed, and a selection of tape has been transcribed.

Conducting interviews with many people in a wide area, such as Ugogo and Ukaguru, generates a variety of responses and, in some cases, significant discrepancies occur in the testimonies. Therefore, as suggested by Jan Vansina, a comparative method of evaluating testimonies has been used in the analysis of data "to arrive at an overall estimate of the relative reliability of the various testimonies."[45]

Vansina further points out that comparisons should be made between testimonies which refer to, or record, the same event. For that reason, nearly

---

43. Marshall and Rossman, *Designing Qualitative Research*, 83.
44. Marshall and Rossman, 84.
45. Vansina, *Oral Tradition*, 114.

all the informants were asked the same questions relating to the themes of this study. In many cases, even during the single-session interviews, the writer sharpened the memory of the informants by framing the same questions differently. This was also used as a method of making an initial assessment of the reliability of the information supplied. Where discrepancies emerged, the writer addressed this by evaluating the reliability of the origin of the story or tradition before the informant received it. Also, information provided by relatives of a former indigenous worker was crosschecked with that of the informants at the locations where he or she served.

It should be stressed that, on the whole, informants exhibited a high degree of integrity in terms of information they chose to share. This was demonstrated by their openness to admit what they didn't know and point the researcher to other people in the local community who knew more about a specific issue, event, locality, or historical figure. Even informants such as Lazaro Ndajilo, Elimerik Mlahagwa, Cleopa Mwaka, and Yusufu Masingisa, who showed considerable knowledge of issues and events in the CMS mission and in Ugogo and Ukaguru, often did the same and sometimes referred the writer to informants younger than themselves. Also, other sources have been used to crosscheck information during the process of interpretation.

Two issues associated with oral tradition should now be addressed. One is the problem of memory and the other is the alleged distortion of oral tradition, particularly through borrowing from printed sources. With regard to the first, it has to be acknowledged that many informants had difficulty remembering details such as the exact dates of some events or the sequence of events. In some cases, an informant mixed the facts. A number of field researchers in East Africa have encountered a similar problem.[46] This writer often jogged the informants' memories by asking whether something occurred during a major event – for example, famine, war, or during the German or British colonial occupation. Again, the method of asking the same questions to all informants ensured that the level of accuracy could be enhanced. Another method used to resolve the problem of dates was to resort to mission and church records which recorded events as they happened, except that CMS missionaries appears to have misinterpreted the meaning of a particular local event they

---

46. See, for example, Karanja, "Growth of the African Anglican Church," 10; Mombo, "Historical Analysis," 12.

recorded. In addition to these measures, secondary (printed) sources have been consulted in an attempt to establish accurate or estimated dates.

The problem of distortion and borrowing from printed sources is much bigger and requires extended response. Both Vansina and David Henige caution against taking for granted oral tradition or oral history. Similarity in testimonies (as indeed was discovered during the analysis of data in this research) could be an indicator that a process of diffusion of tradition had occurred. But, as Vansina points out, this does not become the case if there has been no social, economic, political, or religious contact between the informants.[47] Except in very rare cases, the informants interviewed, whether in Ugogo, Ukaguru, or between the two regions, had never met each other before. They gave independent accounts of the events and perceptions.

But there remains another possible problem – similarity between oral data and archival and printed sources. On a number of occasions, a comparison of oral data and archival material, particularly the mission archives used in this study, revealed such similarity. About this Vansina says, "When there is complete concordance between independent sources, the chances that the events described did actually happen are very much increased and almost amount to certainty, especially if the sources are different in kind as they could possibly be."[48] In this sense, the two sources, oral and documentary, become complementary. Yet this explanation does not fully answer the concern raised by David Henige, one that he refers to as the problem of "feedback" in oral tradition. In his article "The Problem of Feedback in Oral Tradition," Henige says:

> The problem of feedback in the study of oral tradition has become increasingly important, not only to historians of Africa, but to any student of the world's oral societies. Feedback occurs in oral tradition when extraneous material, usually from printed sources, is incorporated into the tradition. Since such matter quickly becomes indistinguishable in form from any truly oral elements in a tradition, historians should never assume that a

---

47. Vansina, *Oral Tradition*, 133.
48. Vansina, 138.

given tradition or set of traditions contains no adulterations from feedback.[49]

In his other study, *The Chronology of Oral Tradition: A Quest for a Chimera*, Henige argues that Christianity and the literacy it introduced, and colonial political domination, especially Indirect Rule, are part of the various stimuli to which oral traditions responded.[50] In another book, *Oral Historiography*, where Henige makes a similar point, he argues, "For most oral societies the written word represented a new orthodoxy that could not easily be rejected because it was accompanied by stark evidence of its efficacy, usually in the form of soldiers, missionaries, and administrators."[51] Incorporation or co-opting of outside data was therefore the "best way to cope with the needs resulting from the introduction of literacy." Consequently, "uncontaminated oral tradition simply does not exist any more, except possibly in the remote areas of Amazonia, the Philippines, or New Guinea."[52]

The point raised by Henige in relation to a body of oral traditions and their chronology, particularly in relation to the political, cultural, or social developments of the so-called oral societies,[53] applies widely and might have relevance for mission historiography. It is possible that oral tradition on the Gogo and Kaguru political systems before the arrival of the colonial governments has been influenced by other sources.[54] It is also true that some of the people interviewed had, in the past, acquired literacy skills.

However, with the exception of a very few of them, there is no evidence that they accessed written material of any historical significance. The documents that might have "contaminated" their knowledge were those produced by the CMS missionaries. The bulk of these – private letters, reports, and minutes of meetings which none of the informants attended – were sent to Britain. The danger of the so-called "feedback" is therefore only a remote possibility as far as the oral data relating to the growth of Christianity in Ugogo and Ukaguru is concerned. One of the reasons similarity may exist

---

49. Henige, "Problem of Feedback," 223.
50. Henige, *Chronology of Oral Tradition*, 95, 97.
51. Henige, *Oral Historiography*, 81–82.
52. Henige, 82, 85.
53. Henige, "Problem of Feedback," 234.
54. See chapter 2.

between certain oral testimonies and archival material is that the Wagogo and Wakaguru have kept their own tradition about their interaction with mission Christianity and have handed it down, though interpreting that process from an indigenous perspective of course.

It has to be said, therefore, that this writer regards the written mission and church archives and the orally transmitted data as complementary, and not mutually exclusive, sources. The former have been selected and interpreted from a perspective that promotes the initiatives, contributions, and experiences of indigenous Christians; the latter are regarded as necessary for evaluating the perspectives of CMS missionaries, for truly, as Henige puts it, "this ability to complement the written record is the principal purpose of oral historiography."[55]

1.3.2.3 Photographs

Photographs can also be used as oral data in historical research, and some scholars recognize this.[56] Therefore, as part of the plan for field research, effort was made to collect relevant photographs of indigenous agents. Two limitations were encountered. First, on the whole, many family members of the people concerned did not have photographs. But a serious limitation was that even though a few did and, indeed, showed or lent them to this writer, lack of quality photographic reproduction facilities in Dodoma meant that only photocopies could be made. The same was done for a selection of photographs found in an album at Kongwa college, sixty miles outside Dodoma. Other photographs have also been photocopied from printed sources. These photographs bring closer the images of some the people mentioned in this study. However, though better facilities have been used to enhance their quality in Edinburgh, it has been decided that the photographs should be placed in an appendix, rather than within the text.[57]

1.3.2.4 Secondary sources

This study also utilizes secondary published and unpublished data sources. Some, such as books and articles, have been obtained from public libraries

---

55. Henige, *Oral Historiography*, 71.
56. Geary, "Photographs as Materials"; Papstein, "Creating and Using Photographs."
57. See photographs in appendix 3.

in Britain and Tanzania. Others are specialist materials such as serial periodicals and annual reports published by the CMS in London or the DCT in Tanzania, as listed in the bibliography.

1.4 A Complementary Role of Data Sources

The three types of data sources employed in this study – oral interviews, church and mission archives, and published secondary material – play a complementary and corrective role for each other. It is hoped that such a combination enhances the level of accuracy and reliability of the reconstruction of the story of the growth of Christianity in Ugogo and Ukaguru attempted in this study which focuses on indigenous initiatives and experiences but begins with an analysis of the Gogo and Kaguru societies.

CHAPTER 2

Gogo and Kaguru Societies in the Late Ninteenth Century

This chapter analyses the Gogo[1] and Kaguru[2] societies – their political, social and religious life before and at the start of the CMS work in central Tanzania in 1876. The examination is largely a historical and phenomenological description of the Gogo and Kaguru traditional life. The purpose is to highlight only those aspects that later became controversial as mission Christianity interacted with the social and religious life of the two societies. The approach adopted is that of a simultaneous analysis of the two societies. Each aspect of their life (political, social, and religious) will be examined separately. It is expected that this will bring out the similarities as well as the differences between the Wagogo and Wakaguru.

Data on the late nineteenth century Wagogo and Wakaguru is scant. Therefore, the analysis draws on oral tradition and firsthand accounts of the nineteenth century foreign travellers and early CMS missionaries. Secondary sources are utilized too, particularly the sociological and anthropological works of Peter Rigby and Thomas Beidelman on the Wagogo and Wakaguru, respectively.

---

1. The Wagogo (the people of Ugogo) uphold a legend that their name derives from the Kiswahili word *gogo* (pl. *magogo*), meaning "log." They believe the Wanyamwezi traders from western Tanzania gave them that name. The traders used to camp in places with large logs in Ugogo as they travelled to and from the coast. See Lazaro Ndajilo, oral interviews, 14 and 16 June 1997; Rigby, *Cattle and Kinship*, 20.

2. The name Wakaguru (the people of Ukaguru) derives from the word *gulu* ("mountain" or "hill"). See Beidelman, *Moral Imagination*, 69, 71; CMIR 3 (October 1878): 645. The Wakaguru are also called Wamegi, possibly a derogatory name given them by the Wamasai and the Wabaraguyu (another Masai-like tribe in the Kaguru neighbourhood). See Yusufu Masingisa, oral interviews, 16 and 17 September 1997; Beidelman, "Chiefship in Ukaguru," 231.

2.1 Geography of Ugogo and Ukaguru

2.1.1 The Geography of Ugogo

The central and western sections of Ugogo are composed mainly of the lowlands, which range between 2,900 and 3,900 feet above sea level. The East African Rift Valley is a notable feature of western Ugogo. The mountainous areas of the southeast include the Kiboriani hills, which have peaks up to six thousand feet above sea level, and separate Mpwapwa and Kongwa. Towards the north, the land is an extension of the Masai plain. The annual average rainfall is about twenty inches. With the exception of small areas, much of Ugogo is suitable for grazing but not for intensive agriculture. Without adequate permanent water sources, the people have suffered frequent droughts and famines (in the past and at present).[3]

Despite these climatic disadvantages, during the second half of the nineteenth century, Ugogo was famous among passing travellers as a land of plenty. Sheikh Thani (an Arab trader who travelled with Henry Stanley during his second journey across Tanzania in the mid-1870s) described Ugogo as a land "rich with milk, and honey – rich in flour, beans, and almost every eatable thing."[4] Based on these and other earlier accounts of Ugogo by other traders, Stanley considered Ugogo to be "a very Land of Promise." At Mpwapwa itself, Stanley recalled enjoying "with unctuous satisfaction a real breakfast and dinner."[5]

2.1.2 The Geography of Ukaguru

If there are notable differences in the physical features of Ugogo and Ukaguru, then it is in the mountainous nature of the latter, as well as its numerous well-watered river valleys. Most Kaguru mountains, particularly in the central area, have peaks up to seven thousand feet above sea level. In the nineteenth century, the majority of the Wakaguru lived in these central mountainous areas, mainly for defensive reasons. Others resided in well-watered river valleys. At the time, the plateau and lowlands were thinly populated. The reverse is true today. Compared with Ugogo, much of Ukaguru enjoys fertile land

---

3. For a chronology of famines in Ugogo dating from 1860 to 1963, see Rigby, *Cattle and Kinship*, 21.

4. Stanley, *How I Found Livingstone*, 131.

5. Stanley, 131.

and good rainfall (up to one hundred inches or more) – hence its prosperity based on an agricultural economy. However, like the Wagogo, the Wakaguru kept sheep, goats, chickens, and to a limited extent, herds of cattle, especially in western and northern plateaux and lowlands with similar climatic conditions as most of Ugogo. As were the Wagogo, the Wakaguru who lived in the lowlands and plateau in the western parts were often prone to enemy attack. Insecurity was one reason the Wakaguru tried to balance the desire to be open to non-threatening neighbours and outsiders while at the same time being "secretive."[6]

2.2 The Formation of the Gogo and Kaguru Societies

The people known today as Wagogo and Wakaguru came into being as distinct ethnic groups after many years. Ecological, economic, and social factors – both within and beyond their control – contributed to their formation. Heterogeneity was one outcome of this evolvement. This stemmed principally from their contact with other ethnic groups through warfare, famine, and the slave trade.[7] In some parts of Ugogo, clans (*mbeyu*) that had been in contact with the Wahehe were nicknamed *wetiliko* (half-bred Hehe-Gogo). In other areas, for example Mpwapwa, some clans took the name *wenyenkulu* – escapees from Arab caravans who sought protection at the palaces of the local chiefs.[8] There were also traders or non-slaves from other tribes who settled in Ugogo of their own will and became "naturalized."

Like Ugogo, Ukaguru witnessed the influx of neighbouring populations too. This was due to warfare and famine. Beside this, it was inhabited by the Wakamba and Wamasai in the central and northwestern parts,[9] and, north of Berega, the Wanguu and Wazigua.[10] Both the Wamasai and the Wakamba

---

6. The Wakaguru who reside in the uplands are referred to as *Wetumba*, and the lowlanders as *Wasika* (deriving from the Kaguru words *itumba*, meaning mountain, and *sika*, meaning lowland). See Beidelman, *Moral Imagination*, 13–15, 69.

7. Beidelman, "History of Ukaguru," 14.

8. Carnell, "Sympathetic Magic," 25.

9. For detailed notes on the Wakamba in Ukaguru, see Beidelman, "Some Notes on the Kamba," 181–194.

10. The suggestion by some, e.g. David Rees, that the Kaguru were part of the Wasagara is clearly a misunderstanding. See Rees, "History of the Church Missionary Society in German

(who migrated from Kenya) often attacked the Wakaguru.[11] There were also some Wanyamwezi traders and their relations who settled in the Mamboya valley. They established their own village,[12] and had their own chief.[13] Those who settled among the Wakaguru and spoke fluent Kikaguru were (and still are) called *Wendiyesi* (a Kikaguru word meaning *dissemblers*). The apparent reason for that name is that such people were regarded as merely disguising themselves as true Wakaguru who accepted Kaguru ways but might have had hidden beliefs and loyalties that could potentially harm or threaten Kaguru stability. Those who couldn't speak Kikaguru fluently were called *Wandubu* (a Kikaguru word meaning *garblers*).[14]

Though it may be difficult to know the total population of the Wagogo and Wakaguru in the late nineteenth century, the estimate made early in the twentieth century gives some idea. CMS missionaries working in Ugogo estimated its population at five hundred thousand in 1902,[15] while in 1923, that of the Wakaguru was estimated at around three hundred thousand.[16]

A significant difference to be noted between the Wagogo and Wakaguru, however, is that, though both are Bantu-speaking groups, the former is a patrilineal, semi-pastoral, and semi-agricultural society; the latter is matrilineal and basically an agricultural society.[17] Despite this difference, the two

---

East Africa," MS, G3 A8/0/1902/19, BUL. The Kaguru were a distinct tribe from the Wasagara who inhabited the "country" south of Mamboya. See *CMIR* 4 (November 1879): 665; cf. Beidelman, *Matrilineal Peoples*, 51, 52–53.

11. Beidelman, "Notes on the Kamba," 182. At times, the Wamasai and Wakamba attacked the Wakaguru when the latter were having dance and drink parties in order to steal cattle more easily. See *CMIR* 14 (March 1889): 171; Semgomba Chitemo, oral interview, 15/9/1997. Yet another reason for frequent attacks was to try to overrule the Wakaguru. See Extracts from the journal of Rev A. N. Wood, 20 August 20–1 September 1888, "Itinerating in Usagara," *CMIR* 14 (January 1889): 24, 26; Beidelman, "Notes on the Kamba," 188. See also Roscoe to Lang, 14 September 1888, quoted in Beidelman, "Notes on the Kamba," 187.

12. *CMIR* 6 (September 1881): 558; Beidelman, "History of Ukaguru," 14.

13. *CMIR* 5 (December 1880): 742.

14. Beidelman, *Moral Imagination*, 69–70.

15. PCMS, 1903, 104.

16. ARCCMS, 1924, 14.

17. For details on the dynamics of Kaguru matrilineality on social ties and religious practice, see Beidelman, *Moral Imagination*, ch. 2–4. Other matrilineal ethnic groups in the Ukaguru neighbourhood include the Wanguu, Wazigua, Waluguru, Wasagara, and Wavidunda. Their patrilineal neighbours are the Masai, Wakamba, Wagogo, Wahehe, and Wabaraguyu.

ethnic groups had (and still have) a number of similarities. Some notable ones including basic political organization, social customs, and religious beliefs.

2.3 Political Organization

2.3.1 Gogo Political System

Like most ethnic groups throughout Africa in the nineteenth century, the political structure of the Wagogo centred on the local chief who ruled a chiefdom. The Wagogo had no central political organization uniting many clans. Each *mtemi* (Kigogo; "political and ritual leader") ruled a clan. The accounts of the European travellers in the mid-nineteenth century who paid *hongo* (passage or road tax) to many chiefs almost on a daily basis is evidence of a decentralized Gogo political system. Oral sources suggest that Chief Chalula of Mvumi ruled quite a large area and that his chiefdom was only divided after his death.[18] The *mtemi* exercised his rule through the subordinate headmen known as *wapembamoto* (sing. *mpembamoto*; lit. "one who keeps the fire burning"). These were the intermediaries between the chief and the people. The *wazengamatumbi* or *wazengetumbi* (sing. *Mzengamatumbi* or *mzengetumbi*; lit. "the builder of a neighbourhood or village") assisted the *wapembamoto*.[19]

In the nineteenth century, the Wagogo chiefs showed their power in at least two ways. First, despite the intense slave trade, and even the kidnapping of children and adults by traders and powerful chiefs, the Wagogo hardly became victims of slavery.[20] Henry Stanley (the British explorer) recalled hearing some Wagogo respond in a "shrill crescendo tone, 'Are we the Wagogo to be beaten like slaves by this Musungu. A Mgogo is a Mgwana [Mwungwana] (free man); he is not to be beaten, – hahcht'"[21] It is not uncommon in speech for people to protest against something done to them as if it hasn't taken place yet. Given Stanley's reputation for ill-treatment of local people during his journeys in

---

18. Lazaro Ndajilo, oral interviews, 14 and 16 June 1997. See "Photograph 9: Chief Mazengo Chalula" in appendix 3 for further notes.
19. Lazaro Ndajilo, oral interviews, 14 and 16 June 1997.
20. Elimerik Mlahagwa, oral interview, 28 June 1997; Lazaro Ndajilo, oral interviews, 14 and 16 June 1997.
21. Stanley, *How I Found Livingstone*, 153, 154.

East and Central Africa,[22] it is quite possible he actually whipped that group of onlooking Wagogo. With the exception of such incidents, and the terror caused by Bushiri bin Salim at Mpwapwa[23] as he pursued the Germans during the Arab-German conflict of 1889, and the frequent attacks on Mpwapwa by the Wahehe,[24] on the whole, the Wagogo defended themselves against abuses.

Second, the Wagogo chiefs showed their strength by imposing *hongo* upon travellers. Other ethnic groups along the caravan routes leading to and from the coast did the same.[25] However, passage in Ugogo was expensive because the chiefs imposed both the water tax[26] and *hongo* upon traders and travellers passing through their land – be they Europeans, African,[27] or Arab.[28] Mvumi chiefdom was particularly dreaded[29] by caravan owners owing to the large amount of tribute extorted by the chief and headmen.[30] Stanley was among those who paid *hongo* to the Wagogo chiefs, including the chief of Mvumi, probably Chief Chalula (Mazengo's father) as his own account testifies:

> We had fixed this day for bearing tribute to the Great Sultan of Mvumi. . . . The Sultan demanded six doti of Merikani, a fundo of bubu, from the Musungu; and from the Arabs and other

---

22. Pakenham, *Scramble for Africa*, 28.

23. For details on the impact of the September 1888 Bushiri coastal uprising on Mpwapwa, see J. C. Price's letter, "The Destruction of Mpwapwa," written 25 July 1889, in *CMIR* 14 (December 1889): 739–743.

24. Stephano Malecela, oral interview, 24 June 1997. Stephano's recollection of the Hehe invasions is supported by documentary sources. For example, the Wahehe attacked Mpwapwa in October 1892, during which they burnt villages and killed a German colonial government officer at the fort. See *PCMS*, 1893, 47; *PCMS*, 1894, 47.

25. See map 2, appendix 4. In Ugogo itself, the caravan routes converged at Mpwapwa, and led to Chunyu, Marenga Makali, and Mvumi. Another less used route passed near Chilonwa village, proceeded to Vyeyula near Dodoma city, joined the Mpwapwa route at Kilimatinde (western Ugogo), continued as far as Tabora and Ujiji (western Tanzania), and led, eventually, to what is now known as the Democratic Republic of Congo (then the Congo). From Tabora, another route branched off northward to Uganda and to Usukuma on the southern shores of Lake Victoria. See map facing title page in Hutchinson, *Victoria Nyanza*.

26. Roscoe, *Twenty-Five Years*, 47.

27. One Terekeza was among the prominent African traders of this period. He possessed a "large caravan" and travelled to Usukuma, south of Lake Victoria, and sold goods in exchange for ivory. See *CMIR* 2 (July 1877): 408.

28. Some of those identified as "Arabs" were in fact Swahili traders from the coast of Tanzania.

29. Stanley, *How I Found Livingstone*, 139.

30. Report of the Usagara-Ugogo Mission (RUUM) for 1909, G3 A8/O/1910/40, BUL.

caravans, twelve doti. In one day from one camp the sultan received forty-seven doti, consisting of Merikani, Kaniki, Barsati, and Dabwani, equal to $35.25, besides even doti of superior cloths, consisting of Rehani, Sohari, and Dabwani Ulyah, and one fundo of Bubu, equal to $14.00, making a total of $49.25 – a most handsome revenue for a Mgogo chief.[31]

The CMS missionaries who formed the delegation to king Mutesa of Buganda (see chapter 3) also paid *hongo* to each chief whose chiefdom they passed through, with negotiations taking up to three days.[32] Besides material goods, African and Arab traders offered kidnapped children as *hongo*. They kidnapped such children from the tribes situated along the caravan routes.[33] It has to be noted that the travellers disliked the demand for *hongo* by the Wagogo chiefs, and to some extent, the amount demanded was excessive. In some cases, brutal measures were taken against those who tried to evade paying water tax or *hongo* or both.[34] That was the policy of many chiefs. However, unlike the chiefs who imposed *hongo*, ordinary Wagogo conducted fair trade with travellers, as Stanley's account indicates:

> The quantity and variety of provisions which arrived at our boma ["fort," used here to mean "camp"] did not belie the reports respecting the productions of Ugogo. Milk sour and sweet, honey, beans, matama, maweri, Indian corn, ghee, pea-nuts, and a species of bean-nut very like a large pistachio or an almond, water-melons, pumpkins, mush-melons, and cucumbers were brought, and readily exchanged for Merikani, Kaniki, and for white Merikani, beads.[35]

---

31. Stanley, *How I Found Livingstone*, 145, 146, 148, 150. Stanley and his Arab companions paid *hongo* to the chief of Matumbulu, as well as of Bihawana.
32. *CMIR* 2 (July 1877): 466, 407, 408.
33. Lazaro Ndajilo, oral interviews, 14 and 16 June 1997.
34. Rees, "History of CMS," MS, G3 A8/0/1902/19, BUL.
35. Stanley, *How I Found Livingstone*, 144.

2.3.2 Kaguru Political System

As in Ugogo, Ukaguru's political life was organized around chiefdoms,[36] each with a chief (*mundewa*; pl. *wandewa*)[37] supported by local clan leaders or headmen, later called *majumbe* (sing. *jumbe*).[38] Beside the chief and headman, there was a *chijiji* (an elder) who controlled a cluster of small hamlets.[39] The Kaguru leadership was hereditary, but the people often elected the headmen.[40]

The Kaguru political system was a decentralized one. "At Kitange," Chitemo recalls, "there was Shimba.... At Berega (Mbuyuni) there was Kiburunge. Mlahagwa succeeded him. Malanda succeeded Mlahagwa. Malanda was ruler until Nyerere era began."[41] These were chiefdoms mainly in the western and northwestern parts of Ukaguru. In central and western Ukaguru, Joseph Last, one of the earliest CMS missionaries in central Tanzania, noted in 1878 the existence of six sultanships or chiefdoms in Tubugwe, Mlali, Rubeho, Kitange, Magubike, and Mamboya – "across each of which it takes a day or more to pass."[42] In June 1879, he described these as "the chief villages on the road to Mpwapwa."[43] The chief of Mamboya is implicated here as just one among many.

However, Kaguru oral tradition, reinforced even by people far from Mamboya, maintains that the famous chief of Mamboya, Senyagwa Chimola, was the paramount chief of the entire "country" of Ukaguru, and "all people revered him."[44] Oral tradition also maintains that when Karl Peters (the earliest German colonist in Tanzania) arrived in Ukaguru in 1884, Senyagwa Chimola summoned other chiefs (apparently under his leadership) from as far as Kitange (western Ukaguru) to the discussions, leading to the signing

---

36. Beidelman, "Chiefship in Ukaguru," 229.

37. *Mundewa* is also used to refer to the paramount chief. See Beidelman, *Matrilineal Peoples*, 41.

38. The use of the title *jumbe* (pl. *majumbe*) for chiefs is an indication of the coastal influence upon the Wakaguru. The title became even more common following the appointment, by the German colonial administration, of coastal Swahili Muslims bearing that title and that of *akida* (pl. *maakida*; "tax collectors") in alien lands in the interior.

39. Beidelman, *Matrilineal Peoples*, 42.

40. Semgomba Chitemo, oral interview, 15 September 1997.

41. Chitemo, oral interview; Berega Logbook No. 51, January 1901–29 May 1915, MH.

42. *CMIR* 3 (October 1878): 645.

43. *CMIR* 4 (November 1879): 664.

44. Semgomba Chitemo, oral interview, 15 September 1997.

of a so-called political treaty with the former.[45] This suggests that though the Kaguru political system was decentralized, there existed a form of political federation well before German colonial activities began, and Chimola presided over that federation.

T. O. Beidelman, who himself accepts and utilizes oral tradition considerably in his ethnographic studies on the Wakaguru, questions – perhaps with an unjustified scepticism – the oral tradition of the *Jumbe* clan on the ascendancy of Senyagwa Chimola as the paramount chief of Ukaguru. But he rightly observes that Senyagwa's paramountship was certainly enhanced significantly through his long contact with Arab traders and the sultan of Zanzibar, and later with the German colonists before his death in 1897.[46]

As in Ugogo, Ukaguru had been in contact with Arab traders during much of the nineteenth century. The influence of the Arab traders over the chiefs along the interior caravan routes, and the chiefs' alliances with them, was notable, especially at Mamboya. Oral evidence points to this:

> When they reached this place they were provided with free lodgings and hospitality. But that was not the case when they reached Dodoma [Ugogo]. There, they were asked to pay tribute (*hongo*) to secure passage to the west. The Arabs didn't mind paying tribute because they could get elephants, ivory and slaves. [But] they passed here free of charge on their way back to the coast. They were impressed by this free passage and formed an alliance with the local chief, Chief Senyagwa Chimola, Saidi.[47]

No wonder Senyagwa Chimola took the name "Saidi" (and became famously known as Saidi Chimola) in appreciation of Arab-Swahili coastal culture and his solidarity with the sultan of Zanzibar in the late 1870s.[48] At this time, identification with *ustaarabu* ("the genteel manners and values of

---

45. Yusufu Masingisa, oral interviews, 16 and 17 September 1997; cf. Beidelman, "Chiefship in Ukaguru," 235; Extracts from the *Proceedings of the Royal Geographical Society*, August 1887, in *CMIR* 12 (October 1887): 614.

46. Beidelman, "Chiefship in Ukaguru," 237, 239.

47. Yusufu Masingisa, oral interviews, 16 and 17 September 1997.

48. Beidelman, "History of Ukaguru," 18; Yusufu Masingisa, oral interviews, 16 and 17 September 1997.

the Arab civilization")[49] was regarded by many chiefs as a noble thing. Arab and Swahili dress was particularly influential.[50]

The wearing of *kanzu* (long tunic dress) and a hat with a tassel was imitated not only by the general public in the interior but also by Christians and indigenous teachers.[51] In most cases, though indigenous teachers wore identification badges supplied at the Mpwapwa fort by the German colonial regional administration, they also dressed in *kanzu* to identify themselves as mission workers. The CMS mission, which disliked Muslim culture, could do little to prevent this other than just discouraging the wearing of such garments.[52]

2.4 Social Structure

2.4.1 Gogo Social Structure

The social life of the Wagogo was organized around clanship and kinship. Among other things, clanship affiliation influenced the kingship system in that it was the foundation upon which ritual activity was organized in different geographical areas known as ritual areas. It was the ritual-area leaders (also called *watemi*, sing. *mtemi*)[53] who performed exclusive rituals such as

---

49. Raum, "German East Africa," 166–167.

50. Iliffe, *Modern History of Tanganyika*, 59; Joelson, *Tanganyika Territory*, 106. A white *kanzu* (long tunic), *kofia ya shada* (embroidered cap), and *kandambili* (open sandals) would be a typical Muslim dress for a man. For women, *khanga* was regarded as a standard and typical dress. Usually, two pieces of a decorated garment would make up a complete *khanga* dress. One piece of *khanga* is worn around the waist, stretching to cover the legs. Another is worn over the shoulders, sometimes partly covering the face. The issue of dress for Muslim women has recently caused controversy between Muslim fundamentalists and the government of Tanzania. For example, on Friday 30 July 1999, police in Dar es Salaam clashed with some demonstrators who demanded that Muslim pupils in primary and secondary schools be allowed to wear *hijab* (head scarves) in school and be allowed to attend Friday prayers. See Mwainyekule, "Kariakoo Bazaar."

51. See photograph 1, appendix 3. I am indebted to Hon John Malecela, MP, for showing the photograph to me and lending it to me for photocopying. His grandfather Yohana Malecela was among the first Kongwa students. Mr Malecela is former Prime Minister of Tanzania and currently the Vice-Chairman of CCM, the governing party in Tanzania.

52. Minutes, EC, 13, 15/11/1909, G3 A8/0/1910/1, BUL; Berega Logbook, No. 51, entry for February 1907, MH.

53. The same term *mtemi* was used for a tribal political leader or chief. Peter Rigby suggests that it was physically and ritually endangering for a ritual leader (whether functioning as both a political and religious leader or not) to come into contact with travellers and strangers, and, for that reason, only his assistants collected *hongo*. See Rigby, *Cattle and Kinship*, 98. However, the evidence (as has been quoted above) from the accounts of travellers and early CMS missionaries who actually met the *watemi* suggests the contrary. See *CMIR* 2 (July 1877):

rainmaking.⁵⁴ Clanship affiliation was also important because it determined patrilineal descent. In Ugogo, a child assumed patrilineal legitimacy whether born within or outside marriage. Slaves or captives captured in war (*wawanda*), or those who arrived in Ugogo because of famine and asked to settle (*kulomba wikalo*), or indeed any foreigner (*mkonongo*; pl. *wakonongo*) had to adopt the clan of the people they first came into contact with.⁵⁵

2.4.2 Kaguru Social Structure

As in Ugogo, the basic social structure of the matrilineal Kaguru society was organized around clanship and kinship. But unlike Ugogo, Kaguru clans and kinships were based on matrilineages. Membership to a matrilineage was achieved automatically by birth. The bond between women and their children formed the ties around which different matrilineal segments were linked together. Tensions existed within a segment, but such tensions often contributed to clan solidarity by emphasizing the necessity for belonging to a matrilineage segment for security and support.⁵⁶

2.5 Aspects of Gogo and Kaguru Social Customs

The social structure of both Ukaguru and Ugogo that has been analysed was a field in which life was dramatized through different customs. Whether in Ugogo or Ukaguru, an important observation to be made is that the right to belong to a patrilineage or matrilineage was taken for granted, regardless of the social circumstances of a person. Nevertheless, the two societies had their ways of enabling their members to participate in wider clan and tribal matters. This was done through rites of passage because, as in many African societies, it was through these rites that the majority of the Wagogo and Wakaguru made the transition from childhood to adulthood, thereby gaining the right to socialize with other members of society. The customs to be analysed here include circumcision, puberty rites, and marriage. Dances will be examined too because they played a key role in the public enactment

---

406, 408, 466. Rigby is right, though, that during the British occupation (1919–1961) the role of the Gogo *mtemi* was somehow secularized.

54. Rigby, *Cattle and Kinship*, 64, 75.
55. Rigby, 78.
56. Beidelman, *Moral Imagination*, 42, 43, 22, 12, 15.

of many social customs. As pointed out in the introduction above, apart from religious practices that will be examined below, it was these rites that became a source of conflict between Gogo and Kaguru on the one hand and the CMS mission on the other.

2.5.1 Circumcision and Puberty Rites
2.5.1.1 Circumcision and puberty rites in Ugogo

In Ugogo and Ukaguru (as in many other African societies), circumcision was performed for three main reasons. First, to mark the maturation of boys and girls into adulthood and their acquisition of the right to public social life.[57] A second related reason was to legitimize the start of sexual relations and entry into marriage.[58] The third was a religious one. The initiation rites of the Wagogo and Wakaguru boys and girls served as a means of purification to "legalize" future participation in the clan rituals and other religious activities.[59]

The Wagogo girls were circumcised before puberty (mostly between the age of eight and eleven). They were taken into the bush where the clitoridectomy (the partial removal of the clitoris) – not infibulation (the complete removal of the clitoris followed by the stitching of the two sides of the vulva, leaving a small opening for passing urine and menstrual blood)[60] – was performed.[61] After circumcision – a term preferred in this study for its familiarity[62] – the girls returned immediately to their homesteads for seclusion in the *kugati* (Kigogo; "the inner room used by one's mother") so as not to be in contact with men until after recovery.

However, a girl did not become marriageable until after puberty.[63] Her first menstruation was marked by ritual seclusion, during which she received instructions in the *kugati* about adult life, particularly about her future life as

---

57. Lazaro Ndajilo, oral interviews, 14 and 16 June 1997.
58. Rigby, "Structural Context," 435.
59. Caplan, "Boys' Circumcision," 27.
60. This form of operation is practised mainly in northeast African countries, for example Ethiopia. The controversial issue of circumcision of girls in Ugogo and Ukaguru and the response of the CMS mission will be considered in chapter 5.
61. See Rigby, *Cattle and Kinship*, 208.
62. The alternative term, "Female Genital Mutilation" (FGM), is becoming increasingly popular.
63. Rigby, "Puberty Rites," 435.

wife and mother.⁶⁴ The seclusion was ended by a public ceremony involving *kuhovugwa* (ritual bathing) and visiting the homesteads to show off "beauty and gentleness." The girl's first menstruation was acknowledged publicly with ceremonies involving dancing, drinking, and joyful shouting to announce to the neighbourhood the fact of the marriageability of the girl.⁶⁵

The nature of the circumcision of the boys (usually in their early teens) was different. A traditional operator (*mhunga*; pl. *wahunga*) performed circumcision at the *chibalu* (the circumcision enclosure or spot) in the bush.⁶⁶ The boys recuperated in the *ikumbi* – the circumcision camp near the homesteads – sometimes for up to a month. As soon as the act of circumcision had been performed, a *nyamuwumbu* sheep was slaughtered and the operator cleansed his knife by driving it through the stomach of the animal, after which the skin could be removed. The blood from the sheep was poured on the exact spot where circumcision took place. The symbolic significance of the *nyamuwumbu* was to "cool down the [hot] blood that flowed from those who were circumcised, to prevent a curse or the sun becoming hot."⁶⁷ Along with the prayers offered by parents on the day of circumcision, the head of *chikumbi* also offered a prayer to the ancestors on behalf of the initiates, uttering the words *Kagona kumtuli mbeho, kumnyamavu* (Kigogo; "go sleep on a tree whose leaves/roots are sweet").⁶⁸

Riddles (*vidari*) and songs (involving "offensive" words) were the chief media by which the teaching was imparted to the initiates at the *ikumbi*. The themes of sexuality, family life – especially the relationship between husband and wife – and the duties and responsibilities of an adult member of society, as opposed to the *wakonongo* (aliens or barbarians), were taught. Good moral behaviour was emphasized too.⁶⁹

During the seclusion period, the initiates left their *ikumbi* temporarily and visited the village in the evening, often eating and sleeping there, but

---

64. Rigby, *Cattle and Kinship*, 208–210; Rigby, "Puberty Rites," 439.
65. Cole, "Notes on the Wagogo," 309.
66. Women were allowed to visit the boys at the *ikumbi*, but the new initiates were warned not to look the women in the face, and the offenders were punished. See Kongola, "Wevunjiliza," 10. I am indebted to the author for giving me access to his personal copy.
67. Lazaro Ndajilo, oral interviews, 14 and 16 June 1997.
68. Ndajilo, oral interviews.
69. Ndajilo, oral interviews.

returning to the *ikumbi* the next morning.[70] However, complete readmission to society did not take place until after the ceremonial washing, followed by the anointing with oil. A few days after readmission into society, the young adults went around visiting different homesteads and receiving gifts.

2.5.1.2 Circumcision and puberty rites in Ukaguru

Similar practices took place in Ukaguru during the period under review. The *Mwana bakwa* ("operator") circumcised the boys in the bush at the *lago* ("small camps"). The initiates' bodies were covered with ash and remained so until the time of full recovery. Contact with women was forbidden during this time. Preparation for adulthood involved teaching by means of riddles and songs. The subjects taught included sexual morality, tribal and clan history,[71] and respect for parents, particularly mothers and maternal relations.[72] As in Ugogo, the traditional elders of the land did all the teaching during the circumcision rite in Ukaguru. The boys stayed at the camp for three months until full recovery.[73] After this, the initiates bathed and a *mlao* ceremony was held to mark their return to the homes. The anointing with oil followed the *mlao*, and the initiates received new names. As with the Wagogo boys, the newly initiated young adults then wandered about, singing and receiving gifts. The circumcised young adults were now obliged to live in the *isepo* or *igane* (the bachelors' hut).[74]

As was the case with the boys, Kaguru girls (*wali*) were circumcised by the *mhunga* in the bush and were brought home soon after the operation. The girls stayed indoors for at least a year,[75] during which they were treated like infants – "nourished, groomed, and domesticated."[76] They were taught prohibitions, sexual morality, domestic responsibilities, artistic drawing, and

---

70. Cole, "Notes on the Wagogo," 308.
71. Beidelman, *Matrilineal Peoples*, 48.
72. Semgomba Chitemo, oral interview, 15 September 1997.
73. Yusufu Masingisa, oral interviews, 16 and 17 September 1997.
74. Beidelman, *Matrilineal Peoples*, 49; Beidelman, *Moral Imagination*, 58.
75. This was a much shorter period compared to that of the confinement of female initiates in other neighbouring matrilineal groups such as Waluguru and Wazaramo girls, which lasted for up to three years. See Yusufu Masingisa, oral interviews, 16 and 17 September 1997.
76. Beidelman, *Moral Imagination*, 58.

how to live peacefully with their husbands and in-laws.[77] The initial period of instruction, *igubi*, was a time when the main ceremony was held. This was followed by *mlao* – the coming out or emergence ceremony. Then, like boys, the girls moved into *ibweti* (special huts for unmarried girls) until the time of their marriage.[78]

2.5.2 Marriage
2.5.2.1 Marriage in Ugogo

Whether in Ugogo or Ukaguru, circumcision for boys and the puberty rite for girls were a doorway to marriage, though not necessarily immediately afterwards. As in many other ethnic groups in Tanzania, and in Africa as a whole, a traditional marriage was both a family and communal affair. In Ugogo, the most common type of marriage was through *kubanya* – betrothal.[79] A successful betrothal mission (during which the proposed fiancée was presented with beads, chains, or other ornaments) was marked with shouting and rejoicing.[80]

Bridewealth was then negotiated.[81] As in other African societies, the giving and receiving of bridewealth legalized marriage, and symbolized the bond between the two families involved. P. Van Velt notes this in his book *Bantu Customs in Mainland Tanzania*: "Bridewealth is the legal form of customary marriage. The surrender of the bridewealth is the conclusion of the marriage contract. It is done before witnesses. It is a certificate."[82] One function of any contract is to act as a guarantee and stabilize the relationship between the parties involved. Thus, Gordon Brown observes, in relation to the marriage among the Wahehe of southwest Tanzania early in the twentieth century, that "a study of Hehe marriage brings one to the conclusion that the primary

---

77. Yusufu Masingisa, oral interviews, 16 and 17 September 1997; Beidelman, *Matrilineal Peoples*, 49.

78. Beidelman, *Matrilineal Peoples*, 49.

79. At times, *kupula* ("abduction" or snatching of a girl) was socially acceptable. But this happened only if the girl's side refused to enter into negotiations that could lead to a *kubanya* marriage. The abduction, *kupula*, was done by the young man, in the companion of his sisters or female relatives. Another form of marriage, *kutizya*, "to run off with" was rare, and antisocial. See Rigby, *Cattle and Kinship*, 211–212.

80. Lazaro Ndajilo, oral interviews, 14 and 16 June 1997; Rees, "History of CMS," MS, G3 A8/0/1902/19, BUL.

81. Lazaro Ndajilo, oral interviews, 14 and 16 June 1997.

82. Van Pelt, *Bantu Customs*, 202.

function of the *mafungu* [bridewealth] is to stabilize marriage."[83] Stability, rather than commercial interest, lay at the root of the custom, a point emphasized by Bishop George Chambers of the DCT (in Ugogo) in the early 1940s: "We speak of a bride-price, but this does not mean that the brides are sold. It is a gift from the bridegroom to the prospective father-in-law as a compensation for his loss of the services of his daughter, and is also a guarantee of good faith."[84] The obvious problem with bridewealth was the size demanded, and if this was high, divorce cases could be difficult to settle, particularly by the woman's family. Yet, many families at the time demanded high bridewealth, trusting that no separation would occur, and in most cases, agreement was reached, opening the door for a wedding date to be set.

On the wedding day, the groom went to bride's home and stayed at a special house where both took off all their clothes and sat on stools. Water was poured into a clean container, usually a gourd (calabash). The bride and the groom then washed in turn in front of everyone present – the groom first and then the bride. The brother-in-law (or if absent, someone appointed by the bride's side) washed the groom, and the bride was washed by her sister-in-law. Then, the round, dry, slippery seeds called *nyilimamba* (also used in flat wooden board games – for example, *bao*)[85] were put in the groom's mouth. The bride opened her mouth and the man spit *nyilimamba* into her mouth.[86] The bride did the same to the groom.[87] By doing that, the man and the woman had become husband and wife.[88] The anointing with oil followed. The parents, particularly the mothers of the groom and bride, admonished their children in the presence of relatives and friends before the bride began the journey to her new home.[89] David Rees (a CMS missionary who arrived at Mamboya in 1897 and then moved to Mpwapwa in 1903) once remarked, "[The Wagogo]

---

83. Brown, "Bride-Wealth," 146.

84. *CTDL*, no. 51 (October 1941): 5.

85. Usually, two opponents play *bao* on a wooden board. The wooden board contains up to fourteen shallow pockets or holes in two opposite rows. The first player to deplete the opponent's balls becomes the winner.

86. Lazaro Ndajilo, oral interviews, 14 and 16 June 1997.

87. Elimerik Mlahagwa, oral interview, 28 June 1997.

88. Lazaro Ndajilo, oral interviews, 14 and 16 June 1997.

89. Cole, "Notes on the Wagogo," 311.

women were treated 'fairly well.' A regular wife could not be sold (as a slave) or put away without an arrangement being made with her kinsfolk."[90]

Polygamy was widely practised in Ugogo. Several reasons caused this: the desire for many children, honour, the ability to entertain guests (when one wife fell ill), long-term cover (just in case one wife died), and gratification of sexual desire.[91] Widow inheritance was another reason, particularly among poor men in Ugogo. As in other societies, one of the reasons for widow inheritance was to enable the brother of the deceased to assume full responsibility for the children left behind.[92] The Wagogo upheld the moral sanctity of marriage and did not sanction adultery. Offenders paid heavy fines, and in some instances, capital offence was applied, particularly if a man tampered with the chief's wife.[93] But such moral standards were only ideal because, as with many societies, men and women had extra-marital relationships, some of which resulted in unwanted pregnancies.[94]

2.5.2.2 Marriage in Ukaguru

Unlike marriage in the patrilineal Ugogo, the matrilineal nature of the Kaguru society meant that some marriages were "uxorilocal." That is to say, a man (usually a poor one) started his married life by residing with his wife's family or kin and offered service to his in-laws for years as a supplement before returning to his father's home. Normally this happened if a man gave small bridewealth (or nothing). Alternatively, after marriage, each spouse stayed with his or her own parents, and the husband visited his wife only occasionally.

The groom's maternal kin and bride's maternal kin were the providers and the recipients of the bridewealth, respectively. Though, in recent years, the groom or his paternal kin have been responsible for the larger share of bridewealth, with his maternal relations making a much smaller contribution. Payment of a large bridewealth presented a man with an opportunity to start married life by living with his wife in his father's home. It also gave him the right to get more support from his children who would normally pay

---

90. Rees, "History of CMS," MS, G3 A8/0/1902/19, BUL.
91. Cole, "Notes on the Wagogo," 311.
92. Lazaro Ndajilo, oral interviews, 14 and 16 June 1997.
93. Rees, "History of CMS," MS, G3 A8/0/1902/19, BUL.
94. Lazaro Ndajilo, oral interviews, 14 and 16 June 1997; Roscoe, *Twenty-Five Years*, 43.

more attention to the needs of their mother and maternal uncles. A feature of Kaguru marriage (quite distinct from that of the Wagogo) was the consummation of marriage in the bride's family home. The custom required that the bride's maternal grandmother should observe and verify that sexual union did actually take place on the wedding day. After this, the man and his wife (now treated as reborn persons just getting into adult life) stayed indoors for four days. Unlike patrilineal groups such as the Wagogo, the survival of Kaguru women depended not on their husbands so much as their children – "the most enduring and powerful of all Kaguru ties."[95] A man could not divorce his wife for groundless reasons. If he did, he lost part or all of the bridewealth he had given.

As may be observed, the differences between the matrilineal and patrilineal marriages of the Wakaguru and Wagogo, respectively, were only in detail, while the procedures were more or less the same. Certainly, the communal dimension and the practice of giving and receiving bridewealth were among the aspects they shared with each other and with many other African societies.

2.5.3 Dance

The significance of dance during the consummation of social customs cannot be over-emphasized. For both the Wagogo and Wakaguru, celebrations (in which dance and drink formed an integral part) were moments of public enactment of social practices whose initial stages involved a degree of secrecy.[96] As has been pointed out above, life in traditional societies was never compartmentalized into strict social, religious, and political regimes. Dances were therefore an integral part of both the circumcision and wedding ceremonies and other religious acts such as rainmaking. In November 1888, John Roscoe wrote from Mamboya, Ukaguru:

> During the past three weeks there has been a great deal of drinking going on in the surrounding villages. This year corn is plentiful, so more ujimbe (Native beer) was made. At two of the nearest towns there was more drinking than I have ever known;

---

95. Beidelman, *Matrilineal Peoples*, 44, 45; Beidelman, *Moral Imagination*, 16, 21.
96. Beidelman, 46; Beidelman, 60.

no doubt a great deal of it was owing to several marriages then taking place.⁹⁷

Some of the common dances in Ugogo included *chasi*, *msunyunho* (variant *sunyunho*), *nindo*, *chipande*, *chisumbi*, *saigwa*, and *mpendoo*. Of these all, *chasi* (common in ceremonies involving circumcision and when a girl's puberty is marked) was perhaps the most controversial because of extreme exposure of the body and the use of the occasion as an excuse for adulterous relationships.⁹⁸ Like *chasi*, *msunyunho* – a popular dance performed at night in the moonlight – was controversial too.⁹⁹ At some stage during the dance, each male dancer approached and picked a female partner at random, whether married or unmarried, and there were no limits to what the pair could share, either in word or deed, as the dance continued or after it had ended.¹⁰⁰ On some occasions, fighting broke out between men or women who competed for partners they had befriended during previous sessions.¹⁰¹ It is for such reasons that even some Wagogo regarded *msunyunho* as controversial.¹⁰² Though also associated with sexuality,¹⁰³ marriage ceremonies, and post-harvest season, *nindo*, *chipande*, *chisumbi*, *saigwa* and *mpendoo* dances were less controversial.¹⁰⁴

2.6 Aspects of Gogo and Kaguru Religions

Dances were a dynamic means by which the Gogo and Kaguru societies celebrated much of their social life. But they were important in religious practices too. An examination of aspects of the religious practices of the Wagogo and Wakaguru will help to show that life in Ugogo and Ukaguru was full of drama that not only involved the living but also the dead. This is important, for, as Donald Green has noted,

---

97. *CMIR* 14 (March 1889): 170.
98. Elimerik Mlahagwa, oral interview, 28 June 1997.
99. Dan Mbogoni, oral interview, 11 June 1997.
100. Lazaro Ndajilo, oral interviews, 14 and 16 June 1997.
101. Dan Mbogoni, oral interview, 11 June 1997.
102. Lazaro Ndajilo, oral interviews, 14 and 16 June 1997; Elimerik Mlahagwa, oral interview, 28 June 1997.
103. Rigby, "Dual Symbolic Classification," 8, 9.
104. Lazaro Ndajilo, oral interviews, 14 and 16 June 1997.

African [traditional] beliefs thus preserve the idea of reciprocity between the living and the dead. Dependence is two-way: the dead need continued respect from and support by the living, and the living need at least benign neutrality on the part of the dead.... It is an affirmation of the essential values of self-discipline and respect for legitimate authority which form the moral basis for society as a whole.[105]

2.6.1 Aspects of Gogo Religion

Sacrifice played a central role in many religious practices in connecting the world of the living with that of the dead whenever a crisis threatened peace and harmony in the two worlds.[106] Sickness was one such life crisis:

> If a child was sick with eye problems a person consulted a diviner. The diviner then told the person, "Oh, it is your grandfather who is making this child sick. He wants you to brew beer for him. He wants meat too." He would then brew beer for sacrifice, and [slaughter] the sheep and take it to the grave of the man's grandfather, ... and give to the deceased the lung portions of the sheep and blood. But people ate the meat.[107]

By cutting meat into pieces and throwing it around (to be left to be eaten by the birds) and pouring the animal's blood over the grave, during a "crisis ritual" of this kind,[108] the worshippers believed that god received their prayers through the ancestor.[109]

Another important ritual in Ugogo and Ukaguru was that of rainmaking. In Ugogo, it was the *mtemi* who became responsible for rainmaking. In his capacity as a ritual leader, the rainmaker kept the *mabwe gemvula* (rain

---

105. Green, "Religion and Morality," 8, 9.

106. The debate on the use of the terms "sacrifice" and "ancestor worship," and on the conceptual separation between the world and role of the living elders and dead elders, may not be adequately explored here. But some scholars argue that "African 'ancestorship' is but an aspect of a broader phenomenon of 'eldership.'" See Kopytoff, "Ancestors as Elders," 140. See also Fortes, "Some Reflections," 122–142. For a valuable and convincing response, see Mendonsa, "Elders, Office-Holders and Ancestors," 57–65.

107. Lazaro Ndajilo, oral interviews, 14 and 16 June 1997.

108. Cox, "Ritual, Rites of Passage," viii.

109. Lazaro Ndajilo, oral interviews, 14 and 16 June 1997.

stones)¹¹⁰ and the *igoda* (stool): "the most important objects in the insignia of ritual office."¹¹¹ The rain stones were kept wrapped in *mwenda mutitu* (a black cloth) which was placed on the stool¹¹² in the ritual leaders hut in his *ikulu* (Kigogo; "palace" or "homestead") and were kept out of sight. Before the rainmaking ceremony, the people wore green leaves and *mbiriri* (bells) and gathered in a ritual area, either at the home of the ritual leader or at a graveyard depending on what the diviner directed.¹¹³ The rainmaker scrapped the soot from the bottom of a pot and mixed it with sheep's fat.¹¹⁴ He then dipped a switch (from the tail of a black cow) into a liquid. After this, he came out of his hut, raised the switch high above his head, and sprinkled the dancers in four directions (north, south, east, and west) to symbolize the summoning of rain.¹¹⁵

Whether it rained or not was a matter of luck.¹¹⁶ The coming of rain was not only important for the people but was also a personal triumph for the rainmaker himself. Lack of rain threatened the survival of both the society and the credibility of the rainmaker. An explanation was therefore necessary. The Wagogo believed that lack of rain was the work of *mkoma-mvula* (the rain-killer) who fed a black snake with medicine and took it to another district or neighbourhood. However, his acts were counteracted by a *mhimbu* – a professional witch-finder – whose task was to locate the snake. If a *mhimbu* found the snake, he recovered the medicine from it, went back to the diviner, and handed it to him. A *mkoma-mvula* who brought the snake into the neighbourhood was identified through the *pugula lugumba* (the casting of lots). He was tied until it rained. But if it didn't rain, he was killed.¹¹⁷

Ugogo had several rainmakers. In the Mvumi chiefdom, for example, Nyama ya Hasi (Kigogo; "meat which is underground")¹¹⁸ was the chief

---

110. The rain stones were believed to be three in number – one small (perhaps the size of a tennis ball) and two slightly larger ones.
111. Rigby, *Cattle and Kinship*, 93.
112. Carnell, "Sympathetic Magic," 30.
113. Rigby, "Dual Symbolic Classification," 6.
114. Rain stones were anointed with sheep's fat.
115. Carnell, "Sympathetic Magic," 30.
116. Lazaro Ndajilo, oral interviews, 14 and 16 June 1997.
117. Cole, "Notes on the Wagogo," 326.
118. Lazaro Ndajilo, oral interviews, 14 and 16 June 1997.

rainmaker in the late nineteenth and early twentieth centuries.[119] He was a contemporary and a joking partner (*mtani*; pl. *watani*)[120] of Ndajilo (the father of Lazaro, one of the informants interviewed for this study). The testimony of Lazaro Ndajilo (probably from late in the nineteenth century or early in the twentieth century) may still give an insight into the practice of witch-hunting and the murdering of suspects who allegedly "prevented" the rain:

> On a certain year, it stopped raining. Then people gathered to make sacrifice for rain.... Msonjela, younger brother of Chalula (Mazengo's father) was the ruler at that time.... It was Mabumo who was killed first.... "He is preventing rain," they said. Then Msonjela said, "This is the man who prevents rain. Go fetch him." So the man was brought near the big trench at Suji. They killed him there... and offered sacrifice, saying, "Cool down, you bad guy who prevents rain."[121]

Witch-hunting and accusations were endless. Indeed, they often took the form of revenge rather than a genuine search for the causes of drought through religious sacrifice. At another time, it was Chituzanzoka, the elder brother of Nyama ya Hasi (the chief rainmaker), himself, who became a victim:

> Despite those murders, it didn't rain either.... "What is this," they asked themselves. "Oh, we know. It is because Nyama ya Hasi's elder brother is a witch."... Then Msonjela, Mazengo's uncle reacted angrily and said, "Why does this man want the people to perish? Go and fetch him. Chituzanzoka."... You know they killed him and threw him into the Mahato dam.... They didn't bury him, because they said to themselves, "If you do throw this man anywhere carelessly, then the drought will

---

119. Bertha Briggs to Baylis, 3 March 1909, G3 A8/0/1909/28, BUL.

120. Unlike the Wakaguru who placed greater emphasis on the role of *watani* in rituals, in Ugogo the role of the *watani* was mainly in the social domain, rather than in religious activities. See Rigby, *Cattle and Kinship*, 88–92. For further details on joking relationships in Ugogo, see Rigby, "Joking Relationships," 133–155. For a discussion on joking relationships in other ethnic groups in Tanzania, see Moreau, "Joking Relationship in Tanganyika," 386–400. For a general survey, see Radcliffe-Brown, "On Joking Relationships," 195–210.

121. Lazaro Ndajilo, oral interviews, 14 and 16 June 1997.

continue. Throw him into the water in order that his medicines may become wet [and lose power] so that it may start to rain again."[122]

Rainmaking continued, but certainly, by early in the twentieth century, public execution and the offering of human beings as an offering for rain had ceased, mainly because the German colonial administration banned them.[123]

2.6.2 Aspects of Kaguru Religion

Kaguru religion and Gogo religion bore significant similarities to each other, not least in the significance they attached to sacrifice. An early foreign missionary (wrongly identified by Yusufu Masingisa as "Mr Price") visited the chief of Mamboya (apparently during an exploratory mission) in the late nineteenth century,[124] and inquired from the chief as to whether the Kaguru believed in God. The chief's response was unequivocal: "Of course we know God. Every tribe knows God. We get rain from God. We get everything from God."[125] Semgomba Chitemo reiterated this: "The black people knew God already.... They knew God.... The Masai had their own religion. This was the same for every tribe. Religion existed already."[126] One of the distinctive features of religious worship in Ukaguru was the use of little huts called *vijumba mulungu* (sing. *kijumba mulungu*, "house of God").[127] Generally, the elders "who knew tradition" built these at the crossroads.[128] David Rees wrote: "The

---

122. Ndajilo, oral interviews.
123. Cole, "Notes on the Wagogo," 326; cf. Lazaro Ndajilo, oral interviews, 14 and 16 June 1997. See additional notes in appendix 3 about Msonjela's imprisonment by the Germans for presiding over killings.
124. Yusufu Masingisa, oral interviews, 16 and 17 September 1997. It is possible that the informant confused Joseph Last with John Price who settled at Mpwapwa in late 1879. Indeed, well before the occupation of Mamboya in 1880, it was Last who visited it seven times as he travelled to and from the coast. The chief (Senyagwa Chimola) often asked him to stay, and the people wanted a missionary to live amongst them. The attitude of the chief and the people made Last conclude that Mamboya was "an eligible spot for a missionary station." See *CMIR* 4 (November 1879): 664. He himself took a permanent residence there in January 1880. See *CMIR* 5 (December 1880): 742.
125. Yusufu Masingisa, oral interviews, 16 and 17 September 1997.
126. Semgomba Chitemo, oral interview, 15 September 1997.
127. In some ethnic groups bordering Ukaguru on the east, e.g. the Luguru, these were called *Vijumba-Nungu* (sing. *Kijumba-Nungu*) and were found in nearly every homestead. See Gwassa, "Kinjikitile," 208.
128. Semgomba Chitemo, oral interview, 15 September 1997.

Wasagara [Wakaguru] worshipped a God, or spirit who they called 'Mulungu.' They built little huts, generally where two paths met. Under the hut they put various offerings, such as a few grains or corn, broken pieces of pottery, or little bows and arrows like those which children played with."[129] The Kaguru paid seasonal homage to the *kijumba mulungu*. Normally, this was after the harvest when food was plenty. Sacrifice was offered to a god (with the various names of *Mateke, Mhonya, Nyalombwe*,[130] *cholile,* or *bode*)[131] – the one who cures the souls of people. The Kaguru god was also called *mundewa*.[132] There was also the goddess *Maduwo – Oniduwo na ng'ombe* (Kikaguru; "the one with a huge belly the size of a cow's"). Both Mateke and she received prayers and sacrifices in times of crisis in the land.

As was the case in Ugogo, sacrifice for rain was a key element in Kaguru religious life. This took place before the planting season. The *watani* slaughtered a black sheep and ate its meat, normally at the graves of reputable departed members of the clan. Household fires were extinguished and homes were swept clean. The new fire to be kindled in the homes had to be taken from the "new" fire kindled during the ceremonies in the bush. If the rain fell, the rainmaker, *mutungu la fula*, got the credit.[133] As in Ugogo, the witch hunting for those alleged to have prevented rain took place as well. The diviners (often the elders) who detected "bad people," such as those preventing the rain, were called *wagonezi* (sing. *mgonezi*). Semgomba Chitemo clarifies this:

> *Semgomba Chitemo:* In the event of lack of rain, they used medicine to *detect the bad person in society*. Then that person was arrested. He was beaten, and then ordered to unlock his magic that prevented rain coming down. Then it rained.
>
> *Mwita Akiri:* . . . Was the act of beating him just enough to bring the rain, grandfather?

---

129. Rees, "History of CMS," MS, G3 A8/0/1902/19, BUL.

130. Semgomba Chitemo, oral interview, 15 September 1997. Mr Chitemo mentioned those various names of the same god of the Kaguru people.

131. Beidelman, *Matrilineal Peoples*, 49. The words are various names of the same god of the Kaguru people.

132. Semgomba Chitemo, oral interview, 15 September 1997.

133. Beidelman, *Matrilineal Peoples*, 50.

Semgomba Chitemo: You! He had to go where he put the traditional medicine he used and undo the magic. Then the rain came down.[134]

If it rained but still the fields failed to yield good crops, the *sembukwa* ("ceremonies of revilement") were held in order to cleanse them. This involved the littering of the fields with "polluting materials" and "persons abused the fields by word and gesture as one might abuse a person."[135] The crop and waste material were then discarded in the bush. This was one of the Kaguru calendrical rites.

Like the Wagogo, Wakaguru offered sacrifices in order to deal with misfortunes. Death of a large number of people was an indication that a serious moral pollution had taken place.[136] Sacrifice had to be offered at the graves of the living dead, and this involved *kushangila kufilalo* (lit. "to sweep a grave"). Beer, flour, tobacco, and, at times, chicken, goats, sheep, or cows were offered, depending on the seriousness of the misfortune, and blood was poured over the ancestral graves.[137] This was Kaguru's way of controlling disruption and enforcing social order in the world of the living.[138]

2.7 Conclusion

The political, social, and religious analysis that has been attempted above shows that life in Gogo and Kaguru societies was full of drama and vitality. The two societies were well entrenched in their beliefs and practices. Maintenance of security and prosperity for the entire society was the responsibility and goal of those vested with authority, such as the chiefs, diviners, and elders. The enthusiastic involvement of the rest of society in customs such as circumcision, marriage, and dance shows that no one wanted to be left behind or kept in isolation. The great care taken to ensure that elaborate social customs and religious practices were performed meticulously points

---

134. Semgomba Chitemo, oral interview, 15 September 1997.
135. Beidelman, *Matrilineal Peoples*, 50; Beidelman, *Moral Imagination*, 123–126.
136. Semgomba Chitemo, oral interview, 15 September 1997.
137. Chitemo, oral interview; Beidelman, *Moral Imagination*, 18, 122.
138. Beidelman, *Moral Imagination*, 114, 111–119, 122; Yusufu Masingisa, oral interviews, 16 and 17 September 1997; Beidelman, *Matrilineal Peoples*, 49.

to the fact that doing the contrary would bring disaster upon the people – something they didn't want. Security and cohesion had to be maintained.

But the Gogo and Kaguru were also open to external influences, especially if these enhanced their aspirations and increased their chances of survival as a people. Their response to the Christian influence was likely to be governed by this concern. As will be seen later, traditional Gogo and Kaguru life continued to survive well into the twentieth century. From the analysis one might conclude, as Ogbu Kalu has observed, that in Africa, Christianity moved into an "alive . . . context."[139]

---

139. Kalu, "African Church Historiography," 173.

CHAPTER 3

Christian Developments in Ugogo and Ukaguru 1876–1900

The thrust of this study lies in a thematic sociohistorical analysis of the initiatives, contributions, and experiences of indigenous Tanzanians (Christians and non-Christians alike) as mission Christianity developed among the Wagogo and Wakaguru whose political, social, and religious setting was analysed in chapter 2. The focus is on the period 1900–1933 – the years that the writer observes to be the first major expansion phase of mission work carried out in Ugogo and Ukaguru under the CMS mission. However, it may be helpful, first, to trace the early Christian developments from the mid-1870s to 1900 – a task which this chapter aims to achieve. This will cover developments in Uganda and Britain that led to the commencement of mission work in central Tanzania and the assessment of that work at the first three major stations – Mpwapwa, Chamuhawi, and Mamboya.

This chapter focuses on how CMS missionaries' understanding, or misunderstanding, of Gogo and Kaguru traditional religion and social practices aided or hindered the progress of work at this period. Equally, attention will be paid to emerging indigenous initiatives.

3.1 King Mutesa of Buganda and Henry Stanley

CMS missionaries were not the first Europeans to come into contact with the Wagogo and Wakaguru of central Tanzania. Richard Burton, John Speke, and James Grant had passed through Ugogo and Ukaguru between the late

1850s and early 1860s.[1] David Livingstone followed shortly afterward, and, in the mid-1870s, Henry Stanley (to whom reference has already been made in chapter 2) passed through central Tanzania.[2] Roger Price of the London Missionary Society (LMS) – whom Livingstone preceded under the auspices of the same society – and one Lt. Cameron were also among those who passed through central Tanzania before any CMS missionary arrived.[3] Of all these, perhaps Stanley's second journey to East Africa had a most enduring connection with the work of the CMS mission in Ugogo and Ukaguru.

The shortcomings of Stanley's conduct during his journeys in Africa, not least in the way he treated the local people he met, sometimes even murdering them, should not be overlooked.[4] The implication of some of his actions for the image of Britain abroad was often a matter of concern even to politicians.[5] However, the purpose here is not to stress his role, but that of Kabaka Mutesa of Buganda, in the commencement of the CMS work in the interior of East Africa.[6] The impression Mutesa made on Stanley in April 1875 was certainly a significant "African" factor in the commencement of sustainable CMS work in the interior of East Africa after early attempts by Ludwig Krapf and John Rebman on the coast three decades earlier. Stanley appealed, on behalf of

---

1. For details of the account of each traveller/explorer, see Burton, *First Footsteps*; Speke, *Journal of the Discovery*; Grant, *Walk Across Africa*; cf. Livingstone, *Missionary Travels*. See maps enclosed in Hutchinson, *Victoria Nyanza*. Map facing title page (n.d.) has routes used by Lt Cameron. It also shows the route followed by Richard Burton and John Speke together in 1857, Speke alone in 1858, and Speke and James Grant in 1861–1862. Another map (by Keith Johnston, 1863) attached to the book also shows the route used by Speke and Grant from Zanzibar to Egypt.

2. Stanley, *How I Found Livingstone*, 122–157. Stanley's first journey was made in search of David Livingstone, whom he met at Ujiji, on Lake Tanganyika, in 1871. His second journey started in 1874 during which he met Mutesa of Buganda in April 1875. See *CMIR* 14 (February 1889): 69.

3. *CMIR* 2 (July 1877): 7; Cameron was at Mpwapwa in June 1873. See *CMIR* 4 (September 1879): 529.

4. See, for example, in chapter 2 where it was noted he probably hit the Wagogo who gathered to watch him. Cf. the shooting of fourteen people at a small island on the western shore of Lake Victoria in April 1874. See Pakenham, *Scramble for Africa*, 28.

5. Pakenham, *Scramble for Africa*, 28.

6. Except in quotations, the name "Mutesa" shall be spelled thus throughout this study, rather than its variant "Mtesa."

Mutesa, to a wider British audience through the *Daily Telegraph* newspaper.[7] It is perhaps worth quoting parts of it at length:

> Mtesa is a great King. He is a monarch who would delight the soul of any intelligent European. . . . Each day I found something which increased my esteem and respect for him. . . . I have already told you that Mtesa and the whole of his Court profess Islam, . . . but by one conversation, I flatter myself that I have tumbled the newly-raised religious fabric to the ground, and if it were only followed by the arrival of a Christian Mission here, the conversion of Mtesa and his Court to Christianity would, I think, be complete. . . . I have indeed, undermined Islamism so much here, that Mtesa has determined henceforth, until he is better informed, to observe the Christian Sabbath as well as the Moslem Sabbath. . . . He has further caused the Ten Commandments of Moses to be written on a board for his daily perusal – for Mtesa can read Arabic. . . . This is great progress for the few days that I have remained with him and, though I am no Missionary, I shall begin to think that I might become one if such success feasible. But, oh that some pious, practical Missionary would come here! What a field and a harvest ripe for the sickle of civilization. . . . Here, gentlemen, is your opportunity – embrace it! The people on the shores of the Nyanza call upon you.[8]

Stanley emphasized that it was not he but "the people on the shores of the Nyanza [who] call upon you." This is significant because, though it is often thought that the appeal came from Stanley, the request for foreign missionaries was not his, but Mutesa's.[9] Stanley merely became the mouthpiece. However, the phrase, "what a field . . . for the sickle of civilization" gives a better indication of what Stanley thought a Christian mission could

---

7. Stanley's letter appeared in the *Daily Telegraph* newspaper in London on 15 November 1875. The appeal was published at the same time in *New York Herald*. See *CMIR* 14 (February 1889): 70; Pakenham, *Scramble for Africa*, 28.

8. Extract from Stanley's letter, Daily Telegraph, 15 November 1875, quoted in full in Hutchinson, *Victoria Nyanza*, 12–18. For the quote, see 14, 15, 16, and 17.

9. Pakenham, *Scramble for Africa*, 28, 297.

achieve – "civilization" of the Baganda. No wonder the British flag and imperialism reached Uganda by the end of 1890.[10] There is little doubt that Kabaka's appeal through Stanley had a big impact upon its intended audience. By 17 November 1875 – only two days after the publishing of the letter – gifts earmarked for the commencement of the Nyanza mission were forthcoming. An anonymous person, who only signed his letter as "an unprofitable servant (Luke 17:10)," wrote:

> The appeal of the energetic explorer Stanley to the Christian Church from Mtesa's capital, Uganda . . . seems to me to indicate that the time has come for the soldiers of the Cross to make an advance into that region. If the Committee of the Church Missionary Society are prepared at once and with energy to organise a Mission to the Victorian Nyanza, I shall account it a high privilege to place 5,000*l*. at their disposal as a nucleus for the expenses of the undertaking.[11]

This offer prompted the CMS, at a special meeting on 23 November 1875, to take up the challenge: "The Church Missionary Society is primarily commissioned to Africa and the East, . . . and undertakes in dependence upon God, to take steps for the establishment of a Mission to the vicinity of the Victorian Nyanza, in the prayerful hope that it may prove a centre of light and blessing to tribes in the heart of Africa."[12] The goal of the CMS was to use the Nyanza mission as a springboard for wider missionary outreach across central Africa. Apart from the first anonymous gift mentioned above, other smaller donations were made to facilitate that mission.[13] Before long, a total of £24,000 had been raised for the initial work of the Nyanza mission.[14] In 1876, a party of eight men was despatched to meet king Mutesa.[15] The king –

---

10. Pakenham, 356, 413–433.
11. Hutchinson, *Victoria Nyanza*, 19.
12. Hutchinson, 19.
13. *CMIR* 1 (January 1876): 49. The second anonymous gift, of £3,000, followed on 29 November. Together with other similar donations, the figure for the second round of donations reached £5,000.
14. *CMIR* 14 (February 1889): 70.
15. The eight men were Rev C. T. Wilson, Lt Shergold Smith, Thomas O'Neill, Alexander Mackay, William Robertson, Dr. John Smith, James Robertson, and George Clark. See *CMIR* 1 (June 1876): 370. James Robertson died at Zanzibar on 5 August 1876 before the trip to the

perhaps keen to demonstrate his acquaintance with international diplomatic procedures – issued a formal invitation to the CMS party before they entered his kingdom. Dallington Scopion Maftaa (his secretary) wrote the two letters, the content of which were as follows:[16]

> April 10th, 1877 TO MY DEAR FRIEND, – I have heard that you have reached Ukerewe, so now I want you to come to me quickly. I give you Magombwa to be your guide, and now you must come to me quickly. This letter from me, Mtesa, King of Uganda, written by Dallington Scopion Maftaa, April, 10th 1877. (On the back of this letter were the following words) April 10th, 1877. TO MY DEAR SIR, – I have heard that you are in Ukerewe, and this king is very fond of you. He wants Englishmen more than all. This is from your servant, DALLINGTON SCOPION, April 10th, 1877.[17]
>
> MY SECOND LETTER TO MY DEAR FRIEND WITE MEN, – I send this my servant that you may come quickly, and therefore I pray you come to me quickly, and let not this my servant come without you. And send my salaam to Lukonge, King of Ukerewe, and Thaduma Mwanangwa of Kageye and Songoro. This from me, Mtesa, King of Uganda.[18]

---

interior began. Clark and W. Robertson only reached as far as Mpwapwa and returned to Britain after falling ill. See *CMIR* 4 (September 1879): 531. Therefore only five men travelled beyond Mpwapwa. These were Lt Shergold Smith, Rev C. T. Wilson, Thomas O'Neill, Dr Smith, and Mackay. The number was further reduced when Dr Smith died as the party reached the south of Lake Victoria Nyanza. Finally, it was Rev Wilson and Lt. Smith who first reached Rubaga, the capital of Buganda on Saturday, 30 June 1877. See *CMIR* 14 (February 1889): 71. Later O'Neill and Lt. Smith were killed on 7 December 1877 after a dispute involving king Lukonge of Ukerewe and Songoro (an Arab trader) about payment for timber that had been used to make a dhow which the latter sold to members of the CMS party. See *CMIR* 3 (February 1878): 313–314.

16. Maftaa (variant Mufta) – the writer of the letters – was a young man from Zanzibar who had learned English at a Universities' Mission to Central Africa (UMCA) school, probably at Kiungani. Stanley requested that he should stay behind at Kabaka's palace to continue the Christian influence while also using his secretarial skills. Maftaa read the Bible to Mutesa in Kiswahili – the language used by Mutesa and his chiefs. See *CMIR* 14 (February 1889): 70, 71. He interpreted for king Mutesa as he listened to the address by Rev Wilson and Lt Smith on 30 June 1877. See *CMIR* 3 (February 1878): 120.

17. *CMIR* 3 (February 1878): 122. Note in parentheses (round brackets) in the original.

18. *CMIR* 3 (February 1878): 122.

The king's invitation to the members of the CMS party was symbolic in that, later, in central Tanzania as in other places in Africa, many chiefs took the initiative to invite missions to commence Christian work in their chiefdoms. Certainly, as will be seen later in this study, the Gogo and Kaguru chiefs did exactly that in places where CMS was operating – less in the nineteenth century but increasingly during the first expansion phase from 1900–1933.

3.2 Mpwapwa: A Place of Significance

In January 1876, the Nyanza sub-committee recommended to the CMS main committee that an intermediate station be formed between the coast of Tanzania and Lake Victoria Nyanza to support the operation undertaken under the Nyanza (Uganda) mission. In this sense, Gordon Hewitt may be right in suggesting that "the CMS mission in Tanganyika was a by-product of its Uganda mission."[19] Indeed, for many years it was Uganda that was the base of CMS work in East Africa, until the diocese of Mombasa was formed in 1899.[20] This interpretation of the developments in Uganda and central Tanzania is to a large extent accurate for, even later (as will be observed in chapter 8), CMS often viewed its mission in central Tanzania as a "burden" that it could well do without.

However, it should also be stressed that the significance of Mpwapwa as a potential mission station in its own right was recognized well before the Nyanza (Uganda) mission was contemplated. A traveller, one Lt. Cameron from Britain who passed through Mpwapwa in June 1873, recommended the place not just as an intermediary resting place but as a mission station.[21] Roger Price (of LMS), who had reached Mpwapwa in July 1876, did the same when he said Mpwapwa was "a most important position to occupy, both as a mission and trading station." Price described Mpwapwa as "a kind of a gateway to vast regions beyond" where all the roads (more accurately, caravan routes)

---

19. Hewitt, *Problems of Success*, 1:180.

20. The division of the diocese of Eastern Equatorial Africa was arranged towards the end of 1897 and was carried out in 1899 when the new dioceses – the Diocese of Uganda and Diocese of Mombasa – were formed. Bishop Alfred Tucker retained the supervision of Uganda, western Kenya, and the area south of Victoria Nyanza in Tanzania. The rest of Kenya and Tanzania became the Diocese of Mombasa under its first bishop, William Peel. See Stock, *History*, 3:731; *PCMS*, 1899, 85.

21. *CMIR* 4 (September 1879): 529–530.

from the coastal towns (Dar es Salaam, Bagamoyo, Sadani, and Pangani) to the lake regions met. It was, he added, "a fresh starting point for caravans after all their trouble and hard labour in the maritime and mountainous regions."[22] Given this publicity, it was almost inevitable that at some point in time, Mpwapwa would to get the attention of a mission society as a suitable place for launching missionary activity in central Tanzania.

3.3 Mpwapwa, Chamuhawi, and Mamboya: The Survivors

In considering the work of the CMS in Ugogo and Ukaguru between 1876 and 1900, one is basically dealing with the developments at three of the earliest stations: Mpwapwa, Chamuhawi, and Mamboya. Mpwapwa was the first station to be permanently established in Ugogo and Tanzania as a whole.[23] George Clark – a member of the CMS party of eight – was particularly commissioned for establishing Mpwapwa. He arrived on 24 August 1876.[24] He tried to build a thirty-foot square house, but by November 1876, he had not

---

22. Extract of Roger Price's letter in the *Chronicle of London Missionary Society*, November 1876, quoted in *CMIR* 4 (September 1879): 530.

23. Most early travellers, e.g. Stanley, regarded Mpwapwa as being in Usagara (Stanley, *How I Found Livingstone*, 130, 139). Some historical maps show Mpwapwa as part of Usagara (see maps in *PCMS*, 1910; Roscoe, *Twenty-Five Years*; Hutchinson, *Victoria Nyanza*). The first CMS missionaries to settle at Mpwapwa, e.g. Edward Baxter and Last, reported visiting Ugogo and wrote, "Mpwapwa, unlike Ugogo, is a bad place for breeding of sheep, goats, and oxen." See *CMIR* 4 (September 1879): 532, 534. In October 1888, John Price reported, "I returned from my last tour in Ugogo." See *CMIR* 14 (March 1889): 168. Some modern writers describe the historical Mpwapwa as part of western Ukaguru. See Beidelman, *Matrilineal Peoples*, 41. But in reality, Usagara is a "country" south of Ukaguru. Travellers such as Roger Price of the LMS who passed through Mpwapwa in July 1876 suggested that the Wasagara and Wakaguru formed the majority population but stated that the Wagogo were present too. (Roger Price's letter is quoted in *CMIR* 4 [September 1879]: 530). Furthermore, in 1879, Baxter reported about "gradually picking up the *Chigogo* language" at Mpwapwa (*CMIR* 4 [September 1879]: 533) and said, "I long for the time when we shall be able to hold services in *Kigogo*" (*CMIR* 5 [December 1880]: 738). Contrary to suggestions in some sources (e.g. *PCMS*, 1900, 113), it appears that there was a large population of the Wagogo among the Mpwapwa inhabitants. A CMS annual report of 1882 noted, "Mpwapwa would be more accurately described as in U-Gogo; the people being mostly of the Ugogo nation (Wa-Gogo); although a pori or desert lies between it and the Gogo territory as generally understood [or misunderstood]." See *PCMS*, 1883, 50. From this, it is better to regard Mpwapwa as the first station in Ugogo, but on the borderline with western Ukaguru (mis-termed Usagara). See Rees, "History of CMS," MS, G3 A8/0/1902/19, BUL; *PCMS*, 1901, 122; *PCMS*, 1877, 44.

24. *PCMS* 1877, 44.

completed it. So he wrote, "taking all things into consideration, I fear I shall have to live under canvas for many months, which I do not mind if rain keeps away."[25] It is unlikely that Clark ever completed the construction of the mission house as he soon fell ill and returned to Britain.[26] Late in autumn 1877, CMS sent four laymen (Dr Edward Baxter, Joseph Last, Alfred Copplestone, and James Henry) to "re-establish the Usagara Mission [Mpwapwa] begun two years ago by G. J. Clark."[27] These arrived at Mpwapwa early in May 1878. Copplestone proceeded north towards Lake Victoria Nyanza, and Henry fell ill and returned to Britain. So it was only Baxter and Last who remained to commence mission work afresh at Mpwapwa.[28] John Price and Henry Cole joined them in the autumn of 1879.[29] In 1880, Chamuhawi (formerly Kisokwe) – located six miles west of Mpwapwa – was started. In the same year, Mamboya (some hundred miles eastward) was opened as the first station in Ukaguru.[30] Kikombo was started in 1886 as an out-station of Mpwapwa but was discontinued in September 1888. By then, two Christians had been baptized there.[31] So, by the end of the nineteenth century, only Mpwapwa, Chamuhawi, and Mamboya had survived and continued. Progress at each of these stations is examined and assessed below.

3.3.1 Some Local Challenges to a Christian Cause

On the whole, little progress was made at Mpwapwa, Chamuhawi, and Mamboya until 1900. A number of reasons contributed to this. First, during the nineteenth century, much of the school work and Sunday worship was mainly among the residents of the mission settlement (freed slaves, builders, interpreters, and guides) who accompanied the first CMS missionaries to Mpwapwa and Mamboya, and these were from Mombasa and Zanzibar.[32]

---

25. *CMIR* 2 (March 1877): 152.
26. *CMIR* 4 (September 1879): 531.
27. *CMIR* 3 (October 1878): 645.
28. *CMIR* 4 (September 1879): 531.
29. *CMIR* 5 (December 1880): 735.
30. See *CMIR* 5 (December 1880): 742.
31. *PCMS*, 1889, 47.
32. *CMIR* 3 (October 1878): 646; *CMIR* 3 (October 1878): 645, 646; *CMIR* 4 (September 1879): 533, 534. Later, Joseph Last (who later moved to Mamboya) brought about forty to fifty "freed slaves" from Zanzibar to Mpwapwa in 1879 to carry out the building work. By the end of 1880, services at Mpwapwa were still for these people alone. See *CMIR* 5 (December 1880): 740.

Ugogo and Ukaguru were vast areas, over 10,000 and 3,600 square miles, respectively. Inevitably, the priority for CMS missionaries was to maintain and preserve the little work done in and around the existing stations.

Second, in addition to the general attitude of self-preservation, CMS missionaries needed time to learn the vernacular languages – Kigogo and Kikaguru. This made them rely on African interpreters as they preached and taught within the vicinity of the stations or during the few itinerations further away. It is interesting to note that the Africans engaged in the task did more than merely interpreting for CMS missionaries. They often engaged in stimulating discussions with the Wagogo and Wakaguru (see below, for example, about Lwanga Tofiki).

Third, CMS missionaries misunderstood Gogo and Kaguru religious life in this period. The nineteenth-century CMS missionaries (as with other missions) were children of their time and cannot be assessed by the standards of the twenty-first century. Moreover, their training was only basic. Even early in the twentieth century it was far from adequate in preparing them for cross-cultural mission[33] – a problem that the World Missionary Conference (WMC) at Edinburgh in 1910 recognized well.[34] The social and religious revival, and enthusiasm for the spiritual transformation of other peoples that prevailed in Europe at the time, was likely to mask such a need and ignorance.

However, an analysis of their encounter with local cultures is important. In November 1876, George Clark – the first CMS missionary to Mpwapwa – wrote:

> Regarding opportunities for mission work, in the first place there are plenty of people in this district, who, as far as I can see, have no form of religion of any kind. Even the fetish houses and charms seen on the road have disappeared here. They fire guns and make a good noise at the new moon's appearance, but seem to have no knowledge whatever of a God.[35]

---

33. For details on the training of CMS missionaries for Africa at Islington College, particularly in the early twentieth century, see Hodge, "Training of the Missionaries," 81–96.

34. See World Missionary Conference, *Missionary Message*, 19, 20.

35. *CMIR* 2 (March 1877): 152–153.

The "fetish houses" referred to were *vijumba mulungu* ("houses of God") that were part of Kaguru, not Wagogo, religious worship. For Clark to expect to find them in Ugogo simply exposes his level of misunderstanding of Gogo religion at the time. Rev C. T. Wilson – one of the CMS delegates to Uganda – also remarked that the Wagogo seemed to "have no religion, and little idea of a God." Yet he described them in religious terms as "superstitious and afraid of evil spirits," a people with "great faith in their 'magangas' [waganga], or medicine-men, who profess to make rain, etc., and stand in great awe of them."[36] Religion was there. The problem was how to recognize and acknowledge it. Writing from Mpwapwa on 14 May 1880, John Price expressed his desire to see the Wagogo believe in the teaching offered, but he also admitted how little understanding existed between him and them:

> May God give them grace to *believe* us when we tell them those things of which they are *confessedly* ignorant! I sometimes hear them use the expression, "Mulunga [Mulungu] kuchanya" (God is above); but on asking them one day if they knew who God is, one replied, "Mvula" (the rain)! How like the old Egyptian with his River Nile. When speaking of the resurrection and life to come, I have been told by them that they know that people will rise to life again, but confess their ignorance as to what becomes of the soul after death. With regard to the resurrection we may have misunderstood each other, for I can scarcely believe they can have much idea of it.[37]

It shows – as John Karanja has noted about the Kikuyu society in their encounter with the CMS missionaries in central Kenya early in the twentieth century – the problems arising from preaching the Christian message which focused on the sharp contrast between earthly life and life after death. Yet, most African traditional societies (the Kikuyu and Wagogo among them) and their religions were basically and acutely conscious of the contrast between the spiritual and the physical world here on earth.[38] In light of the analysis of aspects of the Gogo religion done in chapter 2, the observation that

---

36. *CMIR* 2 (July 1877): 409.
37. *CMIR* 5 (December 1880): 740.
38. Karanja, "Growth of the African Anglican Church," 49.

"the people had no idea of God" was inaccurate. Consequently, the message preached to the Wagogo was far from interacting with their religious aspirations. The sermon Baxter preached at a village on his way to Mpwapwa in May 1878 gives a sense of the basic structure and nature of most sermons preached at the time: "I then spoke to them, through my interpreter Ali,[39] of the Creation, the distinction of man and a beast, the fall, the remedy in Christ; His Life, death, and resurrection; the home in glory, one judgement; and then of God's preserving care over His people as illustrated by Daniel, etc. etc."[40] Price, who had been with Baxter since 1879, always insisted he wanted to baptize only those he was sure had understood the message of Christian religion. This could be one of the reasons for the lack of an early baptism at Mpwapwa. In 1884, though noting the friendliness of the Wagogo, a report from Mpwapwa emphasized how the people were still "indifferent to the teaching and hard to lift above the common wants of everyday life."[41]

The phrase "common wants of everyday life" points to the fourth reason why little progress was made during this period. Given the intensity of the slave trade and the material traffic (for travellers, whether explorers or Christian missionaries – most of whom at this time were from Europe – carried substantial quantities of supplies with them), the local people viewed CMS missionaries as rich people. Attempts to deny this were not always successful. The encounter of John Price with the Wagogo of Mpwapwa, who constantly asked for cloth, indicates this. In May 1880, Price wrote:

> Happily the doctor [Dr Baxter] has all the cloth, etc., in his own charge, so that I am able to tell them I have nothing to give them. They then point to my boots and hat as evidence that I must be a rich man! I tell them I have riches, but they are in heaven, and I have come here to show them the way to that happy place. Sometimes after trying to talk a little seriously to them of eternal realities, and asking if they have understood me, they reply, "Yes, give me some cloth, bwana [sir]."[42]

---

39. Ali (the interpreter) spoke both English and Kigogo.
40. *CMIR* 3 (October 1878): 646.
41. *PCMS*, 1884, 49.
42. *CMIR* 5 (December 1880): 739.

The notion, that the Wagogo would easily concur with Price that he and his fellow CMS missionaries were "poor" was self-deception. Above all, for the traditional Wagogo – and their attitude was in no way unique – riches were to be acquired here and now and not in heaven. Failure to share in or have access to the riches held by CMS missionaries put off the Wagogo from mission Christianity at this time. It has to be observed in passing though, that when later (as will become evident in chapter 5), the mission widened the scope of what it could offer to the Wagogo to support life on earth, more people joined.

3.3.2 First Baptisms at Mpwapwa and Chamuhawi

It has been pointed out that the Gogo religious life was misunderstood, and there were conflicting ambitions between the Wagogo of Mpwapwa and the CMS missionaries. But that is not to suggest that the whole message that was communicated fell on deaf ears. Seven years after Mpwapwa was reestablished, in December 1885, the first baptisms of three people took place there (and included people from Chamuhawi).[43] In July 1889 – nine years after he was asked for cloth, Price now realized how difficult it was to preach about happiness in heaven when the Wagogo wanted it here and now. It is likely that the three first Christians saw that possibility and decided to become members of the mission. An enlightened Price was now able to realize the difficulty of trying to underplay worldly riches while communicating the Christian message:

> One thing I have made up my mind upon – that if am spared to live out here, I will have as little as possible of this world's goods about me. Having so much of it at Mpwapwa in the big house has been a curse to the Mission, as it only excites the avarice of these people, and makes it more difficult for them to understand our real motive in living amongst them.[44]

By the end of 1898, on the whole, Mpwapwa had not found favour with CMS missionaries yet. A CMS report noted that "the native Christians, especially those of years standing, were not altogether satisfactory; and seem to have 'got into a groove,' and all efforts to arouse them were in vain."[45]

---

43. *PCMS*, 1886, 42.
44. *CMIR* 14 (December 1889): 743.
45. *PCMS*, 1899, 100.

3.3.3 Oral Tradition and Stagnation at Mpwapwa

But oral tradition points to quite a different reason for the stagnation at Mpwapwa – one that actually led to its closure later in 1906.[46] One informant, Elimerik Mlahagwa of Chamuhawi, was blunt in his assessment of stagnation at Mpwapwa: "The reason was that when those people arrived at Ving'hawe [which is the name of the exact location where the first station was established at Mpwapwa], they didn't do any serious work. They only preached. . . . Those who worked there did not have better tactics for attracting people. The only thing they did was to ring the bell and invite people to learn how to read, and people didn't turn up."[47] The problems of communication in preaching encountered by John Price have already been noted above. Though it appears that, at a later time, he may have improved his approach to the Wagogo and possibly developed a good relationship with older people whom he invited to the mission house. Indeed, the Wagogo often called him *Bwana Mwalimu* ("Mr Teacher").[48] Apparently, as Esta Chali of Mpwapwa says, he became very gentle in persuading the Wagogo to join the mission, not minding when the elders he gathered took snuff as he preached to them at the mission station.[49]

3.3.4 Missionary Methods: A Key to Success at Chamuhawi

Compared with Mpwapwa, better progress was made at Chamuhawi. Oral sources attribute this to at least three reasons. First, it was the skilful missionary method of Henry Cole. He identified himself with the local people:

> The church grew from here, because when this man arrived he thought about ways of attracting people to the church. That was why he joined their traditional game of *naga*.[50] . . . He went on playing *naga* while the construction of the church also progressed. When the church building was about to be completed, he said, "Now I must also try to draw them to the mission." Therefore he cleared a portion of land as a football ground. . . .

---

46. Details of the closure of Mpwapwa will be found in chapter 5.
47. Elimerik Mlahagwa, oral interview, 28 June 1997.
48. Esta Chali, oral interview, 26 June 1997.
49. Chali, oral interview.
50. *Naga*, which is no longer played in Ugogo, was a ball game, played by two teams, one on each side of the pitch. Players hit the ball towards their opponent's side with the aim of passing it beyond the line. A *naga* ball was made from soft wood or the inner part of a sisal trunk.

> When he had done this he told the local people, "You should now come to my place for a game. There is football. Come and play with me." The local people spread the news among themselves saying, "There is football. Let us go and play."
>
> ... He knew that he would not have gathered such a great number of people had it not been through making friendship with them. He said to the people, "We must start worshipping and learning in this place." There were a lot of people in the church. "We can no longer call this place, *Kisokwe cha Kwanza* [Kiswahili name; "Kisokwe One"]. It shall be called, *Bonde Baraka* [Kiswahili name; "the Valley of Blessing"]. We shall call it so because the church is packed full with people."[51]

Chamuhawi had several freed and escaped slaves from the caravans, and those who had fled persecution from their local communities. So Elimerik Mlahagwa admitted that some of the first church members at Chamuhawi were former slaves. As noted in chapter 2, everyone who settled in Ugogo was naturalized and became a "Mgogo." Some, together with slaves, became members of the early group of Christians. Despite that, Elimerik Mlahagwa was emphatic that "it was the Wagogo who were founders of the church at Chamuhawi because only the Wagogo could play *naga*."[52] In 1883, the planned baptism of Cole's child was made known to the villagers. This became a communal event and attracted people to the church service, including the local chief (probably Dikunguwale Madimilo). After this, the chief promised to encourage children to attend school.[53]

The second reason for better results at Chamuhawi was Cole's appointing of indigenous Christians, very early on, to carry out mission work, at least in the vicinity of Chamuhawi station. Oral tradition testifies to this:

> Without the knowledge of anyone, he was making note of the ones he regarded as brave and talented during the *naga* game, with a view to appointing them to certain responsibilities in the mission, if they turned up. They finished the service and ate the

---

51. Elimerik Mlahagwa, oral interview, 28 June 1997.
52. Mlahagwa, oral interview.
53. *PCMS*, 1884, 49, 50.

food afterwards. He then started mentioning people by names, because he had written all the names already. "So and so, you will be responsible for such a duty, and so on." . . . Cole quit *naga* as soon as he managed to start a congregation.[54]

Cole was wise to engage the Wagogo in the carrying out mission work at the earliest time possible. He was wise because, to begin with, the number of CMS missionaries at this time was small.[55] Sooner or later, African contribution was going to be necessary. The initiatives and contributions of some of the indigenous workers began to emerge. Only a few of these will be examined here.

First, Lwanga Tofiki. Tofiki was a Muganda from Uganda who settled at Chamuhawi but later moved to Mamboya. In 1886, a resident CMS missionary described Tofiki's initiatives in spreading the Christian message:

> Every morning about 6 a.m. he goes (voluntarily) to the chief's house, about three quarters of a mile off, talks to the chief about his soul, then collects his children and brings them to be taught, and takes them about four o'clock in the afternoon. He teaches morning and afternoon, and again at night, besides performing duties of a cook, washerman, etc., etc. I ought to mention that in addition to the above, he preaches occasionally, both in Swahili and Kigogo. His wife, who is also a bright Christian, cooks gratis for the chief's children, who are living here, and scarcely a day passes but that someone is fed from their table for Christ's sake and the Gospel's.[56]

Tofiki's wife was a baptized mission adherent already. But he himself had not been baptized yet. Nonetheless, he was participating in the Christianization programme. It may be concluded that the pre-baptism instruction he had

---

54. *PCMS*, 1884, 49, 50.

55. As stated earlier, only Last and Baxter stayed at Mpwapwa until 1879. Cole and Price joined them that year. Cole moved to Chamuhawi in 1880. In the same year, Last moved to Ukaguru to start Mamboya. His service was terminated in 1885, and Wood took over from 1886. Septimus Pruen was posted to Mpwapwa in the same year, and John Roscoe joined Mamboya staff in 1888. John Beverley was posted to Chamuhawi in 1889. Other reinforcements took place in the last decade of the nineteenth century as follows: Chamuhawi – John Briggs (1892); Mpwapwa – Ernest Doulton (1894); Mamboya – David Deeks (1892), David Rees (1897), Rose Colsey (1893), Elizabeth Waite (1893), and Emily Spriggs (1897).

56. *PCMS*, 1887, 43.

been receiving made him qualify for his job. He was a Christian at heart, even though he had not been signed with the sign of the cross at a public baptism.

The engagement of people yet to be baptized in Christian work became a common pattern in the CMS mission as work expanded in the twentieth century. But this happened mostly when the mission, as will be seen later (especially in chapter 5), came under pressure as it faced secular challenges (the German colonial government, in particular) or its religious competitors (Islam and a Roman Catholic mission). That Tofiki was doing it when no such pressure was visible suggests that the initiative came from him and not from the CMS missionaries present at Chamuhawi. He later moved to Mamboya where, after his baptism in November 1886, he became an indispensable companion of Arthur Wood when they itinerated villages located away from Mamboya station (see below).

Tofiki was not the only the indigenous agent whose ministry contributed to the growth of the church at Chamuhawi. CMS missionaries paid similar warm tributes to one Farahani,[57] as they did to Tofiki. There were also some interesting encounters between young Christians and their fellow Wagogo at Chamuhawi. In 1897, "little bands of Christians" undertook to go daily to the streams where local people either drew water or washed, and preached to them there.[58] One of the young Chamuhawi Christians preached "almost all day long and everyday to people drawing water at one of the streams."[59] These young Christians must have done a lot of work to make Chamuhawi a success because a statistical table from the CMS annual report of 1893 shows that, in that year, Chamuhawi had only two "official" teachers. In 1894, Chamuhawi had four teachers, then five in 1895 and 1896, nine in 1897, and thirteen in 1898 (of whom three were women), and nine in 1899 (including four women).[60]

---

57. *PCMS*, 1887, 43.

58. *PCMS*, 1898, 110.

59. *PCMS*, 1898, 111.

60. See statistical reports in *PCMS*, 1894, 64; 1895, 103; 1896, 132; 1897, 140; 1898, 111; 1899, 101; and 1900, 113. At this time, Mpwapwa had two teachers in 1892, two in 1893, three in 1894, one in 1895, two in 1896, three in 1897, and the same for 1898, and 1899. Mamboya had five in 1892, three in 1893 and 1894, one in 1895 and 1896, two in 1897, and the same in 1898. There were four in 1899 (one of whom was a woman named Persisi, see *PCMS*, 1900, 111).

Third, and finally, the success of the work at Chamuhawi was also due to the friendship of Dikunguwale Madimilo, the local chief of Chamuhawi.[61] The alliance between Madimilo and Cole included mutual defence against potential enemies. Both men had armies composed largely of freed slaves.[62] Cole's army was mainly for defence of the mission station and was occasionally used for intercepting the slave caravans. Madimilo was baptized in 1893[63] – a rare phenomenon among the Gogo and Kaguru chiefs at this time or, indeed, even in the twentieth century.

The initiatives and contributions of the chiefs will be explored more adequately in the next chapter. Meanwhile, it is important to point out that, already, even before the expansion phase began, the pattern "inaugurated" by King Mutesa was taking roots. Variations in attitudes and motives existed, and the situation cannot be simplified. However, the attitude of the chiefs to the mission or the Christian evangelistic endeavour determined the fate of the work in a locality. Mission stations like Uyui (in Tabora province) and Msalala (in Mwanza province) had to be closed because the chiefs displayed an unfavourable attitude to the mission, constantly demanding large taxes or preventing their people from working for the mission.[64]

Yet, at Buigiri (more than forty miles from the "difficult" Mpwapwa and its indifferent chief and people), the Mpwapwa-based CMS missionary John Price was offered a chance to regain hope in his mission work amid the lack of progress experienced at Mpwapwa. Chief Mulimbwa of Buigiri invited him and sent a deputation, first in December 1892 and then sometime before March 1893.[65] Price wrote: "I found the people wonderfully prepared. . . .

---

61. *CMIR* 14 (December 1889): 743; Elimerik Mlahagwa, oral interview, 28 June 1997.

62. Mlahagwa, oral interview. Madimilo, chief of Chamuhawi, and Lukole Lusito, chief of Mpwapwa (famous by the name of "Chipanjilo" for his provision of shelter to passing travellers and escapees), were in constant conflict in the late 1880s. This was partly due to the notion of most people in the neighbourhood that the latter was receiving large gifts from the European and Arab travellers, as well as the Germans, and did not share them. It is not clear whether Cole supported Madimilo against Chipanjilo, but, undoubtedly, Price recognized himself as a friend of both. See *CMIR* 14 (December 1889): 743. Lukole was the chief of Mpwapwa even when Stanley passed thorough in the mid-1870s. See Stanley, *How I Found Livingstone*, 132. Price also used the same name in 1880. See *CMIR* 5 (December 1880): 736.

63. *PCMS*, 1894, 47.

64. See *PCMS*, 1888, 49, 53.

65. Cole does not name this chief. But an oral source identifies him as Mulimbwa. See Nehemia Uguzi, oral interview, 18 June 1997.

Nearly 1000 assembled to hear the Gospel. I had two young men from here with me, who also spoke, so that we were preaching for nearly three hours. . . . I had never seen anything like it."[66] To be sure, Chief Mulimbwa did not invite Price solely for the purpose of wanting to be preached to. Price himself observed that smallpox "had been making great havoc [throughout Ugogo], and I knew he wanted me to go and vaccinate his people."[67]

Such was the nature of the relationship between the chiefs, and indeed their people, with mission Christianity as it expanded its frontiers in Ugogo and Ukaguru. As will be seen more clearly in the subsequent chapters, the aspirations and interests of the Wagogo and Wakaguru motivated them to align themselves with the mission in the late nineteenth century and the pattern continued in the twentieth century.

3.3.5 The Beginnings at Mamboya

With the exception of Chamuhawi, the pattern and nature of work in Ukaguru did not differ so much with that of Ugogo at this time. Much of the work was still carried out in and around the mission station. At Mamboya in Ukaguru, prior to taking permanent residence there, Last, (then residing at Mpwapwa) had visited the place seven times in 1879 (on his way to and from the coast). On all these occasions, he had been exhorted by Chief Senyagwa Chimola and his people to live amongst them.[68] Here again we see the importance of the initiative of a chief in the commencement of a mission station. Last was certainly impressed by the kindness of the Kaguru people. Given the exhortation he had, and, more importantly, the strategic location of Mamboya (its proximity to a caravan route and its being central in relation to the surrounding chiefdoms), he was in no doubt about the eligibility of the place as a mission station. "I feel sure," he wrote, "that anyone sent to settle there would meet with a hearty welcome.[69]

In January 1880, Last himself moved from Mpwapwa and settled at Mamboya:

---

66. *PCMS*, 1893, 46.
67. *PCMS*, 1893, 46.
68. *CMIR* 4 (November 1879): 664.
69. *CMIR*: 664.

The Sultan received me very kindly, and said he was very glad I was [sic] come.[70] The land was mine, I could go over it, choose whatever spot I pleased and begin to build at once. I at once went off with two of my men and the chief of the Wanyamwezi.[71] . . . When the talking was over, he went out and brought a large bowl of honey and gave to my headman for me, and after a little while I gave him a little present of cloth, worth about eight shillings.[72]

T. O. Beidelman has suggested that Last sought to move to Mamboya because he was "the most restless" of the CMS missionaries who reestablished Mpwapwa and, due to quarrels with his colleagues, "sought errands elsewhere and persuaded his fellows and those at home of the imminent danger of 'Jesuit aggression'" – hence the commencement of a new station at Mamboya.[73] If Beidelman is aware of Last's early contacts with the chief of Mamboya and his people, then he disregards that knowledge. He equally does the same for the initiative taken by the chief to invite Last. This observation does not, however, rule out the possibility that Last might have wanted to be at a location where he could take charge of his life and the direction of the local station alone. But oral tradition emphasizes that it was the initiative of the local chief that led to the commencement of the Mamboya mission station.[74]

The place where Last settled (now deserted) was called Nhingulu, and it was on the hills near Maluwe. It was bordered by two steep slopes and was suitable for defence: "The enemies could not climb it. They had to use a path near the chief's palace. Yet, no one could do so because the chief was heavily guarded."[75] It was close to four or five villages with about two hundred people in 1880.[76] By December 1880, the first church building was in use.[77]

---

70. Chiefs in Ukaguru were addressed as "sultans" – the title used for chiefs in the coastal areas and the paramount sultan of Zanzibar. This is an indication of the coastal influence upon Ukaguru, particularly Mamboya.

71. The Wanyamwezi were undoubtedly a large community at Mamboya, such that they had their own chief. It is quite possible that the majority of these were traders who decided to settle there for good.

72. *CMIR* 5 (December 1880): 742.

73. Beidelman, *Colonial Evangelism*, 55.

74. Yusufu Masingisa, oral interviews, 16 and 17 September 1997.

75. Masingisa, oral interviews.

76. *CMIR* 5 (December 1880): 742.

77. *CMIR* 6 (September 1881): 559.

However, a hearty welcome to Last by the paramount Chief Chimola and his people was one thing; subscribing to the message and religious life Last had come to introduce was another matter. Oral tradition points to this:

> You see, some local people were despising them and saying, "What is this man saying? What are they singing?" It was astonishing. I used to ask my parents, "Did the old man who allowed these men to settle here become a Christian himself?" They replied, "No." He never became a Christian. . . . His son too was never baptized, except the children and the grandchildren.[78]

So, it took some time before any progress was made. Joseph Last himself confirms this, especially the difficulty of communicating with the Wakaguru:

> I have always met with unvaried kindness at the hands of the Natives while visiting them; but this must not be taken as a proof that they are in any way interested in what I say. I do not think they are, and it will not be so until the Holy Spirit convince them of sin, and show them their need of a Saviour. As they have no idea of the purity of God, nor of his righteousness which is essential to a person becoming a member of His kingdom, they can scarcely entertain the idea that they are sinners or in unfit state to be accepted by God. They have no literature, nor any traditions likely to lead their minds to discern a higher state of righteousness than that which is before them everyday, viz., the life and conduct of their fellow-creatures.[79]

3.3.6 First Baptisms at Mamboya Hill Church

The slow response of the Kaguru people to the Christian message that Last describes above (which also reveals his misunderstanding of Kaguru religious life) explains the delay in making converts. The first baptism of the Kaguru people (two adults and two infants) took place in 1884 – slightly earlier than

---

78. Yusufu Masingisa, oral interviews, 16 and 17 September 1997. Chief Saileni, who succeeded his father Chimola as chief, later became a scholar and attended baptism class in 1901. See *PCMS*, 1902, 109; *PCMS*, 1903, 102. But, as oral evidence suggests, he never became a Christian. No written evidence suggests the contrary.

79. *CMIR* 6 (September 1881): 559.

at Mpwapwa and Chamuhawi.[80] However, this did not take place at Mamboya itself but in Zanzibar (within the UMCA sphere). Last's service in the mission ended in 1885, only a year after the start of the German colonial activities in Tanzania. Arthur Wood succeeded him in June 1886. The first "proper" baptism at Mamboya may therefore be said to have taken place in August 1886, when three adults (Uledi, Mwano, and Lupanga) were baptized. The baptism of Lwanga Tofiki followed in November 1886, but as stated earlier, he was not a Kaguru.[81]

3.3.7 Difficulties of Communicating the Christian Message

Despite these initial fruits, the structure and content of Wood's message to Wakaguru was the same as that of Last or Baxter, which, by and large, emphasized repentance as a key to life after death. In August 1888, Wood recorded in his journal the encounters he and Tofiki had with the Wakaguru at Berega when he made his first itineration to other parts of Ukaguru far from Mamboya:

> We told them why I had come, namely to tell them the words of God; went on to show them the difference between man and the cattle, the former being destined to live for ever in happiness or woe. The Son of God came from heaven, and died on the purpose to redeem us out of the bondage of sin, and take us to heaven to dwell in happiness for ever. They were told to repent and leave off all their old bad works, to turn to, believe in, and pray to God, who was their father in heaven. I then taught them some of the Lord's Prayer, and explained God's Fatherhood.... Their idea of praying to God is simply dancing around a little fetish hut to the beating of a drum.[82]

---

80. *PCMS*, 1884, 49. One of the two infants was a *mgego* (i.e. had the upper teeth out first). According to the Kaguru custom, such a child was to be killed. The child's father, apparently with the support of chief Msamwenda of Maundike (one of the neighbouring villages), asked the mission to take her to safety. Last and his wife decided to take the child to Zanzibar. Two women – Fayida (and her child) and Sikuzani [Sikudhani] – who had been under instruction under Last accompanied them and were baptized at Zanzibar too.

81. *PCMS*, 1887, 41.

82. Extracts from Wood's journal in *CMIR* 14 (January 1889): 24–25.

The emphasis of the message was clearly on life after death. But this hardly touched deep Kaguru aspirations such as the need for security and survival here and now. The ministerial companionship of Tofiki went some way to help in the effort to communicate the word of God to other Kaguru people present in their entourage – such as the porters whom they hired from Mamboya:

> Tofiki is very good in explaining to the men between times the things we are daily teaching. He is now, as I write, sitting round the camp-fire with the six porters, and telling them about Creation. One man says Adam must have married Eve, *his sister*, as there were only two. "No," says Tofiki, and passes on to tell them how they both fell, and sin came into the world. . . . "Let us repent and turn to God, and give up all bad things." "But" says one man, "Do the white men do it?" "No," says Tofiki, "Bwana [Mr Wood] says they all know about God, but some love evil and Satan more than God, and choose Satan, and follow evil."[83]

Tofiki must get the credit for being one of the early African converts and, indeed, Ganda missionary to share the Christian message with his fellow Africans, first in Ugogo and then in Ukaguru. That he did not make a breakthrough can be attributed to two things. As an outsider (a *Muganda*), he was not free from the difficulties of cross-cultural communication. Second, the nature of the message was the same as Wood's – structured and centred on what CMS missionaries regarded as major doctrines of the Christian church but which failed to connect or relate to the Kaguru religious concerns.

Despite Tofiki's lack of clear breakthrough, and the slow progress in Ukaguru, by the end of 1899 other African teachers at Mamboya – such as Asani Mugimbwa, Yeremia Senyagwa, and Persisi, then the only paid female worker – had already established themselves as major players in the evangelization of Mamboya and Ukaguru in general.[84] So much so that when Arthur Wood became ill and left the Hill Church for Britain in August 1896, Asani Mugimbwa (already a graduate of Frere Town divinity school near

---

83. *CMIR* 14 (January 1889): 30; cf. *CMIR* 15 (March 1890): 184.
84. *PCMS*, 1899, 99; *PCMS*, 1900, 111. Mugimbwa was stationed at the Hill Church, and Senyagwa and Persisi at the Valley Church.

Mombasa, Kenya) "carried on the work single-handed."[85] Periods when CMS missionaries were absent were often the best moments for African members of staff to use their skills "unhindered" and prove their abilities, not only in this period, but also during the expansion phase (as the biographical notes of some teachers will show in chapter 6).

3.3.8 The Valley Church and Its First Fruits

At Mamboya, almost a decade passed after 1880 before it was realized that it was better to start a branch on the Mamboya valley (over three miles from the Hill Church). A church was built there and was opened in February 1894.[86] Apparently, this was where more people lived. There was a cluster of some thirty to forty villages in the valley,[87] including Wanyamwezi settlers, and the place was much closer to the caravan route. It was not until 1898 that the first Christians were baptized at the Valley Church – both of them women – Persisi and Loisi. The proximity to the caravan route, however, proved later to be a problem and affected the school's work in 1899 as more people (mainly young men) joined the caravans as porters.[88]

3.3.9 The Dawn of the "Official" German Colonial Administration

In 1890 – a year before the dawn of the official German colonial occupation of Tanzania – statistical evidence shows that Chamuhawi had sixteen Christians, nineteen catechumens, and twenty scholars. These figures may include Mpwapwa because nothing is indicated for that station in the statistical table. Mamboya had only four Christians – an indication that perhaps the four baptized earlier in 1884, in Zanzibar (as pointed out above), did not return to Mamboya.[89] In both places, Ugogo and Ukaguru, this was relatively small progress after twelve years of mission labour (counting from 1878 when Mpwapwa was reestablished). Nonetheless, the church had been started in central Tanzania.

---

85. *PCMS*, 1897, 108.
86. *PCMS*, 1895, 87; *PCMS*, 1899, 99.
87. *PCMS*, 1896, 108.
88. *PCMS*, 1900, 112.
89. See Beidelman, *Colonial Evangelism*, 57.

The replacement of the German East Africa Company (GEAC) in 1891 by the official German colonial administration was expected to give impetus to the work of the CMS mission, and other missions too, in this period.[90] The previous seven-year unofficial rule (1884–1891) had been characterized by gross human rights abuses in the form of floggings, beatings, and killings under "the notorious Karl Peters" and his colleagues (but see counter accusations).[91] For non-German missions along the coast, the UMCA for example,[92] such abuses tarnished the image of the Europeans, alienated Africans from the mission, and hindered the mission work.

---

90. Until then, German colonial activities were carried out under the Society for German Colonization (from Berlin). This society hoisted the first German flag in Tanzania on 19 November 1884, and Carl Peters made treaties with local chiefs in the north-east and in Ukaguru. See Extracts from the *Proceedings of the Royal Geographical Society*, August 1887, in *CMIR* 12 (October 1887): 614; Pakenham, *Scramble for Africa*, 290–295. The eventual purpose of the treaties was not "protection," as claimed by Carl Peters, Carl Jühlke, and Graf von Pfeil, but occupation and colonization. Oral tradition suggests that chief Saidi Chimola of Mamboya and other petty chiefs whom he summoned to be part of the agreement didn't know the full extent of the agreement until after they had signed it. See Yusufu Masingisa, oral interviews, 16 and 17 September 1997. The German East Africa Company succeeded the society in 1885. See *CMIR* 12 (1887): 614–615. Well before the start of the official rule, the Germans had already established an administrative post at Mpwapwa which was commanded by one Lt Giese. That is why Bushiri Salim attacked Mpwapwa in June and July 1889. See *CMIR* 14 (December 1889): 739–743; *PCMS*, 1890, 54.

91. "Freedom for Small States and Justice for Native Races" (printed leaflet), folio 209, n.a., n.d. part II (but certainly written shortly after the First World War), *Official Papers of the Diocese of Zanzibar (OPDZ), 1864–1963*, Box A.4.1, RHL. For details on the undesirably cruel actions of Carl Peters against Africans from mid-1884 up to the early twentieth century, see "Treatment of Natives in the German Colonies," in *Handbooks* (prepared under the direction of the historical section of the Foreign Office), No. 114, London: HMSO, 1920, NLS; and Carl Peters, *The Eldorado of the Ancients*, 1902, part of which is quoted in *Handbooks*, No. 114, 21. "People are so astonished at the remarkable youth of most of the so called English missionaries.... The brutal usage which Dr Fisher, a credible witness has reported, is not calculated to enable the English missionary to train up useful converts. Fisher tells us of a case of English justice, where the offender[s], whose offence was not an offence in the eyes of the black population ... were tied to a tree, and had to undergo brutal bastinado, one of the delinquents received sixty-five lashes and the other a number which Dr F did not recollect. This took place in the presence of the assembled children of the Mission and missionaries. The doctor of the Mission was present, to decide when the flogging must cease, and this was the only human feature which characterised this dispensation of justice." See *"Colonial Political Correspondence"* (the English translation of a German periodical), No. 18, 1886, "German East Africa", Box C.I., RHL.

92. No wonder, after years of tension, the UMCA strongly opposed a possible reoccupation of Tanzania by Germany after the First World War. See "Freedom for Small States and Justice for Native Races," *OPDZ, 1864–1963*, RHL.

The impact on the work of the CMS at Moshi of the clash between Chief Meli of Uchaga Moshi (northern Tanzania) and the Germans has already been noted in chapter 1. Yet the CMS mission in central Tanzania regarded the political and economic developments after 1891 as advantageous and relevant for the advancement of its evangelistic work.[93] Security, law, and order had been enhanced and tribal wars could not be fought indiscriminately without attracting the reaction of the colonial government. Communication (through the building of roads and the introduction of telegraphic and mail services) was improved too. Even so, with the exception of Chamuhawi, results obtained at Mpwapwa and Mamboya remained only meagre (see table 3.1 below).

3.4 The End of Self-Preservation and the Birth of an Expansion Era

As pointed out earlier, both Mpwapwa and Chamuhawi were home to many social outcasts and freed slaves. These formed the majority of the two mission communities' populations. One outcome of the extension of administrative centres by the German colonial government into the interior was the reduction, and sometimes the termination, of persecutions aimed at such outcasts (for example, those alleged to be witches).[94] Many such people were able to return to their original villages or settled elsewhere. Inevitably, the function of the mission station as a place to take refuge declined. Church attendance dwindled.

By the end of 1899, Mpwapwa had forty-seven Christians and ninety-seven scholars. Christians at Chamuhawi numbered 114 and at least 321 scholars were enrolled in five schools. Time was almost right for the CMS mission to consider extending into what was mistakenly regarded as "Ugogo proper."[95] Reflecting on the work of the mission in Ugogo, John Briggs, who joined the mission in 1892, wrote, "For over twenty years we have been on

---

93. Rees, "History of CMS", G3 A8/0/1902/19, BUL.

94. Witchcraft accusations were numerous in the nineteenth century. For example, when the chief of Kikombo (name not available) died in 1888, charges were brought against "two poor slave men." These were "hacked to pieces." See *PCMS*, 1889, 48.

95. See Rees to Baylis, 8/7/1901, G3 A8/O/1900/34, BUL; *PCMS*, 1900, 112; *PCMS*, 1901, 122.

the borders of the land. Shall we not with the new century upon us enter in to possess the land for him who has bought the precious souls of those there with His own blood?"[96]

Table 3.1: Progress of Mission Work in Ugogo and Ukaguru 1892–1899[97]

	1	2				3				4			
		Mpwapwa				Chamuhawi				Mamboya			
	Year	Christians	Catechumens	Schools	Scholars	Christians	Catechumens	Schools	Scholars	Christians	Catechumens	Schools	Scholars
	1892	22	29	1	51	26	25	1	25	35	40	1	79
	1893	28	57	1	43	59	60	1	82	35	80	1	85
	1894	39	45	1	45	76	88	4	227	56	18	2	148
	1895	35	4	1	30	72	57	3	90	30	10	2	92
	1896	28	22	1	30	70	60	5	135	43	13	2	155
	1897	28	64	1	40	80	51	5	218	49	12	2	126
	1898	42	20	1	96	103	37	5	321	51	6	2	155
	1899	47	17	1	97	114	41	5	*	37	8	5	218

* The 1899 report doesn't show the number of scholars attending the five schools.[98]

The 1899 report suggested that quite a few Wagogo migrated to those areas, namely further west and east of Mpwapwa. Symbolic as it was, the period when the people came to the mission station was coming to an end. Briggs was right. Now the mission had to follow the people where they were. The situation in Ukaguru was similar. By 1899, there were now thirty-seven Christians at Mamboya and 218 scholars.[99] But, by now, a pattern that signalled the end of self-preservation began to emerge. "Progress was manifested

---

96. *PCMS*, 1900, 113.

97. Based on CMS annual statistical tables in *PCMS*, 1893–1900.

98. In part, this was caused by the rapid depopulation in the neighbourhood of Chamuhawi. Some Wagogo emigrated to other parts of Ugogo. See *PCMS*, 1900, 113.

99. See statistical report for 1899 in *PCMS*, 1900, 111.

Christian Developments in Ugogo and Ukaguru 1876–1900

chiefly at the out-stations"[100] – for example, Tangalata, Nyangala, and Berega. Yeremia Senyagwa of the Valley Church and other Mamboya teachers often visited these places.[101] But permanent occupation had not been contemplated.

Soon, a natural disaster struck, ending the nineteenth century very tragically at Mamboya. On 31 December 1899, the church building collapsed during Sunday worship, killing seven Kaguru people – five adults and two children.[102] Yusufu Masingisa explains what he was told happened:

> They came down here to start another church. Now in 1900, 1900, that church fell down. When a strong wind began to blow, the late Mr Rees told people not to leave the church. Therefore, those who went outside had to return. When they returned (but some were still outside) then came another strong wind. This time he too began to run away. It seems a loose pole hit him. He was hurt but didn't die. That woman was trapped inside. The rescuers removed her to safety, but the baby died. Some, like my uncle were struck on the leg. He was squashed, but he was rescued.[103]

The church Masingisa refers to is the Valley Church, not the original Hill Church. Like many oral informants, memory failed him on the date but only just. For he mentions that the church collapsed in 1900, while mission records have 31 December 1899 – very little difference indeed. Mission records written by foreign missionaries tended to be accurate on dates because events were often recorded in logbooks or journals soon after they took place. But they are often at odds with local interpretation because CMS missionaries often misunderstood and misinterpreted the events they recorded. The collapse of the Mamboya Valley church is a case in point.

Despite the fact that CMS missionaries and perhaps some local people thought the collapse was a natural disaster for which no one could be blamed, others – the local population in particular – assigned it to the "white man's

---

100. *PCMS*, 1900, 112
101. *PCMS*, 1900, 112.
102. *PCMS*, 1900, 111.
103. Yusufu Masingisa, oral interviews, 16 and 17 September 1997.

witchcraft."¹⁰⁴ Indeed, some of the relatives of the Christians who died reacted angrily to the news of death of their loved ones and wanted to kill David Rees who was in charge of the worship that day. Yusufu Masingisa tells the story:

> *Mwita Akiri*: Let me ask you a question. When the church fell, what did the local people say about that event, I mean those who were not Christians?
>
> *Yusufu Masingisa*: You see they were used to seeing people go to read there. But they didn't believe that they were doing the right thing. The believers were saddened by that event. But the unbelievers showed contempt and said, "Look. The church has fallen." Not all were upset. The one who was most upset whose name I was mentioning [earlier mixing it with the teacher who died] was *mzee* Kibada. He was a relative of the one who died. I mean the teacher who was killed.
>
> *Mwita Akiri*: What was Kibada's full name?
>
> *Yusufu Masingisa*: Kibada Madihi. . . . He took a gun. He wanted to shoot Mr Rees. But people restrained him. He was crying, saying, "My relative has died. I want to kill this man." Those present restrained him.¹⁰⁵

Chief Saileni Chimola (who succeeded his father, Saidi Chimola, as chief of Mamboya) offered Rees a refuge and helped calm the situation.¹⁰⁶ On the one hand, the event was a tragedy for the CMS mission and the Kaguru Christians. It depressed many people, including Christians. But on the other hand, it played a crucial role in pressing upon the CMS missionaries the urgency of considering opening new stations in Ukaguru. Bishop William Peel noted this:

> The fall of the church in Mamboya in that year, which resulted in seven deaths and the consequent depression of the minds of villagers round about, who seemed to hold rather aloof from

---

104. Rees to Baylis, 6/1/1900, G3 A8/O/1900/6, BUL.
105. Masingisa, oral interviews, 16 and 17 September 1997.
106. Gresford Chitemo, "Historia Fupi ya Kanisa Anglikana Kuingia Ukaguru na Unguu 1879–1979," notes, Morogoro, September 1980, 1.

the Mission, caused the missionaries resident in Usagara [i.e. Ukaguru] to look upon the widely-stretching Berega valley and the uplands of Itumba as fields in which immediate efforts should be made.[107]

Peel's assessment gives a more accurate picture and is confirmed by oral tradition at Mamboya. Yusufu Masingisa's description of the outcome of the event is graphic:

> It was after this event when the missionaries said to themselves, "We have made a mistake, to stay in one place like this. We have *tamed religion* in one location. Now God has shown us that we must move out. We have chosen this place but we have *piled ourselves* up here. It was after this that Mr Wood was sent to Uponela [Itumba]. Mr Parker who baptized me remained here. Mr Deeks went to Nyangala. And Mr Rees was sent to Berega.[108]

In light of the testimonies of both Peel and Masingisa, the interpretation in the CMS annual report for 1900 does not acknowledge the full impact of the event and could be misleading. It only states that "the shock caused by the fall of the church in MAMBOIA [Mamboya] VALLEY in December, 1899, affected the attendance of the people both at services and school for several months."[109] It further attributes the redistribution of staff at Mamboya (hence the start of new stations) to the bishop's visit to Tanzania.[110] It is true that the executive committee of the CMS mission stated, at its meeting on 6 April 1900, that it merely formalized a process that had already started.[111] However, it was at this meeting that the need to start four new districts in Ukaguru was discussed for the first time, and this was based on the event at Mamboya in December 1899.[112] Certainly, the collapse of the church and the indigenous

---

107. W. G. Peel, "Usagara and Ugogo Revisited 1902-1903," MS, G3 A8/O/1903/38, BUL; W. G. Peel, "Usagara and Chigogo Revisited, 1902–1903," in *CMI* 55 (February 1904): 109–119 (first part), and *CMI* 55 (March 1904): 192–199 (second part).

108. Masingisa, oral interviews, 16 and 17 September 1997.

109. *PCMS*, 1901, 118.

110. *PCMS*, 1901, 118.

111. Minutes, EC, 6/4/1900, G3 A8/O/1900/20, BUL.

112. Minutes, EC, 6/4/1900, G3 A8/O/1900/20, BUL.

response to it was a moment of awakening for CMS missionaries.[113] The tragic shedding of the blood of Kaguru Christians marked the end of the tradition of self-preservation that had characterized the CMS mission for much of the nineteenth century.

3.5 Conclusion

An attempt has been made in this analysis to show how the work of the CMS mission began and developed in central Tanzania up to 1900. It has been noted that, after more than two decades of mission work, only meagre results were obtained. However, it has been emphasized that it was also a period in which the African initiatives and contributions (be they of young Christians or chiefs) were "inaugurated," stimulating the growth of the church at the three stations.

Indigenous agents such as Lwanga Tofiki taught; converts at Chamuhawi preached at rather odd places; teachers such as Asani Mugimbwa showed that they could perform their work even better in the absence of CMS missionaries. Slowly, but significantly, out-stations – the cry for expansion – were beginning to get attention. Chiefs such as Mulimbwa of Buigiri took initiative and invited CMS missionaries. From 1900 onwards, all of these initiatives became more visible, magnified, and consistent. The initiatives and contributions of the Gogo and Kaguru chiefs in the foundational stages of the expansion phase is the subject of the next chapter.

---

113. Yusufu Masingisa, oral interviews, 16 and 17 September 1997; Phanuel Makau, oral interview, 12 September 1997; Asdadi Mwinyuma, oral interview, 13 September 1997.

CHAPTER 4

The Initiatives of the Gogo and Kaguru Chiefs

"Hodi (May I come in)?" says a voice. "*Karibu* (Come in)," and on the missionary's veranda walks the headman of a village some miles away. "What is it you want?" "I have a number of children in my village whom I wish to be taught. Will you send me a teacher?" "Yes, if you undertake to get the children and their parents together when the teacher comes." So once or twice a week the village is visited.... "Can the teacher be allowed to live in our village so that he can teach every day?" "Yes, when you have built a school and a house for him, then he will come." The simple hut is built, and the teacher takes up his residence, gathers the children and adults together for school, holds classes to teach them the Word of God, and there is the beginning of a church. It is a new out-station.[1]

An analysis of early Christian developments in Ugogo and Ukaguru indicated that only limited results were obtained in the initial period of 1876–1900. However, as noted, this period was one during which some of the indigenous initiatives and contributions that this study explores began to emerge. This included the limited initiatives of the Gogo and Kaguru chiefs. This chapter now considers the initiatives and contributions of the chiefs in some detail. As the opening quotation indicates above, it explores the positive contribution of the Kaguru and Gogo chiefs to the establishment of mission stations and

---

1. Chambers, *Tanganyika's New Day*, 27.

literacy centres under the CMS mission in Ugogo and Ukaguru. The impact of the social and political context on both the chiefs and the CMS mission at the time is also taken into consideration. Equally, some exceptions in the relationship between the CMS mission and some of the Kaguru and Gogo chiefs, including their response to the question of conversion to mission Christianity, are analysed too.

The year 1900 marked a new phase – indeed the expansion phase – in mission work. The number of principal mission stations grew from two to five in 1900 – Mamboya, Berega, Itumba, and Nyangala in Ukaguru; and Mvumi in Ugogo. By 1904, two more had been added, namely Buigiri (1901) and Kongwa (1904). Chamuhawi, which was classified as an out-station, ought really to be regarded as a mission station because even by CMS's own definition (as explained earlier in the glossary[2]) that is what it was. Reckoned thus, the number of mission stations now rose to eight. Major local sociological and religious factors that prompted the necessity for expansion have been noted already – the collapse of the Valley Church at Mamboya in Ukaguru and the depopulation at Mpwapwa, not forgetting the religious indifference too of the people of Mpwapwa. In terms of scholars and Christians, there is an obvious contrast with the earlier period as table 4.1 indicates.

4.1 Chiefs as Indigenous Agents

Louise Pirouet has noted the involvement of the chiefs in the establishment of mission Christianity in East Africa, for example in Uganda.[3] Little if not nothing has been written in the standard literature relating to the growth of the Anglican Church in Tanzania. As one of the groups covered by the general term "indigenous agents" explored in this study, the chiefs are important.

This is not only for the contributions they made to the expansion of the work carried out by the Anglican CMS mission (as shall be seen below). They are important also because many of them refused to be drawn into Christian conversion and baptism. In other words, for them the price of abandoning their traditional social and religiopolitical obligations to their society was too high, or perhaps unnecessary, so they chose to remain outside. In relation

---

2. See "CMS Glossary" on page 387.
3. Pirouet, *Black Evangelists*.

to the work of other indigenous agents, and the entire expansion phase, the initiatives and contributions of the chiefs laid a foundation upon which literacy and evangelistic work was built.

Table 4.1: Christians and Scholars 1892–1910[4]

1	2	3	4	5	6	7	8
Late Nineteenth Century				Early Twentieth Century			
Year	Christians	Schools	Scholars	Year	Christians	Schools	Scholars
				1900	203	15	356
				1901	226	32	1129
				1902	298	56	2415
1892	83	3	155	1903	375	67	3060
1893	120	3	210	1904	452	65	3195
1894	171	7	420	1905	501	76	2414
1895	137	6	212	1906	543	74	2688
1896	141	8	320*	1907	612	91	3603
1897	80	8	384	1908	694	102	4156
1898	196	8	572	1909†	771	123	4804
1899	198	11	315	1910	810	117	5061

* Figures include 3 seminarists undergoing training for lay ministry.[5]

† The year 1909 marks the end of an era in mission education.[6]

---

4. Based on statistical tables in *PCMS*, 1893–1910.

5. These were Asani Mugimbwa, Andrea Mwaka, and Daniel Chowe at Frere Town divinity school, Mombasa, Kenya. See *PCMS*, 1897, 100; Knox, *Signal on the Mountain*, 148.

6. The introduction of German educational policy requiring chiefs and their sons to acquire reading and writing skills contributed significantly to the growth of schools and the number of scholars in the CMS mission.

4.2 Chiefs and the Establishment of Mission Stations

As was observed earlier,[7] before the dawn of a sustained colonial occupation of mainland Tanzania by the Germans, the political organization of many ethnic groups centred around the local chiefs and their subordinates (sub-chiefs or headmen) who ruled tribal chiefdoms. This did not change very much when the official German occupation began in 1891 and ended in 1918. But from then on, the chiefs' rule had to be relegitimized, and sometimes, government appointees outside the succession line had the title of "chief" or *jumbe* conferred upon them by the coloniser.

By 1900, the legitimacy of the chiefs' rule was symbolized by three things acquired during the ceremony at the local German district *boma* (fort). These were a document (or "certificate"), a special cap which had a tassel attached to it,[8] and a German flag, to be hoisted over the chief's *ikulu* (Kaguru or Kigogo; "palace"; the chief's official residence).[9]

The cap was particularly significant. It was like an identity card for the chiefs to identify them to people who didn't know them within or outside their own chiefdom.[10] An element of the chiefs' rule was the power they had to give or refuse permission to foreign travellers who wanted to pass through or settle in their chiefdoms or kingdoms, and this was a common practice in other countries – for example, Uganda.[11]

In Ugogo and Ukaguru, CMS missionaries had to consult the chiefs and acquire permission to establish a mission station or an out-station. As will be seen below, on many occasions the chiefs themselves were taking the initiative

---

7. See chapter 2.

8. The hat was regarded as a symbol of civilization and was popular among coastal Muslims and *jumbes* (junior chiefs appointed by colonial administration).

9. Normally an *ikulu* was a large traditional flat-roofed hut with walls made of crossed poles and is common in central Tanzania, particularly among the Gogo. See extracts from Bishop Peel's journals, *CMI* 25 (November 1900): 814. The extracts were published after the bishop's first visit to the CMS mission in Tanzania between March and May 1900.

10. *CMI* 25 (November 1900): 815. For example, Chief Chilongola (variant Kilongola; not Kilongolo) had to put on his cap and become a guide to Bishop Peel and Mr D. J. Rees as they travelled to Bagamoyo in Ukaguru (not to be confused with the coastal town of Bagamoyo). On Peel's misspelling, see *CMI* 25 (1900): 815; cf. Kaguru's own spelling "Chilongola" (variant Kilongola). See Isaka Mlahagwa, oral interview, 14 September 1997.

11. *CMIR* 3 (February 1878): 122.

to invite the mission to open teaching and preaching centres in their villages. As noted in the previous chapter, this practice started in the nineteenth century.[12] However, now the enterprise gathered momentum because the number of places permanently occupied by both CMS missionaries and indigenous teachers increased. The contrasting response of the two local chiefs and their people to the start of mission work in Berega makes this location an interesting one for beginning this exploration.[13] Here, merely a valley and stream separated the areas controlled by the two chiefs, but the people were of the same ethnic group – namely, the Kaguru.[14] Malanda Malundo was the local chief at Mbuyuni, the place where the first CMS missionary from Mamboya and his party settled.[15] Malanda's response to the idea of opening a school in his village was positive. He organized his people to build a *kibanda* (Kiswahili; lit. "a hut") for the purpose.[16]

But there was something else that CMS missionaries could not contend with. Drum beating and traditional dances were a phenomenon common in Ugogo and Ukaguru, and this has been noted already in the previous chapter. David Rees, who was in charge of Berega and the surrounding areas, complained about the circumcision ceremonies and dances which he regarded as being "great hindrances to the progress of the work. . . ."[17] He felt they had a

---

12. See the invitation and permission to Joseph Last to open a mission station at Nhingulu, Mamboya, in 1880. See *CMIR* 5 (December 1880): 742.

13. The exact date of arrival may not be known but, from what Bishop Peel wrote, by 26 March 1900, a "church" or "school" had been built already at Berega. See W. G. Mombasa to Baylis, 26/3/1900, G3 A8/O/1900/17, BUL. "W. G. Mombasa" was the official "episcopal" signature of Bishop W. G. Peel, bearing the name of the Diocese he led. Anglican bishops are required (by ecclesiastical law) to sign official letters in that manner. Rees also makes reference to a church built by the people. See D. J. Rees to Baylis, 10/4/1900 G3 A8/O/1900/19, BUL.

14. Apart from the Kaguru (Wakaguru), there were other ethnic groups that lived within or in the vicinity of Berega but in smaller numbers, e.g. the Zigua (Wazigua) and the Kamba (Wakamba). See journal of the Rev A. N. Wood, 20 August–1 September 1888 in *CMIR* 14 (March 1889): 24.

15. Isaka Mlahagwa, oral interview, 14 September 1997.

16. Berega Logbook No. 51, MH. The agreement between Rees and Malanda was that the *kibanda* should be ready by Tuesday, 9 April 1901, so that the lessons could start the next day, Wednesday, 10 April. The lessons did begin, but on Friday, 12 April 1901.

17. Berega Logbook No. 51, MH.

negative influence on the "*hearers* [and] young *readers*."[18] This was common in many places.

However, at Berega (Mbuyuni), the drum beating and dances that upset CMS missionaries were associated with the exorcism of evil spirits, a practice known as *kucheza madogoli* (*kucheza* is a Kiswahili word meaning "to dance" or, in this context, to "activate"; *madogoli* is a Kaguru word meaning "spirits"). It seems that dances took place frequently, possibly more than once a week, and the level of noise, as is often the case, was high.[19] Rees had been in Ukaguru for three years only, and he must have found the noise quite intolerable. He tried to persuade Chief Malanda to stop his people from performing *madogoli* near his camp, but his efforts ended in vain.

Inevitably, a new place for the station had to be sought.[20] Chilongola, described by Peel as "a very nice young fellow, and so nice-mannered and friendly and intelligent," offered a site for the erection of a mission house at Mugugu, his village.[21] Though *madogoli* was practised at Mugugu – a place separated from Mbuyuni only by a stream valley – the attitude of the chief and the people there was more positive than at Malanda's village. David Rees and his successors received more cooperation.[22]

In Ugogo, far away from Ukaguru (about a hundred miles to the west), it was Masenha, chief of Unyangwira, who gave a large piece of land to the CMS mission to establish a mission station at Mvumi in 1900.[23] Like many

---

18. "Hearers" is a term used to refer to people who took the first step and showed interest in Christian instruction with a view to becoming *inquirers*, then *catechumens*, before being admitted into baptism; Berega Logbook No. 51, MH.

19. Isaka Mlahagwa, oral interview, 14 September 1997.

20. Mlahagwa, oral interview.

21. Extracts from Peel's journals in *CMI* 25 (November 1900): 815; *PCMS*, 1901, 20. This is a place where the present Berega mission hospital is located, referred to sometimes as "Berega Mlingoti." When Chilongola offered Mugugu as a site in his village (29 March 1900), CMS missionaries had already been using the name "Berega" in their overseas correspondence and carried on using it even after moving from Berega (Mbuyuni) and relocating to a neighbouring village of Mugugu (only a mile or so away). That is why even the present location of the mission at Mugugu is called "Berega." Berega is named after a creeping green vegetable plant called *iberega*. Though rare to find nowadays, some people – for example, Eunike Mngh'umbi – grow *iberega* at home on their thatch roofs where it can creep easily. This writer was able to see the plant for himself at Eunike Mngh'umbi's home at Berega (Mbuyuni) area.

22. Isaka Mlahagwa, oral interview, 14 September 1997.

23. *CMI* 25 (November 1900): 821.

other places, Unyangwira had been visited before with the view to win the favour of the chiefs, as a 1901 CMS report records:

> Mvumi, fifty miles from Mpwapwa, in Ugogo country, was occupied during the year [1900] by Mr. J. H. Briggs. It was mentioned in last year's Annual Report that he had made an itinerating journey into Ugogo in 1899. In February, 1900, he went again, and especially visited Mvumi to ascertain the views of the chiefs on the question of settling amongst them.[24]

But the chiefs had their own motives. It was noted earlier that Chief Mulimbwa of Buigiri invited John Price twice in December 1892 and early 1893 to visit his chiefdom during the smallpox epidemic, and though he gathered people to hear the Christian message, he wanted his people to be cured with medicine from the mission.[25] Sometimes, chiefs wanted allies who could help them in the fight against enemies, though this became less so as the German administration extended its authority, law, and order in Ugogo and Ukaguru. The desire to share in the material "riches," especially clothes and other movable possessions owned by the CMS missionaries, played a role too. Later, as benefits of literacy became evident, the desire of the chiefs to have literacy centres and worship places for their people became even greater. When Mulimbwa of Buigiri died, his son, Chief Magungu, succeeded him. He too urged CMS missionaries at Mpwapwa to bring teachers to teach his people to read and write, and the request was accepted.[26]

This underlines the introductory remarks above that, in the early days of the expansion of the CMS mission work, a chief's favour or disfavour with the CMS missionaries was one of the reasons a station or an out-station might be established in one chiefdom or sub-chiefdom and not another. A minor factor to be borne in mind is that ecological and health factors were equally important to CMS missionaries when settling in a place, but this was after the chief had granted permission.[27]

---

24. *PCMS*, 1901, 122. See also *PCMS*, 1900, 112.
25. *PCMS*, 1893, 46.
26. Nehemia Uguzi, oral interviews, 18 and 19 June 1997.
27. *CMI* 25 (November 1900): 815. Sites on hill tops were generally preferred by the CMS missionaries, as were sites with less danger of mosquitos and malaria fever.

4.3 Chiefs, Buildings and Literacy Classes

Another sphere of the chiefs' contribution to the CMS mission work was in the erection of buildings for use as worship places and classrooms.[28] At first, in many places, the reading classes and Sunday gatherings took place under the giant baobab trees or similar trees that provided adequate shade.[29] The need for buildings became obvious, though in the CMS mission (and this provides a sharp contrast with other Western missions – for example, the Roman Catholic ones), these were of a very temporary nature. Peel advised that such buildings be erected so that a "much wider area be undertaken" because these were easier to erect, and only required local resources.[30]

Except for the size, these buildings were similar in style to the residential houses used by the local people – that is, traditional rectangular *tembe*. At Chipera, within the vicinity of Berega, six chiefs with their people had built a large and strong church, forty-five feet by fifteen feet and eighteen feet high.[31] There was another church at Tangalata, an out-station of Berega. At Maundike, an out-station of Nyangala, Chief Mwando had erected a church too.[32] By April 1900, Nyangala district had at least three churches, all erected by the chiefs and their people. Such steps by some chiefs had considerable influence on other chiefs, as did the action of the Chipera chiefs on their neighbour, Chief Chambo of Mwandi.[33] Itumba (Uponela) chiefs such as Semropo were no different.

Even before ending his tour of the Ukaguru side of the CMS mission, and moving on to Ugogo, nothing impressed Peel more than the warmth of the chiefs and the people, and their readiness to hear the teaching and willingness to erect buildings for Christian purposes "at their own cost."[34] Many chiefs, for

---

28. A note has to be made, however, that for a considerable time during the early period of CMS work in central Tanzania, a building erected by the local people was multi-purpose. It was used for preaching, teaching, and worshipping. That is why, in some cases, such a building was referred to as a "school-church." See *CMI* 25 (November 1900): 820.

29. Philemon Chidosa, oral interviews, 12 and 13 June 1997; cf. *CMI* 25 (November 1900): 821.

30. Minutes, EC, 6/4/1900, G3 A8/O/1900/20, BUL.

31. *CMI* 25 (November 1900): 815; Peel, "Usagara and Ugogo Revisted," G3 A8/O/1903/38, BUL; *PCMS*, 1901, 120.

32. *CMI* 25 (November 1900): 816; *PCMS*, 1901, 120–121.

33. *CMI* 25: 815.

34. *CMI* 25: 816.

example Msamwenda,[35] chief of Maundike,[36] had promised to do the same. A similar attitude was evident among the chiefs in Ugogo. At Kimagai,[37] Chief Nyanhera and Chief Chedego (variant Cedego) were willing to build a school-church, and because of their enthusiasm, they managed to persuade their reluctant neighbour, Chief Muhehe Fund, to join them in their endeavour.[38]

In most cases, the chiefs erected teaching or preaching places in order to attract teachers to their villages. As Peel remarked about the action of the six chiefs at Chipera: "This then [was] their invitation to us!"[39] A delay in appointing and sending a teacher to the chief who requested one often frustrated the chief and embarrassed the mission. Peel recalls one such occasion, when he met Chief Msamwenda of Maundike during his second episcopal visit to the CMS mission – which he began in the autumn of 1902 and ended early in 1903:

> In 1900, Mr Deeks and I visited him and reproached him for not having built a school as he had promised. He turned the rebuke upon us, saying that we had promised to send him a teacher and had not done so. He then took us to the upper part of his village and showed us a number of poles stacked, ready to be used for the school! We did not feel comfortable. This year [1903] Mrs Peel and I accompanied Mr Deeks and his teachers to Maundike. How surprised we were! We entered a comfortable and cool shed with walls made of crossed poles. Soon it was filled with scholars, young and old. For an hour and a half school was vigorously carried on. The chief and one of his sons were present, learning. About 130 names were on the school register, of

---

35. Msamwenda is used here as a correct spelling for the chief's name, instead of "Samwenda" which appears in Peel's paper. See "Usagara-Chigogo Notes II," typescript, December 1903, G3 A8/O/1904/28, BUL, where the name "Msamwenda" is used by Deeks, a CMS missionary who accompanied Peel on his visit to Msamwenda's, though Deeks refers to the chief as "the headman." See also RUUM, 1909, on 19/3/1910, G3 A8/O/1910/40, BUL, where again the chief's name is spelled as "Msamwenda."

36. Maundike is the correct spelling, not "Makundike" as in *CMI* 25 (November 1900): 817.

37. *Kimagai* is the correct spelling, not "Kimugaye" as in *CMI* 25 (November 1900): 820.

38. *CMI* 25 (November 1900): 820.

39. *CMI* 25: 815.

whom seventy were present. Since my interview with the chief in 1900, a school had been built.[40]

In 1910, at an out-station near Mvumi, Chief Mbogoni built a large preaching place to demonstrate to the CMS mission his desire to have his people taught to read and write.[41] In some places, the local people were paid for the labour they provided, but the impetus and initiative for having people taught to read and write often lay with the local chiefs.

The depression and reconstruction of the 1920s in Tanzania after the First World War,[42] and lack of outright enthusiasm and support from the British colonial government for mission education (based on their doubt over the efficacy of out-schools, as will be shown in chapter 7),[43] reduced the intensity of the contribution of the chiefs in mission education, especially in literacy. Their contribution was further frustrated by the British colonial government's introduction of Indirect Rule ("the principle of ruling through the Native Chiefs")[44] and secular Native Authority Schools (NAS) which became one of the features of Indirect Rule in the 1920s and 1930s. From this time onward, quite a number of the chiefs' sons went to these schools.[45] The stipulation by the CMS mission itself, that a chief and his people must first build a church before a teacher could be sent to them, also had a similar effect in some places.[46]

However, the contribution of the chiefs continued to be noted. For example, at Mvumi Makulu, near Mvumi station, Mazengo Chalula, the paramount chief of Ugogo (see photograph 9, appendix 3), maintained his involvement in mission education and had a good relationship with CMS missionaries at Mvumi station. As a strategist, he wanted many young people in his chiefdom to get employment in their own land and work as clerks, tax collectors, agricultural officers and so on.[47] He had no doubt that the school was the

---

40. Peel, "Usagara and Ugogo Revisited," MS, G3 A8/O/1903/38; *CMI* 29 (February 1904): 114.
41. Briggs to Baylis, 29/1/1910, G3 A8/O/1910/24, BUL.
42. Thompson and Hornsby, "Iss-Feres Tanz. Project," 41.
43. *Report of the Proceedings*, 5–7. See also Mbilinyi, "African Education," 14.
44. Cameron, "Native Administration Memoranda No. 1–8." Donald Cameron was governor of Tanganyika.
45. Furley and Watson, "Education in Tanganyika," 477–478.
46. *PCMS*, 1925, 14.
47. Dan Mbogoni, oral interview, 11 June 1997.

road that led to the achievement of that goal. In his chiefdom, those who registered at the mission to attend a *Shule ya Saa Nane* (Kiswahili phrase; "the two-o'clock school") and made themselves known to him were exempted from government roadwork.[48] This was done as an incentive to enable more people to attend literacy classes.[49] A small requirement for these people was that they should offer free labour at the mission, particularly in connection with the collection of local building materials for the construction of classrooms. During his official meetings with his people, Mazengo often invited the indigenous teacher to be present and often asked him to confirm or deny whether people were attending the school and Sunday gatherings. If the number was small, he exhorted his people not to stay away from the opportunity to learn to read and write, an exhortation that was well heeded by many of his subjects in the chiefdom.[50]

Whether in connection with literacy or attendance at gatherings where Scripture was taught, the influence and power of the chiefs over their people was significant. The chiefs' involvement in traditional religious and social practices also had similar effect on their people.[51] In January 1904, Ernest Doulton (a CMS missionary in charge of the Buigiri district) visited a place called Mukonzi. It was a time of drought, and rain was greatly needed. Upon his arrival, Doulton was informed by Chief Mutwe wa Muhera, (Kigogo name; "the head of a rhinoceros") that a sacrifice for rain was to be offered the next day, and the people would attend. But the chief also promised that after the sacrifice, he would take his people to a meeting where Christian teaching was to be offered, and the promise was kept.[52] At Muhalala, near Kilimatinde in the Mvumi district, Briggs (a CMS missionary in charge of the district) was greatly impressed by Chief Meso Mapya when they met at the chief's court,

---

48. Details on government road work will be given in chapter 5 in relation to the motives for conversion.

49. Dan Mbogoni, oral interview, 11 June 1997.

50. Lazaro Ndajilo, oral interviews, 14 and 16 June 1997.

51. The subject of the interaction of indigenous African religious and social practices with "European" mission Christianity is dealt with in chapter 5.

52. "Usagara-Chigogo Notes I," typescript, September 1903, G3 A8/0/1903/40; "Usagara-Chigogo Notes [III]," April 1904, G3 A8/O/1904/31, BUL.

first because of the way he dressed "like a European"(!) and second for accepting an invitation to attend a night gathering with some of his people.[53]

4.4 Chiefs and German Colonial Education Policy

Already as far back as 1902 – at a time when it might be said that the benefits of literacy had not been adequately appreciated – some of the chiefs and their sons had joined *masomo ya nguo* (Kiswahili phrase; "cloth-classes").[54] This was done by Chief Msamwenda and his three sons at Maundike, who at this time were able to read the New Testament and were about to join the book-class.[55] But, at times, especially when the benefits of literacy had not been realized, chiefs displayed hostility towards the mission. For example, until 1907, the chief of Idifu, south of Mvumi, and his people were hostile towards the work of the mission. But early in 1908, they changed their minds and sent a deputation to the mission station, expressing their readiness to be taught.[56]

Even so, the introduction of educational policy by the German colonial administration in 1910 was a decisive intervention which led to an increased involvement of more chiefs in the literacy programmes offered by the CMS mission. The policy required that the chiefs and headmen, as well as their sons (heirs to the chieftainship) and nephews, enrol to learn to read and write.[57] The ulterior motive on the part of the German colonial authorities was to find and employ suitable men to perform administrative tasks, especially tax collection from within the local chiefdoms where they belonged. This was being taken as a move towards the reduction and eventual replacement of the coastal Muslim clerks and headmen who had been increasingly appointed by

---

53. "Usagara-Chigogo Notes II," typescript, December 1903, G3 A8/O/1904/28, BUL. Briggs described Meso Mapya as "the most civilized Mgogo" simply because the chief came to meet him wearing "European" clothes, turned up at the night gathering wearing a long military cloak, had a well-built house with windows and equipped with "European" chairs, and had a white donkey kept in the stable! It is interesting to observe how *some* early CMS missionaries loved to see their culture imitated by Africans.

54. Peel, "Usagara and Ugogo Revisted," G3 A8/O/1903/38, BUL. The cloths (used instead of a blackboard) had vowels, consonants, and syllables written on them.

55. W. G. Peel, "Usagara and Ugogo Revisited;" Peel, *CMI* 29 (February 1904): 114. The "book-class" was the next stage where readers or pupils went after the cloth-class, and proper elementary reading, often of Bible portions, took place.

56. Peel to Baylis, 11/2/1908, G3 A8/O/1908/20, BUL.

57. *PCMS*, 1911, 57; Nehemia Uguzi, oral interviews, 18 and 19 June 1997.

the German colonial government. They had to be replaced because some of them did not find favour with the local chiefs, and the people in alien chiefdoms in the interior, and this affected the performance of government work.[58]

However, the German colonial administration left the option open to the chiefs and their relations to choose whether to receive instruction at the fort or at the nearest mission school or out-school.[59] By now, the colonial government had at least one school at Mpwapwa, but this would have been inadequate to cater to the educational needs necessary to make the policy as success. So it urged the CMS mission to take up the opportunity and provide education in its own schools and out-schools.[60]

But there was another reason why the colonial government made their preference known. It must have been aware that many Wagogo and Wakaguru pupils feared learning at the fort under direct supervision of the Germans. Their fear was based on the fact that colonial German government officials, mainly those of German nationality, but also some African colonial employees, had a reputation for being cruel.[61] The excessive use of *kiboko* (Kiswahili word; "a whip made out of a hippopotamus hide") as a standard form of corporal punishment was particularly dreaded by Tanzanians. Earlier in 1903, it was the youths' fear of being compelled to attend a German colonial government reading class established by Captain Fonck at the fort that forced them to attend the mission school at Mpwapwa. Like their parents, they did not concern themselves with what went on at the mission station or what it taught. Nonetheless, they "chose that which they regarded as the lesser of the two evils" – namely, the mission out-school.[62]

German colonial district officers were conducting occasional but strategic visits to the chiefdoms under their responsibility to enforce the policy. This worked to the advantage of the CMS mission. An out-station had been started at Handali, near Mvumi, in 1902.[63] It seems that this out-station did not survive, possibly because of hostility from the local chief. Towards the end

---

58. Lazaro Ndajilo, oral interviews, 14 and 16 June 1997.
59. Extract from Westgate's letter in *PCMS*, 1911, 57.
60. Briggs to Baylis, 29/1/1910, G3 A8/O/1910/24, BUL.
61. Philemon Chidosa, oral interviews, 12 and 13 June 1997; Semgomba Chitemo, oral interview, 15 September 1997.
62. *PCMS*, 1904, 97.
63. *PCMS*, 1903, 104.

of 1908, the chief openly told the CMS mission that he would not allow his people to be taught. It is possible this was a different chief from the one who allowed the opening of the station there in the first place. But early in 1909, a shed was built quickly in the village to enable literacy classes and preaching to take place, and an out-school was started at Handali. This was after a visit by Herr Sperling – the German district officer stationed at Mpwapwa.[64] Elsewhere that year – for example, at Buigiri – chiefs were among those who attended the reading classes regularly.[65]

Though some of the chiefs were unhappy about the German colonial government drive, they obeyed the command and placed themselves, their sons, and their nephews under instruction and chose to do that at the nearest mission school, as did almost all in the vicinity of Buigiri and Mvumi.[66] At Mvumi, they were asked to attend the central school at the station, and nearly thirty chiefs or their sons and nephews did so.[67] Later on, a special "morning school" was held for the chiefs' sons at each of the major out-stations within the Mvumi district, with a view to preparing them "to act as pupil-teachers."[68] At Buigiri, a different course of action was adopted in 1910. When presented with two options: either going to the central school at the mission station or paying a Christian teacher six rupees[69] per month to come teach them and their people in their villages, seven chiefs chose the latter option.[70] By 1912, over thirteen chiefs exercising authority in the area were reported to have enrolled themselves as inquirers, and their example was followed "by a large number of their headmen."[71]

---

64. Briggs to Baylis, 31/3/1909, G3 A8/O/1909/26, BUL; *PCMS*, 1910, 57; cf. *PCMS*, 1913, 53.

65. Westgate to CMS, annual letter, 21/12/1909, G3 A8/O/1910/27, BUL.

66. Westgate to Baylis 30/11/1910, G3 A8/O/1910/91, BUL; *PCMS*, 1911, 57.

67. *PCMS*, 1911, 57.

68. *PCMS*, 1913, 54.

69. The rupee is the basic monetary unit of the sub-Indian continent (India, Pakistan, Indonesia, Nepal) and in some African countries such as Seychelles. It was the official currency when Tanzania was under German colonial occupation until 1918. At the time, one rupee was worth approximately eight British pence. This is based on Westgate's estimates in 1915 that Rs20 was equivalent to £1.68. See Westgate, *In the Grip*, 73.

70. Westgate to Baylis, 31/11/1910, G3 A8/O/1910/91, BUL.

71. *PCMS*, 1913, 54.

The CMS mission was particularly charged with the task of providing the elementary education required. But the colonial government made clear to the Mission that if it failed to fulfil the task, those young people would be sent to a government school which would be built within the sphere of the mission, possibly at Mpwapwa.[72] Teachers at such schools were likely to be coastal Muslims.[73]

4.5 The "Threat" of Islam

Until about 1909, the CMS mission was the only Christian mission operating in Ugogo and Ukaguru. While the mission saw itself presented with a golden evangelistic opportunity through the German colonial educational policy, yet, on the other hand, it became threatened. If, as indicated by the German colonial government, more government schools were started in the interior, the government would use coastal Muslim teachers. The reason for this was that by 1910, it was Muslims rather than Christians who had better training from state schools. The state schools were first introduced by Julius Freiherr von Soden (the first German governor of Tanzania, 1891–1893), mainly along the coastal belt.[74] The first was opened at Tanga in 1892, and others were built later at Pangani, Bagamoyo, Dar es Salaam, and Lindi. By 1911, there were eighty-three state schools in the country, with a total of 4,312 pupils. Given the location of the state schools, the majority of their pupils and teachers were Muslims.[75]

CMS missionaries feared that Islam would grow in Ugogo and Ukaguru through Muslim teachers, for they expected those teachers would take every

---

72. Bertha Briggs to Baylis, 3/3/1909, G3 A8/O/1909/28; Briggs to Baylis, 31/3/1909, G3 A8/O/1909/26, BUL. The school must have been built between shortly after 1909.

73. Briggs to Baylis, 31/3/1909, G3 A8/O/1909/26; Briggs to Baylis, 29/1/1910, G3 A8/O/1910/24, BUL. Since 1892, Muslim pupils had been attending government schools such as the one at Tanga and provided much of the civil and administrative workforce for the German colonial government. The subjects taught at the state schools were intended to achieve the following purposes: drafting of letters, writing short reports, writing receipts, filing forms, tax procedures, and simple accounting, as well as developing character towards obedience, tidiness, punctuality, and a sense of duty. See Iliffe, *History of Tanganyika*, 209; Hornsby, "German Educational Achievement," 84.

74. Iliffe, *History of Tanganyika*, 209; Gifford and Louis, *Britain and Germany*, 770.

75. Hornsby, "German Educational Achievement," 87. There were seventy-eight schools with 3,494 pupils receiving elementary education; two schools with 681 pupils in higher education; and three schools with 137 pupils receiving industrial training.

opportunity to introduce the Muslim faith to the sons and nephews of the chiefs and sub-chiefs. And since these were the heirs-apparent, who, like their fathers, were expected to have much influence over their people, the faith would spread quickly. Mission adherents such as Lwanga Tofiki (to whom reference was made earlier in chapter 3) had, it was claimed, gone back to Islam (his former religion), but renounced it when he became ill, and then made a public confession in church after recovery.[76]

As part of the strategy to prevent Islamic influence, the CMS mission requested a grant to start a mission store where mission adherents could buy goods and avoid going to Muslim-owned shops.[77] Islam was to be kept out of the CMS mission sphere at all cost. Many CMS missionaries made this point to the CMS committee in London in their annual letters of 1909.[78] Indeed, to emphasize the so-called "danger" of Islam in central Tanzania, they put the whole issue in a global context:

> The Mohammedan hosts continue to accumulate. They come, they teach, they labour and although we have reason to believe that the Wagogo will not follow the example of the Yao tribe, a strenuous effort with that object in view will undoubtedly be made. . . . The time has come for Christendom to demand and determine [that] from degradation and bondage of Islam, not only the Wagogo but all unevangelised African tribes, shall forevermore be free. Temporizing will do no longer: now is the time for decision, for firm, persistent, resolute action.[79]

But it was not resident CMS missionaries alone who gave this impression of the opportunity in education and the "danger" of the arrival in central Tanzania of Muslim teachers to teach the sons and nephews of the chiefs and sub-chiefs. They were supported by Peel, their bishop. Peel urged the committee to "see the importance of our having bulwark against Mohammedan

---

76. Kate Pickthall to Baylis, 20/11/1909, G3 A8/O/1910/14; Baxter to Baylis, 13/12/1909, G3 A8/O/1910/25, BUL.

77. Doulton to Missionary Leaves Association, 1/12/1909, G3 A8/0/1910/20; Doulton to Baylis, 12/4/1910, G3 A8/0/1910/50, BUL.

78. E.g. Bertha Briggs to Baylis, 3/3/1909, G3 A8/0/1909/28; Ruth Spriggs to Baylis, annual letter, 2/12/1909, G3 A8/0/1910/15; Briggs to Baylis, annual letter, 29/1/1910, G3 A8/0/1910/24, BUL.

79. Westgate to Baylis, annual letter, 31/11/1910, G3 A8/0/1910/91, BUL.

invaders when they do come, as they surely will, later on."⁸⁰ He added: "It will be simply disastrous, if at present, in our condition of just drawing so many thousands to knowledge, by God's loving blessing, the sons and nephews of the chiefs in all the area in which CMS is in evidence and expected to be in evidence, be alienated from us by the influence of Islam."⁸¹ Such a plea was not only in relation to the dreaded potential influence of Muslim teachers. CMS missionaries also expressed reservations about the progress made in the construction of the central railway that had been started by the German colonial government at Dar es Salaam in 1905 and had reached Mpwapwa in 1909. They felt that this could increase the contact of the Wagogo and Wakaguru with other groups of Muslims – for example, traders.

A report, based on letters from CMS missionaries in Ugogo and Ukaguru, noted: "The construction of the railway in German East Africa is proceeding apace, but while facilitating the movements of the missionaries, it brings with it some disadvantages, since 'all along,' Miss E. Forsythe writes, 'as far as it has reached, are little Mohammedan mosques, quite insignificant huts, but still sufficient for scattering broadcast of the seeds of false doctrine.'"⁸²

It should be stressed that the fear of Islam at this time embraced many missions, not just the CMS mission. Writing from Mound Place (New College), while attending the WMC in Edinburgh in 1910, Karl Axenfeld (a missions inspector of the Berlin Mission in Germany) urged the CMS mission to join hands with other Protestant missions to combat Islam, which he perceived to be on the increase. He particularly noted that missions stations situated along the trade route from Dar es Salaam to the interior faced a greater risk because the routes facilitated Islamic propaganda, but at the same time, such stations, like those of the CMS, were best situated to counteract such propaganda.⁸³ Axenfeld actually travelled from Edinburgh to London to meet David Rees, one of the CMS missionaries who was on leave at the time, to discuss the issue further.

To emphasize the sense of urgency for strategic action against Islam, Axenfeld shared with Rees the observation of Albrecht von Rechenberg, then

---

80. Peel to Baylis, 23/3/1910, G3 A8/O/1910/42, BUL; *PCMS*, 1910, 56–57.
81. Peel to Baylis, 23/3/1910, G3 A8/O/1910/42, BUL.
82. *PCMS*, 1910, 56; *PCMS*, 1911, 57.
83. K. Axenfeld to Baylis, 21/6/190, G3 A8/0/1910/55, BUL.

the German colonial governor of Tanzania. Rechenberg expressed concern for Christianity, and urged that effort be made along the railway route rather than in the interior and remote districts, as the CMS mission appeared to be doing.[84] Axenfeld went at length to make several practical suggestions on areas of cooperation, including the writing of articles in a Kiswahili Christian newspaper, *Pwani na Bara* (Coast and Interior) and the retranslation of the Epistles in Kiswahili.[85]

Despite the fears and attitude of CMS missionaries and those of other missions towards Muslims and Islam, there is no evidence to suggest that Muslim teachers or traders entered Ugogo and Ukaguru in large numbers from 1910 onwards. In fact, despite prolonged and continuous contact of the Wagogo (and the Wakaguru for that matter) with Muslim traders and travellers, possibly dating as far back as the second half of the eighteenth century, and certainly from the middle of the nineteenth century, there had been hardly any conversion to Islam in Ugogo and Ukaguru.[86] But the fear speeded the process of the establishment of numerous learning centres and the recruitment of more indigenous staff.

There were two outcomes of the educational policy of the German colonial administration that related to the chiefs and their sons. The first was the increase in the number of scholars attending CMS schools; and the second was the increase in the government employment opportunities for CMS mission adherents. With regard to the first, table 4.1 above indicates that by the end of 1909 the number of scholars had already started rising, from 4,804 to 5,062 in 1910. But the sharp rise began in 1911 when 7,175 attended CMS

---

84. "Notes of the Interview between D. J. Rees of CMS and K. Axenfeld of Berlin Evangelical Society at Livingstone College, 26/6/1910," G3 A8/0/1910/57, BUL; cf. the exhortation by First Lieutenant Styx, Commanding Officer at Mpwapwa, during a conversation with David Rees on 25/1/1907 at Mpwapwa fort, reported at the meeting of the EC, 30/1/1907. Styx urged the CMS mission in 1907 to consider starting work at Kondoa Irangi, north of Dodoma town, to counteract the influence of Islam. A delay of another three years, he noted, would result in the Kondoa area being overrun by Islam, and the religion would spread further south into areas already occupied by the CMS mission. The Kondoa plan was later abandoned for lack of human resources, but the HGF had already started occupying Kondoa Irangi. See Minutes, special meeting, EC, 30/1/1907, G3 A8/0/1907/27; Westgate to Baylis, 15/8/1907, G3 A8/0/1907/50, BUL. To date, Islam still has a significantly larger following in Kondoa and its surrounding villages, but the Muslims there are not Arabs but Wairangi (the people of Irangi).

85. Interview between Rees and Axenfeld, 26/6/1910, G3 A8/0/1910/57, BUL.

86. For details of the sociological and religious reasons that prevented receptivity to Islam, especially in Ugogo, see Rigby, "Sociological Factors," 268–295.

schools. The figures rose even higher to 17,130 and 17,202 in 1912 and 1913, respectively. Obviously, competition with the Roman Catholic missions from 1911 must be included in the factors that contributed to such an increase. This will be explored in more detail in the next chapter. The chiefs and their sons did not necessarily form the bulk of scholars. Nonetheless, it must be acknowledged and stressed that it was the political interest which the German colonial administration showed in them as a group that led to the awakening within the CMS mission for consolidation of educational work. This included the realization by the mission that if it didn't teach the chiefs and their sons, they would end up in the hands of Muslim teachers and consequently adopt Islamic faith. Just as they were influential in the establishment of literacy centres and worship places for Christian missions, they had the potential to do the same for Islam.

As for the increase in the employment opportunities for Christians – and this included the chiefs or headmen who became Christians – a few years back, before the start of the new educational policy (that is, towards the end of 1903), the government had promised the CMS mission that suitable Christians with elementary education would be enlisted for service in the local administration in the interior.[87] Chelwe (variant Celwe) in the Kongwa district had a Christian headman in 1907 named Timotheo Makanyaga (brother of Mugube Makanyaga, the father of Andrea Mwaka).[88] Timotheo not only allowed Christian teaching to be conducted in his village, he himself became a mission teacher and conducted teaching at his own residence.[89] Oral testimonies suggest that the desire of the CMS mission to have Christians in positions of influence in local administration continued for many years, even during the British colonial era. "They wanted us to know to read and write so that we may help the nation and be employed as tax clerks, court clerks and so on. Possibly to become doctors," one informant said.[90]

---

87. D. J. Rees, Secretary, Usagara-Ugogo Mission: Notes of Interviews with [Adolf von] Götzen, the Imperial German Governor of German East Africa, 14 & 16/11/1903, G3 A8/O/1903/45, BUL.

88. Cleopa Mwaka, oral interview, 4 July 1997.

89. RUUM, 1907, G3 A8/O/1908/24, BUL.

90. Dan Mbogoni, oral interview, 11 June 1997; Isaka Mlahagwa, oral interview, 14 September 1997.

By 1908, Christians within the sphere of the CMS mission were now holding responsible positions in the local chiefdoms' administrations. At Mvumi, in Mazengo's chieftainship, a church teacher called Natanaeli held a position which was then regarded as that of a government collector. He had powers to hear and judge criminal or civil cases and to enforce punishment according to the government rules and was working under a German district office.[91] Zakaria Chomola and Abel Zoya became local tax clerks at Mvumi immediately after completing elementary school education at Mvumi mission station school. The two men were sent to school by Chief Mazengo in place of his own sons.[92]

It was common at this time that while chiefs became enthusiastic about literacy within their chiefdoms, they nonetheless wanted to keep their own sons – heirs apparent – away from the mission and mission school. This paradox showed itself in connection with the chiefs' own attitude to personal conversion, as will be explored below. Some of those sent to school by the chiefs were indeed sons of the slaves who had been given as *hongo* by the Nyamwezi traders and other travellers from western Tanzania.[93] Chomola (Zakaria's father) was one such person. The fathers of Mabwai and Eliya Mbungwe, who were sent to the government schools at Mpwapwa, were also given as *hongo*.[94] In Ukaguru, another Christian, identified also by the name Timotheo (not Timotheo Makanyaga), also became a tax clerk. Timotheo was both a local headman and a church teacher.[95]

4.6 Standing by the "Fence": Chiefs and Conversion

Throughout this study, the writer pursues the paradox of indispensable initiatives and contributions of the indigenous agents on the one hand, and on the other, the resilience of the Gogo and Kaguru traditional religions and social practices which formed the context of the agents. The initiatives of the chiefs should therefore be evaluated here. The same will be done in relation to the

---

91. Peel to Baylis, 11/2/1908, G3 A8/O/1908/20, BUL.
92. Lazaro Ndajilo, oral interviews, 14 and 16 June 1997.
93. Ndajilo, oral interviews.
94. Ndajilo, oral interviews.
95. Peel to Baylis, 11/2/1908, G3 A8/O/1908/20, BUL.

catechetical process in which converts were involved (in the next chapter) and in relation to the indigenous teachers in chapter 8.

Whether through direct or indirect action and participation, the contribution of the chiefs in the foundational period of the expansion phase cannot be ignored. Many young people and adults who joined literacy classes and went on to become Christians did so because of the initiatives taken by the chiefs to welcome the mission. But how, at a personal spiritual level, did the chiefs themselves respond to the call to convert to mission Christianity?

If there was anything common among many of the chiefs on this matter, it was their refusal to accept baptism and enter the Christian fold. In the eyes of many early CMS missionaries, conversion of the indigenous people was seen as a natural and ultimate consequence of joining a literacy class.[96] It should be stressed that a number of chiefs did actually become "hearers" and "inquirers," but for many, that was the furthest distance to "Christian faith" they travelled. For example, Msamwenda, chief of Maundike (see above), started attending church "regularly" with two of his wives in 1882; he was "ever ready to listen to any spiritual conversations," and he prevented his people and slaves from working on Sunday but gave them "every opportunity to attend services."[97] He was under instruction in 1902.[98] Yet he died in 1909 without committing himself to baptism.[99] For him and many others, the "road" to baptism had its obstacles, two of which may be considered here to illustrate the point being made.

One obstacle was polygamy – a subject about which more will be said in the next chapter – and the CMS mission was aware of it; religiopolitical obligations was the other. In the first two decades or so of mission work leading up to the end of the nineteenth century, CMS missionaries appeared to have shown a degree of tolerance towards some aspects of Gogo and Kaguru social and religious life – for example, some dances, such as *nindo*, *chipande*, *chisumbi*, *saigwa* and *mpendoo*, which were used in social celebrations.[100]

---

96. "Usagara-Chigogo Notes I," typescript, September 1903, G3 A8/O/1903/40; Usagara and Ugogo Revisited 1902-1903, G3 A8/O/1903/38, BUL.

97. *CMIR* 8 (May 1883): 293.

98. "Usagara-Chigogo Notes I," typescript, September 1903, G3 A8/O/1903/40, BUL.

99. RUUM, 1909, G3 A8/O/1910/40, BUL.

100. Lazaro Ndajilo, oral interviews, 14 and 16 June 1997.

Circumcision too was tolerated in the pre-expansion era. This trend will be revisited again in the next chapter. Meanwhile, it should be realized that this was not the case with polygamy. Yet chiefs tended to be polygamists.

At the start of the twentieth century, more conditions were being introduced, one of which was that a polygamist could only be admitted to the class of catechumens (let alone be baptized) if he made arrangements for putting away all his wives except one.[101] Quite a number of "ordinary" people (that is, those not in influential positions) were often willing to do just that, as was the case for an "accomplished" traditional dancer who was also working as a porter for CMS missionaries at Mvumi.[102] But most of the chiefs never abandoned their cultural and social obligations to the women, who, according to the traditional provisions, they had been legally married to. Accepting baptism and becoming members of an alien religion proved too much for them because it would have alienated them from their people.

Even those whom CMS missionaries described as "friendly" – for example, Chief Masenha of Unyangwira – did not necessarily develop personal spiritual interest in mission Christianity.[103] Masenha was not the only one. In his article to the editor of the "Usagara-Chigogo Notes I," Henry Cole wrote about a chief at Chelwe near Mpwapwa: "The chief is friendly and has a new knowledge of the Gospel, imparted to him, principally by his nephew Andreya. One sometimes thinks that he is on the verge of the Kingdom and would probably enter in were it not that he loves many wives."[104] Anza Lema observes the same kind of rejection of mission Christianity by a considerable number of the Chaga chiefs. Chaga chiefs welcomed the German Leipzig missionaries in the late nineteenth century, partly out of fear because of the latter's links with the German colonial power, and also for the advantages of educational work. However, like their counterparts in Ugogo and Ukaguru, they themselves "steadfastly refused to commit themselves to the new religion."[105]

---

101. Minutes, EC, 6/4/1900, G3 A8/O/1900/20, BUL.

102. Briggs to Baylis, 17 March 1908, G3 A8/O/1908/27. The same incident was reported later by Bertha Briggs. See Bertha Briggs to Friends in England, 3 March 1909, G3 A8/O/1909/28, BUL.

103. Briggs to Baylis, 20/8/1900, G3 A8/O/1900/38, BUL.

104. "Usagara-Chigogo Notes I," typescript, September 1903, G3 A8/0/1903/40, BUL.

105. Lema, "Chaga Religion," 58.

Apart from polygamy, the other obstacle to the baptism of many of the chiefs was their religiopolitical obligations. It was noted in chapter 2 that chiefs had the responsibility of being the custodians of rain stones which were used during the rain sacrifice.[106] Chiefs such as Mazengo Chalula had become inquirers in the days of German colonial rule but remained unbaptized for a long time.[107] When confronted with a choice between relinquishing his power as chief (and, consequently, *mawe ya utemi,* meaning "chieftancy rain stones") and becoming a Christian, or remaining as chief, Mazengo chose the latter. He (as much as the CMS missionary resident at Mvumi) knew only too well that if he chose the former, he would offend the people of Ugogo, who obviously would have regarded him as a traitor.[108]

This attitude was common among the chiefs elsewhere in the country, even outside the geographical area under consideration in this study – for example at Nasa (on the southern shores of Lake Victoria) in northern Tanzania. Though geographically Nasa was located in Tanzania, it fell under the jurisdiction of the CMS mission in Uganda when it was handed over to the Africa Inland Mission in 1909.[109] That is why Alfred Tucker, then bishop of the Diocese of Uganda, visited it in 1906. After his visit, Tucker did not hide his disappointment that despite the many opportunities the chief had to hear the gospel, Chief Kapongo of Nasa could not contemplate forsaking his tribal religiopolitical duties to become a Christian. Tucker wrote:

> Another disappointment was the chief, Kapongo. For long years he has been reasoned with and pleaded with, but still remains a Heathen. The fact is his Heathenism is his living. As chief he is great rainmaker of the tribe, and were he to give up his pretension as a medicine-man his influence with his people would, he believes, vanish, and he himself be deposed. He cannot face the prospect. *Christianity would cost him too much.*[110]

---

106. Lazaro Ndajilo, oral interviews, 14 and 16 June 1997.
107. Stephano Malecela, oral interview, 24 June 1997.
108. Lazaro Ndajilo, oral interviews, 14 and 16 June 1997.
109. *PCMS*, 1910, 73–74.
110. *CMI* 31 (May 1906): 357.

In Ugogo itself, oral testimony suggests that the chiefs were also under pressure from the older generation within their chiefdoms not to accept Christianity. Makanyaga Mugube, chief of Ibwaga, started to receive baptism instructions at Chamuhawi. Ibwaga and Chamuhawi were separated only by Kiboriani hills. He was therefore able to commute. But the local people didn't like the idea. According to Cleopa Mwaka, the grandson of Mugube Makanyaga, chiefs such as Makanyaga were told:

> "You have joined foolishness. You have joined foolishness." Whenever they went to the chief for traditional practices, they found little response. "You are annoying us," [they said]. So the people became very impatient. . . . We fell out of favour. They said, "These have become barbarians. They no longer want to offer sacrifices. If we vote them, they will spoil our land. Let them continue in their madness."[111]

That is how the chiefs who associated themselves with mission Christianity were despised by their own people. In fact, it was not only the chiefs alone who fell out of favour with their people. The people, for example those of Ibwaga chiefdom, feared that voting the chiefs' children who were attending mission schools to traditional duties would further undermine the community's religious life. Reference has been made to Timotheo Makanyaga who was appointed by the German colonial administration to be headman of Chelwe. It may not be easy to evaluate his work as a Christian chief and how he survived the opposition of the traditionalists. But the fact that he was appointed by the Germans could mean that he earned respect not as a traditional leader but as a secular government agent.

4.7 Conclusion

Perhaps this may be an appropriate point to conclude this chapter. An attempt has been made to explore the contribution of the Kaguru and Gogo chiefs to the work of the CMS mission in central Tanzania early in the twentieth century. The chiefs took part in the establishment of the stations and in building literacy centres and worship places. They showed a genuine desire to help

---

111. Cleopa Mwaka, oral interview, 4 July 1997.

their people acquire literary skills and other benefits brought by mission education, and even become Christians. This may be one of the major factors that account for the numerous churches and centres, and a relatively unparalleled following, that the Anglican Church has in Ugogo and Ukaguru in the modern Dodoma and Morogoro provinces, respectively, in central Tanzania.

The intervention of the German and British colonial governments caused some vibrations on the attitude of the chiefs to the CMS mission. But the power to determine the level of participation rested with the chiefs, not the CMS missionaries or indigenous missionaries and teachers. Maintenance of loyalty to tribal order – social, religious, and political – was as much a desire they had as having their subjects "awakened" through literacy. The paradox here is a telling one, for it does not concern the chiefs alone, one group within the category of indigenous agents considered in this study; it involves many of the Gogo and Kaguru people who interacted with mission Christianity in central Tanzania early in the twentieth century, as will be explored and demonstrated further in the next chapter.

It is significant also because it is representative of the tension that African peoples experienced with mission Christianity, whether their subscription to it was partial or full. Those who chose to subscribe to mission Christianity through literacy and remained as converts, or went on to become indigenous missionaries and teachers, experienced even greater tension.

In this regard, though on the whole they remained "outsiders," the Kaguru and Gogo chiefs become an important group within the category of indigenous agents, not simply because they helped Anglican Christianity to take root, mainly through literacy, but also because of their boldness to stay outside. Of course, some of them, such as Mazengo Chalula, accepted baptism at the very end of their lives – a time when they had neither the social nor religiopolitical obligations to fulfil. They were advanced in age. But more importantly, especially for Mazengo Chalula, he chose to be Christian at a time when the political landscape had changed much in Tanzania. The British colonial government encouraged chiefdoms and traditional values through Indirect Rule as a means of controlling the masses (if not keeping each ethnic group in its place).[112] The Tanzanian mainland won its freedom from the

---

112. For details on the philosophy of Indirect Rule and its application in Africa, especially Nigeria and Tanzania, see Cameron, *My Tanganyika Service*; Perham, "System of

British in 1961, and soon afterwards, Julius Nyerere abolished the chiefdoms. The power of the chiefs, including that of Mazengo Chalula, vanished with it, though he continued to receive state benefits as a recognition of his service to the people of Ugogo.

When, therefore, such an influential chief in Ugogo as Mazengo accepted Christian baptism in 1967, he had nothing significant to lose in the religiopolitical sphere except his own soul, which he was free to associate with whatever faith he wished. Ndajilo says, "Ooh, he was baptized after independence. You see he was very advanced in age. He was no longer having an active relationship with his wives. He was living alone, and had become very weak. You know he lived for 107 years."[113] Most chiefs did the same. In the opinion of this writer, perhaps that was a better position, especially if no "concessions" were to be gained from mission Christianity in the general manner it was presented to the Wagogo and Wakaguru. Yet "concessions" would have helped to redefine what being a Christian would have meant for Africans in Ugogo and Ukaguru, be they chiefs or their subjects. Many Gogo and Kaguru who proceeded beyond the hearer or inquirer stage, and became converts, wrestled with these very tensions. The next chapter explores the educational process, particularly that education through which the Wagogo and Wakaguru were turned into baptized converts, and analyses the tensions experienced by many who attempted to travel further than the chiefs did.

Native Administration"; Latham, "Indirect Rule"; Evans, *British in Tropical Africa*; Gann and Duignan, *Rulers of British Africa*; Tagart, "African Chief"; Perham, "Re-statement of Indirect Rule"; Tagart, "African Chief."

113. Lazaro Ndajilo, oral interviews, 14 and 16 June 1997.

CHAPTER 5

Educational Contributions of Indigenous Teachers

> I would call and gather people and preach to them. There was no church building. Baobab tree was my church building. Until when we built a church.[1]

By examining the response of the Gogo and Kaguru chiefs to the work of the CMS mission in their chiefdoms from 1900 onwards, the previous chapter dealt with the foundational stages of the first expansion phase. It was argued that though many of these chiefs refused to commit themselves to mission Christianity, nevertheless they participated in the establishment of worship and preaching places, as well as literacy centres. In a sense, this was a necessary preparation for the educational and catechetical work that followed later.

This chapter analyses and evaluates the use of literacy training as an evangelistic method, and the nature of the catechetical process through which the Wagogo and Wakaguru became church members. Of special interest is how the catechetical process engaged with the religious and social practices of the potential converts and indigenous Christians, as well as the role of indigenous teachers in the process. While suggestions that mission Christianity assaulted and undermined African traditional practices are not wholly inaccurate, the factors that motivated the Wagogo and Wakaguru in central Tanzania to accept mission Christianity must also be taken into account.

This chapter seeks to show that Wagogo and Wakaguru accepted Christianity largely on their own terms and were motivated by the visible

---

1. Lazaro Ndajilo, oral interviews, 14 and 16 June 1997.

benefits offered by the mission. This puts the CMS mission in a disadvantaged position, for it could neither control the process of the conversion of the Wagogo and Wakaguru, nor succeed in enforcing its moral codes upon those whom it regarded as offenders. This, in a sense, was not a battle between CMS missionaries and the Wagogo and Wakaguru converts as such. It was a contest between mission Christianity and African traditional heritage. This chapter argues that it was the former that lost many battles.

5.1 Literacy Training as a Missionary Method

Various missionary methods were adopted in order to evangelize the Wagogo and Wakaguru – for example, literacy training, preaching in churches and in the open air, visiting people at home, and medical work.[2] Each of these contributed to the process of converting the Africans. Nevertheless, it was particularly through literacy training in the out-schools that much of the evangelistic work was done.

One of the reasons that lay behind the use of literacy as missionary method was the notion, perhaps common among many Western missionaries during the nineteenth and early twentieth centuries, that the African was a degraded being.[3] Poikail John George has rightly argued, in his article "Racist Assumptions of the 19th Century Missionary Movement," about how the presumed Western moral "superiority" and duty to "enlighten" and "uplift" the people of other races characterized the missionary movement in the nineteenth century.[4] Opinion on, and assessment of, the Western missionary of the time is of course varied, and the genuineness of the desire to evangelize other people cannot be underestimated. It seems, also, that the notion of degradation, though influenced by the presumed Western moral "superiority" prevailing at the time, and stereotypes about the African people as a race, was probably tied up more with Western missionaries' misunderstanding of African cultural and religious expressions. An example from outside Ugogo

---

2. Rees, "History of CMS," MS, G3 A8/0/1902/19, BUL.

3. RUUM, 1906, G3 A8/0/1907/23; Rees to Baylis, 23 July 1906, G3 A8/0/1906/53, BUL; "The Importance of Education: a report for the Dioceses of Zanzibar and Masasi, 1926–1936," MS 3122, LPL.

4. George, "Racist Assumptions," 271–284.

and Ukaguru is not irrelevant. In 1892, E. H. Hubbard, one of the CMS missionaries at Nasa in Usukuma (south of Lake Victoria) wrote:

> Were a stranger to appear amongst us, he might wonder what has been done to make known God's Word to these poor degraded Wasakuma [Wasukuma]. He would go to the village and see hundreds of almost naked savages, probably drinking *pombe* and engaged in their wild dances, while around the huts facing the cornfields and the lake would be found little houses built to contain the offerings for the evil spirits of the land and lake. . . . Now we usually get between 400 and 500, and often many more.[5]

Though Hubbard wanted to make a contrast between what was happening, and the breakthrough the mission had started to make, the terminology he used to describe the Wasukuma's social and religious expressions is based on misunderstanding. Based on that misunderstanding, Christian teaching, or evangelization, was therefore regarded as a "civilizing" factor. This became a significant purpose – indeed, *the* main purpose – of mission education:[6] "It is the aim of the missionaries to let people understand that, while education is for the purpose of developing mind and character in the right way, the great object of teaching to read and understand books is to secure to each man and woman the privilege of reading God's message to man in His Own Book."[7] This placing of the Scriptures at the centre of literacy training was quite interesting, because it seemed best in the CMS mission (as in other missions) that the person who gained reading and writing skills should also become a Christian.

5.2 The Out-School as Chief Agencies for Evangelization

Like other missions,[8] the CMS mission gave prominence to the teaching of Scriptures in its educational institutions at all levels: at out-schools, stations

---

5. *PCMS*, 1893, 48.

6. Broomfield, "Importance of Education," MS 3122, LPL.

7. Peel, "Usagara and Ugogo Revisited," G3 A8/O/1903/38, BUL; Peel, *CMI* 29 (February 1904): 115.

8. For example, the UMCA and German Lutheran missions. See Broomfield, "Importance of Education," MS 3122, LPL; Wright, *German Missions*, 173.

schools, central (boarding) schools, and teacher training colleges. Esta Chali was a pupil at Buigiri girls' central school in 1928, and gives this testimony:

> There at Buigiri, those who brought the Word of God to us taught the Word of God more than anything else. . . . Ordinary school lessons were taught, but *the Word of God came first*. . . . We started standard one lessons when the Bishop arrived.[9] We continued until standard six. . . . The pupils learnt how the ancient people lived, what God did to them.[10]

Despite such Scripture-oriented evangelistic teaching in central (boarding) schools, the focus of the inquiry in this chapter is more on the out-schools.[11] In most cases, as the opening quote in this chapter indicates, literacy training was first conducted under baobab trees until such time that the people erected a mud and wattle hut. Ndajilo's description in that quotation is the same as that of Bishop Peel, who remarked that, at the out-schools, "beneath some rough shelter or the shade of a large tree, men and women as well as children are taught for a few hours with the aid of a cloth sheet on which have been printed the letters of the alphabet or easy syllables, and afterwards listen to a simple Gospel address."[12] In this sense, they became commonly known as "*bush* schools." Naturally, the out-school became the first point of contact between the majority of the Gogo and Kaguru and mission Christianity,[13] and much of primary and basic evangelization took place there.[14] Out-schools produced what later became known in East Africa as *Kusoma* Christianity.[15] *Kusoma* is a Kiswahili verb meaning "to read," and for that reason, Christians were called "readers" – or *abasomi* in the case of some Bantu speaking groups, such as the Wakuria and Wasimbiti in the Tarime district on the eastern shore of Lake Victoria, Tanzania.

---

9. The bishop who arrived in 1928 is George Chambers – the Australian first bishop of an independent diocese created from the diocese of Mombasa in 1927.

10. Esta Chali, oral interview, 26 June 1997.

11. *PCMS*, 1909, 57; *PCMS*, 1915, 60.

12. This typical description of an out-school was made by Agnetta Peel, the daughter of bishop W. G. Peel in the *CMS Gazette*, June 1908, 182, cited in *PCMS*, 1909, 57.

13. Oliver, *Missionary Factor*, 201.

14. *PCMS*, 1909, 56–57.

15. Anderson, *Church in East Africa*, 111.

Though indigenous teachers were co-teachers with CMS missionaries in the central (boarding) schools and station schools, their evangelistic role was more central and extended in the out-schools. Here, their leadership was exclusive. But before examining and appreciating the place of the out-schools in literacy training and evangelization, it seems convenient that a brief analysis of the station school should be made first because they too were centres of evangelization, though only on a much smaller scale compared to the out-schools.

Between 1900 and 1933, the CMS mission established at least one station school at each of its nine major stations – namely, Mpwapwa, Mvumi, Buigiri, Kongwa, and Kilimatinde in Ugogo, and Mamboya, Nyangala, Itumba (Uponela), and Berega in Ukaguru.[16] The station school was above the out-school in terms of the level of staffing and curriculum.[17] It was under the direct supervision of a CMS missionary, who, in most cases, was a man.[18] The exception to this was the Mamboya station and its school. For a long period after the first expansion phase began in 1900, the school was under the leadership of Kate Pickthall, Emily Spriggs, and indigenous Bible women such as Persisi, Salama, Damari, Viktoria, and Naomi, as well as male teachers, particularly Yeremia Senyagwa.[19] As for the curriculum, while only reading and writing were taught at the out-schools, arithmetic, history, geography, mathematics, hygiene, and English were introduced and taught at the station schools.[20]

Returning to the out-schools – the main focus of analysis here – it has to be stated that in Ugogo and Ukaguru, as in other places in Africa during the nineteenth century, it was the CMS missionaries who first taught literacy classes. But as soon as the potential converts were identified, these started taking part in literacy training and preaching. This was a common phenomenon in CMS missions in other countries – for example, Kenya. In 1898, a

---

16. In 1913, Kilimatinde (1922) had not become a station yet. Mpwapwa was deprived of its status as a mission station in 1906 and was thereafter worked as an out-station along with Chamuhawi. It reopened in 1921 and reclaimed its status as a mission station. See Rees to Baylis, 3/8/19106, G3 A8/0/1906/54, BUL; *PCMS*, 1907, 77; *PCMS*, 1922, 34; Chambers, *Tanganyika's New Day*, 27.
17. Chambers, 29.
18. See Smith, "Missionary Contribution," 105.
19. *CMR* 61 (August 1910): 486; *CMR* 65 (September 1914): 548.
20. Lazaro Ndajilo, oral interviews, 14 and 16 June 1997.

female CMS missionary at Frere Town in Kenya described her partnership with Andreas, one of the indigenous teachers, as follows:

> Sometimes I only read a passage in Kinyika and Andreas does all the teaching. He preaches so earnestly and delights in it.... You may perhaps say, "Why not leave this work to him?" He tells me that they will not come in any numbers when he is alone, but when I go, he sends a child round to all living near to tell them they are called. Bibi[21] has come to teach them, and they come. But though I am there, it is Andreas who does nearly all the work.[22]

Such was the partnership between a foreign missionary and an indigenous teacher on the coast of Kenya. In central Tanzania – especially during the expansion phase (1900–1933) – the role of indigenous teachers became more extended and almost exclusive.[23] It was a campaign in which even mobile guides and porters assisting CMS missionaries during their itineration participated.[24] The indigenous teachers who were attached to the station school also visited the out-schools periodically – three times a week, once a week, once in three weeks, or once a month, depending on the distance from the place where they were based to the out-school.[25] By 1913, there were at least 370 out-stations or "strategic blockhouses" in the CMS mission.[26] Since the out-school was located at the out-station, it could be estimated that at least the same number of out-schools existed at the time. Some districts, for example Kongwa, had at least thirty out-schools attended by over 1,200 adults and children in 1908.[27]

---

21. *Bibi* is a Kiswahili word meaning "grandmother." The other possible meaning is "wife," but this usage is inaccurate, though it is still used in common speech among a number of non-coastal Kenyans. Hardly anyone in Tanzania, then or now, would refer to a married woman as "bibi," and the same is true for the official Kiswahili used in the Kenyan press and media.

22. Letter from M. C. Brewer, quoted in *PCMS*, 1899, 88.

23. Lazaro Ndajilo, oral interviews, 14 and 16 June 1997; Peel, "Usagara and Ugogo Revisited," G3 A8/O/1903/38, BUL.

24. Peel, "Usagara and Ugogo Revisited," G3 A8/O/1903/38, BUL.

25. *PCMS*, 1909, 57; *PCMS*, 1915, 60.

26. *PCMS*, 1914, 61.

27. *PCMS*, 1909, 60.

5.3 The Medium of Instruction in the German Colonial Era

The question of which language should be used as a medium of instruction in mission schools became a controversial issue in both the German and British colonial eras. It is therefore important to review this issue before dealing further with the expansion of literacy training in the out-schools. Only the debate during the German colonial period is covered here. The period of British colonial occupation will be dealt with in chapter 7, since the issue of language was part of the debate on adaptation, which is the subject of that chapter.

The first literacy classes and Sunday services at Mpwapwa in 1878 were conducted in Kiswahili until about 1880. However, the importance of Kigogo was recognized early, and Edward Baxter (one of the earliest CMS missionaries at Mpwapwa) expressed his desire for "a time when we shall be able to hold services in Kigogo."[28] At this time, few Wagogo spoke Kiswahili.[29] Indeed, all other communication between CMS missionaries present (Edward Baxter and Joseph Last) and the Wagogo was done through indigenous interpreters who were from the coast, as was noted in chapter 3.[30] As more Wagogo joined reading classes, it became necessary that the instruction in elementary schools be given in the mother tongue. Religious instruction at the station schools and central (boarding) schools was also given in the vernacular, and this was not unique to the CMS mission. Kiswahili was used mainly for secular subjects.

However, towards the end of 1903, the German colonial government issued policy guidelines on language in schools (including those under missions) in Tanzania. The guidelines demanded that Kiswahili be used exclusively

---

28. *CMIR* 5 (December 1880): 738.
29. Minutes, EC, 18, 19, 21/12/1903, G3 A8/0/1904/12, BUL.
30. Reference was made earlier (in chapter 3) to Ali, who was one of the interpreters. Another interpreter, Swedi, spoke English, Kigogo, and Kikaguru. In addition to that he was "more or less acquainted with all languages of the people from the coast to Ujiji [western Tanzania] at which he lived for more than two years." See *CMIR* 3 (October 1878): 645. He was an interpreter and guide for Joseph Last, first at Mpwapwa (1878–1879) and then at Mamboya (from 1880). See *CMIR* 3 (October 1878): 645, 646; *CMIR* 5 (December 1880): 742. In 1879 he was working with Last to translate the Lord's Prayer into Kigogo. See *CMIR* 4 (September 1879): 533.

as a medium of instruction in all schools.[31] That this policy was somehow implemented is indicated by a report written by a German district officer at Mpwapwa at the end of January 1907, in which he stated that instruction in local schools was now being imparted in Kiswahili.[32]

Despite this policy change, the CMS mission requested, and got permission from the German colonial government, to be allowed to continue using the vernacular languages for religious instruction. The influence of Kiswahili was less intense in Ugogo, but the situation in Ukaguru was rather different. There, Kiswahili was used much more widely, especially at Mamboya and Berega.[33] Proximity to the coast (and, thus, greater exposure to the influence of the Swahili people and their language) may be singled out as a major factor contributing to the popularity of Kiswahili in parts of Ukaguru.[34] The advent of the railway in 1911 in central Tanzania also gave Kiswahili a new impetus.[35]

Apart from the vernaculars (Kigogo and Kikaguru) and Kiswahili, there was also an attempt by the German colonial government, as early as 1901, to introduce the German language in schools, so that it would become a second official language along Kiswahili.[36] In 1907, a report by a German district officer noted that scholars in CMS schools in Mpwapwa had acquired "a nice store of [German] vocabulary."[37] However, the report also acknowledged that a long time would pass before students at mission schools learned sufficient

---

31. D. J. Rees, "Notes of the Interview with Count von Göetzen, the Imperial Governor of German East Africa," 14, 16 November 1903, G3 A8/0/1903/45, BUL.

32. Report by Sytx, Imperial District Officer, on "Examination of Mission Scholars of the Church Missionary Society, Mpwapwa," 1/2/1907 (English typed translation of German), G3 A8/0/1907/28, BUL.

33. Minutes, EC, 18, 19, 21/12/1903, G3 A8/0/1904/12, BUL.

34. J. C. Green to Baylis, 21/11/1910, G3 A8/0/1910/84, BUL. By late 1910, Sunday services at Mamboya were conducted in Kiswahili, but much of the preaching was done in Kikaguru (sometimes called Kimegi or Kisagara). A Kiswahili hymnbook had already been in use for some time.

35. The central railway, which is 1,252 km (approx. 778 miles), was begun in 1905 at Dar es Salaam. It reached Morogoro in 1908, Tabora in 1912 and Kigoma in 1914. See "Tanganyika (German East Africa)" in *Handbooks* (prepared under the direction of the historical section of the Foreign Office), No. 113, London: HMSO, 1920, 45, 46, NLS; *CMR* 63 (March 1912): 156.

36. Imperial Governor of German East Africa to Bishop Peel (Rt Rev), 30 November 1901, reference J. N.7889.1, (the English typed translation of German), G3 A8/0/1902/17, BUL.

37. Report by Sytx, Imperial District Officer, on "Examination of Mission Scholars of the Church Missionary Society, Mpwapwa," 1/2/1907 (English typed translation of German), G3 A8/0/1907/28, BUL.

German.[38] On the whole, little success was made, and the German language never enjoyed similar popularity in schools as Kiswahili did, first in Ukaguru and later in Ugogo.

5.4 Teaching Methods at the Out-Schools
5.4.1 The Cloth Sheet and *Ikangambwa*

Despite the popularity of Kiswahili, much religious instruction for adults and children was done in the vernaculars at the out-schools – and, in part, at the station schools – both in Ugogo and Ukaguru. Through these local languages, adults and children were taught and catechized. The readers were introduced to the basics of literacy – vowels, consonants and syllables. These were written on a white cloth sheet.[39] The cloth was placed against a tree trunk or hung from the branch of a baobab tree which provided sufficient shade from the hot sun.[40] Some informants who taught at or attended the out-schools have vivid memories of the literacy classes under baobab trees: "They hung a cloth up. . . . Then they said, '*Ribwa, Kochwa, Yeijira, Chihamba, Mwanagwe, Yuyo*. Dog, gourd [calabash], cow.'[41] . . . Single letters and syllables were written on *mwenda* [Kigogo; 'cloth']. [They wrote] 'a, e, i , o, u. Ba, be, bi, bo. Sa, se, si, so, su. Da, de, di, do, du.' That's where we started."[42] This was a time when many in central Tanzania had not heard the Christian message. In parts of Ugogo, people often confused the meaning of the call to attend literacy centres even before they started to grapple with the content of the teaching itself. When urged to attend reading classes, particularly during the harvest season, some people thought they were being urged to go to the fields, harvest sorghum, and as usual, arrange it in the baskets. That is the equivalent of the word "reading" in Kigogo. Yet, the kind of reading that was meant was to read "a, e, i, o, u."[43]

---

38. Report by Sytx; cf. Smith, "Missionary Contribution," 91–109; Hornsby, "German Educational Achievement," 83–90.

39. *PCMS*, 1909, 57.

40. To date, baobab trees are a natural and common vegetation in many dry parts of Ugogo and Ukaguru with long, hot months and provide much needed shade for small or large village gatherings.

41. The informant did not go on to name everything he mentioned in Kigogo.

42. Lazaro Ndajilo, oral interviews, 14 and 16 June 1997.

43. Ndajilo, oral interviews.

In addition to the cloth sheet, *ikangambwa* (variant *kikangambwa*; Kigogo; "a traditional rope with three branches or splits for holding and hanging up utensils in the home") was used in teaching the adults to read. Esta Chali recalls:

> They wrote these words, "*Tu tu tundika*"[Kiswahili; "hang up," or "suspend," especially the verb "tundika"].... They asked, "What is this?" The adults replied, "*Ikangambwa*." "What does it do?" the teachers asked. "[It is used for hanging up] a utensil," they replied. They started from there, to help them understand how to pronounce the word. In doing so they demonstrated what that means. That was the beginners' class for adults.[44]

For both adults and older children, the mission's ultimate objective of teaching to read and write was to have them baptized. At a somewhat similar level, but mostly at the station school, literacy classes were known as *Shule ya Saa Nane* (two-o'clock school).[45] Adult classes often followed at four o'clock.

One of the reasons for holding the classes in the afternoon in the early years of the expansion phase was to enable the indigenous teachers to "search" for children in the morning and persuade parents to relieve them from tending cattle in the afternoon.[46] Buigiri village school (located at the station) had a number of indigenous teachers who taught in turn both in the morning and the *Shule ya Saa Nane* (two-o'clock school). Men who taught there were Mikaeli Matonya of Zoisa, Eliya Kamanjenzi, and Matayo Madelemu of Buigiri. Female teachers included Lea Saso, who taught standard 4 pupils, Elizabethi Uledi, Jemima Miyonga, and Dadali Milangasi, who taught children at nursery level and standards 1 and 2.[47] All of these women were Buigiri converts. This was mainly in recognition of their talents because children at that level needed gentle introduction to school life. Lazaro Ndajilo, who was

---

44. Esta Chali, oral interview, 26 June 1997; RUUM, 1909, G3 A8/0/1910/40, BUL.

45. Dan Mbogoni, oral interview, 11 June 1997; Nehemia Uguzi, oral interviews, 18 and 19 June 1997; Philemon Chidosa, oral interviews, 12 and 13 June 1997; Yudith Chidosa, oral interview, 12 June 1997; Esta Chali, oral interview, 26 June 1997.

46. Yusufu Masingisa, oral interviews, 16 and 17 September 1997.

47. Cleopa Mwaka, oral interview, 4 July 1997.

a teacher at Mvumi station school and responsible for standard 3, recalls the presence of Aksa and Elina, his female colleagues at the school:[48]

> They taught reading, [and] writing. You see there were books for small children, *vidudu* [Kiswahili; lit. "tiny insects," – a reference to what today may be called "nursery children"]. They started teaching at the lower level, "a, e, i o u," until they reached a stage where they could use books. By the time they came to my class, they could read the New Testament. Aksa and Elina were teaching standards 1 and 2.[49]

Damari Sagatwa (whose teaching and missionary career will be explored in detail in chapter 6) taught at Mpwapwa station school early in the 1930s and was indeed the only female teacher when the school started. Like Leas Saso at Buigiri, Kaguru women – Mariamu Chausiku, Naomi, and Anna Benyamini – taught in upper classes at the Berega girls' boarding school which opened on 30 October 1926. Others included Damari Shadraki, Ruth Danieli, and Enid Asani.[50] It is possible that all moved to the local day village school when the boarding school closed in 1937.[51]

5.4.2 Traditional and "Modern" Songs

Apart from the cloth sheet and *ikangambwa*, indigenous teachers used traditional songs, first to summon the children to school, and then to sustain their interest and impart the Christian message to them. One of the popular traditional children's songs Lazaro Ndajilo used had this line: *lwala gode'ho*,

---

48. Aksa could as well be the Aksa (a Kaguru woman) who was one of the indigenous teachers at Mamboya in 1901 and might have moved to Mvumi as a missionary. With minor exceptions, use of first names only in the mission and church archives is a major problem in identifying people. Given the distance between villages from where both teachers and pupils came to school at the mission station – and memory loss – even Lazaro Ndajilo could not recall the surname of his colleagues Aksa and Elina.

49. Lazaro Ndajilo, oral interviews, 14 and 16 June 1997.

50. John Briggs, "Circular [letter] to members of the Diocesan Council," 15/10/1937, cited in Berega Logbook, No. 50, 1926-1937, an entry for 1937, MH.

51. Berega Logbook, No. 50, MH. The school was closed due to changes introduced by the British colonial government that required standard 1–4 girls (and boys alike) to be taught in mixed village (day) schools, and not in the boarding schools. Berega had only eighteen girls, who were to complete standard 4 by the end of the year (1937) and had to leave to begin standard 5 elsewhere.

lwala gode'ho yebaya, chenjele nyuma mlamosa, yicha!, baa, yicha![52] In English, this Gogo song could be rendered as follows: "Mother hoe, mother hoe, they hate me. They hate me. But one day when the mouse comes, it will bite them. It will bite them." At the end of the song, Ndajilo revealed who the mother was. He told the children, "Jesus Christ. He has brought me here from Mvumi, therefore do not make him *gode*. He is not [the wooden] *gode*, but the metal hoe."[53] When a sufficient number of children had assembled, the teacher stopped singing and began teaching them the word of God.[54] Ndajilo explains:

> *Lazaro Ndajilo*: When you beat the drum at 2:00 p.m., they would come running fast. . . . Then when many had come, and the number increased, I stopped singing the song. I would then say, "You fellows, Jesus is alive, he is present, he died for you. If you are not serious, know that the devil has already been judged to hell. You will undoubtedly face death, however remember you will suffer, you will suffer. But if you follow Jesus, there will be no hunger, no diseases. It is an everlasting joy, there is no death. Make a choice. If you are thrown into hell, you will be crying day and night. Your finger keeps burning. Your tongue keeps burning. If you are a liar, your tongue keeps burning. If you are beating people, your finger too, if you loved sensuality, your genital parts keep burning. Is that what you want? Is that what you want?"
>
> *Mwita Akiri*: What would they say? Would they answer or keep quiet?
>
> *Lazaro Ndajilo*: [I asked] who wants to become an inquirer? "Me, and that one, and that one," [they responded].[55]

The contrast between Ndajilo's use of the *gode* imagery, and his teaching that focused on life after death, is striking. Yet this was the style and content

---

52. Lazaro Ndajilo, oral interviews, 14 and 16 June 1997.

53. Lazaro Ndajilo, oral interviews, 14 and 16 June 1997. *Gode* refers to a traditional wooden hoe that was used by Wagogo several years ago. The wooden hoe had sharp ends – sharp enough to dig the soil – but didn't last as long as the metal *gode* that replaced it.

54. Ndajilo, oral interviews.

55. Ndajilo, oral interviews.

of preaching, whether by CMS missionaries (as was hinted earlier)[56] or the indigenous teachers.

5.5 Missionary Focus on Children
5.5.1 Reasons for the Focus
As was noted in chapter 3, more than two decades of mission work (1876–1900) gave only poor results. Some of the reasons for poor results were noted, one of which was the underestimation of the resilience of the traditional religious and social life of the Wagogo and Wakaguru. This resilience continued in the twentieth century. For CMS missionaries, prejudices against mission Christianity and long-standing customs and superstitions among adults in Ugogo and Ukaguru were some of the reasons a shift in strategy needed to be made. At Mpwapwa, Henry Cole once complained about the inconsistent nature of the lives of Christians, and how this blocked the chances of the outsiders considering joining the church: "The Wagogo seem to cling as tenaciously as ever to their heathenism. They find strong argument for remaining as they are from the inconsistent lives of the Christians. The few who have kept straight are compromised by their fellow Christians who have gone wrong, and so the heathen look upon them all as a lot of liars and hypocrites."[57] Cole had lived at Mpwapwa since 1879, and his failure to make any progress there may have led him to reach such a conclusion in 1900 about the Wagogo and their customs. Bishop Peel's verdict on Mpwapwa after his 1902/1903 tour was blunt too: "Christians as a whole neither seem to care for the inward comforts of the Gospel, nor the external offered them in the ways of services and meetings."[58] Thomas Westgate expressed similar disappointment soon after arriving in the mission in 1902: "I set myself to the difficult task of initiating the ignorami (these *wapungufu* [Kiswahili; "the void" or "less fulfilled"], the *wajinga* [Kiswahili; "ignorant"], i.e. the Wagogo illiterate)."[59]

---

56. See chapter 3.
57. Henry Cole to Baylis, 12/9/1900, G3 A8/0/1900/41, BUL.
58. W. G. Peel, Usagara and Ugogo Revisited 1902-1903, G3 A8/O/1903/38, BUL; *CMI* 29 (March 1904): 192.
59. "Usagara-Chigogo Notes II," typescript, December 1903, G3 A8/O/1904/28, BUL. Emphasis added.

CMS missionaries attributed this to the negative attitude of the chiefs towards the CMS missionaries. Peel added, "We English are not thought of by the chiefs here who have been well instructed by [German] soldiers that we are nobodies."[60] Probably, as pointed out earlier,[61] poor missionary methods and religious conservatism at Mpwapwa were the major reasons for lack of interest in the teaching offered by the mission. But the decision to dishonour Mpwapwa as the headquarters of the mission was contemplated in December 1902,[62] supported by Peel himself,[63] and carried out in December 1903. Kongwa (separated from Mpwapwa and Chamuhawi only by Kiboriani hills) was started in 1904 as the new headquarters of the mission. Christians at Mpwapwa were distributed to Kiboriani, Kongwa, and Buigiri, and from August 1906, Mpwapwa no longer functioned as a station but as an out-station.[64]

At Mpwapwa, CMS missionaries blamed the lack of response on the presence of the fort and German soldiers. Elsewhere in the mission, complaints about the indifference of the Wagogo to mission Christianity were numerous too. At Mvumi, Rose Briggs, who itinerated with her husband for five weeks in distant places within the Mvumi district in 1902, observed that local people were still "so *thoroughly content* with their own customs and heathenism."[65] It is true to say, though, that as far as Mvumi was concerned, not much had been done in evangelistic work through school or direct preaching. After all, the station was only started in 1900, and by 1902, there were only two indigenous agents at work in the district. But at Buigiri in 1910 – nine years after Buigiri was started as a station – Thomas Westgate, who moved there in 1908, commented on the slow progress of work among the adult Wagogo there:

> They are for the most part very capricious and so far as my knowledge goes Chigogo caprice is as caprice as any. In our Inquirers' class we have some old veterans . . . who constantly remind me of the picture of St George on the tavern sign, always

---

60. Peel to Baylis, 29/12/1902. G3 A8/O/1903/10, BUL.
61. See chapter 3.
62. Minutes, EC, 12-13/12/1902, G3 A8/0/1903/11, BUL.
63. Peel to Baylis, 29 December 1902, G3 A8/0/1903/10, BUL.
64. Rees to Baylis, 3 August 1906, G3 A8/0/1906/54; RUUM, 1906, G3 A8/O/1907/23, BUL.
65. Rose Briggs to Baylis, 10/3/1902, G3 A8/0/1902/20, BUL. Emphasis added.

on the horseback but never riding. They listen to everything in connection with the Gospel, hear everything, criticize everything, analyze everything, believe nothing. The absurdities and moral corruptions of their heathen estate often appear to make them ashamed yet they cling to them for the sake of old association, while the Gospel appeals to them only as cold and abstract theory.[66]

Indeed some Wagogo of Buigiri regarded Christianity as "nonsense brought by aliens."[67] In realizing the indifference of the local people towards mission Christianity, the CMS mission admitted that the task of uprooting such prejudices was to be "a work of time, needing patience, perseverance, as well as constant exhibition by example and precept, of the superiority of Christianity over heathenism."[68]

This demonstrates that far from dying down, the social and religious practices that were prevalent when CMS missionaries first settled in Ugogo and Ukaguru in the nineteenth century (some of which were analysed in chapter 2) continued to be "alive and kicking" well into the twentieth century. So much that informants like Lazaro Ndajilo, who was born in 1900, had no hesitation in making reference to the strength of the Gogo customs at the time. Ndajilo cited the initiation rite of circumcision (which will be considered further below) which he went through:

> I am a man of old age. I was circumcised when all the Gogo traditional life was still in place. I was circumcised without being injected with a needle (with anaesthesia). . . . I was nursed in the bush. Without staying at the *chikumbi* [Kigogo; "initiation camp"] it was a taboo to return home. *Chibalu* [Kigogo; "the spot where the actual circumcision is performed"] where my skin was

---

66. Westgate to CMS, annual letter, 30/11/1910, G3 A8/0/1910/91, BUL; cf. *CMR* 63 (March 1912): 160.

67. Cleopa Mwaka, oral interview, 4/7/1997.

68. Rees, "History of CMS," MS, G3 A8/0/1902/19; cf. Westgate's complaint in 1909 at Buigiri, "To destroy an image or hurl it into the stream is easy, but to extirpate a faith, eradicate time-honoured customs, and establish the true in the place of the false, is not easy." See Westgate to CMS, annual letter,21/12/1909, G3 A8/0/1910/27, BUL.

cut off was in the bush. Everything in traditional Ugogo life was still in place.... A sacrifice was made for me.[69]

One therefore suggests that perhaps the expectation of the early converts in Ugogo and Ukaguru was that becoming a mission adherent entitled one to both the visible, material benefits, as well as the "hidden" spiritual ones, without making a break, or losing touch altogether, with one's pre-Christian heritage. The rest of this chapter attempts to explain the reasons that attracted the majority of the Wagogo and Wakaguru children and adults to mission Christianity and evaluate the nature of the teaching that was given to those who became mission converts. But first, the broader question of African conversion should be addressed.

5.5.2 African Conversion and Motives of Child Converts

In 1909, Westgate wrote,

> The older Wagogo are notoriously conservative and from them we expect but little, but our mission is gradually increasing its grip on the younger generation, and with them rests the future hope and destiny of the tribe. To them we must give our undivided attention, and to my mind there is no doubt but that the concentration of effort will abundantly pay.[70]

The hope for an "easy" conversion of the children was based on the notion that they had not learned as much of the traditional social and religious practices as their parents.[71] The multiplicity of the out-schools as learning centres reflected this new strategy. But the conversion of the children cannot only be explained by the so-called "innocence" they were believed to have. The broader issue here is the need to explain the reasons for African conversion in general – in this case, of the Wagogo and Wakaguru. It cannot be denied that there were converts who responded to the Bible message and Christian teaching offered to them. Indeed, further afield in West Africa, C. C. Okorocha has argued that in the context of Igboland, conversion to Christianity was

---

69. Lazaro Ndajilo, oral interviews, 14 and 16 June 1997.

70. Westgate to CMS, annual letter, 21/12/1909, G3 A8/0/1910/27; cf. Rose Briggs to Baylis, 10/3/1902, G3 A8/0/1902/20, BUL.

71. Rees, "History of CMS," MS, G3 A8/0/1902/19; TBR Westgate to CMS, 30/11/1910, G3 A8/0/1910/91, BUL.

an immensely religious phenomenon. So much so, that the socioeconomic benefits that Christianity offered, to which the Igbo were attracted, should be viewed as constituting that religious phenomenon, and not merely as secular and ulterior reasons for conversion.[72] What happened was a reordering of the Igbo traditional cosmology to cope with Christianity – and, one might add, colonialism and commercialisation.[73] This argument, of the failure of African cosmology, especially the microcosm, is not dissimilar from that advanced by Robin Horton.[74]

Robin Horton, in his article "African Conversion," divides African cosmology into two categories: the microcosm and macrocosm. The former is the domain of the lesser spirits who are involved in the daily events of human concern and are therefore the guardians of morality. The supreme being has direct responsibility for the latter and is less involved in matters of daily concern. Horton continues that when

> people find themselves outside the microcosms, and even if those left inside see the boundaries weakening if not actually dissolving, they can only interpret these changes by assuming the lesser spirits (underpinners of the microcosms) are in retreat, and that the supreme being (underpinner of the macrocosm) is taking over direct control of the everyday world. Hence they come to regard the lesser spirits as irrelevant or downright evil.[75]

To this Horton adds that those who live in rural areas but are engaged in some modern occupation which is integrated with the economy of the macrocosm are associated less with the lesser spirits – just as is the case with someone who goes outside the microcosm and engages in a "modern" (urban) environment. Such a person will be associated more with the supreme being. Horton concludes that, in Africa, the so-called world religions (Christianity and Islam) have been accepted only where "they happen to coincide with responses of the traditional cosmology to the other, non-missionary, factors

---

72. Okorocha, *Meaning of Religious Conversion*, 12, 13, 239; cf. Walls, *Missionary Movement*, 89–93.
73. Walls, 90.
74. Horton, "African Conversion," 101, 102.
75. Horton, 101, 102.

of modern situation."⁷⁶ For that reason, Christianity and Islam only play the role of catalysts, stimulating and accelerating changes which are often already underway in African societies. But whereas Islam has been content to play that role alone, Christianity hasn't, and that is why it insists rigidly that converts should accept its official doctrines.⁷⁷

As has been acknowledged, this theory, which in a way resembles Okorocha's, goes a long way in explaining African conversion. It stresses the genuineness of African conversion, acknowledges the religious heritage of African peoples, and shows that African people have become part of the global Christian movement. However, a few remarks should be made.

First, in the view of this writer, this explanation of African conversion does not take into account the obvious fact that in many missions, certainly in the CMS mission in Ugogo and Ukaguru, it was not the adults, but the children – the "innocent" group – who were the prime target of mission Christianity through the mission school. Whether CMS missionaries were right or wrong in their estimation of the "innocence" of the children – and in fact they were only partially right – there has to be an explanation as to why children were attracted to the school. It is difficult, in the case of the Wagogo and Wakaguru, to exclude ulterior motives. For the majority, it may be right to suggest that conversion might have taken place on the way rather than at the start of the Christian journey. Second, in addition to the point made, one has to grapple with the issue of the resilience of the traditional cosmology against mission Christianity. The suggestion that those who managed it (be it the lesser beings or other religious forces) became discredited when Christianity arrived fails to answer the question *Why after so many years of Christian teaching, both during the era of missions and in the present time, is the traditional worldview still alive and kicking?*

Certainly, several reasons may account for this. But maybe one simple but significant answer lies in the category of the traditional worldview's adherents. Those served by traditional religious and social practices are found not just among traditionalists (non-converts to Christianity), or rural, non-technical people where, apparently, the lesser spirits are still at work, but also,

---

76. Horton, 103, 104.
77. Horton, 105.

significantly, among educated and economically better-off urban dwellers, as well as those who identify themselves as Christian adherents. Therefore, Paul Jenkins rightly argues:

> Replacement of traditional structures and traditional ways of organizing communal life would have been theoretically possible only if missionary forms of organization could have totally replaced traditional ones, which has happened only in exceptional situations in Africa and for relatively short periods. Instead, the characteristic situation is one where traditional structures have been consciously preserved and adapted, a process in which the Christian community itself has often played an important part.[78]

Jenkins makes his observation about the survival of traditional African heritage in relation to the Christian community in West Africa, especially in places where the Basel mission operated – for example, Akropong, Ghana – but his observations are applicable elsewhere.[79] The preservation he refers to occurs particularly because of the desire among converts to maintain a dual identity – to be both African and "Christian."

In this context, one cannot simply spiritualize the new ideas that Christianity brought – for example, literacy – as Okorocha seems to suggest, at least because, as will be shown below, such new ideas and benefits were needed by African people for practical mundane reasons, not for controlling the traditional religious cosmology. Indeed, a CMS report pointed out how, in the 1910s, people in Ugogo and Ukaguru had shown "a widespread desire to read, and there is also a wish for the positions of influence which knowledge opens before Africans. The result is that the people are "clamouring for teachers on all sides."[80] It is important that the motives for child converts be examined more closely to illustrate this point.

Perhaps the "guilelessness" and presumed innocence of the African children meant that simple tactics, if used appropriately, were just enough to draw them into mission Christianity. The first step was to arouse their curiosity about life at the mission station and the elementary school located there. In

---

78. Jenkins, "Roots of African Church History," 68.
79. Jenkins, 67.
80. *PCMS*, 1913, 53; cf. Knox, *Signal on the Mountain*, 168.

a joint interview to which both contributed, Philemon Chidosa and his wife Yudith Chidosa of Mvumi recall what they witnessed during their childhood:

> For younger children, you know the lady missionaries used to put small pins (which were golden in colour) on the windows of their house.... One of those women used to throw those pins outside. As children we liked to go and collect those things. That was the way we gathered there.... When they started separating the church from school, the missionary who was leading it as head teacher had record disks that played songs. Then when the record disks were being played, children enjoyed dancing and jumping. On the educational side, that was how people were attracted.... On the church side, Mr Briggs's own wife used to cook scones, and then put jam and margarine on them [both Philemon and Yudith laughing]. She then cut them into small pieces and distributed them to us when we went there. Children then persuaded their fellows by saying, "Let's go and receive a gift." Children enjoyed that very much.[81]

Dan Mbogoni of Mvumi has a similar recollection to the Chidosas'. He adds empty tins or cans, including empty Kiwi shoe polish containers, to the list of gifts given to the children.[82] Showing off an empty can to other children who were still tending cattle in the bush generated considerable interest and attracted more children to the mission school.[83] Those testimonies are from Ugogo. In Ukaguru, Yusufu Masingisa of Mamboya testifies that he and other Kaguru children had similar experiences:

> The children who went to [day] school came back home with new clothes.... This made each child say, "I must get clothes of that sort. Everybody else is having one."... He who came home with clothes told his/her fellows, "Look I have got a garment." In that way more pupils became available.... People were given

---

81. Philemon Chidosa, oral interviews, 12 and 13 June 1997.
82. Dan Mbogoni, oral interview, 11 June 1997.
83. Mbogoni, oral interview; Philemon Chidosa, oral interviews, 12 and 13 June 1997; Yudith Chidosa, oral interview, 12 June 1997.

gifts. Even I myself was given a book (a Gospel) as a gift when I was eight.[84]

At Berega, Joshua Mkwama, one of the early evangelists there, told Isaka Mlahagwa the same story about clothes.[85] As the testimony of these Kaguru Christians indicate, visible gifts, games, and parties were an important incentive to children.

Another subjective motive that attracted children to the mission school was the desire to be able to read and write. Dan Mbogoni recalls how grateful he was that, despite the objection of his uncles who thought that mission school would spoil him and make him less efficient in carrying out traditional family responsibilities, his mother allowed him to go to school. He regarded his joining of the mission school at Mvumi as the fulfilment of a dream:

> I myself had wanted to go to school for some time. When we wandered in the mission compound, I used to pick up pieces of scattered papers thrown by the missionaries, but I could not read the content. So I became curious to know what was written. My younger brother who went to school before me used to read the papers for me. I wanted to read for myself too.[86]

It was pointed out earlier that the purpose of mission education was to "civilize" and convert the Wagogo and Wakaguru. Therefore, as soon as the children acquired the reading skills, they were given Scriptures to read.[87] The pursuit of education and desire to become a "mission child" went hand in hand. It was a mutual enterprise for both the African children and CMS missionaries even though, of course, the terms of mutuality were never negotiated. Indeed, a UMCA missionary on the coastal belt once complained about lack of worthy motive on the part of boys who joined Magila central (boarding) school in the Tanga region on the northeast coast of Tanzania: "In most instances a heathen child comes because he has a friend here and he thinks it would be nice to live at 'Kizungu' [implying living at the white

---

84. Yusufu Masingisa, oral interviews, 16 and 17 September 1997.
85. Isaka Mlahagwa, oral interview, 14 September 1997.
86. Dan Mbogoni, oral interview, 11 June 1997.
87. RUUM, 1906, G3 A8/0/1907/23; RUUM, 1907, G3 A8/0/1908/24; Bertha Briggs to Baylis, 3/3/1909, G3 A8/0/1909/28; "Usagara-Chigogo Notes I," typescript, September 1903, G3 A8/0/1903/40, BUL.

man's compound]. There is no *worthy motive* at all as a general rule. There is absolutely nothing to keep them except their own pleasures."[88] Obviously, the UMCA missionary expected more from his pupils in terms of the ethos of the school, but since the terms were not negotiated at the beginning, the children didn't fully understand them. It was easier for the UMCA missionary, as well those of the CMS mission, to be disappointed. This shows that African children knew what they wanted from the mission, even though it might appear that the things that attracted them were simple – pins, music from record disks, scones, and the desire to be able to read and write. It appears they had an upper hand in controlling their process of conversion, otherwise foreign missionaries would have had little to complain about.

It was stated in chapter 4 that many chiefs and their subordinates welcomed mission schools in their chiefdoms and undertook to build out-schools themselves. Their purpose was to ensure that their subjects – particularly children – got the opportunity to become literate so that they could increase their chances of getting government jobs. One of the methods used by indigenous teachers to encourage parents to bring children to literacy classes was to point them to the benefits of being served by "one of their own" rather than by "aliens" from other ethnic groups. Ndajilo did just that:

> I said this, "Outsiders are the ones who are collecting tax. Rural agricultural officers who are all outsiders have come to teach your children here at Chikandu. Your own clan, so that they may learn and eventually take over the jobs and become agricultural officers, tax clerks, court clerks, just here, in your midst. You are still asleep. I have come. Bring your own children, bring children of your relatives. I want one hundred children. One will be stupid. The other will be clever. You must serve yourselves."[89]

Politicization of literacy was a strategy that struck its target well among the Wagogo at Mpalanga and Mwitikila near Mvumi. There were indeed "aliens" serving in Ugogo. In the German colonial era, many subordinate

---

88. Woodward to Travers, 5/7/1897, "Letters from Africa," Box E.2, RHL. Emphasis in original.

89. Lazaro Ndajilo, oral interviews, 14 and 16 June 1997.

employees – namely, *maakida*[90] and *majumbe*[91] – were coastal Muslims. Though the British colonial government inherited and retained, temporarily, the "*akida* system"[92] from the German colonial administration, it curtailed their privileges and took away their powers of punishment. Where vacancies occurred, the wishes of the local people were considered when choosing a successor. Where possible, a local man was selected "in preference to an alien."[93] In their review of the mission's work for the year 1907, John Briggs and Ernest Doulton pointed to the "great" influence of the tax collectors who were baptized and educated in the mission and had been working in the districts.[94]

The incentives, ranging from simple gifts to clothes and the possibility of employment in the local area, caused many children and young people to be attracted to the mission school. Oral testimonies and archival sources such as those quoted above – among many others[95] – show that, in the first place, African children had very simple and subjective reasons for acquiring the knowledge that the mission offered.

5.6 Competition with Roman Catholic Missions

It is perhaps appropriate that at this point another factor – namely, the competition of the CMS mission with two Roman Catholic missions – be considered. The purpose is to show that despite the children's own desire to acquire reading and writing skills, the CMS mission was also desperate not to lose those it had attracted and, at the same time, continue to attract new ones.

---

90. "Maakida" is the plural of "Akida." Broadly speaking, an Akida was a junior administrative official (above a "Jumbe") during the German colonial rule in Tanganyika (later Tanzania) especially in the coastal areas but also in the interior as well. In most cases they were responsibe for tax collection. The majority of them were Muslims.

91. "Majumbe" (singular "Jumbe") were junior officials (headmen) below Maakida. As Maakida, the majority of them were Muslims during the German colonial rule.

92. The Akida system of governance was a local system of governance under the watch of German colonial officials in Tanganyika (later Tanzania).

93. *Report on Tanganyika Territory*, 37, NLS.

94. RUUM, 1907, G3 A8/0/1908/24, BUL.

95. For example, Nehemia Uguzi, oral interviews, 18 and 19 June 1997; Lazaro Ndajilo, oral interviews, 14 and 16 June 1997; Yusufu Masingisa, oral interviews, 16 and 17 September 1997.

The impetus given to the mission's educational work by the policies of the German colonial administration in 1910 was mentioned in chapter 4.[96] In addition to this impetus, the rise of the number of scholars (many of whom must have been children) in the CMS mission from 1911 onwards (see table 5.1 below) was also caused by competition with two Roman Catholic missions.[97] These were the Order of the Benedictines of St Ottilien and the Holy Ghost Fathers (HGF) – the former in Ugogo and the latter in Ukaguru. The HGF had been working at Bagamoyo on the east coast since 1868, and further inland at Mhonda near Morogoro town (1877), Mandera (1880), and Morogoro town itself (1882).[98] Until the end of the first decade of the twentieth century, the Benedictines worked in the southern parts of Tanzania and near Dar es Salaam.[99]

Gregory Maddox suggests, in his article "The Church and Cigogo: Father Stephen Mlundi and Christianity in Central Tanzania," that the first Benedictine mission station was established at Bihawana in Ugogo by Fr Seiler in 1909. But he also rightly points out, as might be expected, that hostility and fierce competition with the CMS mission only began after the Roman Catholic mission had become well established.[100] This must be around 1911 because it was at this time that CMS missionaries began to express their concern about the presence of the Roman Catholic mission. In one of his reports in 1911, Bishop Peel wrote:

> The floating of the Roman Catholics into our districts is actually happening *now*, and I have had to deal with the Benedictines on the one hand, and with a French colony of [HGF] priests on the other; for the Benedictines who have now made Ugogo their objective asked us a few months ago to make an agreement with

---

96. *PCMS*, 1911, 57; *PCMS*, 1912, 49.

97. Reports for each preceding year were given in the following year. Therefore, for 1910 statistics, see *PCMS*, 1911, 59; for 1911, see *PCMS*, 1912, 52; for 1912, see *PCMS*, 1913, 56; and for 1913, see *PCMS*, 1914, 62.

98. Bennett, *Studies*, 56, 59, 64–65; Nolan, "History of the Catechist," 2; Anderson, *Church in East Africa*, 10.

99. The Benedictines founded monasteries at Lukuledi in 1895 (then moved to Ndanda), at Peramiho in 1898, and at Madibira in Southern Highlands in 1894. See Oliver, *Missionary Factor*, 163–164.

100. Maddox, "Church and Cigogo," 155.

them which we found was that a line should be drawn from the south to the northeast of the province, passing within a comparatively short distance of Mvumi mission station, CMS, and securing to them nearly two-thirds of the whole territory known as Ugogo. We have proposed other boundaries, but "agreement" we have come to, because of the few Europeans at our disposal. In Ukaguru, similarly, an encroachment was desired by the French Roman Catholics which would have seriously crippled our Berega district enterprises. This has been opposed by us.[101]

CMS missionaries in Ugogo and Ukaguru disliked the presence of the RC missions. Their letters and reports to CMS in London, which in turn reported to its supporters, reveal this. In such reports, the RC missions were called "another foe to Protestant Missions besides Islam."[102] Extracts from Thomas Westgate's letter about the Benedictine mission (printed in a CMS annual report) further elaborates this: "[They are] marshalling and organizing all the forces of knavery, an art in which they thoroughly accomplished, they seem to have deliberately set themselves the task of checkmating and confusing our every effort. They resort to methods utterly inconsistent with their profession."[103] In the same year, J. C. Green reported that the Benedictines in Kongwa district were bribing many chiefs to allow them to open little preaching places and locate African agents, and that some chiefs responded positively but others refused to accept the inducements offered. In Mamboya district, Emily Spriggs complained about that the HGF taking some of the preaching places belonging to the CMS mission, and planting "small crosses on the doors to show they have done so."[104]

---

101. *CMR* 63 (March 1912): 162. Emphasis in the original. Negotiations were actually being conducted between Bishop Peel and the bishops in charge of the two Catholic missions. See *PCMS*, 1912, 50.

102. *PCMS*, 1913, 53.

103. *PCMS*, 1913, 53.

104. *PCMS*, 1913, 53.

Table 5.1: Christians, Catechumens and Scholars 1911–1933[105]

1	2	3	4	5	6	
Year	Christians	Catechumens	Scholars	Year	Christians	Catechumens	Scholars
				1924	3461	3557	15608
1911	924	129	7175	1925	3421	3660	15988
1912	1126	2324	17130	1926	3963	3208	11162
1913	1295	2976	17202	1927	4225	2746	9356
1914–1918	1295*	2976*	17202*	1928	4278	2898	10769
1919	1789	1729	20417	1929	4100	2753	9600
1920	2460	2424	18746	1930	4743	3805	9627
1921	2648	2860	16261	1931	5161	3406	10904
1922	2362	3257	13922	1932	5472	3236	9175
1923	2944	3937	15606	1933	6417	4508	8995

*Figures for 1913. No statistics were compiled during the First World War.

The battle for converts, particularly children, to become scholars was fought vigorously, and the indigenous teachers on both sides were at the forefront of it. The following extended interview excerpt indicates this:

> *Lazaro Ndajilo*: [The] Roman Church was in Bihawana, at a place called Kinyambwa.
>
> *Mwita Akiri*: Did you ever hear that a Roman mission was in rivalry with the Mvumi [CMS] mission?

---

105. Based on CMS statistical tables in *PCMS* 1912–1922 and the Annual Report of the Committee of CMS (ARCCMS) 1923–1934.

Lazaro Ndajilo: ... Oh yes. We were fighting for people. When I went to Mpalanga, the Romans were there too. ... Some liked my place, others the other place. Therefore we worked hard to teach people to listen and understand, and we used a *method*, ... so that people might like the teaching. My counterpart in the Roman Catholic Mission used a Roman *method*, and I too used my Anglican mission method. ...

Mwita Akiri: What kind of method? What exactly did you do, what tactics did you use to draw people to your denomination?

Lazaro Ndajilo: The first method I used was to sing Kigogo songs ... to the children and play games with them. ... Another method [was this]: ... I used to go to Abdallah's shop. From there, I bought beads, some papers with pictures. I played games with the children, then spoke only a few words so that they might not get tired. Then, if a child performed well, I rewarded him/her. ...

Mwita Akiri: ... What about your [Roman Catholic] colleague?

Lazaro Ndajilo: ... My colleague would become angry, *akigwaba*. ...

Mwita Akiri: What does *kugwaba* mean?

Lazaro Ndajilo: "To fail." ... He would be angry. And the more he became angry, *ndio mimi nalala yombwe.*

Mwita Akiri: What does *kulala yombwe* mean?

Lazaro Ndajilo: Literally, it means "to lean forward," that is, I increased the effort to persuade the adherents of his denomination to come to mine.[106]

On the Roman Catholic side, the conduct of one Gasi, a Roman Catholic teacher at Lindi (one of Buigiri's out-stations), in the presence of both Danieli Mbogo and Thomas Westgate is particularly interesting. Danieli Mbogo wrote:

---

106. Lazaro Ndajilo, oral interviews, 14 and 16 June 1997.

Lo! [Gasi] alikuwa mkali kwa sisi akisema tunachukua inchi yake, karibu kutaka kupigana. Bwana Westgate akamjibu sisi tulifika inchi hii kabla hujazaliwa. Maana yake Kanisa la C.M.S lilianza kufika Ugogo kabla R.C hajafika. Nilipoona maneno makali yanazidi, nikamsihi Dr Westgate, Bwana tuondoke tumwache, akanisikia tukaondoka.

Translation:

Lo! [Gasi] became furious, and claimed we wanted to snatch his territory. He nearly started a fight. Mr Westgate replied, "We came to this land before you were born." That is to say, the CMS church started its work in Ugogo before the RC did. When I noticed harsh exchanges getting out of control, I pleaded with Mr Westgate, "Sir, let us leave him alone and go." He listened to my word, so we left.[107]

The situation was similar in Ukaguru. There, it was reported that the Roman Catholics resorted to "intimidation and even compulsion" of indigenous CMS staff to work for them.[108]

Both in Ugogo and Ukaguru, CMS missionaries were well aware of the tactics used by the indigenous teachers, and probably sanctioned them, though Lazaro Ndajilo defends this: "I wasn't binding anybody with a rope, I was merely persuading people tactically."[109] Lazaro served as a teacher from the late 1920s – a time when British colonial administration had long been established. The diverse nationalities of CMS missionaries of different missions working in close geographical areas also became a contributing factor to rivalry between missions.[110] As was pointed out earlier,[111] despite having

---

107. Danieli Mbogo, personal diary. Translation by this writer. Mbogo's personal diary accessed at the Archives of the Diocese of Central Tanganyika (at Mackay House), Dodoma, Tanzania.

108. *CMR* 63 (March 1912): 160.

109. Lazaro Ndajilo, oral interviews, 14 and 16 June 1997.

110. For example, the nationality of 306 educational missionaries in Tanzania in 1938 was as follows: eighty-four British, ninety-four German, forty-four Dutch, twenty-seven Italian, twenty-two Swiss, nineteen American, and sixteen French. See Thompson, "Historical Survey," 48.

111. See "Notes on Names and Terminology," xvi.

recruits from various countries outside Britain, the CMS mission was essentially British in origin. For some Ugogo teachers, this was both an evangelistic tool and source of pride. They persuaded potential scholars and converts (including adults) that it was better to be members of a mission that "had the flag":

> *Mwita Akiri*: In your opinion, who had more people, you or them [that is, the Benedictine Mission]?
>
> *Lazaro Ndajilo*: I had more people because the rulers were British, the mission Europeans were British. It was therefore easy to answer people who asked me about government actions. But the Roman Catholic had no flag.
>
> *Mwita Akiri*: Which country did they come from?
>
> *Lazaro Ndajilo*: They came from France to Chikoa and were at Mpalanga.[112]

Like many other informants, Ndajilo gave insights into the dynamics of mission work, though he sometimes got some details mixed up – but given that Lazaro was ninety-seven years of age in 1997, this should be regarded as a small matter. The Benedictine missionaries who operated in Ugogo came mainly from Germany. Probably Ndajilo had heard about the HGF French missionaries who made an incursion into Ukaguru. His claim that the CMS mission had more scholars than the Benedictine mission could only be verified accurately if figures from the RC side were available for comparison. But judging by the overall rise in the number of catechumens and scholars in the CMS mission from 1911 onwards, his statement may be regarded as trustworthy.

But returning to the effect of the competition, it has to be observed that the number of scholars rose also because out-schools were started very close to each other – at times separated only by a marked boundary. The British colonial government policy to restrict missions to specific spheres of operation in order to lessen or prevent the establishment of out-schools close to each other was largely unsuccessful and was abandoned in 1923. In its place, the colonial government introduced two policies in 1926. The first was that

---

112. Lazaro Ndajilo, oral interviews, 14 and 16 June 1997.

missions should not operate less than seven miles apart; and second, missions were forbidden to occupy land without the approval of the local people under the chief.[113] But these policies prevented neither the phenomenal growth of the out-schools nor the rivalry between missions.

One reason for the failure of the policy was the fact that, after all, out-schools were built not on the so called "mission land" but on communal land and, much more, at the initiative of the chief and his subjects.[114] The involvement of chiefs and headmen in the rivalry between missions became a crucial factor in determining which mission opened a school at a place in the chiefdom. Indeed, some chiefs were bribed by missions to win their favour.[115]

In concluding the account of the competition between the Roman Catholic missions and the CMS mission, it is worth making one further observation. The arrival of the Benedictines in Ugogo in 1911, and the pressure of the Holy Ghost Fathers upon CMS work in parts of Ukaguru (especially Berega) about the same time,[116] only helped to accelerate a development that was already underway. More children had been coming to CMS schools before, and these included the sons of the chiefs who joined the out-schools to comply with the order issued by the German colonial authorities. Consequently, there was going to be more children than adults. However, the effect of the arrival of the two Roman Catholic missions on the school and evangelistic work of the CMS mission, especially in Ugogo, can be seen in the sharp rise in the number of scholars.

Though the overall figures have been given in table 5.1 (see above), an indication of the figures for some stations may make this clearer. In 1910, Kongwa, Mvumi, and Buigiri had 1,201, 723, and 465 scholars, respectively.[117] In 1911, the figures at these stations (respectively) jumped to 1,570, 1,728, and 1,386.[118] They went even higher in 1912, as follows: Kongwa, 4,208; Mvumi, 5,218; and Buigiri, 2,646.[119] In 1913, a significant drop of numbers reduced

---

113. Thompson, "Historical Survey," 47.
114. See chapter 3 of this study; Thompson, "Historical Survey," 47.
115. Thompson, 47.
116. *CMR* 63 (March 1912): 162.
117. *PCMS*, 1911, 59.
118. *PCMS*, 1912, 52.
119. *PCMS*, 1913, 56.

figures to 4,161 at Mvumi, and slightly to 4,096 at Kongwa. But gains at Buigiri (2,868) kept the overall figures high.[120]

5.7 African Conversion and Motives of Adult Converts

It was observed above that the CMS mission readjusted its missionary strategy to focus on children because of the poor results it had so far obtained in converting the Wagogo and Wakaguru adults due to their indifference to mission Christianity. But that is far from suggesting that mission work among the Kaguru and Gogo adults was an outright failure. Within the context of the argument put forward in relation to African conversion (of the need to acknowledge the significance of ulterior motives in that process), after considering the motives of child converts, attention may now be given to adult converts.

To start with, it has to be stated that some Wagogo and Wakaguru were drawn into mission Christianity simply through the love, charm, and joy of the CMS missionaries, though of course not all CMS missionaries demonstrated that.[121] Nehemia Uguzi recalls: "Of course, some were arrogant because human beings love themselves. But truly they showed how to love. For example, Miss Gelding, or Mr Doulton himself. He was mingling with people and identifying with them. Then people began to say, 'Oh, could a European do this?'"[122] It has to be recalled that identification with the indigenous people was one of the reasons that accounted for Henry Cole's success at Chamuhawi. Philemon Chidosa shares the same view as Nehemia Uguzi's:

---

120. *PCMS*, 1914, 62.

121. The moral life of some CMS missionaries – for example, Joseph Last and Charles Stokes – fell short of what might be regarded as "exemplary" Christian life. Both lost their wives while in central Tanzania in the late nineteenth century, after which they got involved in sexual immorality with some Tanzanian indigenous women. This led to their expulsion from the CMS mission. Last returned to Britain in 1886 after scandals at Mamboya mission station. Stokes got married to Limi – a non-Christian Nyamwezi woman who was the cousin of chief Mtinganya of Usongo near Uyui in Tabora, mid-western Tanzania. He was later deserted by Limi, and since he had by then been expelled already from CMS, he went broke and got involved in illegal ivory trade between western Tanzania and what is now the Democratic Republic of Congo (formerly Zaire). He was executed by the Belgians on 15 January 1895. See extract of letters by [John] Roscoe to Wigram, 1 June 1885, and Baxter to Lang, 29 January 1886, CMS archives, both quoted in Beidelman, "Contradiction," 91–92; Knox, *Signal on the Mountain*, 74, 79–80.

122. Nehemia Uguzi, oral interviews, 18 and 19 June 1997.

"When this man started to explain the gospel of Jesus Christ as a place of love, peace and so on, his character impressed them. So they followed him. They saw the difference between a German and a British."[123]

5.7.1 Protection from Cruelty

CMS missionaries preceded the German colonial government officials in central Tanzania. It is generally true that the popularity of any government may suffer because of policies it introduces. This may have nothing to do with the personal conduct of its officials towards the public. But Chidosa's observation about the difference between German colonial officials and the CMS missionaries points to something more than that. German officials and their African subordinates (including the Sudanese soldiers) had a reputation for cruelty.[124] At times, the Sudanese soldiers arrested indigenous teachers or converts belonging to the CMS mission without cause.[125] Protection against cruelty was therefore one of the major factors that drove some adults to associate themselves from mission Christianity. This requires explanation.

During the German colonial occupation, the chiefs and the headmen in the interior often acted as "recruitment agents" for the German colonial government for casual labour on the plantations near home and contract work on plantations on the coast. As an incentive, the chiefs were paid one rupee for each person they recruited.[126] But the German colonial government also obtained illegal labour by imposing the hut tax of not less than five pounds sterling, which was to be paid by all over the age of sixteen.[127] Many could not afford it and had to work for the government as a payment for their

---

123. Philemon Chidosa, oral interviews, 12 and 13 June 1997.

124. Becker, "Material," 43. The article was first published by the author in German as "Materialem zur kenntnis des Islam in Deutsch-Ostafrika" (Materials for the study of Islam in German East Africa) in a German periodical *Der Islam* 2 (1911): 1-48, later reprinted with minor changes as *Islamstudien: Vom Werden und Wesen der islamischen Welt*, Quelle & Meyer, 1932, 63–115.

125. "Interview given to Revd D. J. Rees and Rev T.B.R. Westgate by Lieutenant Lademann at Mpwapwa on 26/1/1906," G3 A8/0/1906/28, BUL.

126. *Handbooks*, No. 114, 21, NLS.

127. Hut tax was first introduced in Tanzania in 1897. See "Tanganyika (German East Africa)" in *Handbooks* (prepared under the direction of the historical section of the Foreign Office), No. 113, London: HMSO, 1920, 23, NLS.

debt.[128] They were put under an escort to the palace (the chief's court)[129] and handed over to German and African soldiers. With this illegal labour went brutal floggings with a hippopotamus or rhinoceros whip. So much so, that German colonies in Africa were often referred to in Europe as the "Colonies of the Twenty-Five" or "Flogging Colonies," where twenty-five lashes were the usual way of corporal punishment or, worse still, a common method of violating human rights and dignity.[130]

Older informants interviewed in Ugogo and Ukaguru suggested that, among many things, escape from the harsh treatment of the local people by cruel German officials and their African subordinates – the *maaskari* (soldiers) and the *wanyapara*[131] – was one of the reasons why some adults joined literacy classes and became inquirers of mission Christianity.[132]

People, particularly the earliest converts, who lived with the mission settlements (which had clear boundaries)[133] stood a better chance of being exempted than those who lived outside. The issue of the isolation and insulation of such people from the local population is a subject that may not be covered in detail here.[134] Nevertheless, it is sufficient to mention that besides constant and intensified labour within the settlements, life in such places tended to be ordered and rigid.[135] Francis Nolan suggests, particularly in relation to Catholic mission settlements in Tanzania, that "there was a deliberate imitation of the monastic ideal of medieval Europe."[136] In 1900, the residents at Mpwapwa mission village numbered two hundred.[137] That must be a sizeable

---

128. "Treatment of Natives," *Handbooks*, No. 114, 20, NLS.

129. Dan Mbogoni, oral interview, 11 June 1997.

130. Rören, *Reichstag*, 3 December 1906, quoted in "Treatment of Natives," *Handbooks*, No. 114, 8, NLS.

131. This usage of *wanyapara* certainly means "foremen" rather than "supervisors" as it does in church contexts, as pointed out in section 5.8.5.

132. Lazaro Ndajilo, oral interviews, 14 and 16 June 1997; Yusufu Masingisa, oral interviews, 16 and 17 September 1997.

133. The boundaries of the Bagamoyo settlement, which belonged to the Holy Ghost Fathers, was at first not clearly marked. Sometimes this caused tension with the local Wazaramo over land occupation. Anderson, *Church in East Africa*, 12.

134. *CMIR* 4 (September 1879): 531; Cole, *History of the ChurchCMS*, 59. It has to be emphasized that this sort of protection also insulated the residents from realistic life outside.

135. See Ajayi, *Christian Missions in Nigeria*, 137.

136. Nolan, "History of the Catechist," 5.

137. *PCMS*, 1901, 122.

number – large enough to cultivate over forty to fifty acres of land that that CMS missionaries acquired at Chamuhawi.[138] In comparison, though, the number of residents at Mpwapwa mission settlement was smaller than, for example, that of the mission settlements that belonged to HGF at Bagamoyo (north of Dar es Salaam) which had more than three hundred "freed" slaves or that of the UMCA in Zanzibar city on the Indian ocean (off the northeast coast of Tanzania) which probably had more.[139]

Of course, not every convert or potential convert lived within the mission villages. But even converts or potential converts from outside the mission settlements feared cruelty at the hands of the German officials. The best way to get nearer to the exemption from government work was to become a scholar. CMS missionaries themselves – for example, David Rees – sought to impress this notion of distinction upon the German district officers who were in charge of *maaskari* and *wanyapara*. Rees argued that the mission had responded to the wishes of the imperial governor of "enlightening" the people through education, and the number of converts who were now "raised" in "morality and intelligence" was growing rapidly.[140] On the basis of what he perceived to be the outcome of the "civilizing" programme, he suggested that "Christians and mission adherents, owing to their intellectual and moral superiority may be generally recognized above the heathen and so deserving different treatment from them."[141]

Though Rees did not seek a complete exemption for mission adherents from offering duty to the government, he nonetheless argued that converts were entitled to different treatment in the hands of the government.[142] An agreement was reached with the local German district officer based at Mpwapwa that certain persons at each mission station be exempted from compulsory labour. CMS missionaries were given the powers to select such

---

138. *CMIR* 5 (December 1880): 736.

139. Bennett, *Studies*, 59; Anderson, *Church in East Africa*, 10. The UMCA started operating in Zanzibar in 1864 and acquired slave settlements at Kiungani in 1866 (later known as St Andrew's College) and Mbweni in 1871. See Wilson, *History of the Universities'*, 26.

140. "Interview given to Rev D. J. Rees and Rev T.B.R. Westgate by Lieutenant Lademann at Mpwapwa on 26 January 1906," G3 A8/0/1906/28, BUL.

141. Minutes, EC, 9/2/1906, G3 A8/0/1906/27, BUL.

142. "Interview given to Rev D. J. Rees and Rev T.B.R. Westgate by Lieutenant Lademann at Mpwapwa on 26 January 1906," G3 A8/0/1906/28, BUL.

people who would offer their labour freely for mission work rather than government work. Indeed, from January 1907, the government agreed that it would not compel a convert of the mission to work on Sundays.[143] All of this must have given the Wagogo and Wakaguru the impression that it was worth associating themselves with the CMS mission.

5.7.2 Employment Opportunities

It was mentioned in the previous chapter that one outcome of the German educational policy introduced in 1910 was the increase in government employment opportunities for literate Christians. In addition to this, employment opportunities within the mission was another reason that motivated adults to enrol as scholars.[144] Apart from the "spiritual" jobs, many people were employed to work as carpenters, masons, and labourers who built mission houses for use by CMS missionaries and schools, churches, and dispensaries at the mission stations. It did not matter whether the person applying for a job was an inquirer or not.[145] However, in many mission stations, those who came to work were obliged to attend prayer sessions during which they were taught the word of God before they started their respective jobs in the morning. In the afternoon they joined literacy classes.[146] In the end, jobs and income rather than an inner desire for conversion to mission Christianity became a driving motive for these people to associate themselves with the mission.

5.7.3 The Influence of Indigenous Teachers over Tax Collectors

Reference has been made above to how the report of the CMS mission for 1907 noted the influence the Christian tax collectors had within the CMS mission. Part of that influence was direct; in some cases, it was indirect but effective. Since local tax collectors were educated at mission schools, they respected the indigenous teachers, some of whom had been their teachers. This was the nature of the relationship between Lazaro Ndajilo and the Christian

---

143. Minutes, EC, 30/1/1907, G3 A8/0/1907/27, BUL.
144. Philemon Chidosa, oral interviews, 12 and 13 June 1997; Yudith Chidosa, oral interview, 12 June 1997.
145. Yohana Muhimili, oral interview, 1 July 1997.
146. Philemon Chidosa, oral interviews, 12 and 13 June 1997.

tax collectors at Mpangala and Mwitikila in the late 1920s and early 1930s.[147] However, as government agents, the tax collectors had to get their job done. Potential taxpayers (some of whom were inquirers and catechumens) observed the influence of the CMS mission teacher over the tax collectors. They often turned to such teachers when faced with arrests or whenever their personal property was in danger of being seized and auctioned to recover the tax they owed the government. Indigenous teachers working under the CMS mission often secured release of the inquirers and catechumens belonging to their mission but declined to offer help to those who had not showed interest in the teaching.[148] One would expect that this seemingly deliberate discriminatory policy would have had a negative effect in the evangelization process. It didn't:

> *Mwita Akiri*: Didn't they say, "This is a bad denomination. They bring people, members of their own denomination, to collect tax. We can't join such a denomination"?
>
> *Lazaro Ndajilo:* No. Look, people were ignorant. They came to me because they wanted protection. They knew that . . . I didn't support sexual immorality or the tendency to take additional money from people or indulge in ill treatment. If they met a man and intimidated him saying, "We want tax," and put him under arrest and brought him to my house, the wife of the arrested man would come to me. Some of those who were arrested happened to be people who were attending the inquirers' or catechumens' class. Such people were released. I offered them bail.[149]

Lazaro did not give money for bail, but only guaranteed that the tax owed would be paid when available. The impact of this power of a teacher on potential converts in times when the people faced imprisonment or seizure of property cannot be overstated. Without discounting the genuineness of conversions that resulted from preaching, the influence of indigenous teachers over tax collectors, together with job opportunities and the need for protection against injustices and harsh treatment during the German colonial era,

---

147. Lazaro Ndajilo, oral interviews, 14 and 16 June 1997.
148. Ndajilo, oral interviews.
149. Ndajilo, oral interviews.

contributed to attracting the local adult population to mission Christianity in the CMS mission sphere.

5.8 The Catechetical Process

Now that the use of literacy training as an evangelistic method has been explored, and its success assessed, including the motives of the children and adults among the Wagogo and Wakaguru for becoming *abasomi* ("readers" or "scholars"), attention may now be given to the process by which the Wagogo and Wakaguru scholars and potential converts actually became members of the visible church. Issues to be explored are the categories of baptism candidates, admission of candidates to the catechumenate, the "policing" of the candidates, and the duration of the process leading to baptism. An assessment of catechism used will be made as well.

5.8.1 Categories of Baptism Candidates

Bishop Peel outlined three categories of baptism seekers throughout the diocese of Mombasa:

> 1. The *Hearer*,[150] who comes for instruction but is not ready to avow himself an Enquirer, and renounce heathenism possibly at a service.
>
> 2. The *Enquirer* who has openly made a renunciation of idolatry, witchcraft and so forth, and professed, in public Service, an earnest desire to find God and be saved by His Blessed Son.
>
> 3. The *Catechumen* who has gone much further, publicly, at service for admission of Catechumen and stands before men as a Christian in life and profession, though not admitted to the privileges of the Church. After six months of probation, the Catechumen is baptised and enters the fourth great class.[151]

---

150. Towards the end of 1907, the term "hearer," meaning someone definitely asking for instruction in Christianity, was dropped. Instead, the term "inquirer" was adopted and became common. See Minutes, EC, 19-20, 26-27/12/1907, G3 A8/0/1908/12, BUL.

151. Peel, "Usagara & Ugogo Revisted," G3 A8/O/1903/38; Peel, *CMI* 29 (February 1904): 119; *PCMS*, 1903, 101; Briggs to Baylis, 17/3/1908, G3 A8/0/1908/27, BUL; Lazaro Ndajilo, oral interviews, 14 and 16 June 1997; Philemon Chidosa, oral interviews, 12 and 13 June 1997.

Though sometimes local timetables varied,[152] in most cases, instruction for hearers and inquirers took place on Mondays. Catechumens had their lessons on Wednesdays,[153] and baptized Christians were taught on Fridays. All involved in the four categories converged in church on Sundays.[154] One of the advantages of the separation of the different groups of baptism candidates and young Christians was that each was able to receive the teaching that suited their level of understanding even though this was not necessarily relevant to their pre-Christian context. Although many dropped out of the instruction at the hearers' stage, the inquirers' classes were generally large. For example, in 1911, the inquirers' class in Mvumi district had 733 people, while, in the same year, Buigiri district enrolled five hundred.[155] In 1913, Zoyisa alone (an out-station in Buigiri district) had two hundred inquirers under instruction.[156] The inquirers received a more detailed course of instruction. In 1901, the executive committee of the mission resolved that courses of instruction for the inquirers be based upon the Apostles' Creed, the Lord's Prayer, and the Ten Commandments.[157]

5.8.2 Duration of Instruction before Baptism

Baptism candidacy lasted for up to three years from the start of instruction. The decision on how soon one should be baptized depended on the policy adopted by individual CMS missionaries and indigenous teachers. To some extent it depended also on the aptitude of individual candidates. The main purpose of delaying baptism was to give the CMS mission "a better chance of reading a man's character" as well as "testing his steadiness in the face of the sensual temptations."[158] Therefore, candidates were not to be rushed to

---

152. See Berega Logbook, entry for 1906, MH. Most adult instruction classes were conducted at 4 o'clock in the afternoon, though in some places, like Berega, some classes started at 2 o'clock.

153. In some places such as Berega in 1906, inquirers'' classes took place on Wednesdays.

154. Lazaro Ndajilo, oral interviews, 14 and 16 June 1997; Nehemia Uguzi, oral interviews, 18 and 19 June 1997; Philemon Chidosa, oral interviews, 12 and 13 June 1997.

155. *PCMS*, 1912, 50.

156. *PCMS*, 1914, 61.

157. Minutes, EC, 6-7/6/1901, G3 A8/0/1901/25, BUL; cf. Lazaro Ndajilo, oral interviews, 14 and 16 June 1997.

158. Minutes, EC, 6-7/6/1901, G3 A8/0/1901/25; Peel, "Usagara and Ugogo Revisited," G3 A8/O/1903/38, BUL; Peel, *CMI* 29 (February 1904): 119.

the stage of catechumenate, lest they went back to the traditional practices in a matter of a month or two after baptism.[159] In 1931, George Chambers still felt that a prolonged candidacy was justified: "It is a long process but we are dealing with raw heathen, steeped in the ignorance and superstition of centuries, and it would be most unwise to allow any undue haste in the preparation of candidates for membership in the Christian Church. Our aim is to build an enlightened Christian community."[160] Prolonging the duration of baptism candidacy did not, however, mean that proper attention was given to the questions that related to the pre-Christian life of the candidates – the consequence of which will be addressed shortly.

5.8.3 Public Admission to the Catechumenate Status

Prior to joining the catechumen's class, candidates were required to make a commitment, at a Sunday service, "in the presence of God and of the congregation, which include[d] many of their relatives and friends." On the day of admission to the catechumenate, candidates stood and turned to the west and faced the congregation. After reciting some readings from parts of the catechism (as outlined in the *Book of Common Prayer*), as well as the Apostles' Creed,[161] candidates were asked the following questions:

> I. Do you renounce false gods and evil sprits and cleave to the one true God and worship Him?
>
> II. Do you renounce sacrificing to idols, fortune telling, charms, witchcraft, heathen medicine men, the pretence of rainmaking, the worship of trees and snakes, that you may worship God in spirit and in truth?
>
> III. Do you realize that lying, thieving, blasphemy, drunkenness, adultery, and such like are evil, and have you decided to forsake them and live a new life?
>
> IV. Will you seek the quietness of a holy life instead of a life according to the lusts of the world?

---

159. Lazaro Ndajilo, oral interviews, 14 and 16 June 1997.
160. Chambers, *Tanganyika's New Day*, 29.
161. Lazaro Ndajilo, oral interviews, 14 and 16 June 1997.

V. Will you try to bring your family and relatives to the Christian religion and earnestly endeavour to come every Sunday to hear the Word of God, and mould your life and that of your family according to the teaching of Christ?

VI. Do you truly repent of all your sins, and is it your earnest desire to forsake all that is contrary to God's will and commandments?

VII. Do you believe on the Lord Jesus Christ as your Saviour, and do you desire to learn His doctrine and be baptized and enter His fold?[162]

It should be emphasized that such questions and admission ceremonies were widespread throughout Africa and were adopted by most missions. The questions give an indication of areas of social and religious life of the Wagogo and Wakaguru over which the battle with baptism candidates and converts in general was fought. They focus on religious context and personal morality. Questions concerning the personal spiritual life and evangelistic obligations of the candidate came last in the series, though the order was probably a matter of chance rather design. The affirmative answer "Yes, I do" was given in response to each of the questions. Then the candidates turned to face the altar at the front of the church. After this, the officiating priest (or, in some cases, the bishop)[163] took each one by the hand and repeated his or her name, and said: "I receive you as a catechumen in the Church of Christ, and may almighty God Who has given you this desire give you the power to persevere that He may perfect His work which he has begun in you, through our Lord Jesus Christ."[164]

5.8.4 Catechumens and Pre-Christian Past

Specific purposes of public admission were that once baptized, the converts would part company with their pre-Christian traditional heritage; second, it was to impress upon those present in church (including friends and relatives)

---

162. Chambers, *Tanganyika's New Day*, 28.
163. *PCMS*, 1902, 104.
164. Chambers, *Tanganyika's New Day*, 28; Berega Logbook, No. 51, MH.

that entry into the church was voluntary.[165] After an act of public renunciation of all that was regarded as incompatible with mission Christianity, it would seem that the catechumens had entered into a contract of loyalty which would regulate the relationship between the two parties even after baptism.

Yet, most inquirers and catechumens (and converts for that matter) hardly abandoned *all things* that were classified as "wrong." Very often, CMS missionaries complained about the failure of the converts to resist the bad influences exerted upon them by members of the local community who were not interested in mission Christianity. Most of those who chose not to become Christian converts, as well as those who joined the baptism classes and then rejected the instruction, did so because they felt Christianity demanded things they were not prepared to offer. An extended analysis of female circumcision will be made in section 5.8.8 to demonstrate that even some baptized adherents could not break with their pre-Christian past.

Meanwhile, a brief mention will be made of some other social and religious practices that the catechumens had difficulties abandoning. As pointed out in chapter 2, these practises were also strong in the nineteenth century when the CMS mission first arrived in Ugogo and Ukaguru. Their survival well into the twentieth century means they had a significant place in society and could not be abandoned easily, whether by traditionalists, those who sought to join mission Christianity, or by baptized adherents.

The practice of offering sacrifices at the graves of the dead for petition during sickness, epidemic, or lack of rain became contentious in the relationship between the CMS mission and potential converts and baptized adherents. Catechumens and Christians who participated in these sacrifices became offenders. But condemnation of such acts without offering in their place an alternative means of explaining or controlling misfortune could only help to promote the relevance of traditional religion in the lives of the people.

Sacrifices to the dead at their graves was an act carried out by individuals or single families. But sacrifice for rain was a religious act with a communal dimension. Evidence shows that these acts were still prevalent in the twentieth century.[166] The events at Mvumi may help to illustrate this. Mention was

---

165. *CMR* 63 (March 1912) 162–163.
166. "Usagara-Chigogo Notes II," typescript, December 1903, G3 A8/O/1904/28, BUL. Doulton might just have been fortunate, but his fellow CMS missionaries had a different

made in chapter 2 of Nyama ya Hasi – the great rainmaker of Mvumi. Even by 1909, he was still alive and had followers.[167] So much so that even when a large python entered a village, it could not be killed. The python and the black mamba were among the sacred snakes in Gogo religion. Whenever such snakes entered a home or village, they were regarded as messengers from the spirits that should not be killed but "tempted" with an offering.[168] About this, Bertha Briggs could only complain, especially against Nyama ya Hasi: "You can imagine how strong their belief in this man's power over the rain is, when they are afraid to kill a creature which is not only a danger to themselves but will probably destroy any number of goats and so on."[169] Though rainmakers did not often bring rain despite the numerous sacrifices they performed, Nyama ya Hasi's reputation was enhanced when, in 1909, he performed sacrifice and it rained. The occasion was so big that CMS missionaries at Mvumi station became aware of it:

> A large number of people went to sacrifice for rain at Nyama ya Hasi's place this week, and the rain has come, but I am glad to say that we also had special prayer for rain last Sunday for the first time this year, and as the rain came on Tuesday, a good many believed it has come in answer to our prayers, as sacrificing has been going on for some time with no result.[170]

It is doubtful if the tradition of praying for rain in church was something that CMS missionaries had experienced in their home countries, except during occasional calendrical prayers (perhaps during the harvest thanksgiving), which may be said in church without there being a real crisis as there often was in Ugogo where drought was common. But at Mvumi, CMS missionaries had to get used to praying for rain in church more often out of the necessity of counteracting the influence of traditional Gogo religion over the potential converts, catechumens, and baptized adherents. Perhaps

---

experience. John Briggs was denied permission to gather and teach people by a chief he refers to as an "inhospitable chief" at Unyambwa (west of Mvumi) because a sacrifice was taking place on the day he requested to speak to the local people.

167. Bertha Briggs to Baylis, 3/3/1909, G3 A8/0/1909/28, BUL. Emphasis in original.
168. See Carnell, "Sympathetic Magic," 31.
169. Carnell, 31.
170. Carnell, 31.

a small but significant consolation for the mission came in 1913, at Buigiri, when "several rain-makers of a wide repute put themselves under instruction," and one of them was indeed baptized and abandoned the sacred rain stones.[171] Fortunately, at Mvumi too, in 1914, Nyama ya Hasi (while still "of great repute" as a rainmaker) showed interest in the Christian teaching, asked for a teacher, and erected small classroom himself where some of his people began learning.[172]

What must be recalled, however, is the fact that from 1910, as was noted earlier in chapter 4, the German colonial government urged the chiefs, but more so their sons, to learn to read and write. Probably this contributed to the rainmakers' change of attitude (many of whom were also chiefs or headmen). It should also be stressed that the dissociation of the Christian converts from sacrifices – whether for the dead or for rain – was a gradual process because, as with most crisis rituals, they explained and controlled misfortune in society.

Polygamy, which was controversial then – and, as F. W. Welbourn observes in his book *East African Christian*, continues to be so today – was another controversial issue in Ugogo and Ukaguru. An issue as wide as polygamy is, in itself, a subject that deserves fuller treatment than can be attempted here, particularly because it touches the status of women too. However, a brief analysis of what went on in the CMS mission is worth attempting.

It was alluded in chapter 4 that polygamy was one of the Gogo and Kaguru social practices that was less tolerated by the CMS mission from very early on. However, by 1900, the position of the mission on the baptism of a polygamist was already hardening. The executive committee resolved that no polygamist would be admitted to the class of catechumenate until he made arrangements for putting away all of his wives except one.[173] Indigenous teachers such as Lazaro Ndajilo were responsible for spreading this teaching:

> *Mwita Akiri*: Did you school teachers and church teachers teach the local people like that, or was it the Europeans who did it?
>
> *Lazaro Ndajilo*: Even us. Every mission teacher had to teach people that whoever comes to Christianity must have one wife

---

171. "The Gleaner," September 1913, 154, cited in *PCMS*, 1914, 60.
172. *CMR* 65 (September 1914): 552.
173. Minutes, EC, 6/4/1900, G3 A8/0/1900/20, BUL.

only. . . . We told such a person, "You must be converted, and leave your other wife, if you want to be a Christian". . . . From the German right through the British era. . . . Until now. If you have two wives, we can't baptize you. . . . Yes. If you have two wives, ah. Lo![174]

This shows that potential converts were informed about the Christian ideal of marriage as soon as they entered the stage of "hearers," and those who complied were admitted to the catechumenate. Yet such a policy had its difficulties, not least for the women it should have helped: "Some men wanted to divorce their senior wife in order to stay with the younger one."[175] Yet in Kigogo culture (as in most African societies), it was the senior wife that was regarded as the "real one."[176]

One can't deny that some Wagogo and Wakaguru complied with the mission requirement. Andrea Kanyanka, a Kaguru headman from Mamboya, was one of those who complied. He joined the inquirers' class under Yeremia Senyagwa, gave up one of his two wives, and was baptized in June 1902 and confirmed into the sacrament of the Lord's Supper by Bishop Peel on 12 January 1903 at Mamboya.[177] But that is far from suggesting that many other polygamists did the same or that the practice was abandoned in Ugogo and Ukaguru.[178]

As was pointed out earlier,[179] among those who were dissatisfied by the teaching of the Christian religion upon marriage were chiefs and headmen who chose to stay away from the church. Polygamy was fought against, but the battle has never been really won on a convincing scale. Part of the reason for this is that Christianity has not provided answers to some of the reasons behind the practice of polygamy: status, childlessness, desire for children of mixed gender – to name a few. Later on, in the early 1930s, the policy on the

---

174. Lazaro Ndajilo, oral interviews, 14 and 16 June 1997; cf. Nehemia Uguzi, oral interviews, 18 and 19 June 1997.

175. Lazaro Ndajilo, oral interviews, 14 and 16 June 1997.

176. Ndajilo, oral interviews; cf. Chambers, *Tanganyika's's New Day*, 35.

177. PCMS, 1903, 101; Peel, "Usagara and Ugogo Revisited," G3 A8/O/1903/38; Peel, "Usagara and Ugogo Revisted," G3 A8/O/1903/38, BUL; Peel, *CMI* 29 (February 1904): 117.

178. Lazaro Ndajilo, oral interviews, 14 and 16 June 1997.

179. See chapter 4.

admission of polygamists to the catechumenate was relaxed, but only just. On this, and on the fate of the dejected women, George Chambers wrote:

> Polygamists are received as catechumens and are kept under Christian instruction until such time as they shall be in a position to accept the law of Christ. . . . While the sanctity of Christian marriage is vigorously upheld by African Christians and they are not prepared to compromise in the matter of polygamy, no general agreement has been reached as to the treatment of the women who are involved when a polygamist becomes a Christian. The cast off wives ought not to become neglected in any way. They return to their parents and their former husband should facilitate their re-marriage under the best possible conditions. Until then he should provide them and their children with clothing from time to time.[180]

How this could be achieved is not spelled out by Chambers. The church could not have such powers to ensure that the former husband fulfilled his obligations to the "cast-off" wives and children. The imperfection of the institution of polygamy can hardly be overlooked. But it should be observed that while the CMS mission (like other Western missions) operating in Africa became preoccupied with ensuring that men gave up their additional wives, it forgot the impact that act would have on the women who found themselves in a forced divorce with confused social status. Consequently, as some scholars have observed, the church's policy on the baptism of polygamists becomes a tool for perpetuating patriarchy.[181]

Dancing was another traditional social practice that was also the focus of the battle between mission Christianity and traditional religion in central Tanzania. The dry season started in Ugogo and Ukaguru at the end of June. This was a time when harvest was finished, and farmers and peasants took a break from work in the fields. With plenty of corn, large quantities of *ujimbi* (local beer) was made, and the dry season became a time for enjoyment. This affected the attendance at instruction classes.

---

180. Chambers, *Tanganyika's New Day*, 35–36.
181. See Nasmiyu-Wasike, "Polygamy," 111; cf. Mombo, *Abaluyia Women*, 137, 138.

Around 1903, Gideoni Ferekani, an indigenous teacher based at Mamboya, could not find more than just three inquirers at Magubike (an out-station of Mamboya) when he went to lead the usual afternoon service with the intention of conducting a baptism class. Other inquirers had gone to a dance-drink party at a nearby village (headed by headman Kisengo). Gideoni showed his evangelistic enthusiasm and followed his "clients" to the party. Over 120 people were in attendance at the party, and it is possible the inquirers formed a good number of them.[182]

At Mvumi in Ugogo, some one hundred miles or so from Mamboya and Magubike, similar drinking and dancing problems were observed. Early in 1909, Bertha Briggs complained about the failure of the inquirers and catechumens who were under instruction to keep the promises they made during the rainy season about giving up drinking and dancing when the dry season arrived.[183] If Bertha Briggs only made a complaint, her husband John Briggs, who had been at Mvumi since 1900, used to go to the homes of the local people in the vicinity of the mission to break beer pots in an attempt to shame the catechumens who joined the drinking parties, but his actions were without much success. Beer drinkers were careful not to respond to Briggs's actions with anger or provoke something that would cost them association with the mission station or their jobs (for those who were employed).[184] Those who refrained from drinking, at least openly, did so to avoid excommunication.[185]

Dance-drink parties continued to be strong even in the 1920s. David Deeks wrote from Berega in 1920: "In October, the leaders of the Church convened a meeting of Christians to pray and work against 'evil of drink and drums,' referring to the heathen dances accompanied by drunkenness."[186] A number of oral informants shared the view that neither CMS missionaries nor indigenous teachers succeeded in stopping the traditional dances and drinking parties at once. The disappearance of some popular dances described

---

182. "Usagara-Chigogo Notes II," typescript, December 1903, G3 A8/O/1904/28, BUL; cf. *PCMS*, 1904, 97.

183. Bertha Briggs to Baylis, 3/3/1909, G3 A8/0/1909/28, BUL.

184. Philemon Chidosa, oral interviews, 12 and 13 June 1997.

185. Lazaro Ndajilo, oral interviews, 14 and 16 June 1997; Cleopa Mwaka, oral interview, 4 July 1997; Elimerik Mlahagwa, oral interview, 28 June 1997.

186. *PCMS*, 1921, 35.

in chapter 2 was only gradual.[187] But some dances, such as *Sunyunho*, have survived to date in parts of Ugogo.[188]

5.8.5 The "Policing" of the Baptism Candidates

Having now assumed the role of givers rather than recipients of the teaching, indigenous teachers had to devise some ways of ensuring that baptism seekers remained "on track." Like CMS missionaries, most indigenous teachers regarded traditional religious and social practices as the "archenemy" of mission Christianity. They were therefore keen to monitor the lives of the candidates. In the monitoring, most attention was paid to the attitude of the baptism candidates towards religious practices and social customs, as well as personal morality:

> You observed whether he was still a drunkard, or whether he/she has started drinking. Or whether he/she liked worldly enjoyments. Or whether he was a settled person. . . . Listen, I cannot just drag them in, only to find that they reject their faith in a matter of days. You don't want to see people rubbing the white clay over their bodies soon after baptism, or making sacrifices. It implies that you, the teacher didn't do your job properly. I cannot rush anyone to baptism. . . . They would return to their former ways because they did not reach maturity. It was important to make a narrow gate so that they enter one after another, slowly. . . . I didn't want problems in the future.[189]

The monitoring of the catechumens' actions and behaviour was even more rigorous:

> You then have to be vigilant with the catechumens, very vigilant with catechumens . . . if they have stopped offering sacrifice, whether he/she has stopped worshipping false gods, and that he/she follows one God. . . . You assess whether he has overcome the

---

187. Dan Mbogoni, oral interview, 11 June 1997; Cleopa Mwaka, oral interview, 4 July 1997; Elimerik Mlahagwa, oral interview, 28 June 1997; Dan Mbogoni, oral interview, 11 June 1997.

188. Dan Mbogoni, oral interview, 11 June 1997; Lazaro Ndajilo, oral interviews, 14 and 16 June 1997; Yohana Muhimili, oral interview, 2 July 1999.

189. Lazaro Ndajilo, oral interview.

bodily desires that tempt him to take two wives, or five, just like that. You observe that the catechumen no longer uses abusive language, no longer fights other people, if he no longer steals sheep belonging to other people.[190]

Lazaro Ndajilo proudly recalls, "I was a teacher, and observed such things if I wanted to accept someone in the name of Jesus. . . . You could easily observe someone's behaviour, because that person was coming to church."[191]

The coming to church on Sunday provided only very little contact to make the task of policing or observation easier. Unlike the early 1970s when most Tanzanians were forced to move into communal settlements known as *Ujamaa* villages, during the German and British colonial era families lived in homesteads scattered across vast areas, which were sometimes distant from each other. Besides this, the desire of the baptism candidates to conceal their misdeeds and misbehaviours rendered the task of monitoring their actions and behaviour extremely difficult.

The teachers were therefore assisted by the lay assistants, or *wanyapara wa kanisa*.[192] *Wanyapara wa kanisa* were appointed or recommended by the local indigenous teacher. There were many such assistants, and each was responsible for a small area and would give feedback on what he or she observed.[193] As part of their policing task, *wanyapara wa kanisa* also exercised some sort of pastoral care. They paid visits to those who didn't come to church or failed to attend instructions because of sickness or the attraction of a social or religious event in the village.[194] Despite this involvement by the elders, it was not easy to keep watch over human beings whose attachment to social and religious practices had developed for many years. Interrogations of the candidates by the teacher and pastor prior to the administration of baptism was hardly sufficient to distinguish between those who kept the agreement they made during their public admission to the catechumenate and those

---

190. Lazaro Ndajilo, oral interviews, 14 and 16 June 1997.

191. Ndajilo, oral interviews.

192. *Mnyapara* is a derogatory Kiswahili term commonly used to refer to Africans who supervised their fellows during the roadwork and building construction, especially during the German and British colonial occupation of Tanzania. It has tended to have negative connotations in the post-freedom era in Tanzania (1961 onwards).

193. Lazaro Ndajilo, oral interviews, 14 and 16 June 1997.

194. Ndajilo, oral interviews.

who did not.[195] The difficulty arose partly from the nature of the interrogation. Candidates were asked to recite the Ten Commandments, the Lord's Prayer, and the Apostles' Creed, and answer questions on God the Father, Jesus Christ, and the Holy Spirit.[196] In fact, it was these elements that formed the major component of the catechism.

5.8.6 The Inadequacy of the Catechesis

The suggestion made by Chambers (as quoted in section 5.8.2) that CMS missionaries (and indigenous teachers for that matter) were dealing with "raw heathen" reflects the assumption, based largely on ignorance common in those days, that the local people had no religion of their own. They were therefore viewed like creatures with empty minds and hollow hearts to be filled with Christian teaching – however irrelevant such teaching might be to their lives. The implication was that "primal religions contained no preparation for Christianity."[197] In this context, it was not uncharacteristic that the content of the catechesis paid little or no attention to the primal worldview.

Whenever cultural or religious studies were conducted by foreign missionaries, they only strove to show "darkness" that needed uprooting among the Wagogo and Wakaguru, as well as other ethnic groups in the CMS sphere.[198] Similar studies in other missions, such as one conducted by Godfrey Dale about the Bondei in northeastern Tanzania in the UMCA sphere, took the same line.[199] Evidence from Dale's study shows that many of the practices he describes were regarded as unacceptable by the UMCA mission and were therefore banned. Indeed, even indigenous clergy and teachers fought against such practices on their own initiative without being urged by Western missionaries.

As has been indicated in connection with the teaching against polygamy, indigenous teachers in Ugogo and Ukaguru were at the forefront of defending Christian ideals as they received them from the CMS missionaries. It would

---

195. *Berega Logbook*, No. 51, MH.
196. Lazaro Ndajilo, oral interviews, 14 and 16 June 1997.
197. Bediako, "Understanding African Theology," 15.
198. Rees, "History of CMS," MS, G3 A8/0/1902/19, BUL.
199. Godfrey Dale, "An Account of the Principal Customs and Habits of the Natives Inhabiting the Bondei" (compiled mainly for the use of the European missionaries), OPDZ, Box A.4.1, RHL, a reprint from *The Journal of the Anthropological Institute*, February, 1896.

therefore be inaccurate to suggest that the fight against traditional African social and religious practices was a task undertaken by CMS missionaries alone. If at times the indigenous teachers appeared "liberal" (in the sense of being less strict, at least for a while) in choosing their tactics when evangelizing fellow Africans, they did so only to bring them in but then intensified the teaching against the social and traditional practices. Ndajilo's testimony shows this:

> Just as how I am sitting here with you, and then tell you, "Come with me." If you are a smoker, I won't tell you not to do so on the first day. Rather, I would tell you, "Take ten cents and buy tobacco, and smoke." I know that if I prohibited someone to smoke, who is young in faith, that person would undoubtedly do the same thing in private. If I met someone who was a beer drinker, I said to him or her, "Here is twenty cent. Go and drink." . . . They drank and smoked. But the moment that person came to the instruction class in church, I taught in depth against such things. *I dug deep, I dug deep.*[200]

The same attitude of being at the forefront in attacking African traditional social and religious practices was common among the indigenous teachers and pastors of the UMCA. For example, at Magila in Tanga province in the northeast of Tanzania, both in the late nineteenth century and early in the twentieth century, some African members of staff, such as Petro Limo, argued that the UMCA missionaries did not know much about what was acceptable and what wasn't.[201] They had to be helped. In hindsight, however, it can be observed that it would have been better if the indigenous teachers had given a lead in analysing the local customs with a view to finding points of interaction with mission Christianity.

---

200. Lazaro Ndajilo, oral interviews, 14 and 16 June 1997; cf. Philemon Chidosa, oral interviews, 12 and 13 June 1997.

201. Woodward to Travers, 23 August 1895, *Letters from Africa*, Box E.2, RHL. For details of the list of practices that were banned between 1896 and 1904, see "Mapatano ya Mikutano ya Wakristo wa Archidiakonat ya Magila 1896–1904" (a pamphlet printed at Msalabani, 1906), OPDZ, Box A.4.1, RHL. It is interesting to note that most of the practices that had been banned before 1900 were being rebanned again. This shows the persistence of the Bondei religious and social practices.

Apart from a general failure in addressing the pre-Christian context of potential converts and believers, the catechesis was characterized by emphasis on the need for candidates to memorize or recite what they were taught from books written for catechetical purposes in Europe[202] But this strategy was hardly successful. No wonder, therefore, that some CMS missionaries complained about the "inability" of the baptism candidates to follow the teaching. In 1909, at Mvumi, Bertha Briggs wrote about some Mvumi women, and said, "sometimes after making them repeat something very simple after one, when asked the question which practically tells them the answer which they have just been repeating, they will look quite surprised and ask, 'How should we know.'"[203] The candidates were right. Lifeless and theoretical teaching, requiring memorization and unrelated to the issues they faced daily, was probably dull and difficult to follow.

As was noted earlier, much of the teaching used for literacy training and catechism was drawn from biblical material. Most indigenous Christians remember this:

> Also about the book of Genesis, [we were taught] how God created Adam and Eve. . . . That is how you taught them. Once they knew how Adam was created, and how Eve was given to him to be his wife, then they stop being inquirers. They became catechumens. Those who understood the lessons (after one year) were admitted as catechumens on a Sunday in church.[204]
>
> Then the candidates went on to learn Ten Instructions [Ten Commandments]. . . . When you finished the first book, and Exodus, and examine what happened in Egypt, and the power of God, how he defeated the Egyptians, . . . you proceeded into

---

202. From 1901, the following books were used in the baptismal instruction: *Steps to Truth Part 1* (for instruction of the hearers), *Steps to Truth Part 2* (for the inquirers), *Catechism: As Far as the Sacraments and Baptismal Service* (for catechumens). Other textbooks such as *Lessons on the Church's Catechism* authored by Cluny Macpherson, and *Foundation Truths* by one Rev Baring-Gould were used also for the same purpose. See Minutes, EC, 6-7/6/1901, G3 A8/0/1901/25; Minutes, EC, 13, 15/11/1909, G3 A8/0/1910/1; cf. "Hundred Texts" of the Irish Church Missions. See Elizabeth Forsythe to Baylis, annual letter, 28/11/1910, G3 A8/0/1910/92, BUL.

203. Bertha Briggs to Friends in England, 3/3/1909, G3 A8/0/1909/28, BUL.

204. Lazaro Ndajilo, oral interviews, 14 and 16 June 1997.

> the New Testament. In the New Testament you started with the birth of Jesus. [Long pause] When Jesus was born he grew up, he did things, he went to John the Baptist to be baptized, he received the Holy Spirit. . . . We were being asked questions: "Where did John the Baptist live? Did he have a house or not?" As for Jesus, the converts were taught that . . . Jesus the Son of God was born, he came from heaven, by Spirit to Mary, the wife of Joseph, he was born by Mary and looked after by her. When he grew up and became an adult, he started preaching saying, "I am the Son of God."[205]

The words quoted above are a small part of what the informant, Lazaro Ndajilo, a 97-year-old former teacher, had memorized when he was a baptism candidate long ago. This confirms one thing among many – namely, the intensity with which Bible material was taught through memorization. Ndajilo, whose information has been used extensively in this study, is an exceptional man. His memory amazes most people at Mvumi Makulu, where he lives, and he is often visited by researchers with different subject interests; this is perhaps so because he was a teacher and had to know by heart what he taught others at a time when much of Christian teaching was done orally. In addition to this, he had been an influential palace official of Chief Mazengo Chalula.

But others, not least those who attended the class taught by Bertha Briggs, as pointed out above, hardly comprehended the lessons at the time of teaching, let alone remembered them years afterwards. One of the reasons must be that little effort was made to explore points of contact with issues in the pre-Christian life of potential converts and converts alike. Instead, the strategy was to get most candidates to the stage where they could become fluent and read an Old Testament book, a portion of it, or the New Testament[206] – depending on the vernacular translations available in Kigogo and Kikaguru (also known as Kimegi).[207]

Though based on Scriptures, one other major feature of the teaching offered to baptism candidates (apart from what has been quoted above) was

---

205. Ndajilo, oral interviews.
206. Peel, "Usagara and Ugogo Revisted," G3 A8/O/1903/38, BUL; Peel, *CMI* 29 (1904): 114, 115.
207. Minutes, EC, 18, 19, 21/12/1903, G3 A8/0/1904/12, BUL.

its focus on personal morality. In particular, there was emphasis on God's judgement on those who violated moral principles. On the surface, it may look as if this struck a chord with moral codes in African traditional religion, where aspects of social and religious teaching also focus on morality and taboos. But unlike the moral codes in African traditional religion, the Christian moral codes were easily and frequently broken.

Godfrey Wilson[208] and Monica Wilson[209] offer one explanation for this contrast between traditional and Christian moral codes. Drawing on their study of the Nyakyusa, they suggest that in African moral systems, the social and religious consequences of disobedience did not only concern the individual but his or her entire community too.[210] For the Nyakyusa, failure to provide hospitality to neighbours is an offence against the community.[211] Therefore, Gogo and Kaguru baptism candidates and converts alike had to disregard and break Christian moral laws that prevented them from fulfilling their traditional obligations – failure of which would have had serious communal consequences. For, as John Mbiti says, "Everyone who is a member of the community must participate in its moral welfare. Whoever constantly or deliberately breaks his community morals eventually finds the community punishing him in return.[212] This covers those very issues such as sacrifice to the dead at the graves to avert an epidemic or sacrifice for rain.

It was not only the adults who broke the moral codes of mission Christianity. Young converts did the same. By 1913, these young converts had indeed become the majority in the baptism classes, giving the impression – as the mission hoped – that they were less conservative and less "spoiled" by traditional practices than their parents and elders.[213] Yet the reality pointed to the contrary. One illustration may be sufficient here.

In the Mvumi area (and possibly other places in central Tanzania), it was common for girls to wear a wire belt apparently for carrying charms. Girls residing within the mission premises were forbidden to wear such a belt.

---

208. See Wilson, "African Morality," 90.
209. See Wilson, "African Christian Morality," 286.
210. Wilson, "African Morality," 90.
211. Wilson, 90.
212. Mbiti, *Introduction to African Religion*, 178.
213. *PCMS*, 1914, 60.

The prohibition was hardly heeded by the girls, and this became a source of constant conflict between the CMS women missionaries and the girls, as Bertha Briggs confirms:

> We had quite a fight over these things! After finding that in spite of orders, they wore them at times on the quiet, the edict went forth that they would be taken from them altogether, if found on them again. Last Friday all our three orphan girls were wearing them so we took them away at once and for the next two days or so Mwendwa was very naughty and disobedient. On Tuesday she had to be punished and in the evening she ran away.[214]

Fortunately, Mwendwa took refuge in the home of one of the local indigenous Christian women and was taken back to the mission and "promised not to be disobedient again."[215] It is difficult to know whether Mwendwa remained obedient throughout the remainder of her time at the mission station, let alone in her entire adulthood. But her story depicts the kind of conflict of understanding between the mission and the local converts, including young people.

One fact was often overlooked. Young people like Mwendwa might have appeared as unsuspecting, passive bystanders during religious acts such as sacrifices, but they must have actually been active participants, noting the significance their parents attached to such events – and this applies even to those who entered the boarding schools.[216] It was not until 1924 that some changes began to be noticed in the attitude among young people towards traditional dances and ceremonies, as well as the rubbing of *husi* (Kigogo; clay "grease") and the wearing of plaited wigs.

Yet, on the whole, as will be seen below, attempts to eradicate aspects of traditional religion were often hardly successful, and where success was obtained, it was very gradual and little, particularly among adults. And in light of the failure of the catechesis to address the pre-Christian social and religious aspirations of the converts, the problem became even more acute

---

214. Bertha Briggs to Baylis, 3/3/1909, G3 A8/0/1909/28, BUL.
215. Bertha Briggs to Baylis, 3/3/1909, G3 A8/0/1909/28, BUL
216. *ARCCMS*, 1925, 14; Yohana Muhimili, oral interview, 2 July 1997; Cleopa Mwaka, oral interview, 4 July 1997.

in the relationship of mission Christianity and the culture and worldviews of the Wagogo and Wakaguru.

5.8.7 The CMS Mission and Traditional Practices

It has to be stressed that the whole issue of mission response to religious and social practices in Africa was a complex one. In his article "The Africanization of Missionary Christianity: History and Typology," Steven Kaplan has made a case for this complexity. While conceding that "the extreme ethnocentricity and cultural arrogance of many Western missionaries cannot be denied," he yet argues that the common assertion that they destroyed African cultures needs qualifying. He suggests that there were sincere and numerous attempts by Western missionaries to Africanize missionary Christianity, and that the process took many forms at different times.[217]

While this remains largely the case, there is little doubt that Kaplan is trying to defend what he perceives to be the unfair attacks on the attitudes of the early Western missionaries in Africa. It can also be observed that his illustrations are taken from the responses that were somewhat "radical" and stood above the rest. However, Kaplan's points are worth noting so that missions are not viewed as homogenous units which carried out a unified policy across Africa without any variations *within* and *between* them. That is the value of his paper.

In fact, there were also a number of creative individual Western missionaries in the field who displayed pro-African attitudes or initiated similar programmes, sometimes to the dislike of their colleagues. Jack Thompson has indicated this in relation to the Scottish missionaries working among the Ngoni of northern Malawi in the late nineteenth and early twentieth centuries. In particular, he has explored the sympathetic attitude of the Scottish missionary Donald Fraser, of the Livingstonia mission, whose support for

---

217. Kaplan, "Africanization," 166–186. He outlines these forms as follows: *tolerance* (acceptance of aspects of African customs though regarding them as "essentially incompatible with a true Christian life); *translation* ("an attempt to express Christian ideas and concepts in an African idiom"); *assimilation* (introduction of non-Christian elements into "essentially" Christian rituals); *Christianization* (creation of Christian versions of a number of traditional rites and practices); *acculturation* (selection and preservation of features of traditional culture considered "valuable and compatible with the development of Christian spirituality"); and *incorporation* (introduction of African concepts into "normative" global Christianity). Kaplan uses these terms, but the description of their meaning has been paraphrased by this writer. It should be observed that these terms overlap and are not radically mutually exclusive.

some aspects of Ngoni culture – for example, the Ngoni custom of marrying a deceased brother's widow – "brought him into open conflict with his missionary colleagues."[218] He notes that Fraser himself was opposed to some aspects of the Ngoni culture, such as polygamy and beer drinking.[219] Nevertheless, he encouraged the development of some of those aspects that he sanctioned as "clean" or "adaptable," for instance the traditional Ngoni songs.[220] This would almost fit in Steven Kaplan's "acculturation mode" – an attempt to preserve features of traditional African culture deemed valuable and compatible with Christian spirituality.[221]

There is no evidence of major differences in the attitudes of CMS missionaries in regard to the Gogo and Kaguru cultures and religious practices during the period under review. Except in cases such as polygamy, the initial period of the CMS mission in Ugogo and Ukaguru was marked with a degree of general tolerance towards the African social and religious practices. Tolerance was mostly based on the notion that the people had no religion, were without "light," and were therefore "ignorant." As one informant notes:

> *Esta Chali:* . . . Let me tell you something. The one who arrived first accepted the Wagogo as they were. Yes. Mr Price.[222] He gathered the elders. You see those traditional elders were tobacco smokers. Some were sniffing tobacco. They used to come to him for conversation. . . . To listen to him. *He accepted them as they were.*
>
> *Mwita Akiri:* . . . Did he not come and say, "You Wagogo people, you must stop doing this or that?"

---

218. Thompson, *Christianity in Northern Malawi*, 153.
219. Thompson, 152.
220. Thompson, 149, 153.
221. See Kaplan, "Africanization," 178.
222. John Price arrived at Mpwapwa in the autumn of 1879. By then Joseph Last and Edward Baxter had been there since the spring of 1878. See *CMI* 5 (December 1880): 735. The informant is certainly referring to Price as "the one who arrived first" because he was one of the best-known foreign missionaries in Ugogo. He was popularly known as *Bwana Mwalimu* (Kiswahili; "Mr Teacher"). Price himself confirms this when describing the Bushiri episode, referring to "Mwalimu" as "the name by which I am generally known out here." *CMI* 14 (December 1889): 742. This may be the reason why the words on the tombstone at the mission graveyard (next to St Luke's church, Vingh'awe's Church, Vingh'awe, Mpwapwa) are inscribed in the Kigogo language. Price died on 23 January 1895.

Esta Chali: No.

Mwita Akiri: . . . Do you think that was a good approach? Could he not tell them to stop doing such and such things?

Esta Chali: Where could he find people when everybody didn't know the word of God? He had to come gently. Very gently.[223]

Taking snuff could be regarded as a minor social habit – one that could have been easily tolerated by CMS missionaries, perhaps, because, after all, some of them were pipe smokers themselves. And Semgomba Chitemo rightly asks: "Which of the Europeans walked without a tobacco pipe? Men such as Mr King . . . Mr Deeks, Mr Bakewell. These days they despise pipe-smoking. But is it not these people who introduced it? [laughing continuously]."[224] The gentle approach was not confined to social habits. Traditional wedding ceremonies were accepted too,[225] and indeed, early in the twentieth century, those who agreed to marry in church were allowed to fulfil their marriages in a traditional way.[226] This was a time when Western missionaries "agreed to accept the continued existence of certain African social customs . . . on the grounds of expediency or functional necessity."[227] This is in contrast to the claims made by some African scholars about the attitude of Western missionaries at this period.[228] Anza Lema is certainly right that during this early period, with the exception of Bruno Guttmann who arrived in Uchaga in 1910[229] – seventeen years after the Leipzig mission had commenced their work among the Wachaga of Kilimanjaro, northern Tanzania[230] – "few Leipzig mis-

---

223. Esta Chali, oral interview, 26 June 1997; cf. Semgomba Chitemo, oral interview, 15 September 1997; Cleopa Mwaka, oral interview, 4 July 1997.

224. Semgomba Chitemo, oral interview, 15 September 1997; cf. Yusufu Masingisa, oral interviews, 16 and 17 September 1997.

225. Lazaro Ndajilo, oral interviews, 14 and 16 June 1997.

226. The only thing that the mission was against was the bride and groom taking off their clothes in order to have their bodies washed by a brother-in-law (for the groom) and a sister-in-law (for the bride). See chapter 2 for details on the Gogo wedding ceremony.

227. Kaplan, "Africanization," 167, 168.

228. See for example, Temu, *British Protestant Missions*, 155; Ayandele, *Missionary Impact on Modern Nigeria*, 242–243, 330–331; Beidelman, *Colonial Evangelism*, 133.

229. Lema, "Chaga Religion," 52, 55.

230. Groves, *Planting of Christianity*, 3:81.

sionaries took the trouble to observe Chaga life in depth or detail."[231] Equally valid is his observation that most CMS missionaries were quick to misinterpret aspects of African religion among the Wachaga, such as sacrifices and libations offered at the family graves as "animism and ancestor worship."[232] However, apart from his comment on the cautious response by the chiefs and the initial apprehension by Chaga elders, perhaps he has exaggerated the destructive power of the attitude and teaching of Leipzig missionaries during the initial period of evangelization and has overlooked the Chaga resistance.

Unlike the early period (pre-1900) when a degree of tolerance was shown towards the social and religious practices, the attitude of CMS missionaries and indigenous teachers gradually shifted. From tolerance came an attitude of contempt, though without legislating to end particular social customs or religious practices. Semgomba Chitemo (a traditional medicine practitioner at Berega who admitted that in the earlier period CMS missionaries were more sympathetic) noticed a change. He observed that some of the "people of the land" joined the mission not voluntarily but by "force" – force embodied in the nature of the message that urged people to forsake their religion.[233] Then came a period when deliberate effort was made to deter people from such practices and even legislate in church and punish the "offenders." However, the three attitudes – tolerance, contempt without legislating, and the punishment of "offenders" – were not mutually exclusive and were taking place simultaneously each time the Christian message was preached to people for the first time in a new place and in the places where Christian work had been established.

But in all this, the thrust of the argument by this writer is that, on the whole, it was mission Christianity and not the Gogo and Kaguru traditional religion that lost the contest. The controversial issue of female circumcision may be used to illustrate the latter phase of the attitude of the CMS mission towards the Gogo and Kaguru traditional practices. It will become evident that even here, the CMS mission hardly won its battle.

---

231. Lema, "Chaga Religion," 53.
232. Lema, 54.
233. Semgomba Chitemo, oral interview, 15 September 1997.

5.8.8 Female Circumcision: A Lost Battle?

For a long time, the issue of female circumcision in Africa has been a subject of much controversy and debate. The consequences of various attempts by some Western missions (or, to be precise, some missionaries within those missions) to eradicate it through banning often ended up dividing local church opinion. This was the case in the 1920s and 1930s in central Kenya when the Church of Scotland Mission (CSM) and the CMS mission opposed the practice among the Kikuyu, as the Africa Inland Mission (AIM) did later among the Maasai.[234] It should be emphasized that even within these missions (as well as others elsewhere), Western missionaries had diverse policies in regard to the different mission stations they superintended. Indigenous opinion was diverse too. Without making a simplistic generalization, it might be said that on the whole, the younger generation (represented by unmarried indigenous teachers or church elders with young families below circumcision age) tended to support the ban.[235] The older generation (parents in particular) often resisted the ban because they didn't want to make their daughters "unmarriageable."

In regard to the CMS mission in Kenya, Jocelyn Murray has explored this reality among the Kikuyu in her article "The Church Missionary Society and the 'Female Circumcision' Issue in Kenya 1929–1932." She argues that though the CMS mission stations – Kigari and Kabare in central Kenya – were only twenty-five miles apart, the mission had two different approaches to the issue of female circumcision for these locations. In the former, the CMS missionary was more rigid in his approach. The church elders supported him and converts who allowed their daughters to undergo the rite of circumcision were excommunicated – and the daughters, if pupils at a local school, were suspended. Yet, in the latter, a moderate form of a "Christian" female circumcision ceremony was allowed, and a baptized operator circumcised girls. Christian families were encouraged to take their daughters to her.[236]

---

234. Waller, "They Do the Dictating," 105–106.

235. Take, for instance, the enthusiasm of young married men with small children at Kabare and Kigari CMS stations in central Kenya who had not been confronted with the issue in relation to their own daughters. See Murray, "Church Missionary Society," 103.

236. Murray, 99, 101. A similar crisis occurred in AIM in 1930. See Waller, "They Do the Dictating," 102–104.

Unlike the situation experienced in central Kenya, in central Tanzania, though CMS missionaries were opposed to female circumcision, neither archival nor oral evidence suggests that the opposition resulted in a crisis or major confrontation. However, the beginning of the twentieth century witnessed a new policy on the rite of circumcision for both boys and girls in the CMS mission in central Tanzania. In 1900, Bishop Peel complained that "our young Christians find this a dreadful snare and are often enticed to the camps which are formed at a certain season of the year."[237] So, in April 1900, with his approval, the executive committee passed a resolution (with a note "for private circulation among the CMS missionaries") declaring that no African boy or girl was to enter the catechumens' class until reasonable satisfaction had been given that the circumcision stage had been passed. The approximate age for entry into the catechumens' class was set at sixteen.[238] It was also decided that only men could be circumcised. Indeed, the mission imitated the Christianization of *jando* attempted by Vincent Lucas in Masasi, southern Tanzania, in the UMCA sphere.[239]

Lucas took a middle ground between what he referred to as ill-considered "vague benediction" of traditional practices based on foreign missionaries' ignorance when they first arrived in parts of Africa and "an indignant campaign of suppression" on discovering aspects of the rites that are contrary to

---

237. Report by Bishop of Mombasa, "Missions of the CMS in the Diocese of Mombasa in 1900," G3 A5/P6, BUL.

238. Minutes, EC, 6/10/1900, G3 A8/0/1900/20, BUL.

239. For details of the Masasi Experiment, see, *Acts of Synod Concerning Initiatory Rites*, Diocese of Masasi, Tanzania, 21–23 November 1927, MS 1468 "Miscellaneous Papers," LPL; Lucas, "Educational Value"; Ranger, "Missionary Adaptation." *Jando* is a Kiswahili word meaning initiation rites, of various kinds, but mostly those involving male or female circumcision, and camping outside the village. *Unyago*, too, is a Kiswahili word, meaning ceremonies connected with *jando* (whether for malemales or femalefemales). See *Standard Swahili-English Dictionary*, 1994, 150, 503. Similarly, "tribal initiation rites" is rendered *jando, unyago, ukumbi* in *Standard English-Swahili Dictionary*, 1st ed., 1939, 290. This certainly is how Vincent Lucas uses the word *unyago* when he says, "just as in the past it was only certain chiefs who had the right to hold a *Unyago*, so, for the present, it is only the Christian priest in each district who has the right to hold the Christian *Unyago*." See Lucas, "Educational Value of Initiatory Rites," 198. Yet, various authors have tended to use the word *jando* as if it applies only to male circumcision riterites, or as if it is a Christianized form of the traditional *unyago*. So, in defence of Lucas's experiment, Ranger writes, "[*Jandos*] remained very different indeed from the traditional *unyago*." See Ranger, "Missionary Adaptation"; Ranger and Kimambo, *Historical Study of African Religion*, 246, 245; cf. Kaplan, "Africanization," 175. Such a confusion is worth avoiding.

Christian morals.²⁴⁰ Among those opposed to the Christianization of traditional circumcision initiation rites was Johannes Raum. Raum acknowledged the educational value of the puberty rites but also summed up his opposition in the following words:

> The introduction of puberty ceremonies into the Christian Church, on the part of a missionary society, is a most regrettable step; it confuses the boundary line between Christianity and heathendom; it must lead to a perplexing of conscience and a weakening of the missionary force of Christianity in Africa. It is also a dangerous experiment: the mental atmosphere of the puberty ceremonies is anything but pure; rites are directed towards awakening the sexual instincts and stand in basic relation to belief in spirits.²⁴¹

It is this sort of extreme view that Lucas felt was unhealthy. Certainly, unlike much of the Christian catechetical teaching which had only a theoretical emphasis, the knowledge gained from the teaching offered during the initiation rite was practical and lasting.²⁴²

Along these lines, an experimental initiation camp was set up in Ugogo soon after the harvest in August 1930. Later, Wynn Jones reflected on it in a document called "An Experimental Initiation Camp Held at Ugogo, 1930."²⁴³ The elders of the land were at first uneasy about a white man getting involved in such an important rite of passage, but their fears were dispelled and concerns addressed. For example, women were not allowed near the camps except to bring food each day at noon and in the evening and hand it over to another person at the camp gate. Also, other things such as the style of the camp and the first operations were decided and performed by a local operator (*mhunga*). The mission doctor then performed the rest without anaesthetic, but used simple modern surgical instruments, so that the elders and the boys could see the difference. The indigenous teachers held a service at the camp, and

---

240. Lucas, "Initiatory Rites," 196–197.
241. Raum, "Christianity and African Puberty Rites," 591.
242. Lucas, "Initiatory Rites," 198.
243. Wynn Jones, "An Experimental Initiation Camp Held at Ugogo, 1930," October 1932, 2, School of Oriental and African Studies (SOAS) Library, IMC/CBMS, Box 201, File F.

the local African pastor prayed for the initiates. Church songs and hymns were sung, and religious teaching was offered.

Jones expressed hope that the camps were a better place to establish Christian influence on issues of morality but also noted that it would take a long time before a breakthrough could be made. Two more initiation camps were held (probably in 1931 and 1932), but Jones gave no details of these when he wrote in 1932. From oral sources, it is clear that the Christianization of *jando* (for boys) continued, though not in the manner described above. By 1940, Kefa Malecela (in Ugogo)[244] and Joshua Mkwama and Daniel Makamba (in Ukaguru)[245] performed the operation. In order to the make hospital circumcision popular at first, especially in Ukaguru, the children of the indigenous teachers and other willing Christians were circumcised first. To a limited extent, hospital circumcision succeeded in challenging the position of the *wahunga* (traditional circumcision experts) in society.

This policy of sanctioning male circumcision and Christianizing it but opposing female circumcision served no useful purpose except to force converts to practice the latter in secrecy. Wynn Jones wrote in 1932, noting that though Christian parents made efforts to prevent their daughters undergoing the operation, the girls pretended to be visiting their relatives "but in reality [went] to the house of some older women of the tribe and there have passed through the rite."[246] It is possible, though, that some or many of those Christian parents actually sanctioned their daughters' secret departures but pretended to know nothing about it. Oral testimony suggests this.

For example, at Mvumi, those who lived near the mission station were sending their daughters away to relatives in neighbouring villages for circumcision. When a CMS missionary inquired about a particular girl, he/she was told, "she is visiting his paternal uncle."[247] The girl who went through circumcision stayed away until the scar healed before returning home near the station. According to a number of oral informants, as far as female circumcision was concerned, the CMS mission was fighting a losing battle all

---

244. Lazaro Ndajilo, oral interviews, 14 and 16 June 1997.

245. Isaka Mlahagwa, oral interview, 14 September 1997.

246. Wynn Jones, "An Experimental Initiation Camp Held at Ugogo, 1930," October 1932, 2, School of Oriental and African Studies (SOAS) Library, IMC/CBMS, Box 201, File F.

247. Lazaro Ndajilo, oral interviews, 14 and 16 June 1997.

the way. "We took action against anyone whom we discovered practising it," says Lazaro Ndajilo who lives at Mvumi Makulu near the mission station, "[but] a Mgogo is never easily defeated in his traditional custom."[248] Cleopa Mwaka, who spent his youth at Buigiri (far from Mvumi), adds in this excerpt:

> *Cleopa Mwaka:* But on the question of our traditional practices, the Europeans were against female circumcision, *but who heeded that? No one did.* [laughing].
>
> *Mwita Akiri:* [laughing]. No one heeded?
>
> *Cleopa Mwaka:* Aa-h. *Neither Christians* nor anyone else. All. *Nor did the teachers.* They were all having their children circumcised.
>
> *Mwita Akiri:* Secretly?
>
> *Cleopa Mwaka:* Openly sir! The reason was that the government did not involve itself in that, therefore the mission had no power to stop the practice. And the custom had become rooted in people's lives since the time of their grandfathers. So they felt that the Europeans were introducing difficult things.[249]

Despite the cost, and the risk of the permanent deformation of sexual organs, which could also lead to death, the practice was never abandoned, and whether secretly or openly, the practice continued. The main reason for its continuation lay in the social significance it carried. Like male circumcision, it signified transition from childhood to adulthood.[250] For many traditional African societies who practice the rite, rendering daughters unmarriageable was viewed first as "a sinister perversion in itself," and second, as something that would also discredit a family socially.[251] Among the Wagogo or Wakaguru, like some other Bantu societies, an uncircumcised person was/is regarded not only as child but also as a "barbarian."[252] Consequently, such a person risked both physical and psychological isolation. Furthermore, some

---

248. Ndajilo, oral interviews.
249. Cleopa Mwaka, oral interview, 4 July 1997; cf. Philemon Chidosa, oral interviews, 12 and 13 June 1997.
250. Mbiti, *African Religion*, 99.
251. Waller, "They Do the Dictating," 106.
252. Lazaro Ndajilo, oral interviews, 14 and 16 June 1997.

the Wagogo believed at the time that female circumcision could enhance a woman's fertility.[253]

Though this study is confined to the historical situation, it should be pointed out that the debate on female circumcision that raged early in the twentieth century continues within and outside Africa today, and the contribution of African women has been notable. Mercy Amba Oduyoye regards female circumcision as a manifestation of androcentrism both in society and in church, and one (among many issues) that denies women full selfhood. She has observed in her article "Christianity and African Culture" that "it is shockingly humiliating for a woman to be presented with pictures of what happens to some women who for whatever religiocultural reasons have to have their genitals violently remodelled."[254] Musimbi Kanyoro takes a similar view, and argues that the church should work towards the eradication of the practice as part of "mission to women" and that the church should teach "something new about culture and human dignity."[255]

All these scholars make valid points. Two observations should be made though. The first is that while some people (including this writer) believe female circumcision – or "female genital mutilation" (FGM), as some refer to it – to be totally unnecessary, yet it should always be evaluated within the broader context of the resilience of African worldviews. It survives and thrives despite the protest from religious and secular circles in Africa and the West. It is estimated that over 130 million women and girls in some twenty-eight countries in Africa, as well as the Middle East and Asia (and also among immigrant communities in Europe – for example, France[256] – and North America), have undergone some form of circumcision and that at least two million are being circumcised annually. In Dodoma (Ugogo), central Tanzania, it is estimated that some 600,000 women and girls have suffered the consequences of female circumcision.[257] More alarming is the fact that it is not only traditionalists with low levels of education who practise it.

---

253. Wynn Jones, "An Experimental Initiation Camp Held at Ugogo, 1930," October 1932, 2, School of Oriental and African Studies (SOAS) Library, IMC/CBMS, Box 201, File F, 1.

254. Oduyoye, "Christianity and African Culture," 87.

255. Kanyoro, "Thinking Mission in Africa," 228.

256. Hawley, "Circumcision Trials."

257. Uledi, "Wanawake 600,000 waathirika kwa tohara Dodoma."

Christians (Catholic and Protestant) are involved,[258] and nurses and midwives in towns and cities perform the operation.[259] The custom is not dying down.

Second, historical experience indicates that during the era of missions, attempts to legislate against it without securing the understanding and co-operation of the participants and practitioners only served to spark negative reactions from women and men who believed it to be an important rite of passage for women. Whether churches or secular governments (for example, the government of Senegal which has recently banned the practice) can hope for a quick solution or easy victory without the cooperation of those who practice female circumcision remains to be seen.[260] However, positive educational steps could be one better way to deal with the practice without antagonising its believers and practitioners.

Surely, the ending of the practice should not mean the ending of the social function it is believed to fulfil. In every society, from East to West, North to South, there is some form of initiation into adulthood – whether that means passing the age-mark of sixteen (as in some European countries, for example Britain) or something else. Teresia Hinga makes this very point. She states that "whereas the campaign to do away with female circumcision is perfectly legitimate, there is nonetheless a case for a reconstruction of female puberty rites as rites of passage to facilitate the transition of the girl child from childhood to adulthood."[261] In certain parts of Africa, for example Kenya, social practitioners have been able to persuade parents to allow their daughters to be initiated through an alternative rite, "Circumcision through Words."[262] This could be adopted elsewhere.

---

258. Dr Charles Majinge, St Gaspers Hospital, Itigi, Singida province (central Tanzania) cited in Okumu, "Circumcising Girls."
259. Mariamu Mwafissi, Permanent Secretary, Ministry of Health, Tanzania, quoted in Makawia, "More Than 100m Girls."
260. Little, "Senegal Bans Female Circumcision."
261. Hinga, "Christianity and Female Puberty Rites," 169–170.
262. In Kenya, several local non-governmental organizations (NGOs) have taken initiatives involving circumcision through words as an alternative to the incision or excision and, sometimes, infibulation. For example, rural families and Maendeleo ya Wanawake Organization (the Kenyan National Women's Group) have organized *Ntanira na Mugambo* (Circumcision through Words) in eastern and central Kenya since August 1996, in cooperation with an American organization, Program for Appropriate Technology in Health (PATH). In Kisii, Western Kenya, Julkei International Women and Youth Affairs (an NGO) has been involved in educational programmes to introduce *Ogosemia Gwekiare* (a similar alternative rite as *Ntanira*

5.9 Conclusion

An attempt has been made in this chapter to show, first, that having made a declaration that the purpose of education was the conversion of the African, the CMS mission (as most missions) used elementary school education to fulfil that purpose, particularly through literacy training and preaching. Second, it has been noted how, without abandoning its work among adults, the mission redirected it missionary effort to children. Third, it has also been demonstrated, however, that African children and adults had their own personal motives for joining the literacy classes and mission Christianity.

The resilience of such social practices as female circumcision, polygamy, and dance, or "crisis rituals" like sacrifice to the dead in times of misfortunes and rainmaking during drought, have been examined. This chapter has questioned the argument that Africans converted to Christianity because it shattered their worldviews. It supports part of Horton's argument (referred to in section 5.5.2) that Christianity insisted rigidly that converts should conform to its moral code. Yet, it has been shown that Gogo and Kaguru adherents often broke those moral codes, and though they became members of the new faith, they maintained a significant degree of loyalty to their traditional practices and worldview.

This chapter has underlined the fact that even the indigenous teachers themselves taught against traditional practices just as much as CMS missionaries did. They were building their church. But this approach was one that was soon to be characterized by much "policing" of converts. As will be seen in chapter 8, some of the indigenous teachers themselves clashed with CMS missionaries over the very issues that caused conflicts between the mission and ordinary converts. The mission's success in persuading some potential converts and indigenous Christians to part with such social and religious practices for the sake of mission Christianity has not been denied. But such success was only of a limited scale and impact. And at best (or worst), African Christians lived with the nightmare of having neither the freedom to be members of the local communities, and traditional practices, nor a sense of belonging and feeling at home in the church.

---

na *Mugambo*). See Turnbridge, "Alternative Rite Ends Mutilation"; *Daily Nation*, "Kisii Women on Warpath"; Reaves, "Alternative Rite."

The analysis of the catechetical process has indicated that it did not deal adequately with the social and religious aspirations of the potential indigenous converts, as well as the baptized adherents. Perhaps, had enough been done to incorporate their worldview in the Christian teaching before and after baptism, the tension and conflict of loyalty they faced would have been lessened or neutralized. This task could have been tackled best through the catechetical process because the Anglican tradition (like other faith traditions) demands that no one should become a member of the visible local church without baptism, even if they may not understand sufficiently what baptism means to them individually and as part of a wider community. But even if someone had been baptized during their childhood, there existed still a chance for receiving a relevant teaching during the preparations for the rite of confirmation (for those in the Anglican communion and episcopal churches), or something similar in other faith traditions, that initiates baptized Christians into "mature Christians" or into being partakers of the Lord's Supper. Opportunities were there, but they were missed.

This, however, does not diminish the enthusiasm that teachers showed in building their church. What has been observed is that they used the tools available to them, but better ones could have made their task more relevant. The next chapter is a continuation of the role of these teachers. It examines other aspects of their role as the builders of the church in Ugogo and Ukaguru, but it focuses both on the collective as well as individual efforts.

CHAPTER 6

Missionary Contributions of Indigenous Teachers

The previous chapter considered the role of the indigenous teachers, particularly in literacy training, catechesis, and in defending the Christian ideals demanded by mission Christianity. It will be observed that the analysis in chapter 5 was largely on the role of the indigenous agents on the educational front – the process by which the Wagogo and Wakaguru were turned into converts. Although literacy training and preaching roles were not mutually exclusive, the latter, and other non-educational activities of indigenous teachers, were not given sufficient attention there. This chapter analyses the contributions relating to missionary work (which includes preaching), and maintenance of work at the mission stations, either by resident teachers or by those who were recruited from outside – the indigenous missionaries.

The first part considers the nature and frequency of the appointment of the indigenous staff, and some reasons for that. The role of the indigenous Christians as pioneer missionaries and as mission strategists is considered too. A special note is made of the contributions of women as mission workers in their own right and as coworkers with their husbands.

The second part is devoted to a study of some of the leading indigenous staff, mainly in the form of biographical notes. The list of the teachers analysed is selective. It is comprised of the individuals who made significant contributions to the growth of Christianity in Ugogo and Ukaguru, some of whom are still remembered by older Gogo and Kaguru Christians today. In most cases, they are the ones who have also been mentioned frequently in the mission archives and printed sources.

The third and final part of the chapter focuses on the contributions of the indigenous teachers and ordinary Christians in Ugogo and Ukaguru during the First World War and their suffering at that time.

6.1 The Nature of Appointments and Contributions

6.1.1 The Appointment of the Indigenous Staff

As pointed out in chapter 5, administrative tasks deprived CMS missionaries the time needed to carry out extensive and sustained teaching and evangelistic tasks, particularly at the out-schools and out-stations. Their number was small too. In 1900 (at the start of the expansion phase), there were eighteen CMS missionaries (including eight wives) and eighteen indigenous teachers. In 1913 (when the number of out-stations and out-schools had reached 370), the number of CMS missionaries was twenty-one, while that of the indigenous teachers was 211.[1] The rapid multiplication of literacy centres and preaching places demanded such a sharp rise in the number of indigenous staff. Thereafter, the number of indigenous staff remained high, with figures reaching 264 in 1933.[2] So Bishop Peel was right in his observation that: "The burden rests upon the chosen African teacher in charge. He and his assistant are responsible for schools, the inquirers, catechumens and the preaching tours. At intervals the European missionary in charge of the district visits him and works alongside him for a day or two, but the training is self-effort."[3] So much so, that very inexperienced Christians or even catechumens were appointed to serve as preachers, teachers, and missionaries.[4] Testimonies from both outside, non-Christian observers – such as Semgomba Chitemo (a renowned traditional medicine practitioner at Berega) – and insiders – such as Lazaro Ndajilo – emphasize this fact: "They started by using *mwenda* (cloth) to teach people to read. . . . Then they continued, and when they saw that one was doing well, they appointed and said, 'You are now a teacher. You shall be teaching your fellows.'"[5]

---

1. See statistical tables, *PCMS*, 1914, xxii, 62.
2. See statistical table, *PCMS*, 1934, x.
3. *CMR* 63 (March 1912): 164.
4. See statistical tables, *PCMS*, 1901, xxiv; *PCMS*, 1914, xxii, 62; "Usagara-Chigogo Notes III," April 1904, G3 A8/O/1904/31, BUL.
5. Semgomba Chitemo, oral interview, 15 September 1997.

> *Mwita Akiri*: Before you became a teacher, was there no requirement that you should go through some stages before you are appointed . . . ?
>
> *Lazaro Ndajilo*: I was just learning. Just learning. Being taught. Then suddenly I was told, "Tomorrow morning, you will be teaching."[6]

However, oral sources indicate that the local population was involved in the choice of a suitable agent:

> When the missionary and his catechist visited a place, they taught the people, and then they singled out one youth and said, "This young man appears to be a suitable person for teaching you here." "Or, yes, he can read," the people said. Then they appointed such a person.[7]
>
> They sought a local person in a particular area. "Who is a suitable person here?" [they asked]. "That person." So they appointed him and said, "Look after the church."[8]

It must also be added that some of the appointees were people who had been in close contact with CMS missionaries. These included domestic assistants (male and female) – for example, Andrea Mwaka, who worked for Henry Cole in the mid-1880s at Chamuhawi,[9] and Nehemia Uguzi, who assisted Eliza Hodgshon (one of the CMS female missionaries) at Buigiri in the mid-1920s, to name a few.[10] Female CMS missionaries were particularly urged to consider employing girls rather than boys as domestic assistants. It was hoped that this would facilitate the process of monitoring the character of the girls. Some of them could be selected and recruited to become "Bible women" and be used in the evangelization of their fellow countrywomen.[11]

Yet other recruits came from among former slaves who had escaped their captors or been rescued by CMS missionaries, sometimes by paying ransom

---

6. Lazaro Ndajilo, oral interview, 14 June 1997.
7. Nehemia Uguzi, oral interviews, 18 and 19 June 1997.
8. Cleopa Mwaka, oral interview, 4 July 1997.
9. Knox, *Signal on the Mountain*, 148.
10. Nehemia Uguzi, oral interviews, 18 and 19 June 1997.
11. Minutes, EC, 24–25/11/1908, G3 A8/O/1909/1, BUL.""

to the caravan owners. These were then housed at the mission settlement.[12] Additionally, a resolution passed by the CMS mission in July 1905 barred domestic slave owners from baptism or entering mission work. Interestingly, Andrea Kanyanka (to whom reference was made in chapter 5) had thirty slaves he had inherited from his father but was nevertheless recruited by the mission, possibly in 1903, perhaps because he was a headman with influence over one of the villages at Mamboya.

This, however, caused controversy within the mission and necessitated Kanyanka's suspension in 1906, though he was later appointed to work as a missionary to Ugogo.[13] After giving up his slaves, he was reemployed as a missionary to Kongwa district, Ugogo, in 1908.[14] In December 1907, the CMS mission also barred domestic slaves from becoming members of the mission staff unless they obtained freedom papers from the colonial government.[15] For the majority of the appointees, however, the ideal qualities required by the CMS mission was the ability to preach and some kind of moral "uprightness." Each CMS missionary responsible for a station or district chose agents locally, but it was the executive committee of the mission that ratified such appointments.

It should be stressed, however, that in some if not many cases, indigenous Christians had their own motives for becoming teachers, especially during the German colonial era. Honour and pride was one of those motives, as Dan Mbogoni points out: "Evangelists offered quickly to go and preach in the villages because an evangelist felt proud to say, 'I can read. I have been chosen

---

12. Elimerik Mlahagwa, oral interview, 28 June 1997.

13. Parker to Baylis, 28/12/1904, G3 A8/0/1905/20. Parker claimed that Kanyanka had twenty-eight to thirty slaves and was asking for eight rupees as ransom money before giving them up. See also Parker to Baylis, 9/5/1906, G3 A/0/1906/42. Rees defended the mission for employing Kanyanka. Marks of beatings constituted evidence of mistreatment by the owner. (For instance, Laoni, a slave woman held by Mwanamanuka, a Nyamwezi chief at Mamboya, obtained her freedom papers from the Mpwapwa fort in 1903 after showing evidence of mistreatment. See *PCMS*, 1904, 94.) But Rees argued that Kanyanka's slaves did not show signs of mistreatment. See Rees to Baylis, 23/7/1906, G3 A8/0/1906/53, BUL. It is possible CMS missionaries at Mamboya knew Kanyanka had slaves but ignored it because they were interested in employin employing Kanyanka.

14. Minutes, EC, 24–25/11/1908, G3 A8/0/1909/1. This decision revoked the one made earlier that required Kanyanka to make a declaration before a German district officer, renouncing all claim to slaves, which, by 1907, were in the hands of his son Masere. See Minutes, EC, 19–20, 26–27/12/1907, and 13–14/7/1908, G3 A8/0/1908/47, BUL.

15. Minutes, EC, 19-20, 26–27/12/1907, G3 A8/0/1908/12, BUL.

by the white man and located to a place where I can teach others to read.'... The teacher who was being sent became joyful and jubilant, because *he felt honoured*."[16] Exemption from compulsory labour was another motive that also played a part. As referenced in chapter 5, the CMS mission and German colonial administration made an agreement in 1907 over the exemption of Christians from compulsory labour for the government.[17]

Whereas the exemption for Christians in general covered Sundays only, the exemption for teachers covered all days, in order to free them for God's work.[18] This contributed to the readiness of some Gogo and Kaguru people to come forward for mission work. Indigenous Christian appointees worked first as helpers, and then as probationary agents, before being promoted to the ladder of teacher, senior reader, and senior catechist.[19]

The number of preaching places and literacy centres opened determined the frequency of appointments. For example, in the first decade of the expansion phase, record shows that appointments were made as follows: six indigenous agents were recruited in 1900, four in December 1901, ten in July 1902, five in May 1905, two in November 1906, six in 1908, and seven in November 1909.

Appointments were probably made in 1903 and 1904 as well, though sources consulted did not show this. The total figure of forty is not very large, and it is not clear whether these helpers and probationary agents were included in the column headed "Native Christian Lay Agents" in the statistical table for 1909, which has forty-two agents.[20] It is important to remember that by 1913, as indicated above, the number of the indigenous staff working in Ugogo and Ukaguru had risen dramatically to 211. This reflects the pace of the expansion programme and the ever-growing need for indigenous workers.

6.1.2 Indigenous Teachers as Pioneer Missionaries

In 1901 at Mpwapwa, Henry Cole complained that some teachers were "lacking in fervour, zeal and earnestness," and required "daily stirring up."[21] He

---

16. Dan Mbogoni, oral interview, 11 June 1997.
17. See chapter 5.
18. Nehemia Uguzi, oral interviews, 18 and 19 June 1997.
19. Details of these categories will be explored in chapter 8.
20. *PCMS*, 1910, 42.
21. Henry Cole to Baylis, 11/12/1900 G3 A8/0/1901/2, BUL.

nonetheless admitted that the success of the work there was dependent on the life and work of local Christians and teachers. This was particularly important because Cole noted how little impact he and other CMS missionaries had made upon the local people – a fact that has been referred to already in chapter 5. During his second visit to Tanzania, which began in October 1902, Bishop Peel made these remarks to the foreign staff: "One lesson of the yearly deficits seems to me to be: depend less on the European; prepare and send forth the converts."[22] A decade or so later, CMS missionaries acknowledged that "the occupation of so many centres would be impossible were it not for the prevalence of the missionary spirit among the Christians and catechumens. Many of the latter, it is said, give the impression that they regard a readiness to take the Christian message anywhere as a necessary part of the duties of the catechumenate."[23] Cleopa Mwaka confirms that, though some CMS missionaries took part in the preaching of the Word of God outside the station, "the teacher who was assigned to work there [at an out-station] was the one with the roots [that is, primary responsibility]. He had to have commitment to persuade people."[24]

The local factors (considered in chapter 3) forced CMS missionaries to concede that work had to be extended beyond Mpwapwa, Mamboya, and Chamuhawi. Christians and catechumens in Ugogo and Ukaguru were therefore involved in the pioneering work from 1900. Oral informants in Ugogo acknowledge that all other stations in Ugogo owe their existence to the indigenous pioneer missionaries from Mpwapwa and Chamuhawi. The testimonies of Cleopa Mwaka and Elimerik Mlahagwa may be sufficient here:

> You see whenever they opened a school, a few people from Chamuhawi had to be appointed together with the European who was to be in-charge of the [new] location. . . . When Briggs went to Mvumi he was accompanied by people from Chamuhawi. [When] Doulton went to Buigiri, he was accompanied by people from Chamuhawi. They were accompanied by people from Chamuhawi when they went to Kongwa. They were

---

22. Peel to Fox, 22/10/1902, G3 A8/0/1902/32, BUL.
23. *PCMS*, 1914, 61.
24. Cleopa Mwaka, oral interview, 4 July 1997.

sent as special people. . . . There was Yohana Malecela who was appointed to Ihumwa. People like Kanyanka, [at] Nyandwa, was from Chamuhawi. . . . But when the [new] mission [stations] became established, they then started to go outside their stations and "spread themselves."[25]

Elimerik Mlahagwa: The people from Chamuhawi who went to other places. . . . They split in groups, and then the local people in one particular place joined in.

Mwita Akiri: . . . To which places did those people go from here?

Elimerik Mlahagwa: . . . Kongwa, Ibwaga, Mvumi. All the surrounding places were evangelized by people from here.[26]

The account of John Briggs taking with him pioneer indigenous workers (baptized Christian and catechumens) from Mpwapwa to Mvumi is documented in a CMS report.[27] It is possible that some of the people who accompanied CMS missionaries to the new locations were "servants" – that is, domestic assistants. But these pioneers formed the first congregations whenever a new mission stations was started and went to evangelize the local people before local appointees became available.[28] Indeed, some indigenous missionaries from Mpwapwa and Chamuhawi to other stations were in fact originally from Ukaguru – for example, Andrea Lungwa (who moved from Mpwapwa to Mvumi in 1900) and Andrea Kanyanka, who first served at Chamuhawi under Andrea Mwaka from 1908 and later moved to Buigiri.[29]

Towards the end of 1907, the executive committee of the mission resolved that after passing the senior readers' exam, suitable men (not necessarily of the same grade) would be sent to work in areas which had not yet been evangelized. This was a change of policy in the mission. Previously, it was thought that the teachers should not be placed more than about twelve miles from the mission station so that they might be in regular contact with the

---

25. Mwaka, oral interview.
26. Elimerik Mlahagwa, oral interview, 28 June 1997.
27. *PCMS*, 1902, 110.
28. *PCMS*, 1902, 110.
29. Doulton to Baylis, 21/11/1910, G3 A8/0/1910/83, BUL. Capital letters in original.

CMS missionary in charge.[30] It seems that such a change of policy was made because of the increasing missionary zeal among the indigenous Christians which grew by that time. With regard to this new zeal, David Rees wrote:

> Our Christians and catechumens alike may be described in their own expressive way as "having shoes on their feet." Their temper in regard to this, the first work of the Church, may be gauged from their letters. For instance, an only son, whose father is dead, wrote to me thus: "In my heart I have seen that it is better to part with mother and friends than with preaching of the Word of Jesus Christ." Another in a letter said, "I am in this work because I have pledged myself in secret, with a pledge known only to God, to serve Jesus unto death." Their prayers, their cheerful and courageous way of meeting privations and dangers, also testify to their zeal and sincerity.[31]

Significant also to the growth of the missionary spirit among the indigenous Christians was the formation of the Native Missionary Association in 1900.[32] In 1902, this was replaced by the Yearly Conference of Africans[33] (also called African Native Conferences). These were evangelistic conferences that were organized once (and occasionally twice) a year, for each district, specifically for the indigenous Christians and non-Christian people who accepted invitations to attend. CMS missionaries were often present at such conferences, but it was the indigenous female (and male) teachers who became the key speakers. Some of the conferences took place at Mamboya in 1902,[34] 1903, and 1908, with the average attendance reaching between two hundred and 250.[35] At Mvumi in Ugogo, an evangelistic conference took place in April 1907 after which seventy-six people were admitted as inquirers. Andrea Mwaka and Yohana Malecela were the principal indigenous speakers.[36]

---

30. Minutes, EC, 19–20, 26–27/12/1907, G3 A8/0/1908/12, BUL.
31. *PCMS*, 1913, 55.
32. Minutes, EC, 6/4/1900, G3 A8/0/1900/20, BUL.
33. Minutes, EC, 14 & 15/7/1902, G3 A8/0/1902/24, BUL.
34. Berega Logbook, No. 51, entry for April 1902, MH.
35. Berega Logbook, No. 51, entry for 3 April 1908, MH.
36. Briggs to Baylis, 17/6/1907, G3 A8/0/1907/46, BUL.

Missionary Contributions of Indigenous Teachers 179

The involvement of the Kaguru Christians in the pioneering work was not different from that of the Wagogo. Baptized Christians and catechumens went from Mamboya to occupy various new places with CMS missionaries. Then from those stations, men and women started to spread the Christian message through preaching and teaching to places near and far. Thomas Mlahagwa (father of Isaka, an informant from Berega) first served as a teacher at Mwandi north of Berega in 1911. Later (at a time Isaka could not remember, but certainly before the First World War), he became one of the earliest Kaguru missionaries to Unguu. He served at Sagasa alongside Stephano Machite. Thomas Mlahagwa and Sephano Machite were not the only Kaguru missionaries to Unguu. Others included Filipo Masingisa of Mamboya (father of Yusufu Masingisa, an informant from Mamboya) and Joshua Sagumo. These served at Tunguli. Yeremia Mlemwa served at Gingi, and Musa Malanda was at Songe.[37] Joshua Mkwama – another early Kaguru pioneer missionary to Unguu – served at Lwande.[38]

Unguu borders the UMCA sphere in Uzigua, north of Bokwa. Muslims were (and are still) the majority population there, as well as in Uzigua.[39] The challenge posed by Islam to the UMCA and German Lutheran missions operating along the coast was a subject that attracted considerable attention in mission reports from Tanzania to parent societies in Europe.[40] Even letters written by the indigenous staff in these missions exhibited the same attitude. From Kwa Maizi in the Tanga region, Peter Limo, an indigenous priest in the UMCA sphere, wrote in 1922: "We have a very great hindrance here now in our work. The Mohammedans are spreading a great deal, and frightens people that the Last Day is near at hand so they must not send their children to the Mission schools, so in some places our schools are getting very low, but we must fight them."[41] Samwel Sehoza (another priest in the UMCA sphere) also

---

37. Yusufu Masingisa, oral interviews, 16 September 1997.
38. Isaka Mlahagwa, oral interview, 14 September 1997. Joshua Mkwama and Daniel Makamba served also at Berega itself. At the same time, they learned the skills of operating the circumcision initiates under Dr Edward Baxter. When Baxter left in 1913, Joshua Mkwama and Daniel Makamba took over his job and provided medical treatment to the Wakaguru at Berega and Mamboya. They worked alone for years before Dr Wallace arrived at Berega in the early 1930s.
39. Isaka Mlahagwa, oral interview, 14 September 1997.
40. For details, see Becker, "Material," 39–42; Raum, "German East Africa," 166–167.
41. P. Limo to Travers, 2/4/1922, *Letters from Africans*, Box A.5, A.6, RHL.

complained about the "unrestricted lifestyle which the Mohammedans lived" before Christians.[42] It is evident that the indigenous teachers and priests, who perhaps grew up and later worked among the Muslims, found it hard to present the Christian message to them. Surely, that task must have been even harder for the indigenous missionaries from Ukaguru who had no sustained contact with Muslims. They hardly made any converts. The following account by David Rees and Ernest Doulton, written in 1913, may give the impression that the work of the schools in the Bokwa area in Unguu progressed well: "One most hopeful feature of the Mohammedanism of Bokwa is that, for the most part, parents do not prevent their children from attending school or church, so that we have most of the young life of the country under the influence of the Gospel three or four times a week."[43] It was likely that the parents had that attitude because the government exempted youths that attended school from poll tax. It was only the CMS mission that had schools there at this time. Equally relevant was the desire for parents to see their children acquire reading skills. However, little progress was made among adults themselves.

In the same report quoted above, Rees and Doulton could not hide their despair:

> Then Islam is up in arms, and parents and husbands vent their ire in beatings, refusals of food, taunts of "Islam up and Christianity down," "Children of swine," etc. . . . Should an opportunity occur of speaking to them, our message is met by a stolidity so freezing as either to depress the speaker or to arouse the natural man in him to desire to shake them up. The bent white-capped head, the expressionless face, give them a statue-like appearance. They pretend not to understand the messenger of the Cross although he speaks to them in a language they daily use.[44]

Bokwa (a name for both an area in Unguu and an out-station) and Muhalala – then the most westward out-station in Ugogo, which temporarily became a mission station in January 1921, before the station headquarters

---

42. S. Sehoza to Travers, 30/9/1922, *Letters from Africans*, Box A.5, A.6, RHL.
43. D. J. Rees and E. W. Doulton, RUUM, 1913, in *CMR* 65 (September 1914): 552.
44. *CMR* 65 (September 1914): 552.

moved to Kilimatinde in 1922[45] – were described by Bishop Peel as "really strategic posts of the first importance to us in the struggle with Islam."[46] But unlike Muhalala and Kilimatinde, where considerable progress was made by 1933,[47] Bokwa didn't bear much fruit. The First World War increased the predicament of the missionary work in Unguu. Details of the arrest of the teachers there will be given later. Meanwhile, it should be pointed out that the Kaguru missionaries, only months after the war broke out, were among the first in the entire country to be captured by the German army. The difficult process of the post-war readjustment did not take off well either.

Referring to the work done by his father and other Kaguru missionaries, Isaka Mlahagwa says, "After the war, they stayed in Unguu in 1919, 1920 and 1921, and then it seemed that there were no people in church. It was only the teachers' wives and children who were going to church."[48] Consequently, most Kaguru workers were forced to return to Ukaguru, and many of the churches were closed.[49]

Yet, the seed of the Christian message sown by the teachers never died. Missionary work resumed in Unguu, and later it was that place that bred several pioneer missionaries to western Tanzania starting in the mid-1930s. This included Yohana Omari Boto – a Muslim convert who later became the first indigenous bishop in the Anglican Church of Tanzania in 1955 and served as an assistant bishop in the historical DCT until his death in 1963.[50] He was the second African to be appointed bishop in Tanzania.[51] Men such as Haruni Mbega and Daudi Muhando, whose life and work will be considered later, were also from Unguu.

---

45. *PCMS*, 1922, 35;*ARCCMS*, 1923, xxix. Original work at Muhalala began in 1911. The station headquarters was moved to Kilimatinde (fourteen miles away) because that is where Nikodemo, the local chief, lived. See "Record of Christians, Catechumens and Inquirers, CMS Muhalala, Kilimatinde District, 1921–1952," MH.

46. *CMR* 65 (September 1914): 545.

47. By 1933, Kilimatinde district had twelve out-stations. The number increased to seventy-three in 1952. "Record of Christians, Catechumens and Inquirers, CMS Muhalala, Kilimatinde District, 1921–1952," 1–6, MH.

48. Isaka Mlahagwa, oral interview, 14 September 1997.

49. Mlahagwa, oral interview; Gresford Chitemo, "Historia Fupi ya Kanisa," 1.

50. Mary Lawrence Chiduo &and Joyce Maiko Mweli (daughters of the late bishop Yohana Omari Boto), oral interview, 9/9/ September 1997.

51. Laurian Rugambwa (later a cardinal), a Catholic from north-western Tanzania, was the first indigenous bishop in Tanzania. See Sahlberg, *From Krapf to Rugambwa*, 186.

6.1.3 Teachers' Wives as Co-Pioneers

So far, the general account of the pioneer indigenous missionaries given above has concentrated on male missionaries. Since many teachers and missionaries were married, it is befitting that the contribution of their wives as co-pioneers be acknowledged too. This reconstruction of the role of women is nonetheless limited by the dearth of sources on women in the CMS mission in general (as in other missions), and about the contribution of teachers' wives in particular.[52] CMS archives and published sources are almost silent about women's contribution to the mission work in Ugogo and Ukaguru. However, even with meagre sources available, it is still possible to have an insight into the role of indigenous women that goes beyond their teaching at elementary and boarding schools, which was highlighted earlier in chapter 5.

Indigenous married women played an important role in the mission enterprise as coworkers with their husbands who were employed as church teachers. With their husbands, they laboured for the conversion of their fellow countrywomen and men. Yet teachers' wives, just like the wives of the CMS missionaries, were not regarded officially as members of the mission staff. Moreover, they were not paid for their work. And, in this regard, Dana Robert makes a point that, "like all caricatures, those of the exhausted wife and the frustrated old maid carry some truth: the underlying message of the stereotypes is that missionary women have been perceived as marginal to the central tasks of mission."[53] The reality, Robert observes, was different. She makes this point specifically about American women missionaries, yet her observation has wider application.

In Ugogo and Ukaguru, the reality was that the influence of the teachers' wives upon the local women in distant places where their husbands were posted made the difference. This was acknowledged in the annual letters written by CMS missionaries in Ugogo and Ukaguru, though of course not

---

52. Cf. For instance, Esther Mombo has observed similar problems about the Abaluyia Quaker women converts. The patriarchal nature of Western missions and African societies are some of the reasons for this. See Mombo, *Abaluyia Women*, 5. In addition to this, David Henige notes that there has been a tendency among researchers to ignore women as informants. See Henige, *Oral Historiography*, 48.

53. Robert, *American Women in Mission*, xvii.

as frequently as the men's contributions.⁵⁴ Such letters were cited in the CMS reports and periodicals:

> The Christian women are giving good evidence of their desire to help in the good work, and some of them are conducting a women's school, to which they willingly give up a great deal of their time, and in the out-stations it has been seen that the wives of the Christian teachers are having a great influence with the women.⁵⁵

At Mwandi, north of Berega in Ukaguru, Penina, the wife of Haruni Mbega became her husband's official church assistant, technically known in the CMS mission as "helper." Penina and Haruni Mbega led a thriving congregation, with numbers at Sunday morning worship sometimes reaching 230.⁵⁶ In Ugogo, Esta Nyembela (the daughter of Joshua Mate who was the first warden of the Buigiri girls' boarding school in 1926) recalls how her mother, Hagulwa, often preached at Chilungu village and surprised many, not least the men, with her courage.⁵⁷ When Joshua Mate died, probably in 1927, he was succeeded by Elieza Balisidya, a Kaguru who had been working as missionary at Ibwaga, near Kongwa. His wife Rebeka shared the job with him. Cleopa Mwaka described Rebeka and Elieza as "good pair." He adds:

> Then they started a girls' boarding school at Buigiri. They brought in Joshua Hunya, or Joshua Mate. He was the patron, and his wife was the matron. . . . But Joshua died later, and Elieza Balisidya succeeded him. Balisidya arrived to work there with Rebeka his wife. They took over the job until when they [CMS missionaries] said, "There is no male teacher at this school, so it can't continue. Let them go to Briggs" [at Mvumi] because he was male.⁵⁸

Cleopa Mwaka's testimony is worth commenting on further. On the succession of Mate by Balisidya, and the transfer of the school, his testimony is

---

54. *PCMS*, 1914, 61.
55. *CMR*, 65 (September 1914): 551.
56. *CMR*, 63 (March 1912): 159.
57. Esta Nyembela, oral interview, 10 June 1997.
58. Cleopa Mwaka, oral interview, 4 July 1997.

supported by that of Esta Chali – a former pupil at the school from 1928.[59] Again, on the transfer of the school for lack of a male CMS missionary, his testimony is supported by published CMS sources. Buigiri had no male CMS missionary from 1927 until 1931. In 1929, there were four CMS women missionaries: Amy Gelding, Eliza Hodgshon, Ada Betteridge, and Ellen Simpson.[60] The school was transferred to Mvumi in 1930, and some of the women CMS missionaries moved there.[61]

Cleopa Mwaka's testimony also gives an insight into the patriarchy in the CMS mission which did not serve CMS female workers well nor pay attention to the educational development of African girls until later in the 1920s. On this point, Hastings has noted that "a largely male-dominated missionary church encountered a largely male-dominated traditional Africa. Two forms of patriarchy appeared to fit together well enough."[62] For example, as stated earlier in chapter 3, with the exception of the Valley Church at Mamboya station, where Rose Colsey and Emily Spriggs were "theoretically" in charge since its inception in 1894 until at least 1900,[63] CMS women missionaries could not take full charge of a station or superintend a district. Esta Chali says John Briggs visited the Buigiri school regularly to teach the Bible "at eleven o'clock."[64] Briggs may have suggested the school be moved to Mvumi where he lived in order to relieve him of the frequent trips to Buigiri.

When Buigiri girls' boarding school was moved to Mvumi, both Balisidya and his wife Rebeka moved too and continued with their service. Prior to moving to Buigiri, Rebeka and Elieza worked hand in hand in pioneering evangelistic work in "the large, populous and as yet little influenced country of Chelwe,"[65] where Chief Timotheo Makanyaga was the headman at the time and had been acting as a teacher too. Lazaro Ndajilo himself told this writer how his wife, Foibe, taught at the *Shule ya Saa Nane* (two-o'clock school) with him at Mpalanga and Mwitikila (part of Mvumi district) where they pioneered

---

59. Esta Chali, oral interview, 26 June 1997.
60. *ARCCMS*, 1930, xxix.
61. *ARCCMS*, 1931, xxix; *ARCCMS*, 1932, xxix.
62. Hastings, "Were Women a Special Case??," 110.
63. Rees to Baylis 10/4/1900, G3 A8/0/1900/19, BUL.
64. Esta Chali, oral interview, 26 June 1997.
65. *CMR* 63 (March 1912): 159.

evangelistic work in the late 1920s and early 1930s. As a gifted singer, Foibe often led people to sing traditional Gogo songs during Sunday worship.[66]

This female factor (of wives as coworkers with men) in the pioneering stages of the mission work is often neglected in African or Western mission historiography.[67] Yet, very often it was the teacher's wife and children who bore the wrath of the ferocious conditions of distant out-stations and the isolation from members of the family. It was nothing like the "luxury" of working in the Ujamaa villages nowadays in Tanzania where up to a thousand families may live in an area less than two square miles. In the past, in many of the villages, the teacher's wife (whether she had some knowledge of reading and writing or none) became the first member of the local out-school and the local congregation (with her school-age children) and, by that example, encouraged other women and children to join.[68] This facilitated greatly the pioneering work among women in distant new places.

6.1.4 The Contribution of Bible women

Besides the teachers' wives who volunteered to work of their own accord, there was another category of indigenous women who received slightly better recognition in the CMS mission. It is interesting that while male indigenous workers were referred to as "teachers," their female counterparts were often called "Bible women." It was these indigenous women workers (in most cases with CMS women missionaries) who were entrusted with the indomitable task of converting the Gogo and Kaguru women by preaching to them and teaching them the Bible. The task was challenging because Gogo and Kaguru women were by no means easy to draw into mission Christianity. In 1904, Arthur Wood, who was based at Itumba from 1900, described the local women there as "solidly indifferent to religious impressions" and observed that even when they did come forward for teaching (as was the case at Chief Ngiga's village), their eagerness never showed up and attendance was poor.[69]

---

66. Lazaro Ndajilo, interviews, 14 and 16 June 1997.
67. Hastings, "Were Women a Special Case??," 110.
68. Lazaro Ndajilo, oral interviews, 14 and 16 June 1997.
69. "Usagara-Chigogo Notes [III]," April 1904, G3 A8/O/1904/31, BUL.

In 1910, John Briggs complained at Mvumi, in Ugogo, observing that women were clinging "tenaciously to traditional customs, ornaments and so on."[70]

Though this was a general trend, it has to be emphasized that the response of women to mission Christianity varied from place to place, and that in some places, women responded better to mission Christianity than men. In his review of the work at Mpwapwa (where he was in charge) in 1902, Henry Cole praised women but described men as a "hopeless set."[71] His description could have been based on the fact that shortly before writing, he had just baptized six adults – five women and a man. Mpwapwa men, as those of other stations and out-stations in the mission, were inclined to be more concerned with wealth, in the form of cattle, and the social and economic power that ensued from it.[72] The manner in which the statistical evidence was compiled makes it difficult to estimate the percentage of men and women converts in the mission.[73] But it may be pointed out that the majority of women converts in Ugogo and Ukaguru came into mission as the result of the work of the Bible women, in conjunction with the CMS women missionaries.

At Buigiri, in 1906, there was Sechelela, the Bible woman. A CMS woman missionary described her influence among the local women as "wonderful."[74] In 1909, Viktoria was recruited officially as a Bible woman and served at Mamboya. Apart from being a Bible teacher, she was also part of the team of women (including CMS women missionaries) who visited the surrounding villages and was "a great help" to CMS missionaries.[75] At Itumba, indigenous women (especially those at Kishambo whom Wood described as "mothers of Israel")[76] – namely, Mariamu (probably the one who moved to Kongwa as a missionary and married teacher Zakaria Malogo of Chamuhawi, about 1906),[77] Lea, Damari and Roda – were already at work in 1903, and their influence was significant. Early in 1904, Mariamu's influence was already being "felt in all villages" where mission work was being undertaken within the Itumba

---

70. Briggs to Baylis, 29/1/1910, G3 A8/O/1910/24, BUL.
71. Henry Cole to Baylis, 23/10/1902, G3 A8/O/1902/29, BUL.
72. Philemon Chidosa, oral interviews, 12 and 13 June 1997.
73. See appendix 1 for details.
74. *PCMS*, 1907, 78.
75. RUUM, 1909, G3 A8/O/1910/40, BUL.
76. "Usagara-Chigogo Notes II," typescript, December 1903, G3 A8/O/1904/28, BUL.
77. Kongwa Logbook, No. 41, 26 December 1904 - April 1950, MH.

district – at Itumba station itself, at Kishambo (its major out-station at the time), and at Ikwamba.[78] Mariamu was based at Kishambo, where she taught the Bible, preached the word of God, and conducted visits to neighbouring villages (possibly including Kisitwi, Kilugu, Kipala, and Unyawo, where church buildings had been erected by the end of 1903).[79]

Mariamu's ministry was focused upon women, but it was by no means confined to that group alone. On one occasion when she was speaking to women at Kishambo, men assembled too. Arthur Wood recalled how the men "seemed decidedly more interested in what she said than the gentler [female sex]. It was a startling thing to them to hear a female of their own tribe preaching."[80] Mariamu's influence continued years after the CMS mission had become a diocese in 1927. In 1941, Bishop Chambers paid tribute to her as a missionary to Ugogo and one of the leading Bible women there. He wrote: "Mariamu our faithful M.U. [Mothers' Union] member and Bible woman, is doing a wonderful work among women. Already some Moslems are worshipping with us because of her friendship and teaching."[81] It is unfortunate that apart from such statements about the work of Mariamu, no data exists that would be sufficient for her life history to be fully reconstructed.

Reference has been made already to the Yearly Conference of Africans or African Native Conference. During these annual conferences, women teachers helped their fellow women, and likewise, men spoke to their fellow men. At the Mamboya conference in August 1903, Mariamu taught Christian life. There were three other indigenous Christian women who also took part in Bible teaching: Yulia, wife of Yeremia Senyagwa of Mamboya, and Persisi. The other Bible woman present was only referred to by Maria Ackerman (a CMS woman missionary at Mamboya) as a "woman of Itumba."[82]

6.1.5 Indigenous Teachers as Mission Strategists

So far, consideration has been made of the appointment of indigenous workers and their role as pioneer missionaries. The contribution of the teachers'

---

78. "Usagara-Chigogo Notes I," typescript, September 1903, G3 A8/0/1903/40, BUL.
79. "Usagara-Chigogo Notes I."
80. "Usagara-Chigogo Notes I."
81. *CTDL*, no. 44 (July 1941): 5.
82. "Usagara-Chigogo Notes I," typescript, September 1903, G3 A8/0/1903/40, BUL.

wives and those known then as Bible women has been noted too. Attention should now be given to the role played by the teachers in missionary strategy. Once in their respective locations, the teachers were involved in making strategic missionary decisions about church growth. This happened even in places where CMS missionaries were stationed. But it was during the absence of CMS missionaries that the indigenous teachers made initiatives that bore what might be described as "spectacular" results. In 1906, when Rees had returned from an extended holiday, he acknowledged the good work done in his absence: "After an absence of 20 months the work at Berega has much impressed me. The teachers seem aggressive and much capable. Judging by the number that came to be taught at the centre and out-schools the people seem to be at last responding to the efforts made in their behalf."[83] It was this absence that was later alluded to in a CMS global annual report: "In the Berega district, during the absence of the missionary, the African teachers of *their own initiative* assembled the leading chiefs and pointed out to them the inestimable value of the Gospel, with the result that the attendance at the station schools trebled, and the Sunday congregations became so large that crowds were obliged to sit outside the church."[84] Information published in the CMS reports was largely based on the letters written by CMS missionaries working overseas. At the time when the promotion of the image of the Western missionary as the sole labourer was almost the norm, such tributes to the indigenous workers as quoted above must have been hard-earned. Commenting on the work of indigenous teachers in the out-stations, David Deeks wrote, "This out-station work, as well as the work of itinerating, have been done almost entirely by Native Teachers during the past year [1908]. Owing to pressure of work I have only been able to make a few tours."[85] The 1908 CMS annual report noted:

> One missionary writes of "the noble band of native workers rallying around" him; another says he has never met with more

---

83. Berega Logbook, No. 51, entry for August 1906, MH.

84. *PCMS*, 1909, 57, 58; cf. Briggs to Baylis, 16/7/1903, G3 A8/0/1903/32, BUL. Briggs was absent from Mvumi for two months visiting Kilimatinde villages, and the mission station church was left in the care of an unnamed indigenous teacher.

85. Deeks to Baylis, annual letter, 29/11/1909, G3 A8/0/1910/10, BUL.

faithful men than the teachers working with him;[86] and a third, the Rev. D. J. Rees, of Kongwa, writes: – "Of the zeal of the five native teachers, who have been *indispensable factors* in the working of the out-schools, it is impossible to speak too highly. Daily at the nearer centres, and at week-ends at those more distant, have these humble and loveable *fellow-workers* plodded for the highest good of their heathen neighbours, encountering fierce sun, rain, flood streams, and at times even beasts – and all so good-temperedly. In their work, they are marked by their patience as by their earnestness."[87] Never shall I forget a personal talk which took place on the path between a teacher and the aged head of the teaching centre, whom we met on our return home, and who had not been present that day. The concise, intelligent, illustrated elucidation of the Way of salvation was wonderful. The trembling, half-blinded old man seemed to take the message in.[88]

Not only did Rees pay a warm tribute to the indigenous teachers, he went on to describe them as "indispensable factors" and "loveable fellow workers." This shows how highly he regarded their contribution to the mission work. Rees might have been prompted to pay such high tribute because, by 1906 (only two years after the opening of Kongwa as a mission station), Kongwa had seventeen out-schools with 634 scholars – the second highest figure in the entire mission (after Berega which had 692 scholars in eighteen out-schools).[89]

Strategic decisions were being made in Ukaguru as well. In 1907, Maria Ackerman and Arthur Wood retired from Nyangala and Itumba stations, respectively.[90] Work did not cease after their departure. But since a place acquired its status as a station only if a CMS missionary or an ordained African resided there (and at this point there were no indigenous clergy yet), the departure of Ackerman and Wood led to the demotion of Nyangala and

---

86. *PCMS*, 1909, 57.
87. J. D. Rees quoted in PCMS, 1909, 57–58.
88. *PCMS*, 1909, 58. Emphasis added.
89. See statistical table, *PCMS*, 1907, 78.
90. Minutes, EC, 19-20, 26-27/12/1907, G3 A8/0/1908/12, BUL.

Itumba to the status of out-stations.[91] Indigenous teachers from Mamboya continued to visit Nyangala in turn, but only for holding Sunday services once a fortnight. However, Nyangala Christians undertook to minister to themselves every other Sunday. They also carried out limited teaching for scholars at the local out-school. This shows that some Christians realized that the survival of the church could not depend entirely on the CMS missionaries nor on the visiting African teachers.

It should be acknowledged though that the number of Christians went down from thirty in 1906 to eighteen in 1907. The number of scholars decreased, too, but only slightly, from 337 in 1906 to 313 in 1907.[92] This may reflect the vibrations felt at the time of adjustment. Nyangala, now an out-station, no longer featured in the mission yearly statistical table from 1908 onwards. It is therefore difficult to assess the performance during the years that followed. Even so, Nyangala hardly lost all its Christians and scholars. It is likely that some joined other congregations within the neighbouring Mamboya district. Evidence shows that after the Mamboya teachers had ceased visiting Nyangala, Nyangala catechumens continued to travel to Mamboya (some ten miles each way) for their preparatory classes each Wednesday.[93]

The demotion of Itumba to the status of an out-station has been mentioned already, and like Nyangala, it was visited by teachers from Mamboya every fortnight. However, unlike Nyangala, somehow Itumba Christians lacked the self-motivation showed at Nyangala, and given the difficulties of climbing steep Itumba mountains (with peaks up to seven thousand feet above seal level), Mamboya teachers probably gave up early. By 1910, the catechetical classes were no longer running,[94] and Mamboya teachers became convinced that work in Itumba would not be easily revived. But that was not the end.

As missionary strategists, these teachers advised CMS missionaries that fresh work should be started elsewhere. They recommended Ngh'olongwa village, and the advice was accepted.[95] This was not the first time an old mission

---

91. RUUM, 1907, MS, G3 A8/0/1908/24, BUL; *PCMS*, 1908, 60.
92. See statistical tables, *PCMS*, 1907, 78; *PCMS*, 1908, 62.
93. Kate Pickthall to Baylis, annual letter, 9/11/1910, G3 A8/0/1910/85, BUL.
94. Pickthall to Baylis.
95. Spriggs to Baylis, annual letter, 31/10/1910, G3 A8/0/1910/86, BUL.

station had been abandoned altogether in the CMS mission. When Mpwapwa station was closed in August 1906 (as was noted in chapter 5), Christians dispersed to Kiboriani and Kongwa stations[96] The practice of abandoning old places in favour of new ones was therefore a familiar feature of mission work in Ugogo and Ukaguru. But it required discernment and wisdom. Indigenous teachers and missionaries were often better placed to assess and judge the situation than their foreign colleagues. In most cases, their judgement paid off, and this is illustrated by the progress made after the abandonment of Itumba.

Besides Ngh'olongwa (the first out-station after the "abandonment"), Lukando, at Chief Mwiyowela's, was started too. This was in 1911. Lukando was served by Yohana Msulwa, Zakaria Mwesongo, and Zakaria Mpunga. Expansion continued in 1912 with the opening of other out-stations at Ikwamba and Mtega, Chief Mng'ong'o's and Chief Chiselema's, respectively. Yeremia Mejugi served at Ikwamba, while Mtega was served by Marko Mtita. In 1913, Marko Mtita left Mtega to serve at the new out-station of Nongwe at Chief Chikonga Mkungile's. In the same year, Ngh'ongh'o at Chief Mhombwe's was started, too, and was served by Lameki Masika.[97]

This pattern continued a decade or so later. In 1924 another out-station was started at Chagongwe (at Chief Mkasanga's) with Lameki Maiwe as its teacher.[98] The Mamboya teachers – though themselves unaware of the implications of their decision to advise against the continuation of work at Itumba station – nonetheless made a significant move that may be relevant for missions at all times: sometimes, the only way to bring new work to birth and move forward is to let the "old" and the dying die.

6.1.6 Indigenous Teachers as Local Church Leaders

Indigenous teachers and missionaries were not only pioneers and strategists. They also sustained the work in the places where they worked, and this in their capacity as leaders. Perhaps the example of women should be sufficient to illustrate the contribution of the indigenous teachers in local church leadership. As in most churches of Anglican origin, each station in the CMS mission had a church council (known in Tanzania today as a "council of elders") elected

---

96. Rees to Baylis, 3/8/1906, G3 A8/0/1906/54, BUL; *PCMS*, 1907, 77.
97. Gresford Chitemo, "Historia Fupi ya Kanisa," 2.
98. Chitemo, 2.

by the local congregation. As was indicated in the introductory chapter of this work, this study is not about church structures and how they functioned; however, some of these structures should be mentioned in connection with the analysis of the role of indigenous women as leaders. A local council of elders (at the level of the congregational or out-station) was chaired by a teacher. The council's task was to implement decisions relating to missionary and maintenance work, and this included the raising of the necessary funds for the task. Mariamu (of Itumba) and Damari Sagatwa (about whom more shall be said below) were members of the church council at Itumba in 1906, together with Damari's husband Nuhu Sagatwa and two other men (both identified in the sources by the name Danieli).[99] In the same year, Nyangala also had female members in its church council, namely Mariamu and Helina, with Barnaba, Petro, and Isaka as their male colleagues.[100] At Kongwa, in 1921, Esta Mabruki, Mary, and Yulia represented their church to the Kongwa district (parish) council, alongside male colleagues Musa Fungo, Madari Mulutu, Benyamini, Haruni, and Atanasio. Female representatives from Chamuhawi were Marita,[101] Susana, Mariamu,[102] and Raheli, with their male colleagues Edward Madimilo, Timotheo Makanyaga, and Reubeni.

Apart from participating in the general church councils, women also served on the "special" bishop's council – the body responsible for church discipline in each district. The disciplinary matters that were dealt with in the bishop's council related mainly to issues of morality facing individual converts and teachers. The council met twice a year or at the chairman's discretion.[103] In most cases, and in the case of offences requiring "severe" punishment, the bishop's approval was sought before a decision could be implemented. Members of the bishop's council came from various stations, and these were often teachers (male or female), as well as "ordinary" church members.

In May 1911, Leah from Itumba, Viktoria from Mamboya, and Penina (whose station of origin is unfortunately not identified in the source material) were the female members of the bishop's council in Ukaguru. The other six

---

99. Itumba Logbook, No. 53, January 20–February 1912, MH.
100. Nyangala Logbook, No. 66, 1901–January 1914, MH.
101. This could be Marita the wife of Andrea Mwaka.
102. Possibly this was Mariamu Malogo.
103. Minutes, EC, 6–7/6/1901, G3 A8/0/1901/25, BUL.

council members were men.¹⁰⁴ In April 1914, the bishop's council had the following female members: Viktoria and Salama (Mamboya), Naomi (Berega), and Rebeka (Itumba). Seven other members were male (four Africans from various stations and two CMS missionaries).¹⁰⁵

The fact that indigenous women leaders were elected by their fellow church members to serve on a panel of "judges," deciding the fate not only of women but of men too, demonstrates that they had leadership gifts that could not be overlooked. Perhaps, as Rose Ampofo has noted in her article "The Contribution of Women to Church Growth and Development in Africa: The Case of the Presbyterian Church in Ghana," the problem was the limited visibility and recognition of women's contribution and not the absence of it.¹⁰⁶ The significance of this contribution is even more meaningful if viewed from the background of the period when it was happening – a time when one might (falsely) think that the African woman's place was in the kitchen!

6.2 Biographical Notes of Some Indigenous Teachers and Missionaries

The outline of the contributions of the indigenous teachers carried out in section 6.1 is not exhaustive. However, in addition to the educational contributions dealt with mainly in chapter 5, it highlights other areas in which the indigenous contribution became significant for the expansion process. But since this has been only a general survey, it is better now to examine the specific contributions of some of the leading indigenous teachers and missionaries who played key roles in the expansion of Christianity in Ugogo and Ukaguru. Since little has been documented about the life history of these men and women, this analysis takes the form of biographical notes. The availability of sources about the life and work of each person has partly determined the extent of the information presented here.

---

104. Berega Logbook, No. 51, MH.
105. Mamboya Logbook, No. 53, 1901–January 1930, MH.
106. Ampofo, "Contribution of Women," 235.

6.2.1 Damari Sagatwa: "A Maidservant of God"

On numerous occasions indigenous women workers served as missionaries in distant places just as some of their male colleagues. The service of Mariamu, a Bible woman and one of the Kaguru missionaries to Ugogo who later married Zakaria Malogo, has already been mentioned. But there was another Kaguru Bible woman and missionary about whom little is known today in Ugogo and Ukaguru. This is Damari Vigowa Sagatwa, whose contribution in the educational sphere was mentioned in chapter 5 and who has been referred to above as one of the indigenous women who served as leaders in Ugogo and Ukaguru during the period under review.

Damari was perhaps the most outstanding of all Bible women in the entire CMS mission in central Tanzania during her time. Damari was born in 1875 at Mamboya and was baptized there as an adult in 1902 by David Rees.[107] Her marriage to a church teacher, Nuhu Sagatwa, took place in 1903.[108] Both Damari and Nuhu served first at Mamboya before being sent as missionaries to Itumba from 1903 to 1906, to serve not only among the Kaguru but also the Masai and Kamba who were among the local inhabitants. Later, they returned to Mamboya. In 1911 she and her husband were sent again as missionaries, this time to Nyangala – one of the three major stations started in Ukaguru in 1900. They served there until 1914 when the First World War broke out. This forced them to return to Mamboya once again.

Damari's other role, as an elementary school teacher, especially at Mpwapwa, was referred to in the previous chapter. What was not mentioned there was the fact that her involvement in school work began at Itumba in Ukaguru long before she and her husband became missionaries to Ugogo in 1921.[109] In 1921, Damari and her husband went to serve as missionaries at Ngh'ambi in Ugogo (over one hundred miles from Mamboya). As in the previous places where she served, Damari continued with her role as a Bible

---

107. *Upanga wa Roho* 8, no. 2 (February 1961): 5, MH; Itumba Logbook, No. 53, MH. In this logbook, 2 April is given as the date of baptism but another source (Berega Logbook, No. 51) has 2 March as Damari's day of baptism at Mamboya, where she was born. Though the month of baptism may not be clear, both sources agree that Damari was baptized in 1902 and that David Rees baptized her.

108. Nuhu Sagatwa, a Masai, was originally from Berega. He first worked as a porter to CMS missionaries before being enrolled for church work. See Philemon Mukuchu, oral interview, Kilosa, 11 September 1997.

109. "Usagara-Chigogo Notes II," typescript, December 1903, G3 A8/O/1904/28, BUL.

woman and taught adults reading and writing. She also taught pre-baptism classes for hearers and catechumens.

It was the tragic death of Nuhu, her husband and missionary colleague, in 1927 that prompted her transfer from Ngh'ambi to Mpwapwa (which, though closed in 1906, had been reopened in 1921).[110] At Mpwapwa, this widowed missionary and Bible teacher continued to work as an evangelist during which she made regular visits to the villages around Mpwapwa. Apart from the ministry of evangelization, Damari was also involved in leading Sunday worship services between 1927 and March 1936.[111] She was the first indigenous female teacher at the Mpwapwa school (Vingh'awe) and was particularly responsible for the younger children in standard 1 and 2.[112] As noted in chapter 5, this was common in many schools. In 1933, her indigenous male colleagues at the school were Yonathan Songola, Yuda, and Gamalieli.[113] Damari's ministry as a Bible woman and missionary continued beyond the period under review in this study. Some details of this have been given in appendix 3, under photograph 3.

She is remembered today at Mpwapwa not only as a prominent Bible woman and missionary but also as one who introduced the message of the East African revival movement, which she experienced herself while working in western and northwestern Tanzania. The revival originated from Rwanda early in the 1930s and spread to Uganda and later to Kenya and Tanzania. As noted in chapter 1, a detailed account of the revival movement would require a separate study, but it may be sufficient to point out here that it emphasized the centrality of the theology of personal repentance and forgiveness and public confession of sin as a mark of salvation.[114]

Both Viktoria Mathiya Sagatwa (Damari's daughter-in-law), and Melea Hango (an acquaintance of Damari who contributed to the interview with

---

110. *PCMS*, 1922, 34. In the event of the death of a church teacher, his widow was asked to move to a nearby mission station where she was looked after by the mission. For instance, Mrs Zakayo Chali who was also asked to move to Mpwapwa when her husband died early in 1917. See Esta Chali, oral interview, 26 June 1997.

111. Mpwapwa Service Register, 1933 onwards, MH. The register originally belonged to Kongwa where it was first used between 1905 and 1916.

112. Esta Chali, oral interview, 26 June 1997.

113. Mpwapwa Service Register 1933 onwards, MH.

114. For a detailed bibliography of the East African Revival Movement, see Murray, "Bibliography," 144–147.

Viktoria) say that Damari encountered fierce opposition from Christians who felt threatened by the radical message of repentance, public confession of sin, and forgiveness. However, Damari stood firm by her message and led a number of people to a new understanding of their relationship with God.[115] In her own testimony shortly before her death, Damari said: "Now Lord you may allow your maidservant [to come to you] for now you have saved and snatched me from the slavery of sin; even now I feel freedom in my heart. If my Lord calls me today I am certain I shall be in his presence."[116] Through these words, she almost compared herself with the prophet Simeon, who in old age uttered the words: "Lord lettest though thy servant depart in peace, according to thy word; for mine eyes have seen thy salvation which thou hast prepared in the presence of all peoples, a light for revelation to the Gentiles, and for glory to thy people Israel" (Luke 2: 29–32 RSV). Damari died on 22 October 1960 at the age of eighty-five.

6.2.2 Andrea Mwaka: A Trusted Leader and a Great Pastor[117]

The next prominent teacher to be considered is Andrea Mwaka. It likely that Andrea knew Damari Sagatwa because Chamuhawi and Mpwapwa are only six miles apart. Andrea Mwaka is one of the best known of the few former indigenous leaders in Ugogo – and, to a great extent, in Ukaguru too. Besides the information shared by some members of his family, several other informants mentioned his name during the oral interviews.[118] The biographical notes about him that follow are perhaps justifiably extended. His kinship name, "Mwakamubi," is often shortened as "Mwaka." *Mwakamubi* is a Kigogo word meaning "tragic year."[119] However, it is the shortened form "Mwaka" that is common and is the one used throughout this study.

Andrea Mwaka, son of Chief Mugube Makanyaga, was born at Kongwa. His date of birth can only be guessed at. Perhaps the date of his baptism may

---

115. Viktoria Mathiya Sagatwa, oral interview, 29 June 1997.

116. *Upanga wa Roho* 8, no. 2 (February 1961): 5, MH.

117. The phrase was used by Bishop George Chambers to describe Andrea Mwaka. See *CTDL*, no. 4 (January 1929): 4.

118. Esta Chali, oral interview, 26 June 1997; Elimerik Mlahagwa, oral interview, 28 June 1997; Dan Mbogoni, oral interview, 11 June 1997; Nehemia Uguzi, oral interviews, 18 and 19 June 1997; Isaka Mlahagwa, oral interview, 14 September 1997.

119. For brief notes on the event that led to Andrea acquiring the name "Mwakamubi," see under photograph 2, in appendix 3.

offer a better clue to his date of birth. Both his son Cleopa Mwaka and the Clergy Register agree that he was baptized in 1886.[120] But Cleopa Mwaka argues that since his father had been circumcised already, and though he might not have been as old as nineteen (as he told his son), he was probably fifteen and not twelve as estimated and recorded by Henry Cole who baptized him. His son's estimate, which based on the age of circumcision, is probably right. This puts his date of birth around 1871.[121]

CMS archival and printed sources, as well as published books, suggest that Andrea was a slave.[122] Oral tradition and family sources refute this, though they agree that there was an attempt by a trader (perhaps a Nyamwezi) at Chamuhawi to deceive Andrea Mwaka (then only a lad) to go with him to the coast. Henry Cole, who averted war between Makanyaga Mugube (Andrea Mwaka's father) and Chief Dikunguwale Madimilo of Chamuhawi – by giving the latter a large piece of garment as the payment for keeping Andrea – requested to keep Andrea at the mission settlement so that he might be taught. During his time at the mission settlement, Mwaka was free to visit his family and was visited by them too, especially his brothers.[123]

While attending school at Chamuhawi, Mwaka worked as a domestic assistant for Henry and Henrietta Cole from 1882 and, because of this connection, was able to visit England twice – first in July 1883 and again in December 1889. On the first trip he accompanied Cole after the death of his wife at Chamuhawi, and on the second he travelled with May, Cole's second wife.[124] His son Cleopa recalls what his father shared with him about his trip to Europe:

Mwita Akiri: Now tell me. How did he get there?

---

120. Clergy Register, CMS Mission and DCT, 1913 onwards, MH; The date given by Cleopa, namely 10 November, differs from that recorded in the Register of Clergy, which is 10 October. The latter is probably accurate on date and month because, with rare exceptions, baptisms were recordedon the day they took place.

121. The Clergy Register puts it at c. 1850, and Sahlberg at 1865, but these estimates are perhaps too early. See Clergy Register CMS Mission and DCT, 1913 onwards, MH; Sahlberg, *Krapf to Rugambwa*, 130.

122. "The Christians at Kisokwe were fortunate in having Andreya [sic], a freed slave, as their quasi-pastor." See *PCMS*, 1904, 98. Cf Cole, *History of the Church*, 66; Sahlberg, *Krapf to Rugambwa*, 130. Sahlberg writes, "In his youth he was a slave. . . ."

123. Details of the kidnapping episode are given under photograph 2, appendix 3.

124. Knox, *Signal on the Mountain*, 148.

> *Cleopa Mwaka:* He said that he was a childminder for the missionaries and looked after their children. In those days travel was only by walking, up to Dar es Salaam. There was no railway. . . . They then boarded a ship. He said when they reached the Dead Sea, they showed him mount Sinai. They told him, "You often hear we read about Sinai. That is mount Sinai." It was from a distance, on the eastern side. Then they passed through Suez and arrived in Maselos [Marseilles] in France. There they took a train, and travelled through France, until they reached the shores on the other side. They took a ship and landed at Dover. They took a machine [train] and arrived in London. In London his responsibility was to look after the children and help with the domestic work.[125]

While in England, Andrea Mwaka did not only mind the children but also had the opportunity to visit various places, including the London underground rail stations.[126] His mature age and humour probably contributed to his ability to cope during his time in Britain because he told his son Cleopa how he often made jokes with his hosts – for example, by referring to the underground stations as "heaven."

By July 1908, Andrea Mwaka had already been a teacher for some sixteen years. This suggests he started his teachership in 1892.[127] He was accompanied by his first wife Debora to Frere Town divinity school in 1896,[128] where he studied with other teachers (Matayo from Chamuhawi and Asani Mugimbwa and Daniel Chowe from Ukaguru).[129] Much of Andrea Mwaka's lay ministry was at Chamuhawi. It is therefore here where his contribution was most notable.

Despite the presence of CMS missionaries at Chamuhawi, it is Andrea Mwaka's name that is often associated with the success of mission work there, especially early in the twentieth century. After meeting him during his earlier visits to central Tanzania (April 1900 and October 1902), Peel wrote,

---

125. Cleopa Mwaka, oral interview, 4 July 1997.
126. Mwaka, oral interview.
127. Minutes, EC, 13–14/7/1908, G3 A8/0/1908/47, BUL.
128. *PCMS*, 1897, 100.
129. Knox, *Signal on the Mountain*, 147, 148.

"Christians and catechumens enjoy a peculiar blessing in the ministry of their quasi-pastor Andreya, whose faithfulness and thoroughness were easily apparent."[130] His decision to appoint him as quasi-pastor as early as 1900 must have been influenced by such qualities.[131] Despite Peel's observation that "this very valuable teacher is not clever," he declared in 1903, "but he is one who ought to be prepared for ordination as a village pastor."[132] In 1904, Peel testified to Andrea Mwaka's good work and leadership at Chamuhawi (formerly Kisokwe):

> The Lord has blessed the people under his care. The Christians at Kisokwe were fortunate in having Andreya . . . as their quasi-pastor. Under his leadership they repaired the church, the school, and another large building, contributing labour and material of the value of more than £20, a considerable sum for such poor people. The adult baptism in the district numbered fourteen.[133]

During the Maji Maji uprising, Andrea Mwaka was left to carry on at Chamuhawi and supervise mission work in other places. His son Cleopa Mwaka refers to that time and what his father did: "There was a time when the Europeans left [their stations]. But during that time they left him behind. They stayed there for some time because they suspected they might be attacked. When they returned, they found him doing a very good work."[134] In 1906, on average, two hundred worshippers attended Sunday service regularly at Chamuhawi. Daily attendance at the local elementary school was about one hundred.[135] From August 1907, Chamuhawi and Kiboriani were without a resident CMS missionary because Westgate and his wife went on holiday to Canada. Despite this, Andrea Mwaka carried on with his work successfully. In that year, Chamuhawi had 223 Christians and twenty-six catechumens,

---

130. Peel, "Usagara and Ugogo Revisited," G3 A8/O/1903/38, BUL; Peel, *CMI* 29 (March 1904): 193.

131. Peel to Baylis, 8/3/1900, G3 A8/O/1900/14; Peel, *CMI* 29 (March 1904): 193; Minutes, EC, 13-14/7/1908, G3 A8/O/1908/47, BUL.

132. Peel, "Usagara and Ugogo Revisited," G3 A8/O/1903/38, BUL.

133. *PCMS*, 1904, 98.

134. Cleopa Mwaka, oral interview, 4 July 1997.

135. RUUM, 1906, G3 A8/O/1907/23, BUL.

far ahead of Mvumi which came second with eighty-three Christians and thirteen catechumens – though of course Mvumi had 520 scholars compared with 413 at Chamuhawi.[136]

In the CMS mission report for 1909, the mission acknowledged Andrea Mwaka's devotion and faithfulness to his duties and described him as someone who continued to give every satisfaction.[137] In his capacity as quasi-pastor, he had indigenous staff to supervise and this included Andrea Kanyanka, a Kaguru missionary to whom reference was made earlier in this chapter.[138] Earlier (in 1905), Mwaka had been allowed to convert a house previously used by Henry Cole at Kisokwe into one that suited his needs and occupy it. The mission allocated sixty rupees for the task.[139] This shows the respect he received from the CMS missionaries. In another show of respect, in 1908, Andrea Mwaka's salary was increased from ten to twelve rupees.[140] This was done in recognition of "the most efficient way in which he carries on the work at Kissokwe [Chamuhawi] and his long service as teacher (and now for sometime as senior catechist or quasi-pastor) extending over 16 years."[141] But that was only a modest sum because, in 1903, a rupee was worth only just over 1.3 shillings.[142] To put this in the context of the British currency (pound sterling) used later, a leap has to be made to a decade or so later. In 1915, twenty rupees (Rs20) was thought to be equivalent to one pound and sixty-eight pence (£1.68p),[143] which suggests a rupee was equivalent to just over eight pence. So Andrea Mwaka's Rs12 was equivalent to only ninety-six pence at the time.

Andrea Mwaka remained at Chamuhawi until 1921 when he moved to Buigiri after his ordination as deacon at Mombasa, Kenya – then the base of the diocese of Mombasa which covered Kenya and Tanzania. Three years

---

136. *PCMS*, 1908, 62.

137. RUUM, 1909, G3 A8/O/1910/40; Ernest Doulton to Baylis, 6/12/1909, G3 A8/O/1910/13, BUL.

138. Doulton to Baylis, 21/11/1910, G3 A8/O/1910/83, BUL.

139. Minutes, EC, 28–29/7/1905, G3 A8/O/1905/40, BUL.

140. Minutes, EC, 13–14/7/1908, G3 A8/O/1908/47, BUL. The issue of wages for the indigenous staff and indigenous contributions will be covered more in chapter 8.

141. Minutes, EC, 13–14/7/1908, G3 A8/O/1908/47, BUL.

142. *CMI* 28 (June 1903): 453; cf. W. G. Peel, "Usagara and Ugogo Revisited 1902–1903," MS, G3 A8/O/1903/38, BUL; Peel, *CMI* 29 (March 1904): 196.

143. See Westgate, *In the Grip*, 73.

later he was ordained as priest in 1924 at Buigiri. Cleopa (his son) was modest about his father being chosen for ordination: "That is known only by the Europeans themselves. But what I think was the reason was that he had been a convert for a long time, and he attended courses at Kongwa several times. These [kind of] reasons. Maybe his character as well. Of being committed, and loving the work."[144] Andrea's commitment, which earned him much respect from both the indigenous Christians and CMS missionaries when serving as a teacher and quasi-pastor, continued even after his ordination. In the early 1930s, George Chambers described him generously as follows:

> Andrea Mwaka is a mine of wisdom, trusted by his fellow men and consulted on all sorts of matters. He has a great sense of humour, and a wonderful power of applying Christians ideals to African conditions when appealed to for his judgement. In all his ministry he ever seeks to bring his people into living touch with their Saviour and their Lord.[145]

Being the only pastor in Ugogo since 1921, he spent up to a month away from his home visiting churches at Zoisa, Itiso, Hombolo, Lindi, Msalato, Ngh'ungu, and Ngh'ongh'ona, as well as Dodoma (at Chief Birinje's on the southeastern part of the modern city of Dodoma). His visits were by no means confined to Tanzania. He also attended church meetings at Mombasa, Kenya.

As a trusted leader, Andrea Mwaka's work in Tanzania involved also looking after parishes whenever a CMS missionary pastor went on extended holiday. In 1928, he served at Mpwapwa briefly when Reuben Flinn went on holiday for a year.[146] He returned to Buigiri towards the end of that year and served there until 1932 when he went to Kongwa to look after the church when Wynn Jones went on annual holiday. Then he began what became the beginning of the end of his work and life. "In the summer [dry season] of 1933" says Cleopa Mwaka, "the construction of the Dodoma cathedral church was completed. They told him, 'You will serve at Dodoma.' From Kongwa he went straight to Dodoma. He didn't return to Buigiri."[147] Even there, Andrea

---

144. Cleopa Mwaka, oral interview, 4 July 1997.
145. Chambers, *Tanganyika's New Day*, 33.
146. Minutes, CC, 3/11/1928, MH; Cleopa Mwaka, oral interview, 4 July 1997.
147. Cleopa Mwaka, oral interview, 4 July 1997.

Mwaka's responsibility extended well beyond the city parish: "It covered the town and the surrounding villages. He became responsible for villages located west of Buigiri, as well as Msalato, Ngh'ungu, Malindi, Zangh'a...."[148]

In the same year, Andrea Mwaka became one of the first four canons (senior pastors advising the bishop on general church work in a diocese).[149] The date Andrea Mwaka was honoured as a canon was historically significant for the Diocese of Central Tanganyika which was established in 1927. The first meeting of the diocesan council met from 27 July to 1 August 1933 at Mvumi.[150] This council was put in place after the promulgation of the constitution of the diocese on 15 July 1933, which brought to an end the exclusive "all-white" executive committee of the CMS mission which had hitherto governed the mission.[151] It was at this council that Bishop Chambers named Andrea Mwaka and his colleague Haruni Mbega as canons.[152]

Unfortunately, Andrea Mwaka, now sixty-two, did not live long after the momentous year during which other indigenous teachers were also ordained.[153] His son, Cleopa Mwaka, says, "In July 1935 he became ill with fever. He died on the last day of August. And since he died after midnight, the Europeans say it was the first day [of September]."[154] Cleopa Mwaka is right, for indeed, that is the date that writers such as Keith Cole have used. Cole writes, "On September 1935 Canon Andrea Mwaka died, and his loss was keenly felt

---

148. Mwaka, oral interview.

149. Haruni Mbega (who was ordained with him in 1921 and made responsible for Ukaguru) and two CMS missionaries, Stanley King (who served mainly in Ukaguru) and Ralph Banks (who served in Ugogo), were also appointed canons at the same time.

150. Minutes of the first Diocesan Council (DC) of the Diocese of Central Tanganyika, Mvumi, 27/7–1/8/1933, MH. The diocesan council is the executive body of the synod (general assembly) in most churches of the Anglican Communion.

151. It must be emphasized that it was not until April 1947 when the African (Canon Yonathan Songola) became a member of the diocesan council. See Minutes, DC, 19–23/4/1947, MH. The number of African representatives in the council was increased to three when the synod meeting of 1948 elected Canon Daudi Muhando and Rev Yohana Omari to join Canon Yonathan Songola. See Minutes of the Synod of the Diocese, Dodoma, 6–10/1/1948, MH.

152. Hewitt, *Problems of Success*, 1:192.

153. Further details on the question of ordination, and the 1933 ordinations in particular, will be given in chapter 8.

154. Cleopa Mwaka, oral interview, 4 July 1997. This writer visited Andrea Mwaka's grave at the old cemetery at Mvumi "mission" hospital. Since, as Cleopa Mwaka notes, the custom in those days was that dead bodies should not be moved from the location where death occurred, Andrea Mwaka was buried there.

by the whole Church throughout the Diocese."[155] Putting aside the cultural difference as to whether a new day starts at midnight or at sunrise the next morning, one can note the generous tribute to Andrea Mwaka by Keith Cole – his death was a loss "keenly felt." In 1937, the diocesan council established a memorial fund for Andrea Mwaka and resolved that a pastor's house be built at a proposed Christian village in Dodoma town in his memory.[156] By January 1939, the house had been built.[157] Later (but before the African bishop was elected in the DCT in 1971), an international primary school designed to cater mainly to the children of Christian and secular expatriates serving in Dodoma was dedicated to Andrea Mwaka. The school is called "Canon Andrea Mwaka Primary School."

That such an honour could be bestowed on an African during the colonial era when many church buildings (whether used for worship or other purposes) were dedicated to Europeans and Australians, or took their names from the Bible, was quite extraordinary and remains one of the visible symbols of Andrea Mwaka's legacy for the church in Ugogo. The modern DCT also decided (in the mid-1990s) to extend the honour already bestowed upon the name of Andrea Mwaka by dedicating a secondary school in the city of Dodoma to his name.[158]

As a person, and a minister, Andrea Mwaka became the complete opposite of what his name, "Mwakamubi" (tragic year), depicted. He became a blessing to many. A number of informants interviewed for this study – people who had either seen him or heard of him – testify to this:

> Mwaka was an exceptional man. He was a calm person, with listening qualities, and was energetic. That was how he was perceived by people. . . . He drew people through his calmness, and his ability to fulfil what people expected of him. . . . That is why

---

155. Cole, *History of the Church*, 66. Sahlberg follows the same date. See Sahlberg, *Krapf to Rugambwa*, 130.

156. Minutes, DC, 1–3/9/1937, MH.

157. *CTDL*, no. 42 (January 1939): 6.

158. In passing, it may be observed that far too many African Christian institutions, churches, and places of worship are named using Jewish ("biblical") and European (extra-biblical) names. The fetishism of equating Western or Semitic cultures with Christianity itself is one reason for this. The other is ignorance about the contributions of the indigenous leaders in the history of non-Western churches.

people loved him, and think it would have been better for him to be here today! But because that is impossible, he is gone. But he is remembered for those things."[159]

Others add, "In fact he was someone with a good sense of humour. He was compassionate. He was much loved."[160]

Such was the life and work Andrea Mwaka, "a trusted leader and great pastor."[161] Beside his work as a teacher and pastor, he would certainly be voted one of the modern indigenous Tanzanian saints who made a substantial contribution to God's work in Ugogo from the late nineteenth and early twentieth centuries.

6.2.3 Danieli Mbogo: Musician and Reliable Companion

Another prominent teacher in Ugogo whose life and work were full of drama is Danieli Mbogo. Danieli Mbogo, a musician who played the trumpet, was the son of Mariamu and Ibrahimu Mbogo – a Mnyamwezi who settled at Mpwapwa perhaps in the late 1870s.[162] Danieli Mbogo was born at Mpwapwa in 1880,[163] and baptized there in 1892.[164] In May 1903, he was appointed by Henry Cole to start working as a teacher at Mpwapwa with his fellow indigenous workers Natanaeli Goigoi and Andrea Kapina. At the request of Cole, Danieli Mbogo went to teach children when a new station was opened at Kongwa in 1904. His missionary career began there. He stayed there for three months only and returned to Mpwapwa in 1905. An extract from his own diary gives an insight into the cross-cultural encounters he had with the Kaguru:

---

159. Nehemia Uguzi, oral interviews, 18 and 19 June 1997.

160. Esta Chali, oral interview, 26 June 1997.

161. The phrase was used by Bishop George Chambers to describe Andrea Mwaka. See *CTDL*, no. 4 (January 1929): 4.

162. Ibrahimu Mbogo was a famous builder who was employed by the CMS mission and became a foreman during the construction of the three major stations: Mvumi (1901), Buigiri (1902), and Kongwa college (1913). See Dan Mbogoni, oral interview, 11 June 1997.

163. Clergy Register, CMS Mission and DCT, 1913 onwards, MH.

164. This is the date written in the Clergy Register. Danieli Mbogo's diary has 1885 as the baptism date (entered by pencil, rather than ink, perhaps by himself but possibly by another person later). See Danieli Mbogo, personal diary.

Tena sikuweza kukaa na Wakaguru maana tabia yao ilikuwa mbali na maisha ya Wagogo. Desturi.[165]

Translation:

I could not live with the Kaguru people because their conduct was different from that of the people of Ugogo. Customs.[166]

Danieli Mbogo's account does not reveal exactly what it was that he found "odd" about the conduct of the Kaguru who lived in the Kongwa area at the time. Nevertheless, it gives an insight into the difficulties the indigenous missionaries from one ethnic group to another were facing. It is not clear whether (unlike most teachers at the time who were either Gogo or Kaguru) his Nyamwezi roots made his cultural adjustment among the Kaguru more difficult.[167]

Fortunately, Mbogo's career as a missionary did not end with his departure from Kongwa. He went back to Mpwapwa, but in 1906 (following the closure of Mpwapwa as a station), he was transferred to Kiboriani to work with Madari Mulutu and Thomas Westgate.[168] He was there for a year. It was during this time that his son, Rev Yakobo Mbogo, says he used to light up a fireball during Easter and Christmas festivals. The fireball could be viewed as far as Mvumi, Buigiri, and western Ukaguru and reminded resident CMS missionaries and teachers to light up their fireballs too.[169] Mbogo returned to Kongwa in November 1907 to work with Ernest Doulton for about two months. This time, he probably coped better. However, his missionary service at Kongwa was interrupted again. Towards the end of 1908, the executive committee of the CMS mission decided that he should accompany Thomas Westgate to work at Buigiri. At this time, part of his financial support came from Christian Union, Kingston branch, Canada. Presumably, this arrangement was made by Westgate, himself a Canadian.[170]

---

165. Danieli Mbogo, personal diary.
166. Translation by this writer.
167. Yakobo Mbogo, oral interview, 30 June 1997.
168. Reasons for Mpwapwa's closure were given in chapter 5. See appendix 3 for Madari's photograph and some notes about his ministry.
169. Yakobo Mbogo, oral interview, 30 June 1997.
170. See Minutes, EC, 24–25/11/1908, G3 A8/0/1909/1, BUL.

Cross-cultural communication was not the only challenge indigenous workers faced. They often gave up their properties for the sake of mission just as men and women crossing national frontiers for missionary service overseas did. Danieli Mbogo wrote painfully about his 1908 transfer from Kongwa to Buigiri, nearly forty miles away:

> Nilikuwa na uchungu kuacha shamba langu. Nilikuwa nimekwisha kupanda mbegu shamba kubwa, tena sikuweza kuchukua uhemba wangu mutama wangu. Ule mtama niligawa kwa ndugu zangu wenyi shida ya njaa, shamba niliuza nikapewa sh. 1.50 basi, nikakaza wito wangu niende niwasaidie watu wa Buigiri.[171]

Translation:

> I found it painful to leave my cultivated plot. I had already sowed seed on a large plot, and I did not take my sorghum. I gave away that sorghum to brethren who had been hit by famine. I sold the cultivated plot and got 1.50 shillings and focused on my calling to go and help the people of Buigiri.[172]

The sorghum that Mbogo is referring to must have been from the previous harvest, not from the plot he just cultivated for the new planting season, which he sold. As pointed out in chapter 2, many parts of Ugogo, including Kongwa, suffered numerous famines owing to poor climatic conditions. Kongwa was no exception, and from this writer's firsthand knowledge of the place,[173] the decision to distribute one's food reserve and forsake a cultivated plot was a brave and generous one indeed. It was brave because Mbogo had to start life midway into the planting season at a new location where the climatic conditions were equally unfavourable. Had it not been that part of his financial support now came from Canada, one might have concluded that Mbogo faced an uncertain future at Buigiri because, at the time, many teachers working under the CMS mission received less than twelve rupees (ninety-six pence).

---

171. Danieli Mbogo, personal diary.
172. Translation by this writer.
173. This writer did a three-year pre-ordination theological training at St Philip's College at Kongwa from 1982–1985.

Nevertheless, one fact remains: Mbogo was dedicated to his work. He became indispensable in mission work. Already, as has been noted, two CMS missionaries (Doulton and Westgate) felt comfortable working with him in new environments. One only has to remember, how he helped Westgate out of a potentially explosive situation at Lindi, when they encountered opposition from a Benedictine mission teacher.[174] His indispensability may be illustrated further. There were other teachers at Buigiri at the time of Mbogo's arrival – Yohana Malecela (about whom biographical notes will be given shortly), Yakobo Kongowa, and Isaka Kibolyani (variant Chibolyani).[175] Danieli Mbogo's main tasks were to teach at the school and do evangelistic work at other villages – for example, Mukwala, Ipala lya Nhambo, Nghoha, Maduma, and Finga (variant Ifinga).[176] In 1912, the re-arrangement of teachers in the Buigiri district took place as follows: Yohana Malecela, who had been there since 1901 when the station was opened, was transferred to Ihumwa; Andrea Kanyanka, a Kaguru missionary to Ugogo who first worked under Andrea Mwaka at Chamuhawi, went to Dodoma;[177] Yohana Meda was sent to Msamalo; Isaka Kibolyani and Yakobo Kongowa were posted to Hombolo and Finga, respectively; Yoshua Madungh'u and Yeremia Chiligati went to Solowa; and Ebeneza Mulilo and Yona Mbogoni were posted to Lindi and Nzasa, respectively.[178]

But Danieli Mbogo remained at the main mission station at Buigiri and was put in charge of junior workers, known at the time as "helpers," such as Nehemiya Masing'oti and Mudachi. In the same year (1912), a school was built at Buigiri, which, according to Danieli Mbogo, "many" pupils attended. In 1908 (the year Mbogo moved there), Buigiri district had 172 scholars.[179] There were now 2,646 scholars in the district, spread between some fifteen

---

174. See section 5.6 in chapter 5.
175. Isaka's surname, "Kibolyani," could also be spelled as "Kiboriani" or "Kiboryani."
176. Dan Mbogoni, oral interview, 11 June 1997.
177. Andrea Kanyanka was probably sent to Dodoma because of his good communication skills. In 1911, Doulton praised him, saying, "Andrea Kanyanka who promises to be a most valuable man and is well worth teaching; he formerly worked as a teacher at Mamboya.... Andrea Kanyanka can preach effectively the gospel in four languages viz. Kiswahili, Chigogo, Kimegi and Kinyamwezi, so his possibility for usefulness in the service of Christ is very great." Doulton to Baylis, 21/11/1910, G3 A8/0/1910/83, BUL.
178. Danieli Mbogo, personal diary.
179. See statistical table, *PCMS*, 1909, 60.

out-stations with some eighty schools and preaching places where the people were taught and the gospel was preached.[180] His encouragement to the junior teachers he visited in the out-stations, especially at a time when competition between the CMS mission and the Benedictines had just started (as noted in the previous chapter), could be one of the reasons why good results were obtained in the district as a whole.

In 1913, Thomas Westgate went to Kongwa to start the construction of a college for church teachers. The first college in-take in January 1914 comprised thirteen senior teachers from various places in the mission.[181] But Danieli Mbogo was not one of them because work at the Buigiri station school depended on him. It was around this time that he was described in a report on the mission work in Ugogo as "an exceedingly intelligent young man, and of great promise."[182] There is little doubt that Danieli Mbogo's contribution made the difference at Buigiri where he served as a missionary and teacher before his ordination. The suffering he and his wife Loi experienced during the First World War will be considered below. Meanwhile, it is sufficient to point out that after the war, he joined the college in 1922 and trained until 1923. He returned to college in April 1932 to train as a certificated teacher qualified to teach at a registered school,[183] but his training was cut short so that he could be ordained. His ordination took place on 29 June 1932. He was made a priest on 16 July 1933, a historic day for the Diocese of Central Tanganyika – a day when, as was stated in section 6.2.2, Andrea Mwaka was made a canon of the diocese.

Though beyond the timeline of this study, a compliment made by deaconess Louise Wilmot (one of the CMS missionaries at Mpwapwa) shows how Mbogo – then the local pastor – was successful in his pastoral work: "The Rev Danyeli Mboga [Mbogo] is a true shepherd to the people. Our success in the Church is due to him. He is a good visitor, understands people, is patient and reverent. He has been a blessing to me and a great help."[184] This further

---

180. *CMR* 65 (September 1914): 550.
181. *PCMS*, 1914, 61. Only twelve of the teachers appear in the photograph in appendix 1.
182. *CMR* 65 (September 1914): 550.
183. Danieli Mbogo, personal diary. More discussion about this type of school will be undertaken in chapter 7.
184. *CTDL*, no. 37 (October 1937): 16.

supports the point made earlier, regarding Mbogo's reliable companionship. This, together with his dedication to his missionary calling, remain one of his significant legacies.

He was appointed canon in 1946, and, after serving in several parishes, he retired in 1959. Danieli Mbogo died in 1961.[185]

6.2.4 Yohana Malecela: A Rainmaker Turned Pioneer Missionary

It is perhaps right that consideration should now be given to Yohana Malecela, the man who served at Buigiri for a long time but had to move to Ihumwa to start new work there after serving with Danieli Mbogo for four years (1908–1912). Yohana Malecela, son of Maula, was one of the prominent indigenous missionaries in Ugogo. He was born at Mvumi, but neither oral nor documentary give his date of birth. The account given by Ernest Doulton, probably late in 1901, and reported in the 1902 CMS annual report, may help in determining his age. When Doulton moved from Mpwapwa to commence a new station at Buigiri on 22 August 1901, Yohana Malecela became his co-pioneer missionary and companion. In 1902, he described Yohana, saying, "about five years ago he was a poor degraded Heathen, but now, by the grace of God, he is rejoicing in Christ as his own personal Saviour and keeper."[186] This description, though loaded with pejorative phrases – common in those days, particularly when referring to the followers of traditional religions – gives us a clue about Yohana Malecela's age. He must have been an adult around 1896.

This is further confirmed by family sources. One such source suggests that Yohana Malecela migrated from Mvumi when he was twenty years of age (or perhaps a little older) and went to live at Msamalo village near Kikombo railway station to learn the art of rainmaking from Mubumba, the local rainmaker.[187] Though Malecela's exact date of birth may not be known, he was probably older than Andrea Mwaka and was therefore born during the mid-1860s.

---

185. Yakobo Mbogo, oral interview, 30 June 1997.

186. *PCMS*, 1902, 111.

187. Lusinde, "Maisha Yake Yohana Malecela," 1. I am indebted to Canon Naftali Lusinde, a grandson of Yohana Malecela, who gave me a copy of the typescript.

After acquiring rainmaking skills, he practised with Mubumba for a few years before moving to Mpwapwa to live with his paternal uncle. Shortly afterwards, the Germans established an administrative centre at Mpwapwa early in 1889.[188] Yohana Malecela was a single man at this time. But a few years later, his uncle died, and he inherited his widow who later gave birth to a son fathered by Malecela.[189] The couple named their son Mudachi (Kiswahili; "German citizen").[190]

Yohana Malecela's nickname, "Kuhodanga," meaning "to destroy,"[191] is a name associated with his art of rainmaking and being a traditional, "destructive" medicine practitioner before his conversion to Christianity. He became converted as a result of the work of Andrea Lungwa, whose life and work will be analysed below.[192]

After resisting the message preached to him by Lungwa for years, two events particularly led to Yohana's joining of the mission. While at Mpwapwa, he and his friend were arrested by a German official and were forced to carry a box of ammunition under escort. His friend was shot dead as he and Malecela tried to escape their captor. Malecela survived and ran away. On another occasion, again with a friend, on a night mission to visit their girlfriends, his friend was bitten by a poisonous snake as they walked down a narrow path surrounded with tall grass. Malecela's friend died shortly afterwards.[193]

After these two "lucky" escapes – and given that he had been in contact with the mission through Lungwa for a long time – he finally agreed to enrol as an inquirer at Mpwapwa. He was now convinced it was God who saved

---

188. Carl Peters completed his treaties with chiefs in Ukaguru and the north-east in 1886. CMS missionaries at Mpwapwa or Chamuhawi do not mention the presence of the Germans at Mpwapwa in their letters written even in November 1888. But they mention the German presence in their letters written in March 1889 in connection with the Arab coastal uprising. It is possible the Mpwapwa fort was established at the beginning of 1889. What is certain is that it was commanded by Lt Giese, who also was in charge when Bushiri attacked it in June and July 1889. See *CMI* 14 (July 1889): 433; *CMI* 14 (December 1889): 433, 739–743; *PCMS*, 1890, 54.

189. As pointed out in chapter 2, widow inheritance was common in Ugogo. However, a widow was inherited by a brother-in-law. Yohana's inheritance of his uncle's widow is therefore unusual but not altogether antisocial in Ugogo.

190. *Mjerumani* is another Kiswahili word meaning "German citizen." This is more common in modern usage.

191. Stephano Malecela, oral interview, 24 June 1997; Lusinde, "Maisha Yake Yohana Malecela," 1.

192. Lusinde, 2.

193. Stephano Malecela, oral interview, 24 June 1997.

him from two dangerous situations during which both of his friends died.[194] To demonstrate that he had now begun a new life, he divorced his first wife (his paternal uncle's widow) and took a second wife named Marita.[195] He also stopped using his nickname, "Kuhodanga."

It was common in the CMS mission (as in other missions) for a convert to be engaged in mission work before being baptized. Yohana Malecela was one of the people who began their Christian vocation in similar circumstances. It is thought that his baptism took place in 1896.[196] As stated earlier, he moved to Buigiri where he and Doulton became pioneer missionaries. At Buigiri, Yohana took initiatives that demonstrated his commitment to God's work. He made possible the recruitment of junior staff through contributions from his own monthly allowance. No one was better placed in 1902 to praise him for this act than Doulton:

> About four months ago Yakobo (of Mpwapwa) expressed the desire to give up the whole of his time to the Lord's work and come here as a probationary agent. Yohana and Isaka, thinking he would be a useful helper in the work, and hearing that there was no provision for another worker, *quite of their own accord and without any suggestion whatever from me*, offered to give Rs3 per month towards Yakobo's support. I thankfully accepted the offer, and by a small addition to this myself, Yakobo was able to come here and enter upon the work. I ought to say also that Yohana was then contributing R. 1 per month towards Isaka's support, and so he is now giving Rs3 per month out of his allowance of Rs10.[197]

"Quite of their own accord, and without any suggestion whatever from me" is the phrase that emphasizes sufficiently the fact that indigenous teachers and missionaries in Ugogo often took initiatives that involved self-denial. This act of self-denial impressed Bishop Peel and his wife during the bishop's second visit to Tanzania (from Mombasa, Kenya). Mrs Peel clearly rejoiced in the

---

194. Lusinde, "Maisha Yake Yohana Malecela," 2.
195. Lusinde, 2.
196. Lusinde, 3; cf. *PCMS*, 1902, 111.
197. *PCMS*, 1903, 105.

commitment shown by Yohana and his colleague. Before she and her husband concluded their tour, she wrote to a friend in England and described, in more or less the same way, what Doulton shared in the quote above:

> We were very pleased with the earnestness and self-denial shown by the teachers there. Yohana, the senior teacher, receives ten rupees a month (13s. 4d.), and has nine members of his family to support, and offered to pay one rupee every month out of his salary to help to provide a second teacher, and both these give two rupees again per month towards the support of a third teacher, who was willing to come for five rupees [6s. 8d.] a month only.[198]

By the time the tour had ended – after which Bishop Peel wrote his reflections on the 1902/1903 visit to Tanzania[199] – Yakobo, "the third teacher," had indeed been employed as indicated in Doulton's account above. As was stated above (in relation to Andrea Mwaka's salary), at this time a rupee was equivalent to just over eight pence. Therefore, Yohana Malecela was receiving about eighty pence a month. The verdict of Mrs Peel at the time was that this was far too little for a teacher who supported a family of nine, hence the emphasis that his giving was an act of self-denial. Perhaps this was part of the reason why, in 1905, the executive committee passed a resolution allowing Yohana Malecela to receive maintenance allowance from the mission fund.[200]

Yohana Malecela was not only able to make sacrificial donations to enlarge the workforce at Buigiri and its out-stations. He was an able leader. In 1906, he was the principal teacher (quasi-pastor) and was assisted by junior members of staff like Yakobo and Isaka. Like other leading indigenous teachers and missionaries, Yohana Malecela's work was even better during Doulton's absence. In September 1905, when the Maji Maji uprising broke out, all CMS missionaries in the CMS mission, including Doulton, were forced to take refuge at Kiboariani for their own safety. They returned to their stations in May 1906. If this was not long enough for Malecela's leadership skills to be tested and commended, Doulton went on holiday to England and returned

---

198. *CMI* 29 (June 1904): 453.

199. Peel, "Usagara and Ugogo Revisited 1902–1903," MS, G3 A8/O/1903/38, BUL; Peel, "Usagara and Chigogo Revisited, 1902–1903," in *CMI* 29. (February 1904): 109–119 (first part) and *CMI* 29 (March 1904): 192–199 (second part).

200. Minutes, EC, 18/5/1905, G3 A8/0/1905/48, BUL.

at the end of November. The mission's 1906 report, to which Doulton contributed, noted:

> It is pleasing to note that during this time, Yohana has proved faithful to his trust, and the work in its different branches has been well maintained on the station and some attention has also been given to three or four of the outlying districts. We are of the opinion that after receiving some further training, Yohana Malecela will in the near future qualify himself to take charge of some district.[201]

During this time of Doulton's absence, "the school on the station was well kept up, several people from outside the station came forward and began to receive instruction. Those who were already under instruction showed sincerity and entered a more advanced class. Nine had been admitted to the catechumenate."[202] Yohana Malecela's leadership gifts and exemplary life couldn't be emphasized enough. In 1908, Doulton wrote, " I cannot speak too highly of his faithfulness and example to the flock over which he was placed, or of his true witness for Christ by life and word."[203] His appointment to take charge of "some district" took place. In 1912, he became a pioneer missionary at Ihumwa village and kept his title of quasi-pastor. It is interesting to note that while at Ihumwa, three of his four sons – Samweli, Daudi, and Petro – were among the junior teachers he supervised, each with his own small out-station away from Ihumwa village itself.[204]

During his time as teacher and missionary at Ihumwa, he managed to convert a former chief. The missionary skills of Yohana Malecela shone here particularly because the chief whom he preached to was also the rainmaker for his area and kept rain stones. Prior to his conversion, the former chief had been "hard and indifferent"[205] – a description befitting some chiefs at this time who opposed the introduction of mission Christianity. Most chiefs, as was demonstrated in chapter 4, were often quick to encourage their people

---

201. RUUM, 1906, G3 A8/0/1907/23, BUL.
202. RUUM, 1906, G3 A8/0/1907/23, BUL.
203. *PCMS*, 1908, 60.
204. Stephano Malecela, oral interview, 24 June 1997.
205. *CMR* 65 (September 1914): 551.

to attend mission schools. However, it was also shown that many of them did not convert to mission Christianity. Yohana Malecela should take the credit for the conversion of someone who was opposed to Christianity all the way until his conversion.

In 1914, Yohana Malecela was among the first thirteen senior teachers to train at Kongwa college. As other leading teachers and indigenous missionaries in Ugogo, he (and his sons) were arrested by the Germans early in 1916 when war intensified.[206] On his release in September along with others, he returned to Ihumwa where he continued to serve as a lay minister until old age and illness defeated him. He died at Mvumi mission on 4 August 1942,[207] and like Andrea Mwaka who died seven years earlier, he was buried there.

Yohana is remembered in Ugogo as a faithful and dedicated servant of God. Unlike most of his contemporaries, he served as a lay person until his death. However, one of his sons, Petro, and a number of his grandsons, such as Naftali Petro Lusinde Malecela and Stefano Daudi Malecela, are well-known clergy in the DCT who first served as catechists for years. His other well-known grandsons – Job Petro Lusinde and John Samwel Malecela – are among senior politicians and have held government position in Tanzania since 1961. The former held various ministerial posts between 1964 and 1985 and has served as an ambassador in different countries. The latter has also served in diplomatic and ministerial positions and was prime minister for several years in the second phase government (1985–1995). He is currently the vice-chairman of the CCM – the governing party in Tanzania. Therefore, whether in church or government, the legacy of Yohana Malecela continues in Ugogo and Tanzania as a whole.

6.2.5 Andrea Lungwa: "One of the Very Best"

The fame and recognition accorded Yohana Malecela can hardly be missed by a careful reader of the CMS archives and printed sources relating to the CMS mission in Ugogo and Ukaguru during the period under review for this study. But there were other humble teachers such as Andrea Lungwa of Mvumi – the man who played a key role in the conversion of Yohana Malecela to mission

---

206. Stephano Malecela, oral interview, 24 June 1997; Lusinde, "Maisha Yake Yohana Malecela," 4.

207. Lusinde, 4.

Christianity at Mpwapwa. As was pointed out earlier in this chapter, it was a common practice that whenever a new mission station or district was opened, CMS missionaries took with them some Wagogo and Wakaguru Christians. Andrea Lungwa, who lived and worked at Mpwapwa (but was probably a Kaguru by origin), was undoubtedly one of the few "baptized Christians and catechumens" who followed John Briggs to commence a new station at Mvumi in 1900. He later became one of the teachers who taught at Mvumi with Javan Haji and was appointed a quasi-pastor there.[208] Ernest Doulton, then secretary of the CMS mission, described Lungwa as "one of the very best in the Mission."[209] Lungwa died from the influenza epidemic that swept Ugogo at the end of 1918.

Several years after his death, the pastor's house at Mvumi was built and named after him in the 1960s. The house is called "Lungwa House." With the exception of Andrea Mwaka and Andrea Lungwa, it has been rare for church buildings or institutions to be named after prominent indigenous ministers (lay or ordained, men or women) who made substantial contributions in establishing the church in Tanzania – and possibly in much of Africa and the non-Western world in general. That a house was named after Lungwa shows the impact his life and ministry had not only on the Wagogo amongst whom he served but on the CMS missionaries too. Surely the naming of the house after Lungwa could not have taken place without the authorisation of the expatriate diocesan bishop. The naming of church buildings and institutions after prominent African leaders and saints should be happening more.

So far, the analysis carried out above has covered some of the prominent teachers and indigenous missionaries in Ugogo only. The list is by no means exhaustive. Since the mission had two branches, the life and work of some of the leading Kaguru members of the indigenous staff should be analysed also.

6.2.6 Haruni Mbega: A Man of Principle

A biographical analysis of the contribution of the Kaguru teachers and missionaries begins with Haruni Mbega. By origin, Mbega was a Mnguu from Unguu, north of Ukaguru, but he served mainly in Ukaguru. But the term "Ukaguru" is used here to refer to the entire eastern branch of the CMS

---

208. Esta Chali, oral interview, 26 June 1997.
209. Dan Mbogoni, oral interview, 11 June 1997.

mission. Mbega's name is as familiar both in Ugogo and Ukaguru as Mwaka's. Many oral informants mentioned him as a colleague of Andrea Mwaka.[210] Lack of sufficient data imposes limitations on what can be said about Mbega. However, it may still be possible to show that Mbega, too, made a considerable contribution in the growth of Christianity in Ukaguru. He was born in 1896 at Bokwa in Unguu. His parents were Lubangala and Muliwa.

On twentieth November 1904 he and Petro Mwendi were baptized by David Rees at Berega.[211] Information on his life and ministry was provided mainly by the Kaguru people – Christians and non-Christians alike. Semgomba Chitemo (a traditional medicine practitioner) described Mbega's physical appearance as follows: "Mbega was a man of imposing personality. He was like a European. If he sat with a white man, you would think both were white. By his body skin. By its lightness."[212] Mbega should not be praised only for his physical appearance and stature. Semgomba Chitemo, who didn't go to church, went on to describe his contribution to church work: "He was called 'Canon.' He helped people who were advanced to become pastors."[213]

One of Mbega's pastoral roles was to nurture senior Kaguru and Nguu teachers whom he felt could have wider ministry if ordained, and he probably recommended such people to the CMS missionaries. The fact that this was known even among people who had little, or nothing, to do with the church demonstrates that he was a well-known figure in Ukaguru, both as a person and as a servant of God.

Mbega had other qualities. Some Kaguru Christians regarded him as a man of principle: "Haruni Mbega was a true priest. It wasn't a joke. . . . First of all it was his principles. If he said to you, 'Welcome home,' or 'wait for a meal,' and you refused his offer, he wouldn't shake your hands the next time you met. He wouldn't greet you. His generosity was excessive."[214] That is how Isaka Mlahagwa (a Berega church elder) described him. One incident might highlight Mbega's character as a man of principle. When David Rees

---

210. See for example, Dan Mbogoni, oral interview, 11 June 1997; Elimerik Mlahagwa, oral interview, 28 June 1997; Cleopa Mwaka, oral interview, 4 July 1997.
211. Berega Logbook, No. 51, an entry for 1904, MH.
212. Isaka Mlahagwa, oral interview, 14 September 1997.
213. Semgomba Chitemo, oral interview, 15 September 1997.
214. Isaka Mlahagwa, oral interview, 14 September 1997.

approached him and his colleague Petro Mwendi about becoming probationary agents, they turned down the offer, asking to be given more time to reflect. Mbega and Mwendi turned down the offer because they observed that indigenous agents were paid low wages, and accommodation arrangements for teachers working away from their homes were poor. Fortunately, Mbega and his colleagues agreed later to work under the CMS mission and were employed as probationary agents on 13 January 1905, starting work at Nguyami, Talagwe, and Magera. Mbega preached his first sermon on 26 February 1905. On 13 December 1905, the rite of laying on hands (or confirmation) was performed on him.

In 1906, when many indigenous teachers protested over the issue of low wages, Mbega resigned to show solidarity with them. He was later readmitted, but his financial support now came from funds donated by the friends of David Rees at the parish of St Peter's Highgate Hill, London.[215] A year later, he and his colleagues Petro Mwendi and Mulosa resigned from work for a while, on account of resenting being rebuked by David Rees, but were restored soon afterwards.[216]

Mbega served at Mwandi and Idibo out-stations for many years. It is difficult to know exactly the whole period of his ministry there, but certainly, by 1911, he had been there for some time. At Mwandi, his achievements could only lead to a warm tribute from CMS missionaries:

> At Mwandi a recent visit found a Sunday morning congregation of over 230. . . . The orderliness of the worship and the quiet behaviour of that heathen congregation in their large, self-built church were alike an impressive tribute to the quiet power and intelligence of the teacher in charge, Haruni Mbega, a shepherd lad at the opening of the Berega station in 1900.[217]

Mbega was merely a young lad in 1900, but by 1912 – the time when the report quoted above was written – he had demonstrated his gifts as an evangelist and a leader capable of maintaining a congregation of that size. No doubt it is

---

215. Berega Logbook, No. 51, an entry for May 1906, MH; cf. Minutes, EC, 10–12/1/1906, G3 A8/0/1906, BUL.
216. Berega Logbook, No. 51, entry for 2 September 1907, MH.
217. *CMR* 63 (March 1912): 159.

such qualities that earned him a place in Tanzania's church history because he became one of the first two indigenous teachers to be ordained in Ukaguru and Ugogo. He was ordained deacon on 21 August 1921 at Mombasa, Kenya, with his colleague Andrea Mwaka, whose life history and contributions have been given in section 6.2.2. Even before his ordination to the priesthood, Mbega's leadership gifts were already evident. He was elected co-chairman of the Church Council of the Tanganyika Mission – a body that was responsible for issues regarded to be "purely African," including the governance of the pastorates and the indigenous workers and their upkeep.[218] Mbega was made a priest on 23 August 1924 at Buigiri.

Many Kaguru Christians today were only children when Mbega was ordained. Even so, they have fresh memories of the sense of pride they felt at the time: "The first time I saw a black man wearing a clerical collar was when I saw those people. The local people were very pleased, because in those days it was only the missionaries who were priests."[219] By "those people" the informant is obviously referring to Mbega and Daudi Muhando (see section 6.2.7). Mbega was stationed at Mamboya, where he took charge of pastoral work in Mamboya and Itumba and their out-stations while Stanley King (the CMS missionary) became responsible for the Berega and Unguu areas. Probably it was King who described him as " a man of God, and when he spoke I felt God was using him. His illustrations were full of meaning, getting much further than we Europeans can ever hope to get. They were taken from ordinary things of every-day life just as our Lord used to do."[220] Early in the 1950s, he moved closer home and worked from Berega until his retirement. Unfortunately, the date of his death could not be established. It is unlikely that he survived longer than the late 1950s or early 1960s. In his pastoral work, Mbega was known (and is remembered) as a soft-spoken, skilful counsellor who often persuaded his clients and opponents alike to make better decisions or change their minds and come to his position. He is also remembered for his contribution in evangelization and his leadership in Ukaguru.

---

218. Minutes, CC, 27/3/192, MH.
219. Isaka Mlahagwa, oral interview, 14 September 1997.
220. Chambers, *Tanganyika's New Day*, 33.

6.2.7 Daudi Muhando: Writer, Preacher, and Pastor

Another prominent figure in Ukaguru to be considered is Daudi Muhando. Like Mbega, Muhando was one of the few first fruits of Unguu – a place where Islamic resistance was fierce and little progress was made in mission work. Muhando was born on 15 April 1895 in Bokwa, Unguu.[221] His Muslim parents were Maligwa Makafu and Salome Chega.[222] He too, like Mbega, served as a catechist at Nguyami and later, in 1924, at Idibo where he joined Thomas Mlahagwa, the father of Isaka Mlahagwa (one of the informants interviewed for this study). He was known for his preaching skills. Though both he and Mbega were originally from Unguu, he took more interest in communicating the Christian message to Muslims perhaps than Mbega: "At times, he used to say, 'Let me read the Quran to you.' . . . He was very *steady* in arguing about Islam. He would not lose [an argument] to a Muslim. . . . In fact, even today, all his relatives are Muslims." With such a Muslim background, his decision to become a Christian should be viewed as a major step of courage and faith. It is possible that he was one of the young people who suffered isolation from family and relatives in Bokwa for associating themselves with the CMS mission. But, as the oral source quoted above suggests, his religious background later became one of his strongest assets in the evangelization of Muslims. As a teacher, he served at Berega, Mkundi, and Nguyami, among other places.[223]

Muhando received no formal education beyond the basic elementary schooling received by many in Ugogo and Ukaguru. Yet he published books and pamphlets in which he sought to adapt traditional Kaguru and Nguu stories for Christian teaching. Some local Christians read these.[224] In 1962 he published *Hadithi za Kiafrika Zimekuwa za Kikristo* (Kiswahili; "African Stories Turned Christian"). His material has not only been used by some

---

221. Clergy Register, CMS Mission and DCT, 1913 onwards, MH. The date on Muhando's tombstone at Berega church cemetery is 1 November 1895. This gives a different day and month for Muhando's birth, but since both sources give the same year, it should be regarded as a minor discrepancy.

222. Loi Muhando, oral interview, 15 September 1997. Loi is the daughter of Daudi Muhando.

223. Muhando, oral interview.

224. Isaka Mlahagwa, oral interview, 14 September 1997.

local Christians of his generation,[225] but also Western scholars such as T. O. Beidelman.[226]

It is no surprise that Stanley King regarded Muhando as a man of exceptional qualities and wrote of him, "He not only possesses considerable intelligence, sound judgement, tact in dealing with people, and the manners of a gentleman, but more important still, he shows increasing spiritual understanding in the things of God and is a keen soul winner."[227] Towards the end of 1928, Daudi Muhando was chosen as quasi-pastor of Idibo in the Berega district.[228] He was ordained deacon on 1 November 1929 at Berega – the third pastor to be ordained in the CMS mission in Ugogo and Ukaguru. His ordination, like that of Mbega, was widely appreciated at Berega, "for it meant the recognition of the fact that Africans were needed to minister in the African Church."[229] His pastoral contributions must have been appreciated by the Kaguru and Nguu Christians who for so long had to depend on one priest:

> Originally, there were only two [stations in the] diocese [of Morogoro] Berega and Mamboya. He [Haruni Mbega] was at Mamboya and was overseeing all the churches in the Kaguru mountains. The European pastor who was based here at Berega was responsible for work on this side that extended up to Msagalu and Songe. Then they appointed a third man, and that was Daudi Muhando. There was no other priest around here. He was assisting the one who was here because this area was very huge. They used to reach different directions.[230]

After serving as an ordained deacon, Muhando was made priest on 16 March 1932 at Dodoma.[231]

---

225. Mlahagwa, oral interview.

226. Muhando, *Hadithi za Kiafrika Zimekuwa za Kikristo*. His other works include two untitled and unpublished manuscripts on the Kaguru, located at Morogoro District Office and Kilosa District Office, Tanzania. These works are cited in Beidelman, *Matrilineal Peoples*, 82; Beidelman, "Chiefship in Ukaguru," 230.

227. Chambers, *Tanganyika's New Day*, 33.

228. Minutes, CC, 3/11/1928, MH.

229. *CTDL*, no. 8 (February 1930): 12.

230. Isaka Mlahagwa, oral interview, 14 September 1997.

231. Clergy Register, CMS Mission and DCT, 1913 onwards, MH; *CTDL*, no. 17 (July 1932): 5.

A few more remarks about his ministry are based on the period after 1933 – the end date of this study – but are worth noting. After his ordination to priesthood, he served at Idibo until 1934 before moving to Kilosa where he worked until 1944.[232] In commending the work done by Daudi Muhando at Kilosa, Ralph Banks, a CMS missionary stationed at Berega, wrote in 1937: "The Rev Daudi Muhando has shown a wonderful spirit and is ready to do anything and go anywhere. He has made a great difference to the work at Kilosa where he has been sent. He is very reliable, with plenty of initiative, and his ability as an organizer is outstanding. . . . He gets on splendidly with all the tribes."[233]

Muhando's ministry extended beyond the borders of Tanzania and Africa. He served in the Middle East as chaplain during the Second World War where he offered baptism and confirmation classes for the Tanzanian soldiers serving in the British army. Some of the material Muhando used was from his own books, particularly his book on worship, which is, unfortunately, no longer in print.[234] Bishop George Chambers who was with him at the time wrote:

> [He] is most respected by the permanent staff. A few days ago I gave a lecture on the East African background to some twenty-five Officers and British N.C.O.s. . . . I took Daudi down to let them hear the beauty of real Swahili after a boy from Uganda had spoken to them in trade "lingua franca" which most Europeans use outside Tanganyika. Daudi, before leaving the tent, asked me to translate, and expressed to them the hope of God that would bless them in their work and give them happiness. . . . As he left the tent the whole twenty-five rose out of respect. You, possibly knowing Daudi, would expect that. Such a man is a great ambassador for goodwill.[235]

There is little doubt that Muhando's mastery of the Kiswahili language was a tool in his career as a writer. Apart from this, his other gifts as preacher and pastor remain a legacy. The nature of the influence of Muhando, and his

---

232. Loi Muhando, oral interview, 15 September 1997.
233. *CTDL*, no. 37 (October 1937): 16.
234. *CTDL*, no. 66 (June 1945): 5.
235. *CTDL*, no. 56 (January 1943): 5, 6.

skills as a writer, on Penina Muhando (one of his granddaughters) may not be fully appreciated until Penina herself is interviewed. She herself has become an accomplished academic and the writer of many literature books used as standard textbooks in secondary schools and higher learning institutions in Tanzania.[236] Muhando died on 1 November 1966, at the age of 71.[237]

6.2.8 Yeremia Senyagwa: "A Man with Insight into Scripture"

Last but not least among the individual teachers whose lives and contributions are considered is Yeremia Senyagwa – a man not well known by the oral informants interviewed for this study or other Kaguru Christians, even at Mamboya Valley Church itself, which was his principal station. Yeremia was a contemporary of Asani Mugimbwa (but the latter started working much earlier at the Hill Church that was built in 1880).[238]

It is not clear when Yeremia started working as a teacher at the Valley Church. But he and Gideoni Ferekani (a Mnyamwezi) were the first two teachers appointed shortly after the opening of the Valley Church in 1894 and were certainly serving there before 1898.[239] In 1900, two CMS women missionaries (Rose Colsey and Emily Spriggs), who had the partial oversight of the Valley Church from its inception, described Ferekani and Senyagwa as "efficient."[240]

Emily Spriggs, who had been at Mamboya since 1897, testified about Yeremia's wisdom in dealing with objections from the people he and Spriggs met during the preaching tours in the surrounding Mamboya villages. On one occasion, Yeremia was faced with a personal challenge. A villager alleged that he (Yeremia) was afraid to drink beer not because he didn't want to but because he feared being found out by CMS missionaries. Yeremia responded to the charge and sought to show that it was his conscience, and not the fear, that forbade him from drinking. Spriggs quoted his response:

---

236. Penina Muhando is the current Chief Academic Officer of the University of Dar es Salaam, Tanzania.

237. The date is taken from an inscription on Muhando's tombstone at the Berega church cemetery.

238. Reference to the Hill and Valley churches were made earlier, in chapter 3.

239. *PCMS*, 1901, 119; *PCMS*, 1904, 95; *PCMS*, 1899, 99.

240. *PCMS*, 1901, 119.

> When you wish to learn to hunt you go to the *mganga* (or medicine man) of hunting, and he inoculates you and teaches you, and then sends you away, and you hunt and kill animals. Who kills the animal, you or the *mganga*? And just so it is not the Europeans who keep me from taking *pombe*; they have taught me, and I now refuse it myself.[241]

Yeremia's statement, and attitude towards the teaching he received, was typical and representative of the attitudes of many other indigenous teachers. This was noted by this writer during the oral interviews, and evidence for this has been presented already in chapter 5 and need not be repeated here. But what is different here is that the challenge Yeremia faced was a personalized one, aimed at discrediting him. In another village, someone argued with Yeremia, asking whether it was really necessary for him to become a Christian (an adherent of the mission) to attain eternal life. The man had helped build the preaching place at the chief's village (the Hill Church) and had specifically helped to fetch water and poles. Spriggs quoted Yeremia's response, with her own words interposed:

> "Look here," said the teacher "if you are sick you take a present to the medicine-man, and he makes medicine and tells you to drink it. If you do not drink it, would you expect to get well?" "No," was the somewhat reluctant reply. "In the same way," continued Yeremia, "if you do all these things, build a house for God, and go to the teaching, but do not receive the word of God, you will not receive eternal life."[242]

The point here is not whether Yeremia's teaching was right or wrong, but that he was able to use simple illustrations to lead his hearers to a different understanding – a gift that was common among the indigenous teachers, except that they did not relate their teaching to the religious and social context. In fact, it was this doctrine of resurrection that, according to reports of some CMS missionaries, was looked upon by the Wagogo as "an idle tale."[243]

---

241. *PCMS*, 1901, 119–120.
242. *PCMS*, 1901, 120.
243. *PCMS*, 1896, 109.

When David Deeks went on leave in 1903, Yeremia was appointed to stand in for him at Berega.[244]

In 1903, Bishop Peel described Yeremia as "a teacher decidedly to be reckoned a holy and earnest Christian [who] has been of great service in this branch of the Mission."[245] This was far from being an exaggerated description by a visitor who might have formed a hasty impression of a teacher he had met only twice during his two early visits to Ugogo and Ukaguru (first in 1900 and then in 1902/1903). For, indeed, some CMS missionaries who had lived at Mamboya before, and to whom Yeremia was a well-known figure, shared similar views of him. When commending him for ordination in 1906, David Rees, who had lived at Mamboya from 1897 to 1902, wrote: "Of Yeremia with whom I am personally acquainted I can speak in the highest terms. His insight into Scripture, his spirituality, his zeal, his graphic and methodical style makes his preaching powerful and attractive. His earnestness in visiting has also frequently impressed me."[246] In 1904, the executive committee appointed Yeremia Senyagwa to be in charge of Itumba station without the knowledge of Alfred Parker, a CMS missionary under whom he worked at Mamboya station. Parker complained to the CMS general secretary and discredited Yeremia. He wrote, "I do not consider him fit for such a responsible post, . . . he is too careless and indolent, besides he cannot do simple rules in arithmetic correctly yet."[247] What hurt Parker most was the fact that the letter of appointment was sent directly to Yeremia Senyagwa! But Rees defended the action of the executive committee to which he himself was secretary and rebuffed Parker: "your knowledge of him extends only over a few months."[248]

The appointment letter (written in Kiswahili) about which Parker complained may be quoted in full to show the high regard Rees and the executive committee had for Yeremia Senyagwa:

> Yeremiah nimpendaye salamu nyingi. Bibi nami sote wawili wazima. Tulipendezwa sana kupokea barua yako juzi. Nataka

---

244. Minutes, EC, 18–19, 21/12/1903, G3 A8/0/1904/12, BUL.

245. Peel, "Usagara and Ugogo Revisited," in *CMI* 29 (February 1904): 116.

246. Rees to Baylis 18/1/1906, G3 A8/0/1906/20; cf. Minutes, EC, 15 /11/ 1905, G3 A8/0/1905/16, BUL.

247. Parker to Baylis, 29/6/1904, G3 A8/0/1904/44, BUL.

248. Rees to Parker, 2/7/1904; an attached letter (found at BUL) without archival reference.

zayidi leo kukuarifu neno moja. Tumefanya sisi shauri uende kwa Itumba kuangalia kazi yake Bwana wetu huko wakati Bwana na Bibi Wood na Bwana Parker wanapokwenda Ulaya. Bwana Wood na Bwana Parker watatengeneza yote nawe. Sasa nakuambia tu mambo yatakayokuja tukijaliwa. Utatangulia na kwenda huko Itumba labuda kwa mwezi mmoja mbele ya kuondoka kwao Bwana na Bibi Wood kusudi upate uzoee na mahali. Lakini Bwana atatengeneza yote. Natumaini Simeoni amepata ruhusa na habari ya Gideoni tutajaribu kusayidia. Sasa kwa heri. Salamu sana kwa Julia na wenzetu wapendwa huko Berega.

Mimi ndimi

Rafiki yako

D. J. Rees.

PS Nataka uniandikie yote ujuayo habari zake Gideoni. Nimesikia kama watu wamesema ilikuwa si mara moja tu lakini mara nyingi amekosa naye Visinda. Nipe mimi habari yote juu yake. D. J. Rees.

Translation:

Beloved Jeremiah, greetings.

My wife and I are well. We were pleased to receive your recent letter. As for today, I would like to inform you about one thing. We have decided [in the executive committee] that you should go to take care of our Lord's work at Itumba when Mr Wood and Mr Parker are on holiday. Mr Wood and Mr Parker will make all the necessary arrangements with you. Meanwhile, I am only giving you advance notice. Perhaps you will have to go to Itumba a month before the departure of Mr and Mrs Wood in order to become familiar with the place. But the Lord will take care of everything. I hope Simeon has been restored; and we will try to resolve Gideon's issue.²⁴⁹ Now goodbye. Greetings to Julia and our beloved brethren at Berega.

Your friend,

D. J. Rees.

PS I would like you to tell me all you know about Gideon. I hear people say he has erred [committed adultery] with Visinda more than once. Give me all the information about him. D. J. Rees.²⁵⁰

Yeremia Senyagwa's other gifts included that of leadership. That is why he was appointed to Itumba. It is certainly also the reason he was appointed to be the quasi-pastor of Mamboya and Berega districts during the Maji Maji uprising when, as mentioned earlier, CMS missionaries took refuge in Ugogo. He was one of the five candidates nominated by the CMS mission in 1906 to be considered for ordination but the plan was halted following a teachers' strike over the issue of wages.²⁵¹

From 1906, a series of events happened that affected Yeremia's life and work. His colleague's wife took remedial medicine from a traditional practitioner but died later. Probably, as a quasi-pastor, Yeremia was expected to inform CMS missionaries, but he didn't. He was suspended from his teachership for a month for allegedly concealing the matter. Unfortunately, again, for reasons not established, he was publicly excommunicated from the church in July 1908, with his colleague Gideon Ferekani.²⁵² The issue of discipline in the CMS mission that was dealt with in chapter 5 (mainly in relation to ordinary Christians) will be explored further in vhapter 8 in connection with the indigenous teachers.

Meanwhile, it should be noted that during the time of Yeremia Senyagwa's absence, the Valley Church experienced setback in the hands of inexperienced

---

249. Gideoni Ferekani of Mamboya is mentioned because there were allegations at the time, probably from Parker, that he had been committing adultery, yet he had a house built for him at Nyangala mission station and was allowed to teach. See Parker to Baylis, 9/5/1906, G3 A8/0/1906/42. Rees refuted these allegations saying by then Gideon was Maria Ackerman"s's personal domestic assistant at Nyangala and was only being used to help at a dispensary and preach to patients. See Rees to Baylis, 23/7/1906, G3 A8/0/19 06/53, BUL.

250. Rees to Baylis 28/7/1904, copy No. 4, letter to Jeremiah, G3 A8/0/1904/47, BUL. Translation by this writer.

251. For details of this issue, see chapter 8.

252. Mamboya Logbook, No. 53, an entry for July 1908, MH.

teachers.²⁵³ It is not clear how his life proceeded after 1908, but like other indigenous teachers who were not ordained, it may be difficult to establish this. Of the two churches of the Mamboya station – Hill Church and Valley Church – it is the latter that has survived to date. Perhaps this is the legacy of Kaguru teachers such as Yeremia Senyagwa who served there from the 1890s.

6.3 Indigenous Initiatives During the First World War

The foregoing section concerned itself with what might be regarded mainly as "peace time" indigenous contributions. The exception to this – but surely only a minor one – was the Maji Maji uprising of 1905–1907 to which references have been made to highlight the indigenous contributions during the absence of the CMS missionaries. Nonetheless, despite the fact that CMS missionaries were absent from all stations for six months, Ugogo and Ukaguru were not affected and work continued without disruption.²⁵⁴

But that was not the case during the First World War, which affected nearly everyone in Ugogo and Ukaguru, if not in Tanzania as a whole. Yet even here, it will be demonstrated that despite the suffering, excellent work was done by indigenous teachers and ordinary Christians. C. P. Groves has suggested that the First World War was "a major injury to the Christian cause" for German missions in German colonies, and that the work done by the German missionaries was "rudely terminated by the fortunes of war" and "left orphaned."²⁵⁵ Groves makes this point specifically in relation to Protestant German missions. But the implication is much broader: the maintenance of the Christian work depended on foreigners and their absence resulted in "injury" to the work done so far. Examples have been given in the foregoing section that contradict this.

In relation to the First World War itself, Louise Pirouet, in her article "East African Christians and World War I," has argued against the paternalistic missionary thinking which Groves reflects – a thinking that had also

---

253. Minutes, EC, 19–20, 26–27/12/1907, G3 A8/0/1908/12, BUL.
254. For an extended discussion on the absence of the CMS missionaries during the Maji Maji, see appendix 2.
255. Groves, *Planting of Christianity*, 4:17.

contributed to a slow development of indigenous leadership. As for the war, she rightly notes that "the real 'injury to the Christian cause' may have lain, not in the removal of so many missionaries, but in their failure to recognize this as an opportunity rather than as a disaster; and in their attempt to put the clock back after the war was over, and try to re-establish the old, pre-war order of things."[256]

Pirouet gives examples from various missions in East Africa – including the German missions in Tanzania (the Moravian mission in the south and the Bethel mission in the northeast) and the CMS mission – of how the indigenous teachers held together congregations during the First World War.[257] The following analysis builds on that position and adds that even ordinary Christians in Ugogo and Ukaguru, who had not exercised any visible leadership roles in the congregations before the war, played a significant role in that task when their teachers were absent. However, though stressing that Ugogo and Ukaguru Christians recovered very quickly to take charge of the congregations, the upheavals in the early days of the war caused considerable disruptions. It has to be recalled that Tanzania was under German occupation when the war broke out, and therefore, like other German colonies in Africa (Namibia, Cameron, and Togo), it became a battle field where German defeat by the British was as important, perhaps, as in Europe itself.

As far as the CMS mission in Tanzania was concerned, it should be stressed that the severity of the war differed from one station to another. One observation is that when the arrests of both indigenous and foreign staff began, services and school work ceased in many mission stations, out-stations, and out-schools. This was due to indiscriminate arrests and intimidation by the German forces in an attempt to ensure that ordinary Christians and teachers associated with the CMS mission (and of course the UMCA) did not aid the British military against them. However, another observation is that when CMS missionaries and leading indigenous staff had been interned at Tabora – and after the Christians had found ways of coping with the intimidation – natural leaders emerged, and, to use Pirouet's phrase, used the gifts "which they did not know they possessed."[258] What follows below is an analysis of

---

256. Louise Pirouet, "East African Christians," 117.
257. Pirouet, "East African Christians," 125, 127.
258. Pirouet, "East African Christians," 123.

wartime indigenous contributions and experiences in Ugogo and Ukaguru. The situation in Ukaguru will be analysed first because the first wave of arrests took place there much earlier than in Ugogo.

6.3.1 Disruption in Ukaguru

Ordinary Christians suffered during the First World War. But, surely, the plight of the teachers was greater. In Ukaguru, the arrest of African teachers working in Unguu (north of Berega), especially at Songe, Tunguli, and Lwande, preceded that of the CMS missionaries and African workers anywhere else in the entire mission. The reason for this was that German forces wanted to isolate anyone connected with the CMS and UMCA missions lest they aided the British troops that would inevitably have attacked them from Kenya, then a British sphere.[259]

Ernest Doulton (then the secretary of the CMS mission) received a letter from the German district officer at Mpwapwa on 26 December 1914 asking if ten UMCA women missionaries (now prisoners of war) could be accommodated in the CMS sphere, to which he agreed. By 8 January 1915, the ladies had arrived at Buigiri, Mvumi, and Berega to stay with the CMS missionaries.[260] The indigenous staff in the CMS sphere working in Unguu and northern Berega were probably arrested at this time.[261]

The disruption in Unguu (in the CMS sphere) was greater, as Isaka Mlahagwa notes: "My father was in Unguu area. He went there since 1912, then he was told to close all the churches, and go into hiding. The churches were deserted.... [He] went back there in 1919 when the war had ended."[262] In parts of Berega (south of Unguu), school and church work was severely affected to the extent that baptismal classes were brought to an end. Semgomba Chitemo, a traditional medicine practitioner, was an eyewitness:

> *Semgomba Chitemo:* ... We had to flee. They fought each other until the Germans were defeated. My own senior uncle [my father's older brother] who lived at a place called Chakwale was killed as he tried to flee with his cows.... I joined the church at

---

259. Groves, *Planting of Christianity*, 4:26.
260. *CMR* 67 (January 1917): 43.
261. "Reports on the Treatment" Command Paper 8689, 6, NLS.
262. Isaka Mlahagwa, oral interview, 14 September 1997.

Nguyami. After that we were "baptized" there.²⁶³ I became an inquirer, then came the war.

Mwita Akiri: . . . When that [war] broke out, you then stopped learning?

Semgomba Chitemo: Yes. Who could teach us when all the teachers had been arrested and taken away? . . . Where would people come from to go in there? . . . I am telling you, all the teachers at our church, who used to teach children and the rest were all arrested.²⁶⁴

6.3.2 Wartime Indigenous Contributions in Ukaguru

Nguyami (variant Ngwiami) was one the northern out-stations of Berega district, and, like Unguu, was worked by teachers from further south. It should be emphasized that other parts of Ukaguru – for example, Berega itself, Mamboya, Nyangala, and Itumba – were less affected. At the beginning, it was the work of the schools that suffered the most, but services survived well. For example, at Berega, Mikaeli Mkwama continued to work despite the withdrawal of the CMS missionaries. Mamboya was served by Lazaro Madumila.²⁶⁵

It should therefore be borne in mind, also, that oral accounts of the disruption as described earlier reflect the situation as it was at the start of the war when panic gripped everyone, and churches and schools were deserted. But even in Ukaguru, the work was quickly reestablished after the release of the indigenous and foreign prisoners of war in September 1916 – well before the hostilities ceased, though of course many CMS missionaries continued to be absent.

Evidence of the work being maintained under the indigenous teachers is given by some CMS missionaries who returned early after their release. When Ralph Banks visited Ukaguru in February 1917, he found that despite what

---

263. Isaka Mlahagwa, an informant who had already been interviewed earlier was now acting as a research guide with the writer. Knowing that Semgomba Chitemo had not been baptized, he asked him to clarify if he really had been baptized at Nguyami, after which the latter said he had not but had been one of the "inquirers" there.

264. Semgomba Chitemo, oral interview, 15 September 1997.

265. Yusufu Masingisa, oral interviews, Mamboya, 16 and 17 September 1997.

the teachers had suffered at the hands of the African soldiers serving in the German army, "most of the African agents had continued the work, and in many places the schools as well as the Sunday services had been carried on."[266] Banks reported specifically about the work at Nyangala.

Reports concerning other stations were equally positive. "The teacher at Berega had got the school in working order before the visit of the European missionaries, and a fair number of men assembled for the services. The mission property has not suffered much."[267] This shows that far from the war being an injury to the Christian cause, the indigenous workers stood firm and maintained the mission work.

6.3.3 Disruptions in Ugogo

Unlike Ukaguru, arrests did not begin in Ugogo until March 1915. But when they began, they became indiscriminate and widespread. Oral testimonies on this are numerous, but only a few may be cited here: "But they arrested people at Buigiri. They arrested people at Mvumi. At Kilimatinde they arrested people. Berega, Mamboya they arrested people.... They were all arrested. They were all taken to Tabora."[268] Also, "The Germans did not trust the African teachers and thought that they might tell the enemy about their movements. Therefore, they wanted to arrest them all."[269] Some indigenous teachers – for example, Paulo Chidinda[270] – were arrested at Handali (near Mvumi) on 25 March 1915. Other Handali teachers – Zakaria Mazengo,[271] Yonathan Mwakamele Mutandala, and Musa Kongola – were arrested in May 1916 along with Mika Muloli of Mvumi.[272] Others arrested at the same

---

266. *PCMS*, 1918, 35.
267. *PCMS*, 1918, 35.
268. Cleopa Mwaka, oral interview 4 July 1997.
269. Isaka Mlahagwa, oral interview, 14 September 1997; cf. Ernest Musa Kongola, oral interviews, 20 and 24 June 1997; Nehemia Uguzi, oral interviews, 18 and 19 June 1997; Elimerik Mlahagwa, oral interview, 28 June 1997.
270. For details of the contribution of Paulo Chidinda at Handali during peace time, see notes below photograph 7, appendix 3.
271. Zakaria Mazengo and his fellow teacher Mika Muloli gave sworn testimonies before a resident magistrate at Mombasa on 18 November 1916. This was part of the compilation of evidence on the treatment of the prisoners by the Germans. In the report the teachers tell how they were tortured to admit being taught heliography by the English but stood firm and denied it. See *Reports on the Treatment* (Command Paper 8689), 24–25.
272. Westgate, *In the Grip*, 70-72, 79–80.

time included Samweli Makanyaga (a teacher at Ihumwa), as well as Andrea Mwaka, Edward Madimilo, Musa Kadulu, and Benjamini Lungwa (all from Chamuhawi). Haruni and Yustino of Mpwapwa were also arrested in May of 1916.[273] At Buigiri, Reubeni (Kapopa) Chidahe of Chilonwa and Isaka Kibolyani of Hombolo escaped arrest, but a Christian known as Yosiya (of Chilonwa) was arrested and charged with hiding them.[274]

The attempt to arrest Danieli Mbogo at Buigiri was unsuccessful, but the anger of the German forces at not being able to do so caused upheaval there, not least to Mbogo's own family (see below about the arrest of his wife). Danieli Mbogo had worked as a colleague and companion of Thomas Westgate at Buigiri for over six years, until the time of the war, and he had learned to play the trumpet (an instrument that Westgate enjoyed playing too). Two lapsed Christians – Dan, son of Yakobo Kongowa who was one of the Buigiri teachers, and John, who later became a polygamist and government official (*akida*) gave false testimony against Mbogo. They misinformed the Germans that, besides music skills, Thomas Westgate had also taught Mbogo the art of heliography, and Mbogo gathered people at Buigiri (allegedly) in order to conspire against the Germans.

For these reasons, Danieli Mbogo became the most sought out teacher of all, to the extent that the Germans promised a reward of two hundred rupees (approximately sixteen pounds at the time) for anyone who handed him over – dead or alive.[275] Buigiri was used as a temporary concentration camp, where, after being held at Kiboriani, all the prisoners (indigenous teachers or foreign missionaries) were kept for two months before being moved to Tabora.[276] This brought home the realities of war to Buigiri Christians.[277]

As pointed out earlier, arrests in Ugogo were indiscriminate when they began in March 1915. Even ordinary Christians were not spared. The German forces recognized Christians associated by the CMS in two major ways. First, Christians were identified by their first names. In most cases, these were the

---

273. Westgate, 70–72, 79–80; Lazaro Ndajilo, oral interviews, 14 and 16 June 1997. Mika Muloli was among indigenous workers from Mpwapwa who accompanied John Briggs to establish Mvumi as a station in 1900 and was probably born at Buigiri.
274. Westgate, *In the Grip*, 75.
275. Danieli Mbogo, personal diary; *PCMS*, 1924, 14.
276. Danieli Mbogo, personal diary.
277. Nehemia Uguzi, oral interviews, 18 and 19 June 1997.

names they acquired during baptism. This happened both in Ugogo and Ukaguru. The second means of identification was in the manner of physical appearance, even dress. This was more so in Ugogo than in Ukaguru. Like most Bantu-speaking groups in Tanzania, the Wagogo had their earlobes pierced. It has to be recalled that the majority of the people who joined the mission were young adults. These had not had their earlobes pierced. They could therefore be easily identified.

Also, at the time of the war, the traditional Wagogo still rubbed white clay (mixed with animal oil) over their bodies. Anyone who did not have such marks over his or her body was arrested on suspicion of being associated with the CMS mission. Christians who knew that they would be arrested resorted to the piercing of earlobes and rubbing of clay in order to allude the Germans.[278] Lazaro Ndajilo of Mvumi recalls this.

> *Lazaro Ndajilo*: They were looking for teachers and mission children. We then had our ears pierced . . . in order that we may not be identified as mission teachers. . . . If they came someone would say to them, "I only put on a rag [*shimizi*], and I have no shoes. Moreover, I have covered my body with leaves" [laughing]. You see, war brings all sorts of things.
>
> *Mwita Akiri*: How did people manage to have their ears pierced quickly just as the soldiers were arriving? . . . Did the ears get pierced and healed at the same time?
>
> *Lazaro Ndajilo*: No. If they came suddenly and found that you had not have them pierced . . . [they arrested you]. Pastor Mika of the mission, now dead, was arrested. One of our colleagues – Zebedayo – was arrested.[279] . . . Zebedayo Mwavwela, a mission teacher.[280]

Lazaro Ndajilo was a teenager during the First World War. He contends that during the initial period, schools were closed. He adds, "we stopped going to school. We were on the run."[281] But he also makes another important point:

---

278. Esta Chali, oral interview, 26 June 1997.
279. Lazaro Ndajilo, oral interviews, 14 and 16 June 1997.
280. Ndajilo, oral interviews.
281. Ndajilo, oral interviews.

"Church work was destroyed for two or three months only. That was when there were no services."[282] He may be referring to the situation at Mvumi station and other places within that district. But this reflects the fact noted earlier: conditions differed from one station to another. That is why the situation at Chamuhawi was quite different. Cleopa Mwaka recounts what his mother told him after her release by the Germans.

> *Cleopa Mwaka*: When she returned home she found all church activity had almost stopped. There were no [church] services. Christians were doing nothing. They were hiding in different places. They thought they too might be arrested. Soldiers were looking for cows. They were looking for flour. They were arresting people. They were seizing cows. Almost anything. It looked as if the Germans were sensing defeat. They then started moving equipment from Mpwapwa [fort] to the south. The cows were [slaughtered] and used as meat. The flour was used by the porters for meals. They kept moving here and there. Convoys from Kondoa arrived. They had to be met and relieved by others from this place. The [porters] from this place went as far as Kilosa, and were relieved by the porters there. So my mother did know I was born. But she recalls that she was freed on May 1st. She said that a week hardly passed before I was born.
>
> *Mwita Akiri*: May 1st of which year?
>
> *Cleopa Mwaka*: Of 1916. . . . My father [Andrea Mwaka] was taken to Tabora. They were imprisoned. Even teachers from Tanga [UMCA sphere], and from all over the places where there were missionaries related to the enemy [the British army]. They were imprisoned there. Africans and Europeans together. Some were girls [women missionaries]. . . . When I asked my mother about the date of my birth, she said, "I don"t know. We were spending much daytime in the bush. We were not worshipping. We had forgotten that there is such a day as Sunday."[283]

---

282. Ndajilo, oral interviews.
283. Cleopa Mwaka, oral interview, 4 July 1997.

Obviously, there was danger in every corner of Ugogo. However, Chamuhawi was a special case and that is why it might have had no church service for a long time. The fort – the seat of the German administration for much of Ugogo and Ukaguru – was only six miles from Chamuhawi. Certainly, the arrest of their famous teachers, such as Andrea Mwaka, left the congregation demoralized and made Christians there more fearful.

6.3.4 Wartime Indigenous Contributions in Ugogo

Despite such disruptions that took place at the beginning due to arrests at different places at different times, on the whole, senior Christians took over the leadership of the congregations.[284] Some of these were people who had not been at the forefront of church work before the war broke out.[285] Other places, like Buigiri, were under constant surveillance of those who acted as government agents, making occasional visits to gather intelligence at the villages around the mission station.[286]

The arrival of the British army at Buigiri enabled Danieli Mbogo (who had gone into hiding) to come out and lead a normal life. He was recruited as a security guard by the British army at Dodoma. Dodoma is about thirty miles from Buigiri. Despite the distance, Mbogo commuted by foot over the weekends to Buigiri to encourage the local congregation there and took the Sunday services for months until complete normality was restored.[287] No CMS missionary was present at Buigiri all this time. So when the 1917 CMS report says, "the church, school, and teachers' house at Buigiri have been burnt, but the spiritual work has been fairly maintained,"[288] it points to the work done by Danieli Mbogo and the indigenous Christians who escaped arrest and didn't go to Tabora.

Evidence of the work at Buigiri being maintained is shown by the fact that, when Ernest Doulton (who was at Buigiri before the war) returned to Tanzania in March of 1918 and visited the stations, he found that the war and persecution had caused great unnecessary suffering to many teachers

---

284. Dan Mbogoni, oral interview, 11 June 1997.
285. Chidosa, oral interviews, 12 and 13 June 1997.
286. Nehemia Uguzi, oral interviews, 18 and 19 June 1997.
287. Danieli Mbogo, personal diary.
288. *PCMS*, 1918, 36.

working under the CMS mission, "yet the work had been maintained, and at some places converts, won by the teachers, were presented for baptism." A total of fifty-nine baptisms took place in Ugogo alone. Of these, thirty-six took place in the Buigiri district.[289]

At Zoyisa (a northern out-station of Buigiri) the local teacher and Christians fled to the mountains briefly for safety at the start of the war. But on the whole, the out-station experienced little disruption.[290] Zoyisa was not the only place where the teacher had shown courage. A CMS report noted maintenance of work at Kongwa and Mvumi:

> Kongwa was visited by the Rev Dr T. B. R. Westgate soon after his release from Tabora, and when Canon Rogers went there all the work was being carried on as usual. In Mvumi district work has been re-established at nineteen out-stations, and at some of them, Handali, the school has nearly 400 pupils, and 107 people were admitted in 1917.[291]

Therefore, even before the return of the three CMS missionaries (for, indeed, others proceeded to Mwanza, then to Kisumu, Kenya, via Uganda, and then to Nairobi and Mombasa for long holidays after their release from Tabora in September 1916), mission work continued in Ugogo and Ukaguru. When the teachers returned, they carried on with the work in the absence of the CMS missionaries who were now on holiday.

At Tabora, the Europeans were assigned to serve at tables, carry water, make leather (from the hides of the oxen slaughtered in or around the Tabora camp), knit socks and trousers for the troops, make boot pegs, riffle-slings, and belts, and clean the latrine buckets.[292] But "black men, chiefly Christian teachers, who had been arrested on different English Missions and interned at Tabora, were brought into our camp, and practically handed over to us as personal servants."[293] No wonder, when Tabora (the stronghold of the German army) fell to the Belgians, the teachers took the risk and walked into freedom

---

289. *PCMS*, 1919, 42.
290. *PCMS*, 1918, 36.
291. *PCMS*, 1918, 35.
292. Westgate, *In the Grip*, 42.
293. Westgate, 56.

away from being both prisoners of war and servants of their fellow prisoners! Cleopa Mwaka remembers what his father Andrea Mwaka told him:

> Now they realized the camp had been taken over. They heard gun shots. They said, "They [the Germans] are now kicked out. They are no longer there." In the morning they came out of their hiding place. But they said to themselves, "If we return there, there we will find new people [in charge]. They will ask us to become their porters. This is our only chance. Let's go home." "Yes, Yes." ... They travelled on the way for nine days. They didn't eat for four days. But in the remaining five days, they ate in the evening, and woke up early in the morning. ... When they arrived they found Westgate there already. He said to them, "We looked for you, but could not see you. Why did you ran away?" They told him, "Lo! We didn't think we would be happy there. We knew we would return to suffering." They looked so thin. Therefore he received them. They continued with their work, and soon the situation went back to normal.[294]

One piece of evidence of the good work done during the war – first, by ordinary Christians during the absence of their teachers and the foreign staff, and later by the teachers themselves during absence of the foreign staff – is that the number of Christians and scholars recorded after the war ended was higher than that recorded at the time of the outbreak.

At the outbreak of the war, the CMS mission had 1,295 baptized Christians and 2,976 catechumens, as well as 17,202 scholars. No statistics were gathered between 1914 and 1918. The first new statistics to be collected were those for 1919.[295] These show that the number of baptized Christians was now 1,789, though that of the catechumens was down to 1,729. Figures for scholars were even better, and now reached 20,417.[296] Though statistical figures are always subject to error, and have to be treated with caution, the statistical

---

294. Cleopa Mwaka, oral interview, 4 July 1997.

295. Though it was not until 1919 that the British officially took over the administration of Tanzania under a mandate of the League of Nations, by December 1917 the German forces had been driven completely out of Tanzania (and Rwanda and Burundi), then called German East Africa. See *PCMS*, 1918, 35.

296. See statistical tables, *PCMS*, 1920, xii, xiv.

tables featuring the above figures contradict a statement, in the same annual report, that "at the end of 1919 the schools numbered 281 against 405 before the war, and scholars 14,000 against 17,000."[297] It is not clear where the figures (281 and 14,000) are taken from, since, at this time, the CMS no longer gave separate annual statistics for each mission – a practice that ended in 1913. It may be concluded that the figures in the written section of the annual report are probably a misquote.

6.3.5 Wartime Experiences of the Wives of the Indigenous Teachers

So far, the analysis above has covered the experiences of men, but women also suffered during the war. Nearly all wives of teachers in Ugogo and Ukaguru suffered psychological trauma during the First World War. None of them could tell the fate that awaited their husbands who had been arrested simply for being ministers of the church. Some of them suffered physical abuses. The wives of Paulo Chidinda, Musa Kongola, and Yonathan Mwakamele (Handali teachers) were tied with cords and ropes and whipped by the German troops. They could only be freed if their husbands made forced confessions that they had been taught heliography and had been "writing letters urging the British troops to come quickly and take colony."[298] Or else the husbands had to buy the freedom of their wives. The teachers refused to make false admissions. Therefore, Paulo Chidinda paid two oxen, Musa Kongola one ox, and Yonathan Mwakamele Rs20 (about £1.68).[299]

Marita (whom Andrea Mwaka married after the death of his first wife, Debora) was arrested at Chamuhawi along with her husband Andrea Mwaka. This was during the second wave of arrests of the indigenous teachers in Ugogo at the beginning of May 1916. Marita was in an advanced stage of pregnancy, expecting her seventh child (Cleopa Mwaka) during the arrest.[300] Others arrested with Marita included the wives of Samweli Makanyaga, Karumu, Edward Madimilo, Musa Kadulu, and Benyamini Lungwa (Chamuhawi

---

297. *PCMS*, 1920, 29.
298. Westgate, *In the Grip*, 72.
299. Westgate, 73.
300. Cleopa Mwaka, oral interview, 4 July 1997.

teachers) and the wives of Haruni and Yustino (Mpwapwa teachers). All were taken to the fort at Mpwapwa.[301]

The arrest of women took place in Buigiri district too. Chindiya, wife of Yosia (a Chilonwa Christian), Sakalani and Suda (Yosia's sister and sister-in-law, respectively), Mugaya (the wife of Josiya's elder brother), Juliya (the sister of Joshua Mate of Ibwaga, who later became patron of the Buigiri girls' boarding school) were among those arrested. Lyazengwa, wife of Lembijima (a close friend of Rubeni Kapopa Chidahe),[302] and Loi, the wife of Danieli Mbogo, suffered the same fate. At Berega (Ukaguru), among those arrested included the wife of Jonathan Mahimbo, who like Marita Andrea Mwaka, was pregnant at the time.[303] All of these suffered considerably.

However, Loi's suffering was far greater than that of any other woman or teacher's wife in Ugogo and Ukaguru. Her experiences should be given in detail. As pointed out earlier, Loi, the wife of Danieli Mbogo, was arrested by the authorities as revenge after her husband narrowly escaped capture and went into hiding.[304] She was then taken to a martial court to which some chiefs were invited – two of whom persuaded the German officials that Loi shouldn't be killed for she could not know the whereabouts of her husband.

The plea by Chief Chiloloma of Hombolo and Chief Birinje of Dodoma saved Loi's life but was probably not enough to secure her release.[305] She and her young child, Helina, were taken to the Tabora concentration camp where she stayed from April 1916 until September 1916, when Tabora was liberated by the Belgium army. While there, she was harassed by a junior guard for some time before a senior officer intervened and gave her a spacious room for herself and the child. She travelled with the CMS missionaries on 3 October 1916 to Nairobi via Kisumu, arriving there on 22 October 1916. She was apparently asked to accompany the CMS missionaries to Mombasa where they boarded ships and went on holiday, each to his or her own country.[306]

---

301. Westgate, *In the Grip*, 78.

302. Westgate, 75.

303. Loi Mahimbo, oral interview, 15 September 1997. Loi Mahimbo is the daughter of Jonathan Mahimbo, a teacher who was also arrested in 1915.

304. Danieli Mbogo, personal diary.

305. Yakobo Mbogo, oral interview, 30 June 1997. Yakobo is the son of Loi and Danieli Mbogo.

306. *CMR* 67 (January 1917): 46.

Daniel Mbogo, who narrowly escaped being arrested at Buigiri, recorded in his diary the story of his wife's long walk from captivity to freedom – a moving story that unfortunately found no place in the CMS missionaries' narratives of the war.[307] He wrote in Kiswahili:

> Mke wangu hakuwapo alikuwa pande za Mombasa, hata apate nafasi ya kurudi. Maana Wadachi waliposhindwa Tabora wao waliachwa na mateka weusi na Waingereza wa Misheni yetu. Basi hawakurudishwa mara hapa Ugogo, Bwana Rev. E. W. Doulton hakumruhusu mke wangu kurudi kwa njia fupi toka Tabora hata Dodoma akifikiri hatari ya adui njiani, basi hivyo walizunguka toka Tabora hata ziwa la Viktoria Nyanza wakaingia gari la moshi hata Nairobi kiisha Mombasa na kule walikaa kungoja nafasi ya kurudi, nafasi ilipatikana walikuja pamoja na bwana Bankis February 1916.[308] O! ilikuwa furaha kubwa. Nilimshukuru Mungu kwa ulinzi wake. Niliua ng'ombe mkubwa nikawaita watu wengi kula kushirikiana nasi katika furaha hii mke wangu ameonekana, ambae . . .

Translation:

> My wife was not present. She was in Mombasa where she stayed waiting for the opportunity to return home. For when the Germans were defeated at Tabora, she was released with black prisoners of war, and the British working in our Mission. They didn't return to Ugogo immediately. Mr Doulton didn't allow my wife to take a shorter route from Tabora to Dodoma because he feared the danger of the enemy on the way. So they took the route from Tabora, travelled [by ship] on Lake Victoria Nyanza, and took the train [from Kisumu] to Nairobi and later to Mombasa. And there they waited for the opportunity to return. The opportunity came, so she travelled with Mr Banks and arrived in February 1916. Oh! What a great joy. I thanked God

---

307. *CMR* 67: 42–47. Doulton only mentions that he and other CMS and UMCA missionaries were interned with "forty-two natives."

308. Certainly Mbogo meant February 1917, for this is the date of the return of Banks from Mombasa to Tanzania. See *PCMS*, 1918, 35.

for his protection [to my wife]. I slaughtered a huge cow and invited many people to celebrate the joy of the re-appearance of my wife, who . . .[309]

Loi (whose date of birth is estimated to be 1890) lived many years after her ordeal during the First World War and died on 2 February 1979.[310]

6.4 Conclusion

This chapter has explored the missionary contributions of the indigenous teachers, besides their work in literacy training and the catechetical process. It has examined the life and work of some of the leading indigenous staff and has analysed their wartime experiences and contributions. It has been noted that their work was indispensable to the expansion of the mission work. The biographical notes of some of the leading teachers have shown that they had different qualities, ranging from Damari Sagatwa, one of the indigenous women missionaries and a prominent Bible woman, who was constantly on the move; to trustworthy leaders like Andrea Mwaka.

The analysis has shown how others, like Yohana Malecela, became poachers-turned-gamekeepers – the rainmaker who became a pioneer missionary and drew other rainmakers into the Christian faith. The contribution of Danieli Mbogo, a reliable companion of many CMS missionaries and a man who often suffered greatly in his missionary career -- and had a price on his head during the First World War – has been noted, as well as the suffering of Loi, his wife. Kaguru leaders with pastoral and communication gifts, like Haruni Mbega and Daudi Muhando (the latter being able to write and publish), have been studied. These indigenous missionaries and teachers assimilated the Christian teaching they received and made it their own, becoming examples to those they led. So much so, that when they were taken away and interned hundreds of miles away at Tabora, the Christians themselves could not let the work suffer and vanish.

---

309. Danieli Mbogo, personal diary. The words quoted are the last in Mbogo's diary. The rest (which include the unfinished story) appear to have been cut out by a sharp object such as scissors or a razor blade. Translation by this writer.

310. Dates were taken from the inscription on Loi's tombstone at the Mlanga Church cemetery.

Yet, it shouldn't be forgotten where it all started: under baobab trees and in mud and wattle huts – the literacy centres and preaching places. Some of the inadequacies of that type of education in helping converts interact with their pre-Christian religious life were examined in chapter 5. Despite that, their contribution as defenders of the "Christian ideal" was acknowledged.

Yet, their contributions and loyalty to their God and the mission during the war was later to be faced with new challenges. The Germans now gone (after the First World War), the British took over the administration of Tanzania. The system of education within which they served – one dominated and characterized by the out-schools – became a focus of criticism. It was viewed as one that failed in other respects, particularly in relating classroom knowledge to real life situations. Its evangelistic and literary nature were now to be scrutinized – a process that began soon after the First World War but gained momentum in Tanzania in the mid-1920s. It is the issues surrounding mission schools in the post-war period, and the supposed redefinition of the role of the indigenous teacher, that are addressed in the next chapter.

CHAPTER 7

Secularization of Mission Education and Its Impact[1]

If the First World War was a challenging time for individual indigenous teachers and missionaries – a test that they endured so well – then the post-war change of colonial government was another test. This time it was not so much a challenge to them as individuals but to the particular way they had been doing their educational work, particularly in the out-schools. Post-war statistics show that there were some 20,417 scholars in the CMS mission in Ugogo and Ukaguru at the start of the British colonial occupation in 1919. This indicates that despite all the imperfections, the educational work of the indigenous teachers had achieved considerable results.

This chapter examines and evaluates the impact of the philosophy of adaptation on mission education, with reference to the out-schools and indigenous teachers in Tanzania, especially in the CMS mission sphere. It notes the reinterpretation of the significance of the out-schools and the role of indigenous teachers from the mid-1920s. Secularization of mission education meant that the evangelistic role of the out-schools and the indigenous teachers – and indeed what missions understood to be the primary aim of mission education – was becoming "endangered." The discourse below seeks to highlight the fact that a key motive behind the concept of adaptation was the desire, by some, to confine the African masses to non-literary education with the implicit purpose of controlling their socioeconomic and political

---

1. This chapter was previously published under the title "Education Reforms in Colonial Africa: Dynamics, Challenges and Impact on Christian Missions" in a book published by Peter Lang Publishing entitled *Reformation Worlds: Antecedents and Legacies in the Anglican Tradition*, edited by Sean Otto and Thomas P. Power, 2016. Used by permission.

ambitions. In the end, though, this chapter argues that, from the perspective of indigenous teachers, the secularization of mission education brought with it some socioeconomic benefits that would have hardly been possible if mission education continued along the basic lines of being primarily evangelistic.

7.1 Background of the Philosophy of Adaptation
7.1.1 The Phelps Stokes commissions

The American influence on African education, and the political impact it had on secular and religious colonial education, has been explored in detail by Kenneth King in his book *Pan-Africanism and Education*. Therefore, only a brief summary may be given here. Early in 1919, Thomas Jesse Jones, then director of the Phelps Stokes Fund (a philanthropic organization started in May 1911 in New York)[2] began persuading his organization about the need for a survey of African education which might eventually show similarities between the educational needs of Africans in Africa and those of African Americans in the southern states of America. By then he had shared his views at the World Missionary Conference (WMC) at Edinburgh in 1910. The Africa section of the report of Commission 3, *Education in Relation to the Christianisation of National Life*, shows that Jones's ideas became influential. The section concludes by pointing out that the value of industrial training and agricultural training for the black race had been "abundantly proved by the experience of the Normal and Agricultural Institute at Hampton, Virginia, and the Normal and Industrial School at Tuskegee, Alabama."[3]

Coincidentally, at that very time (namely, in 1919), the Baptist Foreign Missionary Society expressed, through the Foreign Missions Conference of North America, the need for a study of African education in West Africa to be carried out by the Phelps Stokes Fund. This led to the formation of the first Phelps Stokes commission that toured West Africa, South Africa, and Equatorial Africa between 4 September 1920 and August 1921, sometimes referred to as "the commission to West Africa."[4] It was chaired by Jones. The

---

2. History of the Phelps Stokes Fund is outlined in Jones, *Educational Adaptations*, 15–20.
3. WMC, *Education*, 277.
4. Jones, *Education in Africa*. The commission actually left Liverpool, in Britain, for West Africa on 25 August 1920. See Jones, *Education in Africa*, xvii.

report of the commission proposed what it regarded as "a solution to ... the problem of educated African, the over-supply of clerks, the mission boy, or black Englishman...."[5] Jones later chaired the second commission, this time mainly to East and Central Africa, in 1924, and later authored the reports of the two commissions.[6]

Through these commissions, the ideological and racial assumptions, implications, and controversies that surrounded the education of African Americans in America itself were now being transported to Africa. Essentially, Jones propagated three things about education for African Americans and Africans. First, it should be different from the literary education offered to the white race.[7] Second, it should be "for life" – that is, be adapted to address what was regarded as the economic "backwardness" of African Americans and Africans. Third, it should focus on agriculture – "the key" to the economic future of the peoples of the two regions. Yet, at the heart of the matter was the fact that Jones and his sympathizers believed that by providing alternative education, African Americans and Africans could be "*immunized* successfully against politics"[8] and made to cooperate submissively with Western colonial rulers, settlers, and educators.

But not everyone supported these ideas. Of many African Americans, some of the best known opponents of Jones's ideas were W. E. B. Dubois and Marcus Garvey.[9] Dubois criticized Jones's dislike of African advance through higher education, fear of African independence, and his inclination towards the views and needs of white missionaries in Africa; and Garvey argued that the education offered to Africans and African Americans should be the same as that offered to Europeans.[10] The opposition of the Europeans, particularly

---

5. King, *Pan-Africanism*, 45. For a detailed background and discussion on the politics of industrial education for African Americans in the southern states of America, see 5–20.

6. The report of the second commission was published as Jones, *Education in East Africa* by the second African education commission under the auspices of the Phelps Stokes Fund, in cooperation with the international board.

7. King, *Pan-Africanism*, 253.

8. King, 258.*immunized*.

9. King, 254.

10. The former was a member of the National Association for the Advancement of Colored People (NAACP) and used its journal *Crisis* to advance his case. See, for example, W. E. Dubois, "Education in Africa," in *Crisis* 32, no. 2 (June 1926): 86–89. For Garvey's opinion, see Marcus Garvey, editorial, *Negro World* 21, no. 1 (14 August 1926). Both sources are quoted in King, *Pan-Africanism*, 144–145.

Norman Leys and Roland Allen, will be discussed later because they relate more to the issue of cooperation between governments and missions.

7.1.2 British Government Policy on Education in Africa

In Britain, the Privy Council memorandum on industrial schools for "coloured" races, produced in 1847 by the committee of the Council on Education, was the first serious policy document on education in the British colonies, including those in Africa. It recognized the influence of Christianity in education, especially in character development. Equally it sought "to make the school the means of improving the condition of the peasantry...";[11] to give the "coloured" races "a practical training in household economy..., knowledge of writing and arithmetic,"[12] and to give "the small farmer the power to enter into calculations and agreements."[13] The memorandum singled out day schools and model farms as the two most important institutions required for the achievement of the objects of education for the "coloured" races.[14] It should be pointed out, however, that the impact of this policy was minimal, perhaps because neither the colonial governments nor missions had sufficient resources to implement it.[15]

The second major British policy initiative on African education took place in the twentieth century after the tour of the first Phelps Stokes commission to West Africa. W. Ormsby-Gore writes that "the return of Dr Jesse Jones of the Phelps Stokes Fund of America from his first tour of investigation into the problems of education in Africa was the occasion which led to the holding at the Colonial Office, on June 6th 1923, of an important conference on the future of Native Education in Africa."[16] Apart from government officials

---

11. Privy Council Office, *Brief Practical Suggestions on the Mode of Organizing and Conducting Day-Schools of Industry, Model Farm Schools, and Normal Schools, as Part of a System of Education for the Coloured Races of the British Colonies*, Colonial Office Library, The Privy Council Memorandum 1847, *Miscellaneous Pamphlets*, Vol. 1, no. 1; cf., Scott, "Development of the Education," in Year Book of Education 1938, 708, 711.

12. Privy Coucil Office, Privy Council Memorandum, Miscellaneous Pamphlets, Vol. 1, 2.

13. Privy Coucil Office, Privy Council Memorandum, Miscellaneous Pamphlets, Vol. 1, 2.

14. Scott, "Development of the Education," in Year Book of Education 1938, 708, 711.

15. At least, this was the case in Sierra Leone. See Scott, "Development of the Education," in Year of Education 1938, 711. Efforts made on adaptation, especially by the Basel mission in Ghana and Scottish missions in Malawi to introduce industrial and vocational education, stood as an exception to the general trends. See King, *Pan-Africanism*, 95.

16. Ormsby-Gore, "Education," 748.

serving in occupied African countries and at home, there were also representatives from church, mission, and philanthropic bodies.[17] Among these were J. H. Oldham (secretary of IMC) and Jesse Jones (director of the Phelps Stokes Fund).[18] The conference was convened with the sole purpose of considering a memorandum submitted to it earlier by the Education Committee of the Conference of Missionary Societies in Great Britain and Ireland. In fact, that memorandum, *Education Policy in Africa*, was written by J. H. Oldham.[19]

The parallel to the steps taken in America in 1919 is striking, in that, in both cases, a major step towards African education was being taken after the initiative of an ecumenical body to respond to the opinion that the results of education in Africa, which by then was largely left to the missions, had been unsatisfactory. The conference resulted in the formation of the Advisory Committee on Native Education in Tropical Africa (ACNETA). The committee was officially constituted in the last quarter of 1924, and Hanns Vischer (formerly director of education in Nigeria, and member of the 1924 Phelps Stokes commission) became its first full-time secretary.[20] In March 1925, the advisory committee submitted to the British government its first policy statement, *Education Policy in British Tropical Africa*, often referred to as Command Paper 2374 or merely as Cmd 2374.[21] The former is adopted in

---

17. Those serving in Africa were governors from Nigeria, Ghana, Sierra Leone, Kenya, and Malawi, and the Chief Secretary of Tanzania on leave in England. Those in home service included the Parliamentary Under-Secretary of State for the Colonies, and five senior officials of the Colonial Office.

18. Other church and mission leaders present were the Archbishop of Canterbury and Garfield Williams of the CMS. Garfield later became a member of the second Phelps Stokes commission.

19. Oldham, *Education Policy in Africa*. See also King, *Pan-Africanism*, 99. Scott, "Educational Policy," 413.

20. Jones, *Education in East Africa*, xxi. Beside Jones, other commissioners were James Emman Kwegyir Aggrey (who was also a member of the first commission), James Hardy Dillard (president of Jeanes and Slater funds), Homery Leroy Shantz (agriculturalist/botanist, Department of Agriculture, USA), Garfiled Williams (educational secretary, CMS), Hans Vischer (secretary for the Advisory Committee on Native Education, Colonial Office, Britain; formerly director of education, Northern Nigeria), C. T. Loram (member of Native Affairs Commission, South Africa; also a member of the first commission who joined the second commission only for the tour of Mozambique, Zimbabwe, and Zambia), James W. C. Dougall (from Scotland; acted as secretary of the commission with the assistance of George B. Dillard, USA). Dougall became the first principal of the Jeanes School, Kabete, Kenya, in 1924 and was later appointed education advisor to the Protestant Missions in Kenya and Uganda in 1931. King, *Pan-Africanism*, 100; Ormsby-Gore, "Education," 749.

21. Ormsby-Gore, "Education," 750; Thompson, "Historical Survey," 35, 36.

subsequent references in this chapter. The tone and terminology used even in section titles of this memorandum (and various subsequent memoranda[22]) issued by the Advisory Committee indicate that the committee was significantly influenced by the reports of the two Phelps Stokes commissions:

> Education should be adapted to mentality, aptitudes, occupations and traditions of various peoples, conserving as far possible all sound and healthy elements in the fabric of their social life. . . . Its aim should be to render the individual more efficient in his or her own condition of life, whatever it may be, and promote the advancement of the community as a whole through the improvement of agriculture, the development of native industries, the improvement of health. . . .[23]

This definition was radically different from what the majority of missions had been doing. Even so, missions were still needed onboard if the new policy was to be implemented successfully. They had the mechanism of the educational structure, save for the content of what they taught. But the nature of cooperation, if at all it was achievable, became a subject of much debate within missions and between them and governments, involving politicians, settlers, secular educationists, and Western missionaries. This study limits itself to the debate within missions first, and then between missions and the British colonial government in Tanzania.

7.1.3 Le Zoute Conference and Adaptation

Before considering the impact of Command Paper 2374 on missions in Tanzania (or, in other words, the debate between the colonial government there and missions), it might be helpful to first highlight the debate within missions. This is best illustrated by referring to the Le Zoute conference and

---

22. Some examples: (1) Advisory Committee, *Memorandum on Education of African Communities* (Colonial No. 103), NLS. This memorandum was issued in 1935. It focused on the contribution of the school to programmes of social advance or community improvement and the role of the teacher. (2) In 1941, Advisory Committee, *Mass Education in African Society* (Colonial No. 186), NLS. This put emphasis on educating the whole community, including adults. (3) There was also *Education for Citizenship in Africa* (1948) which was intended as a guide for "making" Africans loyal and responsible citizens. In this chapter, the focus is mainly on the memorandum of 1925, namely, Command Paper 2374.

23. Advisory Committee, *Education Policy in British Tropical Africa* (Command Paper 2374), 4.

its aftermath. It is here also where the views of Roland Allen and Norman Leys (mentioned earlier) will be considered.

Le Zoute conference was convened by the IMC in Belgium in September 1926. The title of the conference was "The Christian Mission in Africa" and this also became the title of the book by Edwin Smith, the official historian of Le Zoute.[24] Over two hundred delegates interested in African education – the majority of whom were Westerners – gathered at Le Zoute. In passing, Jack Thompson's observation about the under-representation of African delegates at Le Zoute is worth noting. Thompson has observed that apart from having "vague and non-committal" comments on the political situation in Africa:

> It could well be argued, however, that over and above any shortcomings of policy, the most serious defect of Le Zoute was the composition of its delegates. With the exception of a few African-Americans and about four black Africans, Le Zoute was basically a conference of Europeans talking about Africa; that this was so in mid-1920s could in itself be seen as an indication of failure.[25]

The four Africans – out of a total of 221 delegates – were N. S. J. Ballunta, the Rev N. T. Clerk, the Rev John Dube, and Z. R. Mahabane.[26] African Americans numbered seven. The participation of the four indigenous African delegates did not alter the thrust of the conference with regard to education in Africa. Nonetheless, their presence was important, during and after the conference.[27]

---

24. Smith, *Christian Mission in Africa*.
25. Thompson, *Christianity in Northern Malawi*, 250.
26. N. T. Clerk was a synod clerk of the Scottish mission in Ghana; John Dube was founder and principal of the Ohlange Institution in Natal, South Africa and a newspaper editor; Z. R. Mahabane was president of the National Congress of South Africa. See Smith, *Christian Mission in Africa*, 25, 26.
27. For example, Smith has noted John Dube's contribution during the devotion times. See Smith, *Christian Mission in Africa*, 34. Equally, Rodney Orr has observed Dube's post-Le Zoute views on the need for African Americans to be accepted as missionaries to Africa despite the fears of colonial governments in Africa that they might be politically influenced by the political views of men such as Marcus Garvey and W. E. Dubois. Dube argued that it would have been better to have "the Black and White work together in Africa. It has its problems, but no more than two Whites!" See John Dube's report on the Le Zoute Conference, International Missionary Council (IMC), Le Zoute files, microfiche 202, School of Oriental and African Studies (SOAS), quoted in Orr, "African American Missionaries," 269ff.

Le Zoute debated and made resolutions on many issues – educational, political, and economic. On education, it debated and made resolutions on issues of policy, curriculum, the education of women, the medium of instruction in schools, and religious education.[28] Those who accepted the idea of cooperation followed Jones's ideas and argued that, though missions had been the chief providers of education in Africa, such education had been largely literary and evangelistic in nature. This needed broadening, if not changing, to become "education for life" – covering health and sanitation; the appreciation and use of the environment; household and home; and recreation.[29] In his paper at Le Zoute, "The Relation of Christian Missions to the New Forces That Are Reshaping African Life," J. H. Oldham called for "a fresh advance, a further step forward, an *enlargement* of our conception of the mission of the Christian Church."[30] In general, official resolutions at Le Zoute were favourable to the idea of adaptation and of cooperation between missions and governments to implement policies based on that philosophy.

As stated earlier, Roland Allen (an Anglican missiologist) and Norman Leys (an educationist in Kenya) were among those opposed to the idea of adaptation. In response to those who supported cooperation, and to Oldham's paper cited above, Rolland Allen accused Oldham of what he regarded as a liberal thought which encouraged missions to become government agents by forsaking their "proper work" of evangelism. Allen appealed to historical experience – for example, in England[31] – arguing that British government intervention in education, particularly in elementary education through regulations and supervision, had served only to weaken church schools

---

28. Smith, *Christian Mission in Africa*, 56–72, 108–118.

29. See Jones, *Four Essentials of Education*, 1926, cited in Smith, *Christian Mission in Africa*, 62. In his own address to the conference under the title "New Forces in Africa," Jones stated that, "education is not limited to the three Rs [reading, writing and arithmetic].... To give life and to give it more abundantly is now more truly than ever the desire and purpose of every missionary who really understands the Christian command.". See Smith, *Christian Mission in Africa*, 133.

30. J. H Oldham, "The Relation of Christian Missions to the New Forces That Are Reshaping African Life" in Smith, *Christian Mission in Africa*, 162, 163. Emphasis added.

31. Curtis, *History of Education*. For the struggles between church and state in eighteenth- and nineteenth-century education in Britain, see especially ch. 6, "Elementary Education in the Age of Philanthropy," 184–229, and ch. 7, "From the Beginning of State Intervention to the Revised Code, 1862," 230–271.

while government schools became stronger.[32] The same was likely to happen in Africa.

If Allen's objections centred on the future of the evangelistic nature of mission education, objections made by Norman Leys took a different line. He focused more on the political implications of adaptation for the future of Africans. He cited the Kenyan context to support his case, but his argument had wider application. The aim of mission education, Leys argued, was to "enlighten," and given the meagre resources missions possessed, he reckoned that the task had been done well. Yet, under the influence of men such as J. H. Oldham, he noted, the kind of partnership between government and missions that was envisaged was one that altered the nature of mission education. It would not necessarily achieve its stated goal of "enlightening" – that is, being for life. It aimed at "wealth production of a special type."[33] The purpose of adaptation, Leys went on to state, was to induce rural Kenyans to leave the land and work for wages for Europeans. If missions entered into partnership with a government that refused Kenyans any rights in land ownership, and Kenyans realized that in Christianity "missions offer[ed] them something less than the fullest life they can realize, they will as the years pass increasingly turn elsewhere than to the Church. They will be right in so turning, since the church that refuses to the least of its brethren the best of God's gifts has lost its Christianity."[34]

With this representative picture of the complex debate even among Europeans, and within missions, it is now possible to proceed and consider the implementation of Command Paper 2374 in Tanzania. It is hoped that this will shed some light on the issues raised in the debate at Le Zoute on the impact of partnership between government and missions. Le Zoute, though attended by people of differing views, nonetheless made resolutions that exhibited the influence of the Phelps Stokes commissions upon some of its leading organizers and delegates.

The two issues raised by Allen and Leys are of interest here. Did cooperation between the British colonial government in Tanzania and missions, including the CMS mission, lead to the erosion of the evangelistic role of

---

32. Allen, *Le Zoute*, 11, 12, 15, 35, 36.
33. Leys, "Missions and Government," 13.
34. Leys, 13.

mission education hitherto offered, as Allen feared? What impact did adaptation have on the socioeconomic life of the indigenous teachers? What was the opinion of the indigenous teachers in all this?

7.2 British Educational Policy in Tanzania

7.2.1 Educational Policy 1919–1924

Until 1918, Tanzania was under German occupation, though, in fact, by November 1917, German forces had surrendered in Tanzania.[35] Germany giving up its African colonies at the Treaty of Versailles,[36] and the drawing up of the "Tanganyika Mandate,"[37] was a mere formality.[38] Until then, education in Tanzania was largely in the hands of missions. Early British colonial political and educational policy in Tanzania under governor Horace Byatt (1916–1924) was similar to that of the German colonial administration.[39] Like its predecessor, the priority of the British colonial government at this time was to build up a supply of low ranking administrative personnel. Christian missions (except those of German origin) also continued their activities with a relative degree of independence in terms of education administration, finance, and use of Christian schools for evangelistic and "civilizing" purposes.[40] This continued until 1924. Put briefly, the government and missions pursued separate educational enterprises.[41]

---

35. *PCMS*, 1918, 35.

36. Other German colonies in Africa were Namibia, Togo, and Cameroon.

37. The Mandate was drawn up by the Council of the League of Nations and was confirmed in August 1922 and 1923. See *Official Journal of the League of Nations* 3 (1922): 793, 865, cited in Buell, *Native Problem in Africa*, 1:430.

38. Cameron and Wood, *Society, Schools and Progress*, 58; Buell, *Native Problem in Africa*, 2:430.

39. It has to be recalled that, by September 1916, German colonial administration had almost collapsed, and British colonial administration begun. However, Tanzania became a British mandate in 1919, though the mandate was only officially confirmed in 1922. Austen, *Northwest Tanzania*, 148; .Cameron, *My Tanganyika Service*, 24.

40. German missionaries were expelled *en mass* from Tanzania in 1919 and were only allowed to return in 1926 after Germany's admission into the League of Nations in 1926 and the intervention of the IMC. See J. Cameron, *Society, Schools and Progress*, 61.

41. Cameron, *Society, Schools and Progress*, 60; cf. Cameron, *My Tanganyika Service*, 127.

7.2.2 Educational Policy 1925 Onwards

The arrangement just described was, however, short-lived. Some of the issues raised in the Command Paper 2374 and highlighted at Le Zoute were bound to affect the work of missions in Tanzania, directly or indirectly. Mission education was never the same from 1925 onwards. Of immediate interest is how Command Paper 2374 affected the status of the out-schools because it is in this school category that much of the evangelization took place, and the contribution of the indigenous teachers was most notable.

Command Paper 2374 did not impose an injunction upon the development of post-primary and higher education for Africans in the 1920s and 1930s. The reason was mainly that the British colonial government depended on central schools, and industrial, technical, and teacher training to raise much of the manpower for its administrative and industrial needs. Yet, for social and political reasons, it appears that the protagonists of the philosophy of adaptation, and those who wholeheartedly subscribed to it (the colonial government officials and key mission leaders such as J. H. Oldham), realized that it would not succeed unless weighty attention was paid to the out-schools.[42] So Oldham wrote: "The small village or bush schools may from the scholastic standpoint leave everything to be desired. They are nevertheless the centres through which new ideas are reaching the masses of the population."[43]

There was another reason why education offered by missions in the out-schools attracted attention. As pointed out earlier, until 1924, the mechanism for the cooperation between government and missions was not in place yet, and the policy was that missions should carry on their educational work without government influence or intervention. Yet it should be emphasized that, even at this period, British colonial administration in Tanzania under Horace Byatt (the first governor, 1916–1924) was nervous about the potential political consequences of leaving scattered out-schools unsupervised. S. Rivers-Smith (then the colonial director of education) expressed this anxiety: "Experience has shown that the revolutionary element may also come through the mission boys, and it is for this reason that I hold the opinion

---

42. Jones, *Education in East Africa*, 50.
43. Oldham, "Educational Work," 50; cf. Dougall, "Development," 317. This article bears the title of an article by Scott, "Development," 693–739.

that the state should have voice in what Missions do unless their work can be limited to religious instruction."[44]

7.2.3 A Re-definition of the Role of Out-Schools and Indigenous Teachers

Such political concerns as quoted above were present. However, the main criticism against missions in Tanzania (as elsewhere in Africa) centred largely on their failure to enable out-schools to live up to "their" potential for adaptation, dwelling instead on literary education. Poor supervision was singled out a major cause of that failure. For, indeed, Jesse Jones had already given sufficient negative publicity about the state of the out-schools and the indigenous teachers who taught at such schools. To him, out-schools were "'little nothings,' neglected, poor and unsupervised. Their buildings are often ugly shacks with no equipment, distinguishable from Native huts only by their size."[45] As for the pattern of teaching, he noted: "Children attend these poorer schools with great irregularity; often, indeed, the hours of instruction are limited to an hour or two in the early morning and an hour for a few stragglers in the late afternoon."[46] On the qualification of the African teachers assigned to the schools, Jones was equally critical:

> A large number of their teachers are ignorant and untrained, "blind leaders of the blind," either futile as regards community influence or exercising an influence which has no basis in reality.[47]

> The majority of the teachers have not had more than the equivalent of three or four years of schooling. Sometimes they seem to be but little above the standards of the primitive people whose children they are teaching. . . . It is hardly necessary to note how wasteful and unfair it has often been to send Natives who have but superficial knowledge of education and religion to change the life of their primitive communities without direction and

---

44. Minute Secretariat Mission Papers (SMP) 3118/2A, quoted in Thompson, "Historical Survey," 30.
45. Jones, *Education in East Africa*, 59.
46. Jones, *Education in Africa*, 44
47. Jones, *Education in East Africa*, 59.

encouragement regularly received from the central station....
The complete supervision of educational activities in a colony
both involves the government and missions.[48]

To a degree, Jones's description of the physical status of out-schools and the qualification of most of their teachers was not entirely off the mark. But that is far from suggesting that he and members of the commissions called for improvement so that out-schools might do better in imparting literary and religious education and continue as evangelistic centres. Jones's comments must be viewed in the context of his political, and perhaps racial, motives.

From the point of view of the government and the Phelps Stokes commission, the drive to improve the out-schools remained an unfinished business. The remedy had to come from the American Jeanes system of supervision.[49] James Dillard (president of Jeanes and Slater funds in America and a member of the second Phelps Stokes commission) agreed, for he himself viewed the out-schools as "the most outstanding problem."[50] So Jones proposed:

The Jeanes Fund system of supervisory teachers so effective for improvement of rural Negro schools in America probably offers more suggestions for the type of supervision required than any other system known to the Commission.... The Education Commission is emphatically of the opinion that this system of supervisory teachers could be introduced by colonial governments and mission societies for the supervision of the village schools in every part of Africa.[51]

As part of the plan to improve the supervision of out-schools in Tanzania, and in accordance with the recommendation of the second Phelps Stokes commission, the British colonial government (now under Donald Cameron, who succeeded Byatt as governor in 1925) indicated its "approval of the plan of itinerant teachers to guide and encourage little schools throughout the

---

48. Jones, *Education in Africa*, 44

49. For a brief history of the Jeanes school system, and how it functioned in the southern states of America, see Davis, "Jeanes Visiting Teachers," 14–25.

50. Jones, *Education in East Africa*, xxi; notes on a conversation between James Dillard and J. H. Oldham, 7 May 1924, File Q-G, Edinburgh House, London, cited in King, *Pan-Africanism*, 151.

51. Jones, *Education in Africa*, 44

territory."[52] Also, among the various types of grants approved in the 1927 Native Education Ordinance (NEO) up to one hundred pounds could be given to missions for peripatetic teachers for a number of village schools.[53] But it is doubtful if supervision through itinerant teachers ever gained prominence or became an ongoing government educational policy in Tanzania in the manner it did through Jeanes schools in Kenya, Malawi, Zambia, and Zimbabwe.[54]

Soon after the visit of the second commission of the Phelps Stokes Fund in 1924 to Tanzania, the British colonial government in Tanzania held a conference with missions in 1925 under the chairmanship of the newly appointed governor, Donald Cameron. The release of Command Paper 2374, with its emphasis on adaptation, coincided well with his arrival in Tanzania. Cameron saw relevance and applicability of his administrative style of "Indirect Rule" for African education, for it emphasized the use of indigenous institutions. So, arguably, more than Byatt (his predecessor), Cameron was eager about educational reforms.

Following the broad guidelines outlined in Command Paper 2374, the 1927 NEO provided for African representation, but, inevitably (and given the point in time), the Europeans became the majority. This was the case in all countries under British colonial rule.[55] Only two indigenous Tanzanians attended: Matola, a head teacher (possibly an appointee of the missions because

---

52. Jones, *Education in East Africa*, 192.

53. Contrary to other sources, W. Furley and T. Watson give an inaccurate date of 1928 for the Native Education Ordinance. See Furley and Watson, *History of Education*, 140; cf. Richter, *Tanganyika and Its Future*, 65; Thompson, "Historical Survey," 38; Oldham and Gibson, *Remaking of Man in Africa*, 163. The last three authors give 1927 as the date.

54. The first Jeanes school in Africa was started at Kabete in Kenya. For details, see Dougall, "School Education," 49. For further details of the political precedence, and assessment of the Jeanes school in Kenya, see King, *Pan-Africanism*, especially ch. 4, entitled "The Jeanes School: An Experiment in Phelps Stokesim," 150–176. For an insider's own view of the Jeanes schools in Kenya, Malawi, Zambia, and Zimbabwe, see *Report of the Inte-Territorial Jeanes Conference*. For critical views, see, Heyman, "The Initial Years," 105–123, and Murray, *School in the Bush*, 261. This book was first published in 1929. The locations of the Jeanes schools in each country were as follows: Zomba (Malawi), Mazabuka (Zambia), and Domboshawa and Hope Fountain (Zimbabwe). See *Report of the Inte-Territorial Jeanes Conference*, especially 381–419.

55. Oldham and Gibson, *Remaking of Man*, 151–171, 163. In Tanzania, there were three government representatives (Director of Education, Director of Medical and Sanitary Services, and Secretary for Native Affairs), eight mission representatives, and two representatives of the Chambers of Commerce and Planters' Association.

missions were given the opportunity to appoint one of the two African representatives), and Samwel Chiponde (a government employee).[56]

The question of supervision, and the status of the out-schools and the indigenous teachers, formed part of the discussions at the conference. S. Rivers-Smith, Director of Education in Tanzania at the time, told the 1925 education conference in Dar es Salaam:

> Large numbers of little out-schools unless properly staffed and regularly supervised will make no appreciable contribution to any general education; in fact I think all admit that there are few greater dangers to civilisation than the ignorant teacher. From all dependencies of the Empire complaints are today being received as to the sinister danger of the multiplication of these little schools conducted by teachers without training and inadequately supervised by any qualified educationist.[57]

One could hardly miss the resemblance of this description and that of Jones quoted earlier! This was a major indicator that the British colonial government in Tanzania had taken onboard the call for the transformation of the status of out-schools and indigenous teachers. Indeed, it was suggested by some that a transformed teacher would "give a new direction and impulse to education in regard to the home life of the people."[58] J. H. Oldham noted this significance of the teacher of the bush school too. The role of the church and its teacher-catechist (who is both preacher and teacher) in this venture was crucial because he or she was the "bearer of new ideas" – if he or she was properly supervised.[59]

Until 1925, seventeen missions in Tanzania (of which twelve were Protestant and five Catholic) were the major providers of education – much of it through the out-schools.[60] A report of the department of education

---

56. W. Bryant Mumford, "Education and the Social Adjustment," 154. Only the single name, "Matola" is given in the source. Furley and Watson, "Education in Tanganyika," 477;. Cameron, *Society, Schools and Progress*, 62.

57. *Report of the Proceedings*.

58. Dougall, "School Education," 51.

59. Oldham and Gibson, *Remaking of Man*, 70; cf. Jones, *Education in Africa*, 60, cf. Jones, *Education in East Africa*, 60; cf. Mumford, "Malangali School," 281.

60. Jones, *Education in East Africa*, 179. Jones's list has nine Protestant and four Catholic missions. The Protestant missions were CMS, UMCA, Bethel Mission (Beilefeld), Leipzig

written two years earlier (that is, for 1922–1923) showed that there were 2,200 mission schools attended by 115,000 students and 2,200 African teachers supported by 157 foreign missionaries.[61] This was a far larger number than the sixty-five government schools, with their 135 African teachers, supported by five Europeans. Soon after the 1925 conference, the Advisory Committee for Native Education (ACNE) was formed in 1926. Two meetings, first in March 1926 and then in February 1927,[62] were charged with the consideration of draft ordinance and further examination of the drafted one, respectively. With their prominent position in the provision of education, missions had hoped that the formation of ACNE in 1926 would make the government recognize the role of missions even further and foster their cooperation. In fact, they felt that Command Paper 2374 itself, and more so the 1925 conference, had vindicated their practice, particularly on the following points. First, "all elementary instruction to be [given] in the mother tongue;" second, "religious instruction to be one of the main subjects as the chief means of character building;" third, "elementary schools and the training of teachers for them to be the special task of the missions"; and fourth and last, "as far as possible the schools were to be fitted into the background and requirements of native life."[63] Yet, in light of the description of the status of the out-schools and the indigenous teachers given by Rivers-Smith at the 1925 Dar es Salaam conference, it looked almost certain that the fate of the out-schools, the African teacher, and the evangelistic role of the elementary mission schools was now sealed.

Mission, Berlin Missionary Society, Moravian Mission, Africa Inland Mission (AIM), Seventh-Day Adventist (SDA), and London Missionary Society (LMS). The Catholic missions were the Holy Ghost Fathers (Congregation of the Holy Spirit), Benedictines of St Ottilien and Uznach, White Fathers (Society of Missionaries of Our Lady of Africa), and Capuchins. Richter's list also has Augustana Lutheran Mission (Board of Foreign Missions of the Augustana Synod, USA), Neukirchen Mission, and Friends Service Council; and for Catholic missions, he adds Consolata (International Missionary College for Foreign Missions). See Richter, *Tanganyika and Its Future*, 93. Taken together, both lists bring the total of missions to seventeen.

61. Jones, *Education in East Africa*, 183. He gives the figure 150 on page 179, but probably the figure 157 is correct. See Thompson, "Historical Survey," 35.

62. Minutes, Advisory Committee for Native Education (ACNE), Tanganyika, 21 & 22/2/1927, IMC files, SOAS Library, IMC/CBMS, Box 258, "East Africa, Tanganyika: Education," Microfiche No. 370. Samwel Chiponde was absent, and Agustino Ramadhani, rather than Matola, was now the African delegate.

63. Richter, *Tanganyika and Its Future*, 65.

7.3 Government Educational Policy: Conflicting Responses

7.3.1 Frustrations of Missions

Soon, mission representatives became frustrated about the failure of the colonial government to assure the missions that ACNE would function mainly along the original London memorandum (Command Paper 2374) and not according to local interpretation by the colonial government in Tanzania.[64] Indeed, as Julius Richter notes, "the missionaries were rather surprised and puzzled when on 25th February, 1927, a comprehensive 'Native Education Ordinance' was published in Dar es Salaam which laid down a pretentious Government educational programme along the lines which to some extent diverged from those of the preceding conferences."[65]

There were six main points in the NEO that alarmed the missions. Their significance to the relationship and "equality" between missions and the government, and their impact on the future of the out-schools and African teachers, make it necessary to quote them in full:

> (a) *All* schools shall be put under Government supervision. No school may be opened *unless registered*. New schools must satisfy the Provincial Education Committee that they are necessary and that they have a minimum staff. *Bush schools which do not conform to the Government syllabus be closed within five years.*
> (b) Instruction to be, *even* in the bush schools, exclusively in the Swahili language. (c) Central Schools (Intermediate) with a four years' course to be exclusively in English. (d) Teachers of the first grade must have passed at least Standard IV of the Central schools and have had four years' teacher training; second grade teachers must have passed the vernacular school and have had two years' training. No person shall be allowed to teach in a Government or *assisted [mission] school* who is not registered as a first or second grade teacher, or is at least on the provisional list. (e) *Religious instruction to be allowed only outside of the regular school hours.* (f) Approved schools shall get Government

---

64. Thompson, "Historical Survey," 39.
65. Richter, *Tanganyika and Its Future*, 65.

grants up to two-thirds of the salaries paid to African teachers and to £300 for the European staff.[66]

The conditions spelled out in the 1927 NEO sounded like a death sentence to the freedom of missions to carry on educational activity along evangelistic lines. The second meeting of ACNE at Dar es Salaam, though attended by mission delegates,[67] made it clear that unregistered schools would not be inspected, but neither could they get grant-in-aid until registered. It added that those teaching there must be paid according to government scales; the expulsion of pupils was possible, but missions had to report, through their education secretaries, to the Director of Education; and teachers were not to be recruited simply for their spiritual enthusiasm. Missions were now faced with the prospect of closing their out-schools that did not conform to government standards. All this – let alone the obvious marginalization of religious instruction in the school timetable – was a serious blow.

With a sense of urgency, Protestant missions, particularly those of German origin,[68] responded to the 1927 NEO by convening a meeting at Marangu, Kilimanjaro province in northern Tanzania, in September 1928. The meeting was sponsored particularly by the Leipzig and Bethel missions.[69] Anglican missions (the CMS and the UMCA) were invited as guests because they too shared similar concerns.

The following responses were made. First, that religious instruction be taught in all schools, including those under grants-in-aid system, and this be done in a Christian atmosphere and within regular school hours. Second, missions should not be restricted in opening unregistered and unassisted out-schools as they wished for evangelistic purposes because Muslims were allowed to open similar schools, *kutabs*. Third, instruction in the first years at the elementary schools should be in the vernacular, with Kiswahili taught as a main subject and this latter language becoming the medium of instruction

---

66. Minutes, ACNE, 21 & 22/2/1927, IMC files, SOAS Library; cf. Richter, *Tanganyika and Its Future*, 65, 66. All emphases added.

67. Missions delegates included Rev John Briggs (CMS), Bishop Wilson (HGF), Bishop Zelger (Swiss Capuchin Fathers), Rev J. J Raum (Lutheran), and G. Broomfield (UMCA). See Minutes, ACNE, 21 & 22/2/1927, IMC files, SOAS Library.

68. The Lutheran missions were Leipzig, Bethel, and Berlin. Non-Lutheran missions included CMS, UMCA, and AIM. See Thompson, "Historical Survey," 42.

69. Wright, *German Missions*, 173.

in later years. Fourth, indigenous teachers should be trained in Kiswahili, with English taught only as a subject. Fifth, grants for teachers should be paid not directly to the teachers but to the school – apparently to avoid fostering the spirit of independence among teachers. Sixth, that missions and schools concerned be notified of inspection visits by government inspectors beforehand to avoid being caught off-guard.[70]

To these, Rivers-Smith offered only minimum assurances, and on the whole he maintained the government position as stated in the NEO of 1927.[71] Even the meeting between L. W. Weichert of the Berlin mission and Rivers-Smith, with other officials at the Colonial Office in London on 19 September 1927 to clarify issues of salary for indigenous mission teachers and the need for the government not to negotiate with mission teachers without the knowledge of the mission concerned, did not give the adequate assurances sought.[72]

The issue of the basis on which government grants-in-aid should be disbursed to registered or "assisted" mission schools also became contentious. In theory, guidelines in Command Paper 2374 of 1924 established that voluntary agencies (that is, missions) would be given grants-in-aid because it was economically viable for the government to do so and missions had a long experience in providing specialist education, especially one that assisted character building. These points were highlighted again in the 1933 policy document, *Memorandum on Educational Grants-in-Aid*.[73]

Despite this, grants-in-aid to mission schools were disbursed on the basis of the quality of secular education, not of religious teaching. In fact, far from missions acquiring an "automatic" recognition, they had to earn their status and place in the new national educational front through efficiency. That is to say, "grants-in-aid were rewards for efficiency rather than the means to attain efficiency."[74] The contemporary tide of opinion in Europe itself – what

---

70. Resolutions, Conference of Evangelical Missions, Marangu, September 1928, IMC/CBMS files, SOAS Library; cf. Richter, *Tanganyika and Its Future*, 66.

71. Response to Marangu resolutions, Microfiche 372, IMC/CBMS files, SOAS Library.

72. Conference at Colonial Office, London, between Rivers-Smith, Major Vischer, Professor Westermann, and L. W. Weichert of Berlin Mission, 19/9/1927, IMC/CBMS files, SOAS Library.

73. Advisory Committee, *Memorandum on Educational Grants-in-Aid*, 5; cf. Ormsby-Gore, "Education," 756.

74. Thompson, "Historical Survey," 67; c. f. Murray, *School in the Bush*, 265.

Victor Murray refers to as "the relativist temper of the age" against traditional missionary values in the 1920s – and then the world economic recession of the early 1930s did not help the financial situation of many missions.[75]

In 1930, missions secured important clarifications and modifications from the director of education. One such clarification was that most of the restrictions imposed on mission schools applied only to the ones which received, or would receive, grants from the government – schools known as *assisted* or *aided* schools. However, these clarifications seem not to have satisfied everyone, for at this time, some, like Raum, were still expressing concern.[76] Raum's concern over the marginalization of the religious instruction in mission schools, let alone in those run by the government itself, reflected not just the opinion of German evangelical missions but of most missions (Protestant and Catholic alike) in Tanzania.[77]

Later, in 1936, the government distinguished between two types of out-schools. First, those classified as "catechetical centres." Here, minimal secular instruction was offered. These kinds of schools were excluded from registration. The second type was the out-schools where both religion and simple, basic secular education (that is, the three Rs of reading, writing, and arithmetic) were taught regularly. These did not automatically qualify for government assistance but could be upgraded and registered to become part of the government educational system, not least if they had registered teachers on the staff.

By 31 March 1931, Protestant and Catholic missions had a total of 142 registered or "assisted" out-schools and were receiving a grant of £4716 out of £34,683,[78] which included the DCT (CMS sphere).[79] The remainder of the

---

75. Murray, *School in the Bush*, 262–264; Oliver, *Missionary Factor*, 231–232.
76. Raum, "Educational Problems in Tanganyika," 564–565.
77. Listowell, *Making of Tanganyika*, 102. It is at this time that the famous advice was given by Archbishop Arthur Hinsley (a papal delegate) to Catholic missions: "Collaborate with your power; and where it is impossible to carry on both the immediate task of evangelisation and your educational work, neglect your churches in order to perfect your schools." Thompson, "Historical Survey," 44, 45.
78. "Annual Report of Education Department 1931" for Tanzania, cited in Thompson, "Historical Survey," 54.
79. Of 142 schools, four belonged to the DCT (CMS sphere) and received a grant of £142. This was rather a small sum compared with £1,903 given to the UMCA dioceses, namely Zanzibar (£1,767) and Masasi (£136). Equally the grant for the two central schools in the DCT (Kikuyu and Katoke) was only £568, compared with £2,101 given for two central schools in the

government grant was for teacher training centres, central schools, industrial schools, and girls' boarding schools in the missions.

Despite tokens of "smooth" cooperation reflected in clarifications given by the British colonial government, and its giving of grants to mission institutions that fulfilled the criteria set out in the 1927 NEO, some missions viewed the government's intervention as disruptive and marginalizing. At first some Protestant missions (Africa Inland Mission, the Mennonite Mission and the Moravian Mission), as well as Catholic missions (for example, the White Fathers in Bukoba, western Tanzania), declined to seek grants-in-aid in order to keep their autonomy.[80]

For some missions though, particularly those with meagre financial resources such as the CMS mission, the system of grants-in-aid was crucial for the success of their work. The CMS mission was probably among the first to apply for a government grant in 1921, and was certainly fortunate to be the first to benefit from the grants-in-aid system in 1926, well before the 1927 NEO (after which the CMS sphere was now called the DCT). The UMCA also received a grant in 1927.[81] That both these missions were Anglican could be the reason (beside financial limitations) why they accepted government funds at a time when non-British missions feared the erosion of their freedom and autonomy. However, like other missions, they were equally frustrated by the educational restrictions imposed on all missions by the British colonial government.

The economic depression of the early 1930s forced the British colonial government to revise its policy on the type of schools to assist. Under the policy revised in 1934 (in which there was a shift of emphasis from central to elementary schools with a rural emphasis or "industrial schools"), grants-in-aid for Catholic and Protestant mission central schools in 1937 was reduced to £2,000 compared to £10,771 given in 1931.[82] Since the number of educational

---

UMCA sphere. Interestingly, unlike any other missions, DCT received the highest grant award in 1931 for girls' boarding schools. Mvumi and Berega boarding schools received £1,550 and £359, respectively, compared with £785 for the same number of girls' boarding schools in the sphere of the UMCA. See Thompson, "Historical Survey," 55.

80. Thompson, "Historical Survey," 40.
81. Thompson, 34, 39, 40.
82. Thompson, 61, 62. In 1930, the government had eight central schools catering to 1,732 scholars. See Richter, *Tanganyika and Its Future*, 64.

institutions other than the out-schools were small, it must be concluded that it was the out-schools that suffered most.

Indeed, due to the lessening of grants by CMS Australia (which took over the CMS mission in Ugogo and Ukaguru from 1927),[83] and by the colonial government in Tanzania, the DCT in the CMS sphere of influence was forced to close many of its out-schools.[84] Educational statistics for 1934 show that in that year there were 218 educational institutions (teacher training colleges, central schools, and elementary and bush schools). In 1935, the number had fallen to just nineteen.[85]

The issue of the standard of education in out-schools in Tanzania (the quality of their teachers and syllabi) remained a contentious one between government and missions for a long time after the introduction of the 1927 NEO. Indeed the government's criticism of such schools never ceased, for, as late as 1945, A. A. M. Isherwood (the colonial director of education who succeeded S. Rivers-Smith) described them almost in an identical manner as Jones did in reports of the first and second commissions to Africa in 1922 and 1924, respectively. Isherwood wrote:

> Children attending these schools receive once or twice a week biblical and catechetical instruction from a peripatetic evangelist who is sometimes almost illiterate and teaches only by rote. Again the conditions of work at many of these schools are soul destroying; it is frequently carried on in an old, dark, unhygienic, vermin-infested hovels, places inimical to enlightenment and positively dangerous to the health of children. Such places should be abolished.[86]

A. A. M. Isherwood accused some missions of being vocal about cooperation and fairness from the government, "but an interpretation of their

---

83. For details, see chapter 8.
84. *PCMS*, 1935, 5.
85. *PCMS*, 1935, xii; *PCMS*, 1936, xii. The number of CMS educational institutions rose sharply again to 169 in 1936 – possibly a reflection of the signs of economic recovery and assistance the DCT was now receiving from the government for elementary schools. See *PCMS*, 1937, xii.
86. Isherwood to Chief Secretary, 12/1/1945, SMP 28867, quoted in Thompson, "Historical Survey," 65, 66.

view often appears to be that the state should pay everything and the church control everything."[87]

In reflecting on the frustrations of the missions, one has to observe that, far more than the government, it was the missions who now wanted to adhere to the question of adaptation and "carry the flag" along the lines of Command Paper 2374 as was interpreted and implemented by the British colonial government in Tanzania. Most missions in Tanzania were "convinced that educational wisdom is on their side; if the danger of an intellectual inflation and of an unhealthy caricature of 'White' civilization is to be avoided, native education must be fitted in with the natives' background and surrounding."[88]

In fact, when Rivers-Smith was about to retire in 1930, Broomfield (of the UMCA) wrote to Oldham, urging him to ensure that Isherwood was appointed to succeed him because his predecessor had given more attention to central schools and the teaching of the English language to the neglect of the village (station schools) and out-schools. Broomfield urged:

> Strong efforts need to be made to counteract the present tendency of *so much education*, i.e. to draw the more intelligent boys from the villages and attract them to Government and commercial service. . . . I think Mr Isherwood is the right man. Under him, education in Tanganyika would progress along the right lines. . . . If you can do anything to bring about the appointment of Mr Isherwood, you will be doing a good work.[89]

For such a comment to be made from within mission circles is interesting. It reveals something typical of some missions in Tanzania and other British colonies in Africa at this time. They complained bitterly against government interference and control of mission education at all levels. They feared the erosion of the influence of the out-schools as evangelistic and catechetical centres. Yet, it is these very missions that seemed, in principle, to be more at home with the philosophy of adaptation of education. They objected to the

---

87. Isherwood to Chief Secretary, in Thompson, 40.
88. Richter, *Tanganyika and Its Future*, 67.
89. Broomfield to Oldham, 12/12/1930, IMC/CBMS files, SOAS Library. Emphasis added.

use of English as an exclusive language of instruction in central schools and preferred Kiswahili instead.[90]

7.3.2 Language Debate and Adaptation

At this point, it may be appropriate to revisit the Le Zoute conference. One of the issues that featured at Le Zoute, which continued to dominate discussion on African education as has been indicated above, is that of the medium of instruction in schools, including mission schools. The core of the debate on language was whether English or the vernaculars be used in schools. If the former was introduced, should it be taught as one subject among many, or be adopted as a medium of instruction, and if so, at what level?

But there were those who argued that the vernaculars should be given preference especially at the elementary level of education. It has to be observed that the whole issue of the vernacular languages was closely linked to the politics of education for the masses and of "preservation" of African institutions.[91] The *official* resolution on language at the Le Zoute conference in 1926 supported this idea.[92] That is to say, it favoured the use of the vernaculars as a medium of instruction in elementary education. English could then be introduced in the latter years. The other major alternative view at Le Zoute did not feature in the official conference resolutions. The view (which, according to Ade Ajayi, was also present among indigenous people in Nigeria in the mid-nineteenth century) recognized that the Africans attending schools wanted to be taught in English and not in the vernacular.[93] C. T. Loram, who was a delegate at Le Zoute, noted that Africans

> knew that the key to the attainment of the white man's power lies in the white man's language. Any attempt to adopt the vernacular as the medium of instruction would meet with strong opposition of certain classes of literate Africans who would feel that the door of opportunity was slammed in the face of their children. Moreover, English is in some regions the language

---

90. Broomfield to Oldham, 12/12/1930, IMC/CBMS files, SOAS Library, 66; cf. Thompson, "Historical Survey," 42; Raum, "Educational Problems," 567.
91. See Advisory Committee, *Mass Education in African Society* (Colonial No. 186), 33–34.
92. Smith, *Christian Mission in Africa*, 68.
93. Ajayi, *Christian Missions in Nigeria*, 139–140.

of Government and commerce, and the African who does not know English is placed at great disadvantage – he is at the mercy of unscrupulous white men.[94]

The memorandum on the *Place of the Vernacular in Native Education* in 1927 (which focused on the socioeconomic and even political aspirations of Africans) echoed this view:

> There can be no doubt that one of the main incentives, if not *the* incentive, of African parents in sending their sons to school is for them to acquire a knowledge of English. A knowledge of English is naturally regarded by them as the principal means whereby economic advance can be obtained by them in later life. Any attempt, therefore to delay unduly the introduction of English into African schools would be regarded as an attempt of the Government to hold back the African from legitimate advance in civilisation.[95]

Yet, all subsequent efforts showed that concerns voiced by people like Loram – that African aspirations had to be taken into account – were almost being ignored. In an effort to promote the vernaculars in schools, and deal with the so-called "language problem" in Africa, the International Institute of African Languages and Culture was founded in 1926 at the initiative of ecumenical mission bodies in Britain. The institute was charged with the dual tasks of rendering selected African vernacular languages into literary form, as well as promoting the preservation of "valuable elements" in the African cultures.[96]

---

94. Smith, *Christian Mission in Africa*, 68–69.
95. Advisory Committee, *British Tropical Africa* (African No. 1110), 10, 11.
96. The Le Zoute conference described the institute's services as "(a) to solve linguistic problems, (b) to remedy and to prevent expensive mistakes in the choice of orthography, (c) to prepare text-books adapted to the needs and conditions of African life, (d) to prepare a better understanding of the distinctive character and contribution of African peoples, (e) to bring about an increasingly sympathetic attitude on the part of Government towards African vernaculars, and towards valuable elements in the African heritage." See Smith, *Christian Mission*, 116–117, 166. The institute has since then used its journal *Africa* as a forum for discussions and debates on various issues related to African cultures. See Schmidt, "Use of the Vernacular," 137–145. The article was read at the meeting of the executive council of the institute, November 1929. In its meeting in October 1930, the institute adopted the Le Zoute resolution on the use of the vernaculars at an early stage in school. See a resolution quoted in Oldham and Gibson, *Remaking of Man*, 149–150.

Indeed, the issue of the vernaculars in African education lead, in 1927, to ACNETA drawing up a memorandum on *The Place of the Vernacular in Native Education*.[97] This document outlined three major "problems" – though this characterization was primarily from the viewpoint of Westerners interested in African education at the time. First, the multiplicity of African languages and dialects; second, the difficulty of training indigenous teachers in a multiplicity of languages so that they may teach a subject in a second or third language; and third, the difficulty of producing textbooks and literature.[98] In 1931, the Institut Colonial International in Belgium was commissioned to look further into the problem and draw up a memorandum on the issue.[99]

But it has to be noted that one of the concerns of the philosophy of adaptation was that literary, or "bookish," education was unrelated to the life of the masses and created a class distinction between the few and the many in African society. Adaptation was meant to correct this trend. Yet, if the use of English as a medium was to be delayed until post-primary school levels (and introduced from year 5 or 6 – the secondary school stage – onwards), then, technically, the majority of children (the masses) would hardly benefit from it.[100] This could lead to policy failure, and at worst, it was bound to create class distinction, which the philosophy of adaptation itself opposed.[101]

Apart from the issue of class distinction, the whole concept of "preservation" and adaptation was almost being dishonoured. Adaptation was

---

97. Advisory Committee, *British Tropical Africa* (African No. 1110). See also references to the memorandum in Ormsby-Gore, "Education," 757–761; Scott, "Educational Policy," 431–433.

98. Advisory Committee, *British Tropical Africa* (African No. 1110), 7, 8.

99. Scott, "Educational Policy," 414. The memorandum also covered the question of the appropriate staff – another "problem" in education in Africa.

100. Smith, *Christian Mission in Africa*, 69.

101. For example, "the lack of a knowledge of English in such areas as Northern Nigeria is to-day [1927] clearly preventing the entry of valuable elements of population into technical services of Government, such as the Railway, the Public Works, and even Agricultural Departments. One of the consequences is that English-speaking natives have to be imported from the Southern Provinces into Hausa-speaking areas to undertake such types of activity." See Advisory Committee, *British Tropical Africa* (African No. 1110), 10; cf. Advisory Committee, *Memorandum on Education of African Communities* (Colonial No. 103); Scott, "Educational Policy," 433. See Advisory Committee, *Mass Education in African Society* (Colonial No. 186), 33: "It is our conviction that a popular mass education movement must be based in the mother tongue." However, the statement was qualified with the acknowledgement of "(a) the complexity of the vernacular language situation in Africa; and (b) the differences of opinion among Europeans and Africans about the place of English in any educational system."

concerned with the preservation of the "good" elements in African cultures. Language was one of those elements. Unfortunately, the multiplicity of African languages and dialects was regarded as a liability rather than an asset.[102] The suggestion that textbooks could be produced first, or only, in the languages of the larger ethnic groups was bound to marginalize the social and educational needs of the smaller groups.[103]

It is the view of this writer that, in places like Tanzania, a *lingua franca* such as Kiswahili,[104] and English as well, were a better solution to the so-called "language problem." These had the potential of uniting pupils from different ethnic groups and wider geographical locations who converged to receive instruction at the out-schools and station schools, without enhancing, or humiliating, the social pride of one group. Perhaps nowhere in Africa has a non-European "neutral" language such as Kiswahili served positively both the educational and political purposes as it has in Tanzania, particularly since Tanzania won freedom from Britain in 1961.

The discussion in the preceding two sections has so far centred on the debate within missions and between them and the colonial government, especially in Tanzania, and has traced the debate on language back to the Le Zoute conference and the socioeconomic implications of using English or the vernaculars. The language issue was at the very heart of adaptation and the level of education to be given to Africans. For example, Raum argued that "for a long time to come, the average African needs only a moderate amount of school knowledge and only such as will be practical use to him when applied to his own wants."[105] But what did the indigenous teachers in Tanzania think about the changes in educational policy, and the level of education hitherto provided by missions? Was it "so much education" as some Western missionaries working in Tanzania suggested? For the purpose of this chapter, and the framework of the study as a whole, it might be sufficient to document the views and experiences of indigenous teachers in the CMS mission.

---

102. Ormsby-Gore, "Education," 758.
103. Scott, "Educational Policy," 43; cf. Smith, *Christian Mission in Africa*, 69–70, 113.
104. By 1932, Kiswahili was already an official language in Tanzania, Kenya, and parts of Uganda.
105. Raum, "Educational Problems," 572.

7.3.3 "Eagles Not Chickens": Aspirations of Indigenous Teachers

In its battle with missions "for the Africans," the British colonial government in Tanzania believed that, on the issue of educational advance, it had Africans on its side because Africans wanted better academic education. At the heart of this was the quest for knowledge of the English language. Of course, it is known that the government's motive was to build the task-force to assist in its administration of the country. But despite those ulterior motives of the British colonial government, the fact remains that Tanzanians noted that the level of education in some missions, such as the CMS mission, was lower. That the government helped to improve it was welcomed by many indigenous Tanzanians.

First a "national" standard syllabus for mission and government schools was introduced – and this was appreciated not only by teachers but by parents too. The immediate effect of this was that, unlike the earlier period when the indigenous teachers had to wander looking for children, "there were no more search for children to persuade them to come to school. They came voluntarily."[106]

As was noted earlier, some educationists such as C. T. Loram (a member of Native Affairs Commission, South Africa, and of the two Phelps Stokes commissions) made observations at Le Zoute about the aspirations of Africans. He argued against making Africans "feel that the door of opportunity was slammed in the face of their children."[107] So despite the fear, on the part of some missions, of government intervention and the consequences of secularizing mission education, most Africans, not least the indigenous teachers themselves, wanted an academic qualification that would enhance their social and economic status in society. Their interest was not to participate in the process designed to tie them to rural agriculture, which after all, would keep them "in their place."

In his article "A Comparative Survey of Educational Aims and Methods in British India and British Tropical Africa," Arthur Mayhew saw a parallel between indigenous teachers in Africa and the Indian *intelligentsia* in the late

---

106. Yusufu Masingisa, oral interviews, 16 and 17 September 1997.
107. Smith, *Christian Mission in Africa*, 68, 69.

1920s and early 1930s. Earlier, colonial government restrictions on higher education of the intelligentsia in India for the sake of the masses was viewed as a "political device for keeping the Indian in his place."[108] Therefore, despite a renewed similar policy dating as far back as 1857, plans for mass education were hardly implemented, such that, by the early 1920s, only 17 percent of school-age children were in schools where instruction was exclusively given in the vernacular.[109] Yet higher education in the English language flourished.[110]

Africans wanted to be "eagles" who could fly, not "chickens," and in this sense, a word should be said about the man who used the saying "you are eagles, not chickens." James Kwegyir Aggrey (a member of the Phelps Stokes commission) wholeheartedly supported the issue of cooperation between the government and missions and, apparently, the philosophy of adaptation.[111] Though he did not go to Le Zoute, his impact on the question of cooperation between government and missions in Africa was significant. He was, as Kenneth King rightly stresses, as "the prototype of the good African" – someone willing to cooperate with the whites on their terms, for Africa. But his impact on his fellow Africans was for reasons quite different from the adaptation he stressed. And that was because of his "literary" academic achievements. He himself "had studied in the [United] States for over twenty years, and he insisted on adding qualification after qualification to his name."[112]

He is remembered in parts of Tanzania, which he toured during the Phelps Stokes commission in East Africa, for the respect he commanded among the whites, to the extent of staying at the governor's residence, and more so, for his famous saying to African audiences: "You are not chickens [who can't fly]; you are eagles." Yusufu Masingisa has vivid memories of his emphasis on that very issue:

> In 1924, (let me think), oh yes, it was twenty-four [1924], Dr Aggrey came here. He was from Ghana. He landed at Dar es

---

108. Mayhew, "Comparative Survey," 178.
109. Carnoy, *Education as Cultural Imperialism*, 105–108.
110. Mayhew, "Comparative Survey," 179.
111. See Aggrey's letter to Jones on his disappointment for not being invited to Le Zoute, in which he also stresses the need for missions to embrace the philosophy of adaptation. See Aggrey to Jones, 14 August 1926, extract in Smith, *Aggrey of Africa*, 256.
112. King, *Pan-Africanism*, 232.

Salaam. He went to meet the governor and told him, "I have been sent to see the people of this land. It is sometimes said that they have tails and that the government people are saying that these people are not intelligent, and that it must take oh how many years...." After only a short stay in Dar es Salaam he requested to go to the hinterland. He broke his journey at Kilosa. At Kilosa he didn't go to the DC's [District Commissioner's] residence. At Dar es Salaam he stayed at the Governor's residence. There it was the governor's cook who was preparing meals for him. But at Kilosa he went to stay with Aram Gondwe, chief town clerk. He was an African ... Aram Gondwe. He [Aggrey] said to him, "I have come to see you. I have broken [off] my journey at this point, but I am on a trip further to the hinterland. You must have cooperation among yourselves. *You must have cooperation in education. It seems there is no progress made here on education. The government seems to pursue its own programme, and the missions are doing the same.* Then he described that saying, "You are not chickens. You are eagles." After that discussion he proceeded to the hinterland.[113]

There is documentary evidence that very often in his speeches to Africans on the issue of cooperation with the government, and even with European settlers in implementing the philosophy of education for life, Aggrey told the story of an eagle that wouldn't fly because it had been tamed as a chicken. Smith, his biographer, recorded one of Aggrey's speeches: "My people of Africa, we were created in the image of God, but men have made us think that we are chickens, and we still think we are; but we are eagles. Stretch forth your wings and fly."[114] At the time of the interview just quoted, Yusufu Masingisa (the interviewee) was ninety-three years old. The interview with him took place in 1997 – seventy-three years after the Phelps Stokes commission visit to Tanzania. Masingisa remembers that Aggrey and the commission visited places such as Kilosa and Tabora. What Jones himself wrote verifies this: "March 30 to April 12 [1924] – Tanganyika Territory, Messrs. Jones, Aggrey,

---

113. Masingisa, oral interviews, 16 and 17 September 1997. All emphases added.
114. Smith, *Aggrey of Africa*, 1929, 136, 137.

Garfield Williams and Dougall, accompanied by Mr S. Riversmith, and by the Bishop of Mombasa, travelled by train to Tabora, visiting Government Schools at Dar es Salaam, Dodoma, Tabora, Kilossa [sic] and Morogoro, and also numerous schools of the Church Missionary Society and the Roman Catholic Missions."[115] In 1906, the CMS mission had conceded in its annual report that "in the matter of education, for instance, although we have a great many schools, and return a great number of scholars; the education we give is of the most elementary character, and we never had anything approaching a normal school or an institution of any kind of education."[116] It is therefore possible that the poor condition of the out-schools belonging to the CMS mission, and the obvious need for their improvement (thus a good case for cooperation between missions and government) could be the reason the CMS mission and its officials (Garfield Williams – Educational Secretary of the CMS, London – and Bishop Peel, who by then still had the oversight of the CMS mission in central Tanzania) were so closely involved in the tour of the commission.

Indigenous teachers were obviously frustrated by the poor educational level in the CMS mission, particularly because teaching was not done in English. Yusufu Masingisa (quoted above) resigned his job as a church teacher to become a medical assistant. He gives his reasons:

Mwita Akiri: Were you a teacher as well?

Yusufu Masingisa: That's right.

Mwita Akiri: From when?

Yusufu Masingisa: From the year twenty-one [1921] to twenty-six [1926].

Mwita Akiri: Until twenty-six (1926)?

Yusufu Masingisa: That's right.

Mwita Akiri: Why did you stop being a teacher so early?

Yusufu Masingisa: For six years. I spent four here at Mamboya and two at Berega.

---

115. Jones, *Education in East Africa*, xxiii.
116. RUUM, 1906, G3 A8/0/1907/23, BUL.

> *Mwita Akiri*: Why did you leave so early?
>
> *Yusufu Masingisa*: Yes, I left early because some other young people and myself felt that the kind of education that we were being given was very inadequate. Therefore we resolved to go far away. We wanted to go to Nyasaland to gain further education.
>
> *Mwita Akiri*: Did you ever go there?
>
> *Yusufu Masingisa*: No. We never reached the place. Shortly before our departure I was chosen to go and study medicine.[117]

Unlike the CMS mission, Masingisa praised the level of education in the UMCA and the Scottish missions in Malawi. He was in no doubt where the difference lay:

> *Mwita Akiri*: What I am asking you is this: what did the UMCA and the people of Nyasaland do to have a better education than the Missions on this side. Were you told the reason for that?
>
> *Yusufu Masingisa*: The UMCA were teaching in English. The Nyasaland people had workers from Britain, from Scotland, the place where ... Dr Livingstone came from. The Scottish taught in their language. But those who came here [at Mamboya – namely, the CMS missionaries] first translated into Kikaguru, and then in English. Our teachers had a college before World War I. They had a college at Kongwa, but the level of education offered didn't differ so much, because they didn't go deep. What was offered was very little. ... I went to college myself, and indeed it was religious courses that were taught.[118]

From this conversation, it appears that knowledge of the English language was a significant factor in the African opinion as to what constituted "better" education. The colonial educational policy wanted this, but the missions felt it was "too much education." That is not to suggest that the government policy and practice pleased everyone in Ugogo and Ukaguru. Some, like Isaka Mlahagwa, felt that the British colonial educational policy was rather discriminatory.

---

117. Yusufu Masingisa, oral interviews, 16 and 17 September 1997.
118. Masingisa, oral interviews.

"You see the British were not serious about helping the African through education. The schools were graded differently. For example, the Indians and the Europeans always went to high grade schools. Therefore, it was a matter of just wanting to be seen to be fulfilling their responsibility, but nothing serious."[119]

7.3.4 Socioeconomic Benefits for Indigenous Teachers

However, despite the reservations expressed by Isaka Mlahagwa, one of the significant outcomes of the impetus given to education by the British colonial government in Tanzania in the mid-1920s was the enhancement of the social and economic prospects of some indigenous teachers in the CMS mission. This concerns those who received teacher training courses at Kongwa in the late 1920s. This is a period which some of the former teachers in the CMS mission interviewed by this writer often referred to as a time when the level of education went up. As Uguzi's testimony indicates, "when the level of education went up, and more people went to school, that is when they started grading education so that those who reached a certain level could get a job."[120] The upgrading of the standard of the out-schools meant also the raising of the qualification of teachers because they were regarded as lacking in teaching methods.

As in some missions, for example the UMCA in Tanzania, central schools received pupils both from the station schools as well as the out-schools.[121] However, unlike the UMCA, where pupils in central (boarding) schools reached standard 5 or 6,[122] in the CMS mission in central Tanzania, central (boarding) schools only offered formal education up to standard 4. Nonetheless, most of those who completed their studies in these schools became elementary school teachers, but some continued as evangelists at the out-stations. As part of residential education, perhaps boarding schools were one of the centres where Western and African traditional values competed. Life in the boarding schools was rigid, rigorous, and designed to test the patience of the African child and his or her desire to become literate. The experience at a UMCA boarding school for boys gives a picture of school life:

---

119. Isaka Mlahagwa, oral interview, 14 September 1997.
120. Nehemia Uguzi, oral interviews, 18 and 19 June 1997.
121. Chambers, *Tanganyika's New Day*, 44–45; G. Ward, "The Magila District," in *The UMCA Atlas* with Printed Maps of the Mission Stations (1885–1915), 1903, Box D7, RHL.
122. Broomfield, "Importance of Education," MS 3122, LPL.

> There are hurried bells at 5:45 a.m. A ruthless teacher turning them off their bed and worse still hurried them down to a cold stream where they must wash. But even if they enjoy that another bell sends them up the hill again to learn their simple prayer and so it goes all day – school bells, roll call and punctuality enforced and no leave to return home when they like.... [But] the food at home is nicer than mission food, which being bulky can never be made so tasty.[123]

Those who endured rigorous life at the boarding schools and pleased foreign missionaries in character and performance were selected to train at teacher training colleges. Teacher training was the apex of the educational ladder in most missions.[124] The fact that only schools with properly trained and certificated teachers could become registered and receive government educational grants has already been mentioned.[125]

Training at Kongwa and acquisition of government certification brought with it better economic and social rewards.[126] Nehemia Uguzi was one of the teachers who joined Kongwa in 1929 and trained for three years in order to gain teaching skills, something that most former teachers described using the English word, *method*. On completion, he taught at the Buigiri village school but under probation from 1931 to 1934 before being licensed in 1936. Though working under the mission, like all licensed teachers, he received his salary from the government.[127] Better training meant a bigger salary.

No one among the informants interviewed for this study was more candid about this than Cleopa Mwaka (a former teacher):

> *Cleopa Mwaka:* They said if you want bigger salary, – at that time teachers who passed [examination] were paid sixteen shillings. So our goal was to get sixteen [shillings]. I went to Kongwa in 1933.... I completed standard six in November [1935], and was

---

123. Woodward to Travers, 5/7/1897, "Letters from Africa," Box E.2, RHL.
124. *PCMS*, 1914, 1; Hewitt, *Problems of Success*, 1:199.
125. See chapter 5.
126. For more details on Kongwa college, see chapter 8.
127. Nehemia Uguzi, oral interviews, 18 and 19 June 1997.

> examined. I passed and was employed as teacher. . . . I started working when the salary had been increased to twenty shillings.
>
> *Mwita Akiri*: How much did you get before you went to Huron [Kongwa]?
>
> *Cleopa Mwaka*: . . . Five [shillings]. You received two [shillings] cash. The other three you gave to the person who gave you food [laughing].[128]

Through Kongwa college, a good number of mission schools were staffed with teachers who not only held government certificates but also received their salary from the government. With better salary, and government regulations that somehow safeguarded their job security, indigenous teachers acquired a new sense of freedom. Apart from the insistence on introducing the English language at early stages, and during their training, these other aspects (salary and enhanced job security) were other benefits of adaptation they enjoyed. Of course, they continued to perform their "traditional" dual task: the work of the school and the work of the church, including evangelization.

> *Mwita Akiri*: What was the difference in those days between a school teacher and a church teacher?
>
> *Cleopa Mwaka*: The difference was just that . . . the former taught secular subjects and religion. But the latter taught religion only, and the regulations of the mission was that in any case, a school teacher must be a member of the church, in any case. If he was not committed [to church], then he was counted unfit. If he didn't want to belong to the church. . . . Until he agreed to serve in the church, and on Sunday lessons, leading prayers, and so on, and preaching, and then go to teach in school. . . . Yes. We helped the pastors a great deal. *Very much. Very much.* . . .
>
> *Mwita Akiri*: Was that compulsory or voluntary?
>
> *Cleopa Mwaka*: That was *compulsory* for a school teacher.[129]

---

128. Cleopa Mwaka, oral interview, 4 July 1997.
129. Mwaka, oral interview.

It should be emphasized, that most if not all the indigenous teachers worked for the mission with great commitment and loyalty. But on the other hand, the interview excerpt quoted above indicates that the requirement to fulfil two tasks became compulsory. And CMS missionaries in the CMS mission (along with those belonging to other missions) were perhaps rather unprepared to deal with the new sense of freedom among African teachers – the main possible reason being that they made serious miscalculation about the aspirations of the Africans. The philosophy of adaptation had almost highlighted, perhaps more sharply than before, the distinction between the traditional church teacher and the new schoolteacher who helped in church mainly in order to keep his largely secular job.

A teacher was in a mission-owned school. At the same time, both education and educational standards in such a school were under government control, and it was the government that paid the salary of teachers in the registered schools. For the indigenous teacher, it was like serving two "masters." Yet, serving two "masters" is often a difficult task and experience. Someone often pays the price, and in this case, it was not the indigenous teachers but one of the "masters." The drama that unfolded, from the early 1930s onwards, may justify the following extended interview excerpt:

> *Cleopa Mwaka:* . . . . The teachers began strikes. [They] observed that the government paid *better salaries*, and yet there were no salaries for mission teachers. There was a wave of protest by teachers. They left until the time when the mission itself negotiated that it was better that teachers be paid by the government. . . . The government agreed to pay salaries to mission teachers . . . That is when the protest died down. E-eh. *So they retained teachers who had no certificate and paid them twelve shillings.* But when a teacher obtained a *grade two* certificate (it was called *Grade Two*)[130] . . . He started with a salary of thirty shillings, and a bonus. Anyone who was in long service got as

---

130. According to the NEO of 1927, a grade 2 teacher was one who had completed sub-standard or standard 1 and 2 at a village school, and then trained for two years at teacher training college. Grade 1 was the next level on the ladder, that is, a teacher with standard 4 formal education who had done four years training at a teachers' college. See IMC/CBMS files, SOAS.

much as one hundred! Lo! [But as for us in the mission] we were nailed down with twenty only [laughing].

Akiri: How did you feel? Because...

Cleopa Mwaka: Very badly. There was a lot of *secret departures*, sir! *People were quitting.* You heard suddenly that someone had become a tax clerk. Another one ...The mission would go to *beg* him to return to work saying [to the government], "you have stolen our teacher" [laughing]. E-eh. [They said] "you see, my colleague who started [working] in the same year, now he/she is earning sixty, yet mine [my earning] is only sixteen. He *applied*." "Come you will become a clerk somewhere. Come, you will be a clerk somewhere. Go to such and such a school." [The mission asked] "where is our teacher. You government, you have stolen our teacher. We want him back." They [the government] said [to the teacher], "your people want you. Leave, and return" [laughing].[131]

In the context of this wave of departures from the mission to government schools, or mission schools controlled by the government, it is no surprise that some informants – though dissatisfied with the level of education in the CMS mission – yet insisted to this writer that the mission was supplying workers and teachers to the government.[132]

The account just narrated by Cleopa Mwaka in the interview excerpt above reflects African experience and aspirations and how teachers dealt with their two "masters." It shows an aspect of the effects of government intervention in mission education and a degree of the freedom it brought to the indigenous teachers. It opened to them the door to better economic life through government employment.

Socially, too, government educational policy and its emphasis on the need for qualified, certified teachers brought benefits. First, pride. Lazaro Ndajilo explains how he felt about changing from being a humble pupil-teacher who was trained through in-service semi-residential courses, to being a full

---

131. Cleopa Mwaka, oral interview, 4 July 1997.
132. Yusufu Masingisa, oral interviews, 16 and 17 September 1997.

teacher:[133] "When I completed the New Testament, I went to do some courses at the mission. I taught in the mornings. At two o'clock in the afternoon, I too became a pupil."[134] He continues, "I became a full teacher only after returning from training at college [in 1933]. I became responsible for standard 3 [pupils]. I knew geography, I knew health [hygiene], I knew grammar. So I was somehow able to teach. . . . I wasn't a pupil anymore."[135] With at least two qualified teachers (Lazaro Ndajilo for standard 3 and Javani Musambili who taught standard 4 pupils) part of the Mvumi village school at the station was registered by the government and received financial assistance.

Another social benefit of the government demand was that there was now a degree of protection against frequent suspensions or dismissals on the basis of "offences" or allegations that were not related to the capacity to fulfil their professional duty. Now, even when teachers refused to carry out some of their "expected" duties, they could not be easily sacked.

> *Cleopa Mwaka:* The teachers who were teaching just for the sake of it evaded teaching religion. E-eh. Those who were willing continued to do so.
>
> *Mwita Akiri:* Were they not dismissed?
>
> *Cleopa Mwaka:* No.
>
> *Mwita Akiri:* [I mean] those who were evading [teaching religion]?
>
> *Cleopa Mwaka:* They were now in government hands, and had signed an agreement with the government. How could they [the mission] dare dismiss them! . . . They could file a complaint, and the mission could not win. If they said, "he [the teacher] is not teaching [religion], [and] is not attending church," [the government reply would be] "that is not our concern. All we are concerned with is teaching [secular subjects] in school." [laughing].[136]

---

133. For details of in-service semi-residential courses, see chapter 8.
134. Lazaro Ndajilo, oral interviews, 14 and 16 June 1997.
135. Ndajilo, oral interviews.
136. Cleopa Mwaka, oral interview, 4 July 1997.

It would be misleading, however, to suggest that the powers of the CMS missionaries to dismiss teachers were completely undermined at this time. Indeed, decades after the period under review – a time when government employment regulations appeared to offer better protection to the mission teacher, "unfair" dismissals occurred. Cleopa Mwaka himself became a casualty in 1957.

> *Cleopa Mwaka:* I taught there in fifty-seven (1957) and quit teaching.
>
> *Mwita Akiri:* Did you just quit?
>
> *Cleopa Mwaka:* I was dismissed. I was given a notice alleging "You are lazy. You don't teach. You get a salary for nothing." Ah-ah [I said to myself]. I kept quiet and built my house very quickly and moved from that place.
>
> *Mwita Akiri:* Was it possible at that time that the Europeans could simply dismiss people from their job without cause?
>
> *Cleopa Mwaka:* The missionaries?
>
> *Mwita Akiri:* Mmh.
>
> *Cleopa Mwaka:* Aa-h. Without following the rules. Ata-ta-ta [an acclamation, implying, "don't ask"]!
>
> *Mwita Akiri:* Didn't people refuse [to quit]? Could you not defend yourself?
>
> *Cleopa Mwaka:* People used to defend themselves, but I didn't want to do so. Because I felt they lied.
>
> *Mwita Akiri:* Where did people appeal?
>
> *Cleopa Mwaka:* To the Education Secretary. There were nowhere further to go to. . . . They were places where too much discrimination existed.

Apart from such experiences like those of Cleopa Mwaka, and possibly many other teachers, the fact remains that government intervention in mission education had given teachers more room to manoeuvre than before.

7.4 Conclusion

This chapter has traced (briefly) the American background of the philosophy of adaptation, noting how, through the Phelps Stokes Fund, and its two commissions to Africa, the philosophy was embraced by the British government for its colonies in Africa. It has highlighted the wider influence of the philosophy of adaptation upon ecumenical bodies such as the Le Zoute conference in 1926 and certain individuals. But it has been emphasized, too, that there was a multiplicity of perspectives on African education both within the missions themselves and within government circles.

Tanzania has been used an example to illustrate the vibrations of the philosophy of adaptation, as well the implication of local interpretation of a British government educational policy for the bush school system and the African teacher. The limiting of time for religious education in the timetable was perhaps unfair to missions. The other unwelcome part of the government educational policy, of course, was the fiction of community-oriented adapted rural education and its political implications. But, thankfully, that fiction never succeeded to the level of suffocating the African quest for that which is highest through literary academic education. Several years later, some African statesmen such as Julius Nyerere of Tanzania advocated similar educational orientations, but emancipation has been their motive, not keeping the African in his or her "place." Certainly politicians such as Nyerere have sought to rescue their people from Western political and economic domination, not the contrary.

One positive outcome of the British government education policy, particularly the Command Paper 2374, has been emphasized – the emphasis on higher educational standards in out-schools and their teachers. It may be observed that prior to the government initiative in education some missions had, perhaps, become too complacent about the quality and level of academic education and dwelled too much on education for conversion. No matter how uncomfortable some missions, including the CMS mission in Ugogo and Ukaguru, felt about government intervention in mission education, such intervention brought new social and economic prospects for most African pupils and their teachers in mission schools and training institutions.

The departure of teachers for better jobs or salaries in the secular sector led to another deficiency in mission education, especially in the teaching of religious education. Cleopa Mwaka laments:

> When school teachers left their job [in the mission], the tragic consequence was that pupils could no longer be taught religious education. E-eh. Because the teachers who [succeeded them] and taught religious education, let's say they had no proper training. Some only came to preach [in schools] and merely wanted pupils to be converted. Just that. But they did not want to teach catechism, or the nature of apostle's creed. It was just preaching. Therefore the level of religious knowledge went down in schools. In fact, to date, the level of the religious knowledge in schools is down.[137]

The category of teachers without proper training is undoubtedly that of the traditional church teacher who regarded their task mainly as evangelistic. The CMS mission could not keep the indigenous teachers with both intellectual and spiritual calibre in the church. Even though this study is historical in nature, an observation could be made that mission churches have often struggled to attract younger Christians with better secular education into church service to work in "secular" church departments or to join the lay and ordained ministry. Just as in the past, congregations were deprived of the potential of well-trained lay ministers, so are mission churches today in Tanzania, not least the branch of the Anglican Church that has historical links with the CMS mission. Yet, as Cleopa Mwaka puts it in the quotation above, those who remained had "no proper training." The next chapter examines the nature of training offered for the traditional church teacher in the CMS mission in Ugogo and Ukaguru.

---

137. Mwaka, oral interview.

CHAPTER 8

The Training and Development of Indigenous Teachers

An attempt has been made in the previous chapter to show how the British colonial government educational policy altered the landscape of mission education, particularly by reinterpreting the place of the out-schools and indigenous teachers in the educational development of Tanzanians. But it was also observed that from the point of view of most indigenous teachers – some of whom were interviewed for this study – the changes brought new prospects for educational and economic advance. Indeed, some left the mission schools to teach in government schools. Those who made such a step now felt less obliged to teach religious education.

In a sense, this was a landmark – a period when the indigenous quest for higher educational standards became more obvious. Whether strictly as a secular school teacher, or as a traditional church teacher, being a mission worker was no longer an excuse for being content with the lower education offered by some missions, not least the CMS mission.

The purpose of the present chapter is to explore and evaluate the training offered by the CMS mission in Ugogo and Ukaguru and the development of indigenous teachers as leaders in the church. This statement needs qualifying. This study, of which this chapter is a part, is neither an institutional history of the CMS mission nor a study of the institutional development of the African church and its organization in Ugogo and Ukaguru. Therefore, the analysis of the structures that allowed greater African participation in church governance is beyond its scope. Two reasons may be given.

First, such an undertaking would have excluded at least one group of the indigenous agents explored in this study, namely the chiefs – many of whom did not become church members.

Second, it would also have necessitated dealing with issues of indigenization of the ministry. That line of investigation would have been a "church" history rather than a mission history, although this does not mean that the two are exclusive to one another. For that reason, the examination of the training and leadership development of the indigenous teachers in this chapter does not engage in the theological discussion of the practice of ordination. But the issue of ordination will be discussed below simply because it tended to become the climax of leadership development in many Christian churches of episcopal and non-episcopal traditions.

With these qualifications, the specific concerns of this chapter may be listed. It evaluates the in-service (semi-residential) training – a type of training which, despite minor exceptions, was prominent in the latter part of the nineteenth century until around 1913. Residential training for church teachers from 1914 until 1933 is examined too,[1] and the place of indigenous women in the training programme will be highlighted. It is argued that the the requirement for ordination in the CMS mission, and the level of training for teachers, was lower. This is more so if what the CMS mission offered is compared, for example, to what the UMCA and the Livingstonia mission in Malawi offered to indigenous teachers and their ordinands.[2] The final part of this chapter will analyse some of the factors that caused the delay in indigenous clergy in Ugogo and Ukaguru being ordained, but early ordinations will be noted.

---

1. As in other chapters, effort to identify teachers by both first and surname has not always been fruitful. For that reason, some teachers are mentioned here by their first name only. Where similar first names occur, differentiation is made either by noting the date of recruitment or, where possible, the location of recruitment and whether the teacher was from Ugogo or Ukaguru.

2. Thompson, *Christianity in Northern Malawi*, 164–168, 214–217.

8.1 In-service Semi-residential Training
8.1.1 The Nature of Weekly Courses

By 1871, barely seven years since the start of operations in Zanzibar, the UMCA had already begun offering residential training for teachers and catechists at Kiungani in Zanzibar, most if not all of whom were former slaves.³ But it took more than three and a half decades before the CMS mission in central Tanzania had its own institution for the residential training of indigenous leaders in 1914 at Mlanga, Kongwa, about which more details will be given below. For all the preceding period, therefore, school and church teachers could only be offered in-service semi-residential training. This was common in other CMS missions in Uganda and Kenya, and in missions of other denominations – for example, the Livingstonia mission in Malawi.⁴

In Ugogo and Ukaguru, courses under this scheme often took place at major mission stations which were also the headquarters for each district. For example, teachers from Finga, Chahwa, Hombolo, Ihumwa, and Dodoma (at Chief Birinje's) received their training at Buigiri station.⁵ But it appears that teachers from almost all Ukaguru stations often received their training at Berega.⁶ Normally, a day was set aside each week and groups of teachers were summoned to the mission station.⁷ The courses lasted for at least three hours a day, but certainly not more than four, and were conducted by a CMS missionary.⁸ As the syllabi will indicate shortly, the courses were for all categories of teachers – from beginners to the most experienced ones. The historical titles used were "helper," "probationary agent," "junior reader," "senior teacher," and "junior catechist." The status of senior catechist or quasi-pastor was introduced, too, but no syllabus was written for this, and it was generally conferred upon teachers on an honorary basis.

---

3. Anderson-Morshead, *History of the Universities' Mission to Central Africa 1859–1896*, London: UMCA, 1897, 54. See also the revised edition, *History of the Universities' Mission to Central Africa*, vol. 1, *1859–1909*, London: UMCA, 1955, 39.
4. Thompson, *Christianity in Northern Malawi*, 164.
5. Nehemia Uguzi, oral interviews, 18 and 19 June 1997.
6. RUUM, 1909, G3 A8/O/1910/40, BUL.
7. Yusufu Masingisa, oral interviews, 16 and 17 September 1997.
8. Minutes, EC, 19–20, 26–27/12/1907, G3 A8/O/1908/12, BUL; Dan Mbogoni, oral interview, 11 June 1997; Cleopa Mwaka, oral interview, 4 July 1997. Doulton to Baylis, 1/12/1909, G3 A8/O/1910/2, BUL.

8.1.2 Syllabus and Course Contents

Since the leadership development of indigenous workers rested so much on the culture of "examination," it might he helpful to outline – with original titles retained – the syllabi used for in-service semi-residential training. As stated already, with minor variations, the examination for the teachers were conducted by a CMS missionary in-charge at each mission station.[9] An initial comment to be made here is that it is proposed that it will be better to summarize each syllabus first and make a general evaluation of the syllabi later. This will help to avoid repetition. Therefore, comments (in passing) will be made on individual syllabi only where it appears convenient and necessary.

8.1.2.1 Syllabus of examination for the status of helper

Helpers were examined in each of the following subjects: (1) reading; (2) writing; (3) dictation; (4) the Apostles' Creed (memorized); (5) the Ten Commandments (memorized); (6) the New Testament: the Gospel of Mark (or, if another book was chosen, the corresponding amount of material was to be used); and (7) Kiswahili: a translation of a page of the book *Masomo Mepesi*.[10] Helpers were often working under the direction of experienced indigenous teachers – for example, Andrea Mwaka who was supported by Andrea Kanyanka (a fellow teacher and missionary from Ukaguru).[11]

8.1.2.2 Syllabus of examination for the status of probationary agent

Like helpers, probationary agents assisted teachers in the local work of church and school, but the level of their responsibility exceeded that of helpers. Besides arithmetic and catechism, the structure of their course was basically the same as that of helpers, except that the Apostles' Creed and the Ten Commandments were omitted, probably because these had been covered already. The course content was therefore as follows: (1) reading: a passage or passages in the four gospels; (2) writing: from any "easy" dictation selected anywhere in the four gospels; (3) New Testament: knowledge of the life of Jesus between his birth and baptism and "from Gethsemane to His

---

9. Minutes, EC, 19–20, 26–27/12/1907, G3 A8/0/1908/12, BUL and Doulton to Baylis, 1/12/1909, G3 A8/0/1910/2, BUL.

10. Minutes, EC, 9/2/1906, G3 A8/0/1906/27, BUL.

11. Doulton to Baylis, 21/11/1910, G3 A8/0/1910/83, BUL.

Ascension"; (4) arithmetic: simple addition and subtraction; (5) Kiswahili: translation into the vernacular of one page of the book *Masomo Mepesi*; (6) catechism: all standard parts, with the exclusion of the section on the sacraments.[12]

8.1.2.3 Syllabus of examination for the status of junior reader

Junior readers formed the bulk of teachers in the mission and undertook much of the school teaching and evangelistic work. Their course covered a little more detail. (1) Reading: morning and evening prayer and the books of Scripture under study at the time (see below). (2) Dictation was from the Gospels selected for study (see below). Also, the spelling, writing, capitals, punctuation and proper division of words at the end of a line were to be taken into consideration when marking the candidate's paper. (3) Composition: a two-page letter, to be written at the time of the examination on any subject of the candidate's choice. (4) Arithmetic: "simple" addition, subtraction, multiplication, short division, and long division (limited to two figures only). (5) Geography: candidates for junior readership were required to have "simple general knowledge of the world, embracing the names of the five continents, five oceans, as well as the definitions of the following terms – mountain, volcano, lake, river, gulf, isthmus, cape, island, peninsula, gulf, strait, plain, sea, desert and valley."[13] For the geography of Africa, the following was learned: "political divisions, rivers, mountains, lakes, islands, seaports, towns of the continent, and principal towns (district centres) in German East Africa."[14] (6) Scripture – Old Testament and New Testament were studied as follows: for the Old Testament, candidates learned the book of Genesis, and in the New Testament, the Gospel according to St John. The *Cambridge Bible for Schools and Colleges* was used as a textbook for both New Testament and Old Testament.[15]

---

12. "Syllabus for the Examination for the Status of Probationary Agent," MS, G3 A8/0/1910/3, BUL.
    13. "Syllabus for the Examination," MS, G3 A8/0/1910/, BUL.
    14. "Syllabus for the Examination," MS, G3 A8/0/1910/, BUL.
    15. "Syllabus for the Examination," MS, G3 A8/0/1910/3, BUL.

8.1.2.4 Syllabus of examination for the status of senior reader

The senior readers' course went into even more detail and comprised of the following components. (1) Scripture: alterations were made to the Scripture examination in 1906. For Old Testament, Exodus, chapters 1–20, and the book of Joshua were added to Numbers (but genealogical portions had to be omitted). In New Testament, Colossians was substituted for Romans.[16] But, by 1909, further revisions had been made. The new syllabus now contained the following subjects. For the Old Testament, Exodus and Numbers (each taken as separate examination papers), and for New Testament, the Acts of the Apostles was studied. The textbook used for studying the books was the same as that for the junior readers' course – namely, *Cambridge Bible for Schools and Colleges*. (2) Reading: morning and evening prayer, the litany, and the books of Scripture studied (see above). (3) Dictation: from the books of Scripture, as well as spelling, writing, capitals, and punctuation. Proper division of words at the end of a line was to be taken into consideration when marking the paper. (4) Arithmetic: "simple" long division, reduction, addition, subtraction, multiplication, and division of the following "moneys" used during the German colonial era: *pice*[17], *hellers*,[18] and *rupees*.[19] (5) Geography: Canaan in the time of the Israelites including the Sinaitic peninsula, Mesopotamia, Syria, Phoenicia, Palestine in the time of Jesus, and the geography of the Pauline missionary journeys. (6) Composition: a two page letter to be written at the time of the examination on any subject the candidate might choose.[20]

8.1.2.5 Syllabus of examination for the status of junior catechists

The syllabus included the following subjects. (1) Scripture: an earlier Old Testament syllabus had Exodus (chapter 21 on) included with Deuteronomy and Joshua.[21] A later version had only the last two. (2) New Testament: the life of Jesus as contained in the four Gospels. First and Second Corinthians were studied in the earlier syllabus but were later substituted with Romans.

---

16. Minutes, EC, 5/3/1906, G3 A8/0/1906/34, BUL.
17. A *pice* is worth 1/64 of a *rupee*.
18. *Heller* is an old sub-unit of the German and Austrian currency.
19. A description of *rupee* was given earlier. See chapter 4.
20. "Syllabus for the Examination for the Status of Senior Reader," MS, G3 A8/0/1910/3, BUL.
21. Minutes, EC, 19-20, 26-27/12/1907, G3 A8/0/1908/12, BUL.

(3) Prayer Book (that is, the main Anglican order of church service at the time, know as the Book of Common Prayer). Items studied here included order for morning and evening prayer, contents of "occasional prayers" and prayers of thanksgiving (which were not to be memorized), and "Collects for Sundays of the year – learnt by heart; the Order of the Church Year."[22] Articles of Religion 1–8 (possibly up to article 10) were also studied under the heading "Prayer Book" and were memorized.[23] (4) Geography: the continents of Africa and Europe. For Africa, the candidates learned the outline of a map showing colonial protectorates, principal rivers, lakes, and mountains. As for Europe, the candidates learned names of countries, capital towns, principal rivers, lakes, and mountains. (5) Arithmetic: based on the textbook *Chuo cha Pili cha Hesabu* (Kiswahili, *Second Arithmetic Book*), with the exception of English weights and measures. (6) Composition: original composition on any familiar subject. (7) Reading was to be based on chapter 1–14 of Robertson's *Kitabu cha Mambo Madogo Yaliyolipata Kanisa la Mungu* (rendered in an archival source simply as *Swahili Church History*, Part I.[24] (8) Kiswahili: translation of any page of St Mark's Gospel from Kigogo or Kikaguru (Kimegi).[25]

8.1.3 Some Weaknesses of In-service Semi-residential Training

Having summarized the syllabi, it is appropriate that their evaluation be made now, though a few brief general comments should be made first. CMS archival records have several reports of examinations for teachers at various levels,[26] particularly before the start of Kongwa college in 1914. Passing or failing an examination for a particular level meant promotion or lack promotion to the next level. In general, the performance of indigenous agents was good,

---

22. Berega Logbook, No. 51, an entry for 1908, MH; Minutes, EC, 19–20, 26–27/12/1907, G3 A8/0/1908/12, BUL.

23. Berega Logbook, No. 51, an entry for 1908, MH; Minutes, EC, 19–20, 26–27/12/1907, G3 A8/0/1908/12, BUL.

24. Minutes, EC, 19–20, 26–27/12/1907, BUL.

25. "Syllabus for the Examination for the Status of Junior Catechist," MS, G3 A8/0/1910/3. See also Minutes, EC, 19–20, 26–27/12/1907, G3 A8/0/1908/12, BUL; Berega Logbook, No. 51, an entry for 1908, MH.

26. Minutes, EC, 19–20, 26–27/12/1907, G3 A8/0/1908/12; Minutes, EC, 13–14/7/1908, G3 A8/0/1908/47; Minutes, EC, 28–29/6 & 5–7/7/1909, G3 A8/0/1909/38, BUL; cf. Berega Logbook, No. 51, an entry for 1908, MH.

and many passed their examinations in the first instance of sitting, though a few had to resit.

A significant observation is that more than anything else, the analysis of the failed examinations shows that most of the teachers failed in Scripture subjects (Old Testament and New Testament)! There may have been other reasons why this was the case, but the main reason could be nothing other than the fact that the subjects were taught in such a theoretical and uncontextualized manner that they seemed to have little relevance, thus making them more difficult for most teachers, especially those who were less gifted in academic subjects.[27]

A few other problems with in-service semi-residential training may be listed. One was that CMS missionaries did not have enough time to run the courses due to administrative and supervision tasks. Consequently, the scheme of offering three-hour weekly training lacked regularity, and the appeal to CMS in London for a person who could deal specifically with training appears not to have received a favourable response.[28] It was a problem the CMS missionaries themselves were acutely aware of.[29] Though, for slightly different reasons, the 1908 report suggests that this trend was common even in the CMS mission in Uganda, particularly in the Buganda province:

> The training of native agents is of almost vital importance to a Mission, but unhappily in Uganda, through the absence of some missionaries on sick leave and of others on furlough, it has been difficult of late to arrange for the Classes for Candidates for Ordination and for the posts of lay reader and senior teacher, which are held at Mengo, and only one man was available for this work during the greater part of 1908.[30]

A second weakness of in-service semi-residential training was that of using examination as a means of assessing and promoting teachers to the next higher status. From the above outline, and the brief evaluation of the syllabi made, it may be observed that the examination culture not only introduced

---

27. Minutes, EC, 19–20, 26–27/12/1907, G3 A8/0/1908/12; Minutes, EC, 13–14/7/1908, G3 A8/0/1908/47; Minutes, EC, 28–29/6 & 5–7/7/1909, G3 A8/0/1909/38, BUL;

28. *CMR* 61 (August 1910): 488.

29. Doulton to Baylis, 1/12/1909, G3 A8/0/1910/2, BUL.

30. *PCMS*, 1909, 66.

and built up a lay ministry based on academic "classroom" performance, it introduced a hierarchical ministry too. A young convert, employed as teacher/catechist on the basis of acquaintance with a CMS missionary, offered some training, and then placed in a responsible position could easily have misunderstood the nature of his ministry – especially if those who appointed him did not show a good example to be emulated.

All this was done without regard for the fact that such a diligent teacher might not necessarily have the leadership qualities that society would have cherished in anyone it gave a responsible position. There is no evidence, certainly from within archival sources consulted, to suggest that the CMS mission sought to contextualize or incorporate traditional African leadership models into its training programme or follow the "chiefly" model. Indeed, in some CMS missions, for example in Uganda, Taylor rightly notes how a "more clerical and more filial" form of leadership, signified by the arrival of Alfred Tucker (the third Anglican expatriate bishop in the Uganda mission), became prominent in the late 1890s. He attributes this to "the new generation of missionaries . . . [who] shared also the impoverished conceptions of those days [indeed for many years that followed] regarding the position of the laity in the [sending] church."[31] It replaced "the African leadership" in which early catechists (some of whom were chiefs and sub-chiefs) had leadership experience in the secular society. In doing so, CMS missionaries in Uganda created a foreign conception of "separate hierarchies of church and state . . . and implied a dualism which Ganda thought has only accepted with the greatest reluctance."[32] Ministry was mistakenly identified with church leadership.

In other words, recruitment into church service, and "theoretical" training, were thought to be capable of conferring leadership qualities. That was hardly how most traditional leaders were chosen. Critics have often claimed that African church leadership emulates the traditional chiefly model but this misses the point. To understand traditional leadership models, the focus should be on numerous people who exercised some group leadership responsibility, from the family level upwards, not just the "political rulers."

---

31. Taylor, *Growth of the Church*, 71.
32. Taylor, 72.

Max Warren is certainly right when he says, "in Africa the younger always give way to the older."³³ But probably like many others, he misunderstands the office of chieftaincy in the past when he suggests that "the Chief is emphatically not a servant. And the African pattern of ministry took that shape from the beginning. . . . There is no shepherd figure in African life except among a few pastoral tribes."³⁴ Warren himself acknowledges that "the missionary had authority over the teachers who were often the first evangelists, and frequently the first clergy. . . . The African clergy continued to see impressive demonstrations of the ministry in terms of authority, of teaching, of administration, yes and of control of finance. They had very few object-lessons in 'shepherding,' in the work of a pastor."³⁵ Use of classroom examination as a means of assessing an individual's abilities (especially his or her intellectual or even work performance) – and as a way of bestowing a new status through promotion – was a model that CMS missionaries borrowed from the societies they came from, not from traditional African leadership models.

A third weakness – perhaps a much more serious one – was the lack of local relevance in the syllabi. This was alluded to in passing above but more details should be added. The importance of scholastic development and satisfactory performance in examinations for those who were serving in the mission at the time cannot be underrated. After all, as noted in chapter 7, one reason that even indigenous teachers joined government schools was to aspire to better education. However, a major deficiency in the syllabi outlined above was their failure to incorporate subjects that would have exposed teachers to their own everyday religious, pastoral, and social concerns – and the concerns of other indigenous Christians and non-converts in society.

This contextual poverty was not addressed in 1909, when it was purported that the syllabi for the examination of the five levels mentioned above were "thoroughly revised."³⁶ But the only purpose of the revision was simply to "raise standards" – if any standards at all! During the same period, a new condition for qualification was introduced, particularly for the status of junior catechists. The candidate had to exemplify good house management with a

---

33. Warren, *Problems and Promises*, 49, 50.
34. Warren, 49, 50.
35. Warren, 51.
36. Minutes, EC, 28–29/6/1909 & 5–7/7/1909, G3 A8/0/1909/38, BUL.

Christian wife *able to read* and willing to cooperate with him.[37] Under this condition, by the middle of 1909, only Danieli Mbogo of Buigiri and Musa Malanda and Haruni Mbega (both from Berega) had been singled out by the executive committee as eligible candidates who could take the examination for the status of junior catechists.[38]

Yet, training and developing an indigenous leadership was not only, or simply, a matter of passing examinations, getting promotions, and acquiring better wages (the last one being another contentious issue, as will be examined in detail a little later). As the syllabi outlined above indicate, the promotion was from the very junior status of helper to junior catechist and senior catechist (the titles being those used by the mission itself, and other CMS missions elsewhere, though with slight variation).[39]

The syllabi were part of the in-service semi-residential training and could have been anchored in the daily social, religious, and spiritual issues and problems encountered by teachers, so that they were able to live, teach, and lead in context. Had this been done, the in-service semi-residential training for lay ministers would have been useful not just in the era of missions but in the post-missions (or, as some put it, "post-missionary") era too. A brief examination of the consequences of the teachers' lack of contextualization (or sensitivity to the social and religious context) may illustrate this point. The focus is on the effect it had on the personal lives of some teachers.

As members of the society, church teachers had similar social and religious aspirations as most people living at the out-stations and out-schools where they served. Interaction with such aspirations could possibly have aided leadership development and induced a process of better character development on the part of potential candidates. No wonder indigenous teachers were often seen by CMS missionaries to be "erring" in a number of areas. Yet, on the other hand, their frequency of "erring" was partly a failure of the mission

---

37. Minutes, EC, 28–29/6/1909 & 5–7/7/1909, BUL

38. At times the name Malanda is wrongly spelled in some archival sources as "Mandala." See for example Minutes, EC, 28–29/6 &/& 5–7/7/1909, G3 A8/0/1909/38, BUL.

39. The title of "probationary agent" was first used in 1900 to describe indigenous workers above the status of helpers. See Minutes, EC, 9/2/1906, G3 A8/0/1906/27, BUL. Other titles used in Uganda included "junior teacher," "senior teacher," and "lay reader." See *PCMS*, 1906, 74–75; *PCMS*, 1907, 84; *PCMS*, 1909, 66. But some of these, e.g. "lay reader," eventually became standard titles even in Tanzania; c.f. *CTDL*, no. 36 (July 1937).

as an institution. Some of the issues that resurfaced frequently included approaches to traditional medicine, taking a second wife, and personal morality – to name a few.

In June 1906, Andrea Kanyanka, one of the Mamboya teachers, was suspended from his job and then excommunicated from the Lord's Supper by the mission for visiting a traditional medicine practitioner for advice on account of an illness he had been suffering from. He obviously made his intention known to David Deeks, because he was counselled by him, and perhaps by other CMS missionaries, well in advance of the visit. But he insisted on making the visit to the traditional medicine practiotioner and did so. An entry in Mamboya logbook by a foreign missionary disappointingly reflects anger, for it states: "very sad case of obstinate resistance to all spiritual council [sic]."[40] Fortunately, Kanyanka acknowledged "the wrong" he did and was reinstated to his job and readmitted into the Lord's Supper in June 1907.[41] But the point remains: those upon whom the hopes of future leadership rested were as pressed with personal social and religious issues as ordinary Christians and other members of the Gogo and Kaguru societies.

Another issue that faced teachers was that of polygamy. Asani Mugimbwa, a teacher at Mamboya, was one of the first teachers to be sent to Frere Town near Mombasa, Kenya, for training in 1895.[42] Sometime in his ministry he took a second wife, and, as a result, could not stay as teacher anymore. Yusufu Masingisa recalls the incident:

> *Mwita Akiri*: Was there anyone here at Mamboya who was dismissed because he took a second wife?
>
> *Yusufu Masingisa*: There were some.
>
> *Mwita Akiri*: Who was dismissed here because of taking a second wife?
>
> *Yusufu Masingisa*: There was Asani Mugimbwa. It was those very people who went to Kisauni, [Frere Town] Mombasa. They left the work. They were cursed [excommunicated]. The bishop

---

40. Mamboya Logbook, No. 53, entry for 27/6/1906, MH.
41. Mamboya Logbook, No. 53, entry for 27/6/1906, MH.
42. *PCMS*, 1896, 98.

came and pronounced curse upon [excommunicated] them. He warned other Christians saying, "Don't have fellowship with such a man. If he dies he should not be buried [according to Christian rites]." There were strict rules. That is what they [CMS missionaries] did.[43]

Devising strict rules and enforcing them (without the cooperation of those they are intended for) can be tempting. But getting people (in this case, the indigenous teachers) to appreciate the rationale behind the rules can be a different matter. Church archives support Masingisa's oral evidence on the excommunication of Asani Mugimbwa by David Rees on 25 January 1913. The logbook states it was done publicly in church.[44] This could be the reason why, over eighty years later, Yusufu Masingisa (only nine years old at the time) could still remember it in 1997. In fact, only a year later, Asani Mugimbwa's colleague, Daniel Chowe – who was also among the first Kaguru teachers to train at Frere Town – was excommunicated, too, on 18 January 1914 for taking two additional wives beside his wife Mina.[45]

Dismissal from church ministry, as happened to Asani Mugimbwa and Daniel Chowe, may not have been viewed by the indigenous teachers as a great loss. But excommunication was likely to hurt. Social exclusion (or being "cursed") in traditional African society, even from church, is often embarrassing and is therefore disliked if not dreaded. It is interesting that in the interview excerpt above, Yusufu Masingisa, a Kaguru, uses the word "cursed" rather than "excommunicated." In most cases, the latter, especially when interpreted in Kiswahili, should simply mean *kutengwa* – being separated from others – something like a "temporary forced exclusion." Being cursed is much more than being "excommunicated." Its burden was/is dependent on the value the "offender" placed on the social ties and fellowship in the community he/she was being expelled from, and this varied/varies from place to place and clan to clan. Given the ritualistic nature of the Lord's Supper, and the spiritual value most Christians anywhere in the world (who observe it as a sacrament) place on it (which can easily find resonance with African

---

43. Yusufu Masingisa, oral interviews, 16 and 17 September 1997.
44. Mamboya Logbook, No. 53, entry for 25/1/1913, MH.
45. Mamboya Logbook, No. 53, an entry for January 1914, MH.

religious beliefs), excommunication would have been a blow to such teachers as Asani Mugimbwa, Gideoni Ferekani, and Yeremia Senyagwa (see below).

This would remain the case whether a lesser or greater form of excommunication was used. The latter was rare and meant a permanent expulsion from the Christian community or congregation. At Mamboya, it was applied to a Christian named Lazaro for abandoning Christian teaching for over six years, not yielding to counselling, defecting to Islam, and becoming a teacher of that religion.[46] The former, "lesser" excommunication, was executed for such offences as drinking beer, adultery, taking a second wife, consulting traditional medicine practitioners, and other offences of a similar nature. At times, "a continuous absence from all church services and devotional meetings" warranted a lesser excommunication.[47] A Swahili text of a lesser excommunication used at the time was as follows (though it contains broken Kiswahili, for which correction is given in square brackets, and a translation provided):

> Taratibu ya Kumpiga Mtu Marafuku [sic] [Marufuku] ya Kanisa. Ni [Na] ndiyo iliyo na Hukumu Ndogo. Kwa Hukumu ya Askofu wa kanisa la Kiingereza katika Ubispibi [Ubishopu] wa Mombasa.
>
> *Translation*:
>
> The Order of Excommunication in Church. This being for a Lesser Excommunication. By order of the Bishop of the Church of England in the Diocese [Bishopric] of Mombasa.[48]

At one time it was applied to Gideon Ferekani and his colleague Yeremia Senyagwa (a senior teacher) at Mamboya on 6 July 1908. The order of excommunication had to be read *in public* on four consecutive Sundays. For the two teachers, it was announced on that day that:

> Gideoni Ferekani na Yeremiya[sic] Senyagwa wametengwa, wasikaribie Meza ya Bwana muda wa miezi 12. Tena, watakapokuwa tayari kushariki [sic] [kushiriki] Ushirika Mt: watatoa

---

46. Mamboya Logbook, No. 53, an entry for January 1914, MH.
47. Itumba Logbook, No. 53, MH.
48. Mamboya Logbook, No. 53, MH. Translation by this writer.

hesabu ya mali jinsi walivyohukumiwa makosa yao. Habari hii inatangazwa leo July 6, 1908. David Deeks.

Translation:

Gideon Ferekani and Jeremiah Senyagwa are excommunicated, so they should not approach the Lord's Table for 12 months. Furthermore, when they shall be ready to partake the Holy communion they shall give sums of money in accordance with level of the offences for which they have been judged.[49] This announcement is made today July 6, 1908. David Deeks.[50]

It is doubtful if the pattern of suspensions and dismissals, as adopted by the mission, brought any relief or gave room for interaction with the issues that prompted such actions.

Reference was made in chapter 7 of the departure of some indigenous teachers from mission service to secular employment beginning in the early 1930s following the educational changes introduced by the British colonial administration. Oral evidence points to the fact that some teachers did not just leave their jobs in the mission. They abandoned mission Christianity too and went back to such social practices as traditional dances (for example *nindo*) which were deemed corrupt. Cleopa was an eye witness:

Mwita Akiri: On the church side, didn't people quit in a similar manner [as mission school teachers did]?

Cleopa Mwaka: Many church teachers left too. Some became peasants. [It was common to hear that] a teacher or an evangelist assigned to a church has quit after two or three years. Others even went back to *nindo* [traditional dance] [laughing].

Mwita Akiri: Did you witness people doing that?

---

49. The Kiswahili phrase, "watatoa hesabu ya mali yao" could equally mean "they shall give an account of their deeds." But this writer has rendered it literally as "they shall give sums of money." The reason is that it was a common practice in the CMS mission that those found guilty and excommunicated were often asked to pay compensation both to the injured party and to the mission fund. Certainly this was done in marital cases, including adultery. For an instance of this, see Bishop's Council ruling on Petro, Mamboya Logbook, No. 53, entry for 7/4/1914, MH.

50. Mamboya Logbook, No. 53, MH. Translation by this writer.

Cleopa Mwaka: E-eh.

Mwita Akiri: For instance where? At Buigiri or some other place?

Cleopa Mwaka: For example at Buigiri there was a man called Yosiya. He disappeared and never cared about anything. I could give a countless list.[51]

The fact that some teachers who left their jobs in the mission stopped being adherents of mission Christianity as well suggests that, despite the training they had received, little had changed in their commitment and loyalty to traditional social and religious practices. Though it can be difficult to know exact number of those who backslid, the indication given by Cleopa Mwaka in the interview excerpt is that such cases were numerous. The CMS mission was paying a price for giving considerable attention to theoretical aspects of training, even in Scripture lessons – whether during the in-service semi-residential training or residential training at Kongwa – without dealing with the pre-Christian context of the teachers. Teachers like Yosiya of Buigiri (mentioned in the quote above) can hardly be judged merely as "rebels." Doing so would be a denial of their pre-Christian experience and the attachment they had to it.

Denial, rather than recognition, that these social and religious issues constituted real concerns was unhealthy to both sides. On the one hand, it closed the door for teachers to engage in a constructive criticism of aspects of social practices and religious beliefs in society. On the other, it prevented CMS missionaries from having a sustained and unaltered positive view of the leadership potential of the teachers despite what might have been regarded as personal failures. CMS missionaries' occasional appreciation of the qualities of indigenous teachers would not, therefore, have depended on the teachers staying on the "safe" side of social practice and religious belief (as understood by CMS missionaries)[52] – or only on performance in examinations.

---

51. Cleopa Mwaka, oral interview, 4 July 1997.
52. See chapter 6.

8.2 Residential Training
8.2.1 Justification for the Need

The provision of in-service semi-residential training for teachers as shown above was mainly due to fact that the CMS mission in Tanzania had no resources for a local residential training centre. However, even after the start of residential training at Kongwa (which is examined shortly), evidence shows that monthly courses at the central stations continued until the late 1920s and were offered when teachers went to receive their monthly wages.[53] The point, therefore, is that the two types of training were not mutually exclusive.

But the inadequacy of in-service semi-residential training was well recognized not just by CMS missionaries but also by indigenous teachers themselves. An excerpt of the letter written by some teachers in Ukaguru to "elders" in London reflects this:

> Letter from African Church Elders at Berega (Yusufu, Luka, Musa, Petro, Yeremia, Paulo, Haruni, Isaka), to the Elders of the Church which is in London, 31 August 1910.[54]
>
> Na sisi wasaidizi tunataka sana kufundishwe Kolleji, kama wenzetu wa pwani Unguja, na Mombasa, na Uganda, jinsi wanavyofundishwa, maana sisi tunapata mafundisho katika mwezi mmoja siku nne tu, bassi. Kwa hiyo tunataka tufundishwe zaidi. Twawasihi sana enyi *Wazee wa Kanisa* mtusikie, kwa maneno haya tuliowambia[.] Mtupelekee walimu zaidi, mkiona vema. Mtuletee, ah, twawasihi sana. *Kwa herini Wazee wa Kanisa.*
>
> Ni sisi Yusufu, Luka, Musa, Petro, Yeremiya, Paolo, Haruni, Isaka.

---

53. Minutes, CC, 27/3/1926, MH.

54. Letter from African Church Elders at Berega, to the Elders of the Church which is in London, 31/8/1910, G3 A8/0/1910/82, BUL. This, however, was not the first time Kaguru Christians had appealed to CMS to send more workers. Earlier, in 1892, twenty-seven Christians at Mamboya did the same. See letter of August 1892, G3 A5/0 264, cited in Knox, *Signal on the Mountain*, appendix K, 254.

Translation:

And we helpers want very much to be taught in a college,[55] like our fellows at the coast [that is] Zanzibar, and Mombasa, and Uganda, because we are [currently] receiving teaching only four times a month, that's all. Therefore we would like to receive more teaching. We beseech you so much you elders *of the church*, to listen to the matter we have presented to you. Send us more teachers, if it pleases you. Send them to us, oh, we beseech you so much. *Goodbye church elders.*

We are [Yours] Joseph, Luke, Moses, Peter, Jeremiah, Paul, Aaron, Isaac.[56]

Mention of Unguja (Zanzibar) is definitely a reference to Kiungani (later St Andrew's) College where the UMCA offered teacher training and theological courses for ordinands. Divinity schools at Mombasa and Uganda belonged to the CMS missions in Kenya and Uganda, respectively. The signatories of this letter probably chose one of their colleagues to write the letter on their behalf. At the time of writing, many if not all of the signatories were teachers and not technically "helpers" or "elders" as implied in the letter. For example, Luka, Musa, and Isaka had been probationary agents since 1902.[57] Yusufu Mgwele had been working as a probationary agent since 1900 and was promoted to the status of junior reader in 1906.[58] Petro Mwendi was employed as probationary agent on 13 January 1905 and was made senior reader in February 1906.[59] Paolo (Paulo) Mwegoha, too, was recruited in 1909 to work as a probationary agent at Berega.[60]

Moreover, as a general policy, it was teachers who were sent to college, not elders. The decision to use the term "elders" at the head of the letter may

---

55. The term "helpers" is definitely not used here in the technical sense as a status in the ladder of grades.

56. Letter from African Church Elders at Berega, to the Elders of the Church which is in London, 31/8/1910, G3 A8/0/1910/82, BUL. Emphasis in original. Translation by this writer.

57. Minutes, EC, 16 & 17/12/1901, G3 A8/0/1902/8, BUL.

58. Minutes, EC, 9/2/1906, G3 A8/0/1906/27, BUL.

59. Berega Logbook, No. 51, entry for 8/1/1905, MH; Minutes, EC, 9/2/1906, G3 A8/0/1906/27, BUL.

60. Minutes, EC, 13, 15/11/1909, G3 A8/0/1910/1, BUL.

therefore have come from the foreign missionary resident at Berega. The motive would be to give the impression that it was a group of elders from a single local church in Ukaguru addressing their counterparts in London, probably at the Parish of St Peters, Highgate Hill.[61]

The appearance of all their names may signify their resolve to make a collective appeal to highlight the need for better training for teachers in the mission. In the earlier part of the letter (not quoted), the "elders" expressed gratitude for the CMS missionaries who first taught them the word of God. But they went on to argue that there were still many people in other places who had not been reached with the gospel. They cited, as an example, the people of Gairo (where Yeremia was appointed to work in 1905), Kisitwi, Mlali, Ngh'umbi, Kisambo, Gingi, and Bokwa. It was important that the present teachers received better training so that they could reach out to others who might in turn offer to serve God as evangelists and teachers.

8.2.2 Lack of Resources, CMS Missionaries and Indigenous Spirit

Right at the start of his episcopacy in East Africa, Bishop Peel recognized the lack of adequate training facilities for lay and ordained ministry not just in Tanzania (which was obviously poorly served) but in Kenya too.[62] In his report, entitled "Missions of the CMS in the Diocese of Mombasa in 1900," sent to a major committee of the CMS in London (the "parent committee"), Peel wrote: "I cannot convey to the Committee, in words or in letter, how serious I consider to be the need of preparing and providing *African* clergy, readers (evangelists), and catechists, school-masters and school mistresses, for the coast district [of Kenya] and Usagara-Ugogo Mission [in central Tanzania]. The dearth of clergy and evangelists after so many years of occupation is lamentable."[63] Reference in the report to the "dearth of clergy and evangelists" should be understood to reference the lack of ordained African ministers. The phrase used was little more than an effort to convey a sense of urgency, and in some ways, Peel was right – there was always a need for ministers in

---

61. Berega Logbook, No. 51, an entry for May 1906, MH. It was this church that supported Haruni Mbega from 1906 onwards.
62. William Peel was made bishop of the Diocese of Mombasa in 1899.
63. Report by Bishop of Mombasa, "Missions of the CMS in the Diocese of Mombasa in 1900," G3 A5/P6, BUL. Emphasis in original.

both categories. But he acknowledged in the same report that "there are many good school teachers, but they are *all*, I think, *untrained*."⁶⁴ To this problem, Peel's proposed solution was the provision of relevant institutions. Yet his immediate obstacle was resources. So he wrote to London and declared, "I am appealing for funds for a building in which theological and normal training may be carried on with all the advantages we can command."⁶⁵

It is interesting to note, however, that despite such enthusiasm for trained indigenous personnel, the bishop was also concerned about the consequences of providing such training to leading African Christians. On the one hand, this would promote a spirit of independence, a quality that he felt was needed for "erudite preachers and teachers." But on the other (and this concerned the mission hierarchy most), the trained leading indigenous Christians would not "cringe and yield when their discontent has the sanction of their intelligence." CMS missionaries were therefore warned "not to unduly express the spirit of assertion."⁶⁶ Yet even without such training, indigenous teachers were from time to time exhibiting the spirit of independence which CMS missionaries didn't know how to cope with except by carrying out suspensions or dismissals.

The dispute over wages, especially that of 1906, may illustrate this. It is clear that the CMS mission had fewer resources, and this, perhaps rather than the idea of self-support, was the reason for the introduction of two local funds. The two local funds – the Native Church Fund and *Fungu la Mungu la Kila Siku* (God's Daily Portion Offering) – were initiated in the CMS mission for the support of the teachers and erection of buildings at the out-stations. The former was started in 1900 and drew its funds mainly from two Sunday offerings from each of the seven major mission stations (in February and August).⁶⁷ The latter was initiated towards the end of 1907, but probably came into operation in 1908.⁶⁸ The Fungu Fund was raised when Christians reserved for God part of what they normally used for daily food – for example, maize flour. Once accumulated, this was turned into money and given to the

---

64. Report by Bishop of Mombasa.
65. Report by Bishop of Mombasa.
66. Report by Bishop of Mombasa.
67. Minutes, EC, 6/4/1900, G3 A8/0/1900/20, BUL.
68. Peel to Baylis, 23/12/1907, G3 A8/0/1908/3, BUL.

treasurer of the fund.[69] An out-station that adopted such an initiative acquired the status of a Fungu station.[70]

However, the annual collection from such funds was not sufficient to meet the needs they were intended for. On average, annual figures reached only 216 rupees (approximately seventeen pounds).[71] In 1906 about £168 was spent on the maintenance of thirty-five indigenous staff. The total grant from the CMS for 1906 was £2,046,[72] but the bulk of it was spent on the maintenance of the CMS missionaries (who numbered about half the indigenous staff). Their salaries were almost ten times more than that of all the indigenous staff put together. In this context of meagre resources, it was likely that the disputes over wages were going to emerge.

During its meeting of 10–12 January 1906, the executive committee resolved that the wages hitherto paid to indigenous teachers were "ample." It appears that these "ample" wages were those reduced in April 1900.[73] Until the end of 1902, teachers' salaries were paid in clothes, but rupees were to be used from 1903 onwards. The rates were fixed as follows. Teachers who received ten pieces of clothing received 8.5 rupees, and 7.5 and 5 rupees were paid to those who received eight and six pieces of clothing, respectively.[74] This time (January 1906), the only consideration given by the executive committee was that absence from home did involve extra expenses. For that reason, an additional four pice a day for food was to be paid for each full day a teacher spent visiting an outpost and sleeping away from home.[75]

But teachers felt this was inadequate. They could not afford new clothes following an increase in prices. So they went on strike. At Mvumi, Benyamini Lungwa, Paulo Chidinda, Lazaro Hembokamu, and Simeoni Muya were dismissed from their work for demanding eighteen rupees (approximately £1.44) for monthly wages, instead of seven rupees (approximately fifty-six pence) which they were currently being paid.[76] The first three agreed to return to

---

69. *CMR* 63 (March 1912): 164; *PCMS*, 1912, 51; *CMR* 65 (September 1914): 547–548.
70. *CMR* 65 (September 1914): 547–548.
71. *PCMS*, 1903, 105; *PCMS*, 1907, 79.
72. *PCMS*, 1907, xxxix, 453.
73. Minutes, EC, 6/4/1900, G3 A8/0/1900/20, BUL.
74. Minutes, EC, 12–13/12/1902, G3 A8/0/1903/11, BUL.
75. Minutes, EC, 10/4/1906, G3 A8/0/1906/46, BUL.
76. Minutes, EC, 10/4/1906, G3 A8/0/1906/46, BUL.

work a month later at the old rates of pay. But Lazaro Hembokamu remained out of his job possibly because he was still unhappy with the way the question of wages had been handled.[77]

In Ukaguru, too (one hundred or so miles from Ugogo), and at about the same time, the wage-crisis raged. It is difficult to know how these teachers, separated by vast forests and with no means of personal communication, could manage to express a similar concern at the same time. Two of the nominees for ordination from Ukaguru – Yeremia Senyagwa of Mamboya and Petro Saileni of Nyangala – were involved in the strike. In response to their involvement, the executive committee resolved in April 1906 that even if the CMS in London approved the nomination of Yeremia Senyagwa and Petro Saileni for the diaconate, as had been recommended in January 1906, the matter was to be put on hold for at least a year from the date when the executive committee met. This decision affected other potential ordination candidates from Ugogo too.[78]

This demonstrates how, in cases where the indigenous staff expressed what they undoubtedly regarded as genuine concerns, and asserted the spirit of independence, CMS missionaries often resorted to punishment. The reason for this, Peter Williams points out, was that in most cases and many places, CMS missionaries often felt threatened by the desire for independence on the part of African converts and teachers.[79] To some extent this explains why, as Dan Mbogoni observes, CMS missionaries often appointed for teachership only those they reckoned to be "gentle" and "submissive."[80] To their surprise though, at times, some "dissenters" came form among the teachers whom CMS missionaries regarded as "loyal and submissive" – for example, Yeremia Senyagwa.

The executive committee agreed to revise wages for teachers in February 1906,[81] as follows, with figures in rupees and approximate British pence in parentheses (round brackets).

---

77. Minutes, EC, 9/2/1906, G3 A8/0/1906/27, BUL.
78. Minutes, EC, 10/6/1906, G3 A8/0/1906/46, BUL.
79. Williams, "Necessity of a Native Clergy," 36.
80. Daniel Mbogoni, oral interview, 11 June 1997.
81. Minutes, EC, 9/2/1906, G3 A8/0/1906/27, BUL.

The Training and Development of Indigenous Teachers

Table 8.1 Rates of Allowances for Indigenous Staff, 1906[82]

1	2	3
Position of Teachers	Married	Unmarried
Helpers	1–6 (8–48)	1–6 (8–48)
Probationary Agents	7.5 (60)	6 (48)
Junior Readers	8.5 (68)	7 (56)
Senior Readers	10 (80)	8 (64)

These revised allowances were not paid immediately, but Yeremia Senyagwa wrote on behalf of his fellow Kaguru teachers to inform the committee about the readiness of Mamboya to accept the old wage levels and their intention to return to work. Their apology was accepted in March 1906, with the committee agreeing to consider letters (one official and another private) written by him. Yeremia had always been held in high regard by foreign missionaries,[83] and it is possible that the committee, because of this, while upholding the original stance of January 1906, resolved to write a "kind letter" to the teachers, accepting their apology.[84] However, as a result of this dispute, Joshua and Haruni were now supported from "high profile" and stable funding sources.[85]

Beidelman rightly notes that mission employees in the CMS mission were expected to work for less pay than those "comparably" employed outside the mission. However, his claim that "the missionaries' wide demands of their African workers resemble the awesome demands many Victorians made upon their household servants"[86] – though it carries some truth – is a misinterpretation. The example he uses, of Tofiki Lwanga's commitments at Mpwapwa

---

82. Minutes, EC, 9/2/1906, G3 A8/0/1906/27, BUL.
83. Rees to Baylis 18/1/1906, G3 A8/0/1906/20; cf. Minutes, EC, 15/11/1905, G3 A8/O/1905/16, BUL.
84. Minutes, EC, 5/3/1906, G3 A8/0/1906/34, BUL.
85. The financial support for the former came from the Bishop's Diocesan Fund and support for the latter came from the Parish of St Peters, Highgate Hill, London. See Berega Logbook, No. 51, entry for May 1906, MH.
86. Beidelman, *Colonial Evangelism*, 168, 169.

(indeed, the same source used by Beidelman was quoted earlier),[87] proves that he does not see Tofiki's commitments in the light of indigenous initiatives.

However, it might be observed still that, whether with or without better training for the indigenous teachers, tensions occurred between the indigenous teachers and CMS missionaries in central Tanzania (and, indeed, in other CMS missions throughout Africa). One reason was that indigenous staff resented the paternalistic treatment they experienced from the CMS missionaries, who also underestimated their social and intellectual abilities.[88] This hardly aided the process of indigenous teachers' leadership development. CMS missionaries would not have stayed in leadership in Ugogo and Ukaguru forever. It was therefore significant that the example of leadership they introduced be one of genuine mutual respect between those in hierarchical positions and the colleagues whom they led and not one of perceived threat or fear on both sides whenever difficult issues arose.

There is little doubt, as will become evident shortly, that whether explicitly or implicitly, paternalism played a major role in the decision not to send the indigenous teachers to Mombasa for training after 1900.

8.2.3 Obstacles to Overseas Training

The sending of Asani Mugimbwa and Musa Malanda to Frere Town even before Peel became Bishop of Mombasa has been alluded to already.[89] Daniel Chowe, Andrea Mwaka, and Matayo went too.[90] The training at Frere Town lasted between twelve and eighteen months. Throughout Africa, within the CMS missions, colleges such as the one at Frere Town were known as divinity class(es) or training class(es).[91] But the scheme was not popular within the CMS mission in Tanzania.[92] Frere Town was not favoured for several reasons, some of which, in hindsight, reflected nothing but the sheer paternalism that

---

87. See chapter 3.

88. See. Henry Venn to Beckles, 21/5/1867, C A1/L8, 147–151, p. 148, quoted in Williams, *Ideal of the Self-Governing Church*, 40.

89. Peel became Bishop of Mombasa in 1899.

90. Wood to Baylis, 30/10/1894, G3 A5/0/1895/155, BUL; c; f. Knox, *Signal on the Mountain*, 134, 147–148.

91. *PCMS*, 1896, 100. For instance, the divinity/training class at Mengo for training teachers in Buganda. See *PCMS*, 1900, 121; *PCMS*, 1906, 74.

92. Minutes, EC, 6/4/1900, G3 A8/0/1900/20, BUL.

prevailed in those days (remnants of which may still be found in the attitude of some missions today).

First, it would have involved more expenses – for example, for travel and upkeep. Second, there was a claim that indigenous teacher-students would be "spoilt" if they trained in a foreign country because it was alleged that teachers trained at Frere Town had the "habit of using many things" that they could not have in Tanzania, except at a higher price.[93] The third reason (not entirely different from the second) had to do with morality. It was alleged that the moral state of those sent to the coast for training was a "disgrace." Asani Mugimbwa, one of the first to go to Frere Town was cited as an example.[94] Whether Asani Mugimbwa would have accepted this view of himself is questionable.

The fourth reason was cultural: the divinity school at Frere Town adopted Mombasa Swahili for communication and instruction. The dialect was different from Zanzibar Swahili. It was the latter that was in use in the sphere of the CMS mission in Tanzania and the interior in general. In addition to this, unlike the coastal belt, it was not Kiswahili but two major vernacular languages that were popular in the mission in central Tanzania. These were Kigogo and Kikaguru (Kimegi).

The fifth reason, and probably the most important, was the issue of the economy of the work force. CMS missionaries were concerned that a year-long absence of experienced indigenous teachers from their work in church and school could mean stagnation in the expansion programme that had already begun. Therefore, no more teachers were sent to Frere Town after 1900.[95] The proposals to start a temporary divinity school at Mpwapwa where teacher-students would train while continuing to offer service to the mission were not implemented.[96] So, in 1901, a new proposal was made that, instead of a full school, a divinity class be started at Mpwapwa and courses be in Kiswahili.[97]

---

93. Rees to Baylis, 16/8/1900, G3 A8/0/1900/37, BUL.
94. Rees to Baylis.
95. Knox, *Signal on the Mountain*, 134.
96. Rees to Baylis, 16/8/1900, G3 A8/0/1900/37, BUL.
97. Minutes, EC, 6–7/6/1901, G3 A8/0/1901, BUL.

By the end of 1909, the contemplated divinity class had still not been started for evangelists and catechists. The idea of a joint institution with the CMS mission in Kenya was dropped too.[98] A change of strategy of appeal to London followed. Ernest Doulton wrote to Frederick Baylis (general secretary of the CMS) and reiterated the fact that the participation of CMS missionaries in evangelistic work was limited and the hope of reaching more people rested with indigenous Christian teachers, many of whom he described as "most promising from a spiritual as well as an intellectual point of view."[99]

8.2.4 Ecumenical Possibilities

The year 1910 began without a residential training in the CMS mission. Out of a sense of desperation, the CMS mission was now open to another possibility. As noted in chapter 4, 1910 was a year of both opportunity and danger. Opportunity because mission education acquired a new impetus through the German colonial educational policy, and "danger" because Muslim teachers would be used at government schools if missions failed to provide education to the public, especially to the chiefs and their sons. It was therefore a time when a number of Protestant missions in Tanzania were united about the need to "prevent" the spread of Islam into their spheres of operation.

Karl Axenfeld's initiatives on this in 1910 were alluded to in chapter 4. Axenfeld brought to Baylis's attention the existence of two seminaries belonging to the Berlin mission – one at Kidugala in Iringa (southwestern Tanzania), and one in Manow (northwest of Lake Nyasa) – which offered residential training for indigenous teachers and catechists.[100] There is no evidence to suggest that this invitation was ever taken up. But in 1912, Axenfeld took yet another ecumenical initiative. He and Schumann (a Berlin mission pastor) held a conference with the executive committee of the CMS and pastor Loebner of the Moravian Mission, at Buigiri, to consider a proposal for the establishment of an ecumenical seminary for the three missions. Kiswahili would have become the main language of instruction. The proposal was

---

98. Peel to Baylis, 29/9/1909, G3 A8/0/1909/41, BUL.

99. Ernest Doulton to Baylis, 1/12/1909, G3 A8/0/1910/2; Ernest Doulton to Baylis, 6/12/1909, G3 A8/0/1910/13, BUL.

100. K. Axenfeld to Baylis, 29/7/1910, G3 A8/0/1920/60, BUL. Earlier Axenfeld had written to Baylis on 21/6/1910 and, on this occasion, was replying to Baylis's response letter of 22/7/1910.

endorsed. However, like Axenfeld's other proposal, there is no evidence that the proposed college was ever established.[101]

In light of these failures, the idea of sending teachers to Frere Town – so firmly rejected in 1900 – was now being reconsidered. Ernest Doulton wrote:

> Andrea Mwaka well supported by Andrea Kanyanka with three others, two of whom are quite juniors, carry on the work and give satisfaction, but one feels that these teachers really want teaching themselves and this remark applies to all our stations[.] The fact is, we are so few in this mission that amidst our many other duties we find it impossible to give the time which these young men ought to get from us and we are now beginning to feel that there seems little hope in the near future of getting a DIVINITY SCHOOL in this Mission and a missionary set apart for the work[.] Despite there being objections to send men to the Coast, it will be desirable to send our senior teachers (a few at a time) to FRERE TOWN DIVINITY SCHOOL FOR TRAINING.[102]

8.2.5 Kongwa Teachers' College

Such a reversal of policy on Frere Town was the only option now left to the CMS mission, and it seemed right that steps be taken to implement it. At a meeting of the executive committee in November 1910, CMS missionaries in charge of mission stations were instructed to bring to the next committee meeting the names of teachers of status not lower than senior reader – one from each of the seven districts: Berega, Mamboya, Nyangala, Itumba, Buigiri, Mvumi, and Kongwa – to be sent to Frere Town. However, there is no evidence that a new wave of students was ever sent to Frere Town between 1910 and 1913.

Fortunately, a new initiative taken in 1913 to establish a residential training college at Kongwa bore fruit. However, even this project was supported *not* by the British CMS but by Canadians through CMS Canada. Thomas Westgate, a Canadian working for CMS in central Tanzania since 1902, secured a grant of

---

101. *PCMS*, 1913, 52.
102. Doulton to Baylis, 21/11/1910, G3 A8/0/1910/83, BUL. Capitals letters in original.

£300 from the alumni of Huron college after which Kongwa was first named.[103] The college became operational in 1914.[104]

The basic and initial purpose of the college was to train teachers who would fulfil the dual task of leadership and evangelistic work in church, as well as teaching in mission out-schools and station schools.[105] Thirteen teachers were enrolled for the opening course (see photograph 1 in appendix 3).[106] Unfortunately, the work of the college was shattered by the outbreak of the First World War which forced its closure. Training resumed not in 1919, as suggested by Gordon Hewitt,[107] but in 1920.[108]

Unlike the 1920s, the 1930s were basically a difficult period for the college. It was closed in May 1935 mainly due to financial shortages. It is possible that world economic recession – hence the reduction in government grants to mission schools and teacher training colleges – contributed to this. The financial problems of the college must have been publicly known to many local people, especially the teachers who were in attendance at the college at the time, such that some remember it well. They knew of the initial and continued Canadian financial support and the time when it vanished.[109] The college reopened in August 1941 in the middle of the Second World War.

8.3 Women's Training

It has to be noted that during the period under review in this study, Kongwa college existed exclusively for male teachers. Though, as has been indicated, the standard of both the semi-residential and residential training for men was low, the educational development of indigenous women was even poorer. Though this was common in most CMS missions, in some places, for example in Uganda, CMS missions provided training for indigenous women

---

103. *CMR* 65 (September 1914): 546.

104. *PCMS*, 1914, 61.

105. Isaka Mlahagwa, oral interview, 14 September 1997.

106. It is unfortunate that only twelve teachers appear in the photograph. Lazaro Hembokamu is the thirteenth person missing from the photograph.

107. Hewitt, *Problems of Success*, 1:199.

108. *PCMS*, 1921, 35. It is shown here that the college reopened on 14 July 1920 with twenty-five students. Compare with an unpublished student enrolment list compiled from college sources by Hugh Prentice as part of a study on the history of the Kongwa college.

109. *PCMS*, 1921, 35.

workers early in the twentieth century. Hoima training classes had seven "female evangelists" in 1910, and eighteen were at Kabarole (Toro) in the same year.[110] Beside these, divinity classes for women existed also at Iganga (Busoga) and Mengo.[111]

In Ugogo and Ukaguru, the women who became Bible women only had catechetical training and attended out-schools. There were references to "education for girls" in the CMS mission, but unlike the training for men, education for girls was viewed largely in the context of marital life. In 1931, George Chambers, the Australian bishop of central Tanganyika declared, "education for women is vital. . . . Our Christian men cannot get Christian wives and the tragedy is that a heathen wife so often means the degradation of the husband and family."[112] Girls' boarding schools were established at Berega and Buigiri in 1926.[113] But the stated aim of these was to "prepare girls for their future lives as wives and mothers, and also to train as teachers for kindergarten and Standards I and II such girls as appear to have a vocation."[114]

Yet, for boys, the primary purpose of boarding schools, and indeed of education in general, was to "produce Christian citizens and leaders who would return to their village life and contribute to the uplift of their community."[115] The wording of the statement somehow reflects the contemporary emphasis on education and the influence of the British government education policy of the 1930s. At this very time, proposals were being made for a training school for evangelists and teachers to be established, to enable them to teach up to standard 3.[116] But this would have been beneficial to men who, after all, were the "teachers" and had been training at Kongwa anyway.

Though well beyond the period under review, it might be helpful to point out that it wasn't until 1947 that the DCT, which had replaced the executive

---

110. See *PCMS*, 1911, 257.

111. *PCMS*, 1914, 225.

112. *CTDL*, no. 13 (June 1931),, MH; cf. Chambers, *Tanganyika's New Day*, 45.

113. As pointed out in chapter 6, the boarding school at Buigiri was transferred to Mvumi in 1931, the one at Berega was closed in 1937. See *PCMS*, 1931, xxix; John Briggs, "Circular [Letter] to Members of the Diocesan Council," 15 October 1937, cited in Berega Logbook, No. 50, an entry for 1937, MH.

114. Minutes, DC, 3–5, 8–9/8/1938, MH.

115. Minutes, DC, 3–5, 8–9/8/1938, MH.

116. Minutes, DC, 3–8/8/1939, MH.

committee of the CMS mission, began to contemplate opening a training school for Bible women and leaders of the Mothers' Union (a women's voluntary organization originating from the Church of England in Britain). But it must be stressed that it was the impending retirement of two prominent Bible women in Ugogo – Damari Sagatwa and Mariamu Malogo – that prompted this idea.[117] There is no evidence, however, that such an exclusive training centre for women workers was ever established. It is possible the idea languished the very year it was conceived because Chambers himself retired in 1947. Several years passed before women candidates were admitted to Kongwa in their own right and as wives of ordinands.

8.4 Ordination as a "Climax" of Leadership Development

8.4.1 Earliest Prospect of Ordination of Africans

Given the nature of training for women that has been assessed above, as well as the tradition in the Church of England which excluded women from ordination (as was the case in other denominations at the time), the analysis of ordination that follows concerns male teachers only. On ordination, Louise Pirouet rightly notes that "to be ordained as a priest is not, of course the only way of becoming a Christian leader."[118] Indeed she herself has demonstrated that lay leadership played a major role in the establishment of Christianity in Uganda,[119] and this study has concerned itself with the very subject.[120] John Taylor's work, *The Growth of the Church in Buganda: An Attempt at Understanding* is another evidence of this phenomenon. Pirouet makes another observation, that "the extent to which missions were willing to train men for ordination is fairly a good indicator of the extent to which they were willing to hand over responsibility."[121] Taylor's observations about the separation of ecclesiastical and secular leadership have been noted already.[122]

---

117. *CTDL*, no. 73 (September 1947): 6.
118. Pirouet, "East African Christians," 118.
119. Pirouet, *Black Evangelists*.
120. See especially chapters 5 and 6.
121. Pirouet, "East African Christians," 118.
122. Taylor, *Church in Buganda*, 71.

Ordination was regarded as the apex of leadership development, and leadership was therefore concentrated in clerical hands.

The CMS mission in Ugogo and Ukaguru was far behind its sister CMS missions in Uganda and Kenya in ordaining indigenous teachers. First ordinations in Uganda took place in 1893 when Henry Wright Duta, Yairo Mutakyala, Yonathani Kaidzi, Nikodemo Sebewato (and two others) were ordained by Bishop Alfred Tucker.[123] In Kenya, W. H. Jones and Ishmael Semler were ordained in 1885; J. R. Deimler in 1896; and Lugo Fussell Gore in 1903.[124] By 1913, the UMCA (another British mission in Tanzania) had already ordained seventeen African clergy in the diocese of Zanzibar, out of a total of thirty-nine.[125] In his review of the work of the CMS mission in Tanzania since 1878, Rees was clear about some of the major objectives that had not been achieved by 1902. These were lack of indigenous clergy, licensed catechists (that is, those with "lawful" church authorization), self-supporting industrial agency, and an institution for training African agents.[126]

Yet, it was not until 1906 when the possibility of ordination of African teachers was contemplated. The five longest serving teachers – Andrea Mwaka of Chamuhawi, Madari Mulutu of Mpwapwa, Yohana Malecela of Buigiri, Yeremia Senyagwa of Mamboya, and Petro Saileni of Nyangala – were named by the executive committee as prospective candidates, subject to the approval of the parent committee in London. These men were said to have demonstrated spiritual qualities and evidence of steadfastness. As secretary of the

---

123. Stock, *History*, 4:94. By 1914, Uganda had forty-nine indigenous clergy, thirty-nine of whom appeared on the 1915 list, the reduction being caused by deaths and suspensions. For a critique of the fact of early ordination and the misleading nature of the figures, see Pirouet, "*East African Christians*," 118–119. This critique includes the lower standards of education required for ordinands (compared with longer, more rigorous training by Catholics in Uganda), "unsuitable" candidates (at least ten) being ordained then removed by 1914 (see Church of Uganda, *Record Book*, cited by Pirouet), and the few teachers coming forward for ordination from within the large number of converts between 1899 and 1914 indicating "regression and rather than progress."

124. All – as were most coastal Christians in the nineteenth and early twentieth centuries – were former slaves. Jones and Semler were sent to train to, and were later baptized at, the CMS mission at Nasik, India, and then sent to Mombasa to work with John Rebmann. They were ordained by Bishop James Hannington. Deimler and Gore were baptized and trained at Frere Town, Mombasa, and ordained by bishops Alfred Tucker and William Peel in 1896 and 1903, respectively. See Stock, *History*, 4:77.

125. Robinson, *History of Christian Missions*, 345.

126. Rees to CMS, 25/3/1902, G3 A8/0/1902/19, BUL.

executive committee, Rees gave further explanation to Baylis regarding the five candidates. He described them as "men of long standing in work, of proved fidelity and of irreproachable character."[127] Rees added, "I may say that the missionaries who have similarly associated with others speak well of them."[128] To emphasize his point, he noted the fact that all of the men were *personally* known to the European missionaries – and it may be added – "personally liked" by them. Strange as it might be, it is inconceivable that anyone would have been nominated to any ministerial position in the mission except in the context of such relationship.

Indeed, Peel was so impressed by the five men that that he was prepared to exempt them from formal examination – an indication that performance in the examination (so firmly adhered to as a major criterion by which lay promotion was determined) could be subordinated in this case. He and the executive committee anticipated an objection from CMS in London and therefore began putting up defences, as well as points to "soften" the request. First, they argued that if the nomination was confirmed, the five candidates would only serve in a probationary position as village pastors, possibly under CMS missionaries who had the oversight of the districts. Second, their wages would not be more than twelve rupees (approximately ninety-six pence per month).[129] And, indeed, funds collected locally from African Christians would be used for the upkeep of these men, not funds from London.[130]

8.4.2 The Duration of Testing Time

The question of how long the five teachers, or indeed any other teacher, would stay in the deacons' order was discussed by Peel. He favoured a lengthened diaconate as a good test (though he did not specify the period).[131] In May 1907, subject to the bishop's approval, the executive committee was determined to put forward to the parent committee in London the names of Yohana Malecela of Buigiri and Andrea Mwaka of Chamuhawi ahead of other teachers whose

---

127. Rees to Baylis 18/1/1906, G3 A8/0/1906/20, BUL.
128. Rees to Baylis 18/1/1906, G3 A8/0/1906/20, BUL.
129. Minutes, EC, 10–12 /1/1906, G3 A8/0/1906/17, BUL.
130. Peel to Baylis, 3/7/1906, G3 A8/0/1906/50, BUL.
131. *Memorandum of Interview with Bishop Peel*, 11/5/1906, G3 A8/0/1906/39, BUL. The interviewer is not named, but it probably was Rees, then secretary of the CMS mission in central Tanzania.

names were proposed for ordination. The committee suggested a minimum period of three years and, during that interval, the candidates would be required to prove themselves "spiritually and mentally fitted."[132] The UMCA required its ordinands to train for three years at a theological college. In Malawi, it took up to ten years before candidates for ordination were ordained in the Livingstonia mission, though, especially in the 1920s, one reason for this was the implementation of the policy that a congregation could not appoint a minister unless it was able to provide his upkeep.[133]

As in most missions, those selected to train for ordination were already long-serving teachers who had "proved their worth" in schools and churches.[134] Tucker's description of some teachers he ordained to deacons' orders at Mengo on 28 May 1899 in Uganda shows that only those with considerable experience were ordained. His remarks on two of the six ordained that day may be sufficient here:

> Tomasi Semfuma has served as licensed reader for the last six years. . . . He is a man of very independent character and of considerable ability. He is a Church worker of at least ten years' standing and has done us yeoman's service. . . . Nua Nakiwafu is also a man of considerable experience. He has been licensed as lay reader for the last three years. He has been tested and tried in many ways.[135]

As has been observed above, no promotion to the next higher level of lay ministerial hierarchy would have taken place without some form of written (and sometimes oral) examination. For that reason, the executive committee suggested that, for the period (of a minimum of three years) when Yohana and Andrea would be under observation, they would be taught subjects appropriate to the ministerial levels higher than those they currently held. However, since the committee was keen to ensure that they were ready for nomination at the right time, it resolved that Yohana and Andrea be assessed

---

132. Minutes, EC, 2–4/5/1907, G3 A8/0/1907/40, BUL.

133. Thompson, *Christianity in Northern Malawi*, 214. Thompson notes, however, that indigenous teachers became frustrated for having to wait up to ten years after leaving theological college before being ordained. Thompson, 166–167.

134. Broomfield, "Importance of Education," MS 3122, LPL.

135. *PCMS*, 1900, 115.

on the basis of the progress they made in the subjects rather than making examination results the yardstick by which their advancement to the next stage on the ministerial ladder – in this case ordination – depended.[136] In fact, the executive committee took a similar decision in November 1906 when it recommended that Yohana Malecela and Andrea Mwaka be promoted to the status of "senior" catechists.[137] It is possible that the reason at the time – as when they were being considered for ordination – was that the two men were not among the intellectually gifted teachers in the mission.[138]

8.5 A Delayed Ordained Ministry: Some Factors

8.5.1 Poor Educational Standards among Teachers

Peel did not regard Andrea Mwaka as a "clever" person. Given what was said about Yeremia Senyagwa as well, it might be generalized that all of the five earliest potential ordination candidates were like him, even though they must have differed in certain respects. Indeed, when one analyses the credentials most referenced by the mission when seeking the approval of the CMS at home with regard to these teachers' ordination, as has been noticed above, it becomes clear that emphasis was put on spiritual qualities, work performance, and CMS missionaires' personal knowledge of the teacher. Little or no reference was made to the educational achievements of the candidates. For ordination, it seems, only spiritual qualities mattered.

This was in contrast to the practice of the UMCA, for example, where the policy demanded almost the same length of training for indigenous ordinands as their foreign colleagues, and some were even sent to train in Britain in the late nineteenth century. The UMCA's high view of priesthood meant that African ministers had to be trained at standards similar to those used for British clergy. Indeed, after training for a time at Kiungani, Zanzibar, indigenous ordinands in the UMCA were sent to colleges in England.[139] Some

---

136. Minutes, EC, 2–4/5/1907, G3 A8/0/1907/40, BUL.
137. Minutes, EC, 22–24 & 26/11/1906, G3 A8/0/1907/1, BUL.
138. Peel, "Usagara and Ugogo Revisited," G3 A8/O/1903/38, BUL.
139. Anderson-Morshead, *History of the Universities' Mission*, 1897, 446, 447, 448. For example, Cecil Majaliwa went to St Augustine's Canterbury (1883–1885) and Petro Limo to Dorchester Missionary College. Others were James Salfey and Samwel Sehoza.

were even ordained in Britain.[140] This was a universalization of the "Holy Orders," which could be described as a *"pre-structured Africanization"* – a pattern in which ordination of indigenous clergy was made a goal from the start of the mission.[141]

The CMS mission in Ugogo and Ukaguru (like some other Protestant missions) seemed to have adopted an *"evolving Africanization."*[142] Though not exclusively different from "pre-structured Africanization," missions that followed an evolving Africanization often observed indigenous teachers for many years and then ordained them on the basis of proven character. But in some cases, this could mean character that posed no threat to the foreign personnel. Equally, demands caused by church growth tended to induce the need for ordaining indigenous clergy. In the CMS mission, it must be added that the reason for the emphasis on spiritual rather than educational qualities might be that the qualification gained through in-service semi-residential training was too little and not worth counting. References have been made already to CMS missionaries' acknowledgement of the lack of time to concentrate on such courses, hence the low academic levels achieved through them.

Oral sources suggest that, in addition to the factors considered already, lack of better education for most church teachers was known to be a setback towards an early ordination. When things improved, and Kongwa gained prominence from the 1920s for training both school teachers and catechists (church teachers), the school teacher training branch was moved to Dodoma in 1928, leaving Kongwa exclusively for training catechists.[143] Since Kongwa became dedicated to the exclusive training of catechists alone, its level of education was not up to the mark. Yusufu Masingisa was one of the scholars:

> Our teachers had a college before World War I. They had a college at Kongwa, but the level of education offered didn't differ so much [with that offered earlier through in-service training], because they didn't go deep. What was offered was very little. Even Mr [German] governor was telling Mr Westgate [first principal],

---

140. Samwel Sehoza was ordained at Iona in Scotland in August 1894. See Anderson-Morshead, *History of the Universities' Mission*, 1897, 344.
141. Anderson, *Church in East Africa*, 142. Emphasis original.
142. Anderson, 143. Emphasis original.
143. Hewitt, *Problems of Success*, 1:199.

"Don't teach these people heliography." But he [Westgate] said, "Oh I am teaching them the basics. But on the whole I teach them religious courses, and some additional small things." I went to college myself, and indeed it was religious courses that were taught.[144]

It is very likely that this move further encouraged mission school teachers to "go secular." The move to separate the groups (church catechists and school teachers) was undoubtedly aimed at ensuring that the mission got the best out of both worlds. That is, getting government grants for training teachers for work in schools and keeping the freedom to teach other catechists how to do church work without the obligation to uphold government standards. But this policy deprived the church of the people who might have exhibited not only spiritual abilities – the ability to teach and preach – but also intellectual gifts. Only later did things improve, and indigenous teachers noted this, some long after retirement. Ndajilo observes, "When they introduced the courses, we were able to get African pastors. . . . First of all, the early pastors didn't understand English. . . . When our children understood English, they became bishops, [government] ministers (when we became independent). Now we have our own children. Bishops, men like [Bishop Mdimi] Mhogolo [of the Diocese of Central Tanganyika], they know English."[145] It was noted in chapter 7, in connection with the changes introduced in secular education by the British colonial government, and again here in relation to the education required for ordinands, that, for indigenous teachers, educational advance was defined in terms of knowledge of the English language –given the period under review in this study, lack of English meant educational "backwardness."

Mention has been made already of the UMCA policy of better training for both the indigenous and foreign clergy, which does not need repeating here. CMS missions in Uganda and Kenya did not necessarily have high quality training colleges, but at least, despite some shortcomings, there was some form of fairly consistent local training in divinity schools or classes. In the 1920s and early 1930s, the majority of indigenous teachers serving purely as catechists in the CMS mission did not have knowledge of English.

---

144. Masingisa, oral interviews, 16 and 17 September 1997; Lazaro Ndajilo, oral interviews, 14 and 16 June 1997.

145. Ndajilo, oral interviews.

Mention has been made already (in chapter 7) how Masingisa and a few colleagues intended to go to Malawi, as they were convinced that education in the Scottish missions was better than the CMS because their school teachers and catechists knew English.[146]

8.5.2 The Threat of Withdrawal

Even if indigenous teachers had attained educational advancement, the CMS mission in Ugogo and Ukaguru was faced with another major problem which equally contributed to the delay of the ordination of indigenous clergy – the possibility, or indeed the "threat," of closing altogether or handing over the CMS mission in central Tanzania to another mission. The rationale for delaying the ordination of indigenous leaders "as long as necessary" was based on the CMS's claim that it was pointless to introduce in Ugogo and Ukaguru a tradition of ordained ministry which a successor mission could easily abandon, if it didn't share that tradition.[147] The issue of closure or withdrawal was of paramount importance not just in respect to ordination but for the entire CMS work in Tanzania. For this reason, it is perhaps appropriate to give a detailed account of it here.

By 1907, the issue of CMS closure in Ugogo and Ukaguru had been raised within the CMS at least three times: April 1890, March 1893, and February 1904.[148] On each of these occasions, either the question of lack of resources or suspicion based on Tanzania being part of the German political sphere were cited as reasons. To some extent, the unease of operating in a territory under German occupation was justified – if one takes into account, for example, the demand by the German colonial administration that the CMS mission (indeed all non-German missions) should have someone fluent in the German language.[149] Nonetheless, the whole issue appears to have been blown out of proportion in London and was based on sentiment rather than facts.

---

146. Masingisa, oral interviews, 16 and 17 September 1997.

147. Knox, *Signal on the Mountain*, 195. Under this policy, it was decided that confirmation – a bishop's laying of hands on baptized members – should not be stressed. The Holy Communion, too, was to be celebrated infrequently.

148. Cust to General Hutchinson, 8/4/1890, G3 A5/0/1890/75; Leipzig Lutheran Mission to CMS, 10/3/1893 G3 A5/0 1893/75; Peel to Baylis 10/2/1904 G3 A8/0 1904/16; Rees to Baylis, 30/1/1907 G3 A8/0 1907/27, BUL.

149. See chapter 5.

The defence put forward by both Peel and the CMS missionaries in Tanzania against the idea was often vigorous. For example, in 1904, while admitting that a year earlier he would have favoured the idea of hand-over to another mission – for example, the Lutherans – Bishop Peel now told Baylis, then CMS general secretary, "My contribution to the debate [on the possibility of closure] is that I consider our mission in Usagara-Chigogo [that is, the CMS mission] full of encouragement whether we looked at the Government or at the people or at the missionaries."[150] Probably playing on Protestant "evangelical," and anti-Roman Catholic, sentiment at the time, he added: "We must occupy Ugogo, or else the RCs will be in. Then trouble will come. If we occupy, the [German] authorities will not allow them to come. This points to our opening the projected station near Kilimatinde."[151] For the moment it appeared that the mission had been saved from closure or hand-over, if only temporarily. The issue resurfaced again in 1907. This time Baylis directed the CMS mission in Tanzania to reduce its annual budget for 1908. This grieved CMS missionaries who felt the estimates were already low. David Rees, the secretary of the mission, even asked the CMS general secretary himself to point out what item(s) should or should not be left in the budget![152]

Kate Pickthall (then based at Mamboya) suggested to Baylis:

> Does it not rather mean that friends at home realising what "retrenchment" means, will rally their forces and come to our help in the war against Satan, so we shall be allowed to continue it here? . . . Oh! How we do hope and pray it will be otherwise. Don't think dear Mr Baylis[.] I am willing to quit and go wherever God sends me, but I feel sure *this* is my sphere of work. . . . Excuse my troubling you, I felt so strongly I *must* write to you, [I] hope it is not too late.[153]

In the same letter, Pickthall suggested to Baylis to consider recruiting and sending to Tanzania people who were prepared to be self-financing. On his part, Peel had even decided to start a Mombasa Diocese Church Missionary

---

150. Peel to Baylis, 10/2/1904, G3 A8/0/1904/16, BUL.

151. Peel to Baylis. It will be observed that despite this, Roman Catholic missionsmission mission entered Ugogo and Ukaguru in 1909. See chapter 5.

152. Rees to Baylis, 9/7/1907, G3 A8/0/1907/47, BUL.

153. Kate Pickthall to Baylis, 15/10/1907, G3 A8/0/1907/55, BUL. Emphasis in original.

Fund, which he promised would go directly to the headquarters of CMS in London for general purposes.[154]

On the question of operating in the German political sphere, Ernest Doulton refuted the falsehood of the information published in the January 1908 issue of one of CMS's periodicals, the *CMR*:

> I believe the implication that the German Government here is unfriendly to English missionary effort, is incorrect and not warranted by facts, and that is my reason for writing. . . . Surely, the fact that we are under the German flag is not sufficient reason [for withdrawal]. . . . May the Committee and all concerned, at this time be so filled with the Spirit that they may understand what the will of the Lord is.[155]

Doulton cited the support shown to the CMS mission by the German colonial administration – granting greater freedom for missionary activity by allowing the acquisition of land for missionary purposes, the importation of goods duty free, and showing sympathy and support for mission schools in educating the local people.[156] Any discomforts that occurred to CMS personnel were isolated acts of mischief by individual German officers and not a consequence of the official policy of the imperial government. To these points, Peel added that the security of the CMS staff was not an issue and articles from both the Berlin Act of 1885 and the German Protectorate Law promulgated in 1900 encouraged foreign missionaries other than those of German origin to reside in Tanzania.[157] He pointed out that by 1907 even converts connected with the CMS mission were being given responsible positions by the Germans with the result that non-Christian chiefs were being stirred up to seek education for people in their areas.[158]

There was a suggestion, by CMS London, that its personnel in Tanzania be transferred to Kenya. This was also refuted on the basis that other missions

---

154. Peel to Baylis, 23/12/1907, G3 A8/0/1908/3, BUL.
155. Doulton to Baylis, 15/2/1908, G3 A8/0/1908/21, BUL.
156. Doulton to Baylis.
157. Reference for both documents is G3 A8/0/1908/16 and attached to Minutes, EC, 19–20, 26–27/12/1907, G3 A8/0/1908/12, BUL.
158. Peel to Baylis, 11/2/1908, G3 A8/0/1908/20; Peel to Baylis, 23/12/1907, G3 A8/0/1908/3; cf. Doulton to Baylis, 15/2/1908, G3 A8/0/1908/21, BUL.

(for example, the Church of Scotland Mission and America Inland Mission – later Africa Inland Mission) had already occupied much of central Kenya, and as they had large staffs and more resources at hand, they had plans for expansion already. In light of colonial government regulations in Kenya, and by agreement between missions, CMS could not open work within three miles of a mission station occupied by another mission. And other parts of central Kenya were still inhospitable for CMS missionaries or settlers.[159]

Despite these persuasive arguments, the CMS committee despatched Fred Wright to Kenya to investigate the state of the mission stations belonging to the Leipzig mission in Ukamba, Kenya. His report was that the Leipzig mission was willing to consider an exchange and added that such an undertaking would be to the advantage of the CMS.[160] This influenced the CMS committee responsible for Tanzania.[161]

To this Peel could only respond with dismay. Only a month after responding to the Wright report, Peel could not hide his frustration regarding the refusal of CMS in London to offer grants to support indigenous teachers during an earlier period, perhaps shortly before the issue of withdrawal or hand-over resurfaced in 1907. He wrote:

> You in Salisbury Square [CMS office in London] have refused us grants for AFRICAN TEACHERS in the period under mention, not because you had no funds, but in the instance of which I am thinking, because you insisted that the people whom we wished to influence should pay a good portion of the evangelists' stipend. This has ever been disquieting to me, for the Society exists to evangelize. . . . Again, money has been given us by friends for TEACHERS with a view to enabling us to employ more than you in Salisbury Square were disposed to grant. But on *your discovering that such money was being given, you* TOOK AWAY *your* GENERAL GRANT to an equivalent amount, and appropriated the extra gift to the current expense in the Mission, thus setting

---

159. Peel to Baylis, 23/12/1907, G3 A8/0/1908/3, BUL.

160. Wright to Baylis, [from Nasa, south of Lake Victoria, Tanzania], 15/5/1908, G3 A8/0/1908/70, BUL.

161. Meeting of Committee of Correspondence, 7/5/1907, G3 A8/O P1, BUL.

free your grant for some other part of the world, and *preventing any expansion on our part.*¹⁶²

The bishop reminded CMS that when the issue of withdrawal resurfaced in 1904, the mission in Ukaguru and Ugogo had only twenty-two CMS missionaries.¹⁶³ This was a much lower figure compared to sixty-two in Kenya. In 1908, the figures were seventeen for Ugogo and Ukaguru and forty-seven for Kenya.¹⁶⁴ The indigenous staff numbered about thirty-two. Yet the results of mission work obtained in Tanzania were far better through the support that CMS missionaries had given to the indigenous teachers who actually carried out the bulk of the work.¹⁶⁵

Such a vigorous defence by the bishop and the CMS missionaries in Tanzania bore fruit. It resulted in a comprehensive review of the future of the mission by the committee responsible for CMS work in Africa – Group No. III Committee on 16 October 1908 – after which it made recommendations to the Committee of Correspondence, which met on 20 October 1908. A month earlier, Group No. III Committee heard a personal presentation and plea from David Rees, one of the staff in Tanzania who was on leave in England in 1908.¹⁶⁶

Far from expressing regret that Tanzania had no ordained pastor at the time, the committee used this as one of the arguments in favour of transfer. The implication was that the successor mission would have less problem accommodating thirty-two or so lay teachers than if these were ordained ministers.¹⁶⁷ However, Group No. III Committee concluded its report by indicating to the Committee of Correspondence: "It will be realised that the Group No. III Committee would not be in favour of abandoning the German

---

162. Peel to Baylis, 9/5/1908, G3 A8/0/1908/38, BUL. Capital letters in original. Italics added.

163. The number reached twenty-five in 1905, of whom five were ordained ministers, and the rest were lay people. By 1908, only one of seventeen foreign staff was an ordained minister.

164. The reduction was a result of unfilled vacancies caused by finished tours, sickness, or death.

165. Peel to Baylis, 9/5/1908, G3 A8/0/1908/38, BUL.

166. Memorandum of Interview of Rev D. J. Rees with Group No. III Committee, 22/9/1908, G3 A8/0/1908/53, BUL.

167. Memorandum of Interview of Rev D. J. Rees.

East Africa Mission if it cannot be taken over by some other mission"[168] How much this influenced the decision to retain the mission (at least for while) is difficult to tell.

While the debate continued within the CMS, the UMCA stepped in and urged the CMS to "avoid weakening 'English' missions," and avoid the German colonial government "sitting on us foreigners."[169] But its offer, made through Duncan Travers (then UMCA general secretary) to take over stations belonging to the CMS mission in Ugogo and Ukaguru was rebuffed. Baylis even downplayed the idea of the hand-over had been contemplated.[170] Nonetheless, it is possible that the interest shown by the UMCA "injected" something into the minds of the CMS leaders that "induced" a rethink of the withdrawal/hand-over mindset and policy and halted the whole idea (along with the protests and pleas from CMS staff in Tanzania themselves). Indeed, on 8 January 1909, Baylis wrote to Doulton, then the current secretary of the CMS mission in Tanzania, informing him that the parent committee of the CMS had been led to repeal their resolution regarding a possible transfer of the mission! Doulton's reply summed up the end of a year-long anguish: "we rejoice at the news and praise God."[171]

8.6 A New Era for Indigenous Leadership Development?

With the assurance of the continuation of the CMS mission in Tanzania now secured (as has been reviewed above), the scene was now set for some kind

---

168. Memorandum of Interview of Rev D. J. Rees.

169. Duncan Travers to Bishop Ingam, 18/11/1908, G3 A8/0/1908/59, BUL. Bishop Frank Weston of Zanzibar made the request through Travers, then General Secretary of the UMCA. The UMCA had strained relations with the German colonial authorities for many years. The German authorities complained, too, about the UMCA. See, for instance, a letter written about protection of British staff as the war broke out in 1914: "I regret to say that the case of the UMS [Universities' Mission] is different [from CMS].... In political matters too, the UMS has given the Colonial gvt much causes for complaint. The German farmers also have complained repeatedly of the UMS missionaries and their political attitude." K. Axenfeld to F. Würz Riehen, 11/9/1914, "German East Africa," Box C.1., RHL.

170. Duncan Travers to F[rederick] Baylis (Rev) 20/11/1908, attached to G3 A8/O/1908/59, BUL. Travers was writing in reply to Baylis's letter dated 18/11/1908, which almost denied that the Bishop of Mombasa and CMS were considering a hand-over.

171. Doulton to Baylis, 15/2/1909, G3 A8/0/1909/20, BUL.

of new beginning. However, eight years passed before the moment that led to the ordination of the first indigenous teachers arrived. Bishop William Peel (Bishop of Mombasa) died on 15 April 1916. Richard Heywood (a senior clergy and secretary of CMS Bombay Committee of Correspondence in India) was appointed to succeed him. Heywood was consecrated in Bombay on 21 April 1917.

But it was not until 1921 when CMS ordained its first two indigenous pastors – forty-five years after the CMS mission arrived in Ugogo and Ukaguru. By this time, Andrea Mwaka (from Ugogo) was the only survivor from the original list proposed for ordination in 1906. It is not clear why the rest, Madari Mulutu and Yohana Malecela (also from Ugogo) and Yeremia Senyagwa and Petro Saileni (from Ukaguru), were no longer considered for ordination.[172] But it was Andrea Mwaka and Haruni Mbega who were nominated for ordination as deacons at Mombasa on 21 August 1921.[173]

The ordination of these two teachers did not break with the tradition regarding the length of lay service as an almost exclusive prerequisite for ordination in those times and many years that followed. Mwaka probably began his ministry in the mission in 1892.[174] Mbega was definitely younger than Mwaka but had been a teacher since 1905.[175] On the other hand, there was a break with a different tradition. These teachers were ordained only as a result of Heywood's extraordinary decision to break the tradition that governed the relationship of an Anglican bishop of an overseas see (episcopal jurisdiction) and CMS in London. The UMCA gave considerable powers to the bishops overseas to plan expansion strategies and acquire resources without having to do much "justification."[176] For CMS, consultation with London and permission from there was necessary before new places could be occupied or key personnel recruited. Heywood neither consulted nor

---

172. It is most probable that these men were now dead. See Knox, *Signal on the Mountain*, 167.

173. See profiles of both men in chapter 6. Clergy Register, CMS Mission & DCT, 1913 onwards, MH. Hewitt, *Problems of Success*, 1:185; Knox, *Signal on the Mountain*, 200.

174. Minutes, EC, 13–14/7/1908, G3 A8/0/1908/47, BUL.

175. Berega Logbook, No. 51, MH.

176. "The direction of the work in Africa was from the first 'vested in the Bishop and such English priests as he may have with him in Africa.'" See Anderson-Morshead, *History of Universities' Mission*, 1897, 436.

sought the advance approval of the CMS! Perhaps justifiably, but with a slight over-involvement, CMS often feared the prospect of being committed to new expenditures, especially wages for teachers, let alone for ordained ministers – as has been stated already.

By ordaining Mbega and Mwaka, Heywood was even making the possibility of a future CMS withdrawal from Tanzania a remote one. Whether he did this consciously or unconsciously remains unclear. But when CMS complained about his decision, he reassured the parent committee that the stipend of African ministers would be met by the local Christians through the appropriate local councils.[177] In 1922, the church council that brought together districts in Ugogo and Ukaguru recommended that Andrea Mwaka and Haruni Mbega be ordained as priests in 1923.[178] For reasons not given, this was delayed until 23 March 1923 when the two were ordained at Buigiri.[179]

Unfortunately, the issue of closure or hand-over of the mission in Ugogo and Ukaguru, which was discussed at length earlier, resurfaced in 1926. This time there was no escape. The only difference this time was that after many contenders had been considered, CMS Australia and Tasmania moved in to rescue the mission and took over the administrative and financial responsibility for Tanzania in 1927. The offer from the UMCA to take over responsibility for Tanzania was turned down once more, mainly due to differences in church polity and perhaps doctrines.[180] A combined effort made by Richard Heywood and CMS leaders in Britain and Australia resulted in the hand over of responsibility for Tanzania to the Australian CMS and the consecration of George Chambers (an Australian) as first Bishop of Central Tanganyika.

The creation of the Diocese of Central Tanganyika (DCT) in 1927 from the Diocese of Mombasa opened up a new chapter in the ordination of other indigenous teachers. On 1 November 1929, Daudi Muhando was ordained deacon and then made priest on 16 March 1932.[181] He was the third to be ordained in the CMS mission. It was from this year on that rapid ordinations of other senior teachers in central Tanzania started. Besides the presence

---

177. Hewitt, *Problems of Success*, 1:185–186.
178. Minutes, CC, 22/1/1922, MH.
179. *PCMS*, 1924, 13.
180. Murray, *Proclaim the Good News*, 197.
181. Clergy Register, CMS Mission & DCT, 1913 onwards, MH.

of a resident bishop in an autonomous diocese, oral sources attribute this to educational advance – though, of course, experience and long service in lay positions continued to be key factors considered before ordination. The following were ordained deacons in 1932: Danieli Mbogo, Rubeni Chidahe, Mika Muloli, and Yonathan Songola from Ugogo; and Mikaeli Mkwama and Yohana Mbele from Ukaguru.[182] All were made priests on 16 July 1933 at Dodoma cathedral.[183] Further ordinations were made in subsequent years, but these fall outside the time-scope of this study.

8.7 Conclusion

This chapter has examined and evaluated the nature of in-service semi-residential training for lay ministry in the CMS mission. It has noted the stress laid upon better academic performance in examinations but went on to observe the lack of relevance in the syllabi used. Some manifestations of the consequence of such deficiency have been analysed. The introduction of residential training in the mission has been examined too. An observation has been made that there was a tendency, within the CMS mission in Ugogo and Ukaguru, of developing poorly educated teachers as future church leaders. Nonetheless, a significant fact has been recognized: even these kind of teachers were men of independent spirit, and some did not like the paternalistic attitudes that CMS missionaries exhibited towards them from time to time.

Coupled with constant threats of possible closure or hand-over of the mission, the prospect of developing an indigenous leadership to a standard level (within the existing clerical tradition) looked remote. However, the creation of the Diocese of Central Tanganyika brought new prospects – for, after 1927, more indigenous teachers now participated in the pastoral care of their fellow Wagogo and Wakaguru.

---

182. *CTDL*, no. 17 (July 1932): 5.
183. Minutes, DC, 27/7–1/8/1933, MH.

CHAPTER 9

General Conclusion

9.1 Aims of Study and Chapters Revisited

The aim of this study was to explore and assess the actual initiatives, contributions, and experiences of indigenous agents in the growth of Christianity in Ugogo and Ukaguru (central Tanzania) from 1876 to 1933. It began by exploring the political, social, and religious context of the Wagogo and Wakaguru in the late nineteenth century and highlighted some of the practices that later became controversial in the relationship between those two societies and the CMS mission as Christianity grew. It has noted that the traditional life in the two societies was "alive and kicking" at the time of the arrival of the CMS mission. The early growth of Christianity in Ugogo and Ukaguru from 1876 to 1900 has been examined too. The examination has demonstrated that only meagre missionary results were obtained during this period. Even so, this study has noted that the initial twenty-four years became a period during which indigenous initiatives and contributions, whether by converts or non-Christians – including chiefs – began to emerge.

Starting with the chiefs, the study has explored in detail the initiatives and contributions inaugurated in the earlier phase. The chiefs, it has been observed, aided the inception of mission Christianity in Ugogo and Ukaguru, yet the majority of them remained committed to their sociopolitical and religiopolitical obligations – for example, on a personal level, by maintaining polygamous marriages and, in an official capacity, by continuing in their role as rainmakers. The initiatives and contributions of other indigenous agents – catechumens, baptized adherents, and teachers – have been examined too. Building on the foundation laid by the chiefs, they evangelized their fellow

Wagogo and Wakaguru through literacy training, preaching, and catechesis, which took place mainly in the out-schools, or the so-called "bush" schools. Unlike the chiefs, many ordinary Wagogo and Wakaguru decided to become members of mission Christianity, and some were employed by it.

But this study also demonstrated that the Gogo and Kaguru social and religious practices continued to be forces to be reckoned with – to the extent that potential converts and a good number of baptized adherents and teachers could not disengage from them easily. Consequently, it appeared, particularly to CMS missionaries, that converts failed to live up to the expectations of the mission Christianity they had introduced, and which was propagated by the indigenous agents. The "policing" of converts, done principally by the indigenous agents, failed to secure total obedience. In relation to this, the study has analysed the catechesis and found it wanting because it did not address the aspirations and issues arising from the pre-Christian heritage of the converts.

Though educational and missionary contributions were not mutually exclusive, an analysis of the latter brought to the fore the collective, as well as the individual, contributions, qualities, and missionary skills of some prominent teachers. This has proved even further the indispensability of the indigenous agents to the process of Christianity's growth in Ugogo and Ukaguru – a fact that the majority of CMS missionaries in the field recognized, appreciated, recorded, and reported. It is striking that they did this rather generously at a time when the majority of Western missionaries, as well as their sending (parent) missions, were keen to promote (among their home supporters) the image of an "indispensable missionary" offering a sacrificial service in order to convert and "civilize the heathen."

One of the key observations that this study has made is that teachers and indigenous missionaries performed even better during the voluntary absence of the CMS missionaries (for example, when on leave), and much more so during the forced absences, particularly during the Maji Maji uprising (1905–1907) and the First World War (1914–1918). The suffering experienced by the indigenous teachers during the First World War, and the role of the indigenous Christians and their teachers (after their release in 1916), exhibited their determination that the work for which they had given so much should continue despite the long absence of foreign missionaries.

Nevertheless, like everyone in society, Gogo and Kaguru teachers had their yearnings for social and economic advancement. This study has demonstrated that this was the case, for when a window of opportunity finally arrived through the educational policies of the British during their colonial occupation of Tanzania, some of them did not hesitate to take it. They became government-registered teachers and earned better salaries than those offered by the CMS mission.

The analysis of the educational and leadership development of these teachers demonstrated that the CMS mission offered low quality education which could not have been of much use for building up a workforce capable of responding to the challenges posed by the socioreligious and sociopolitical context of Ugogo and Ukaguru and Tanzania as a whole. Despite the shortcomings of the secularization of mission education, there was a lesson that the CMS mission could have learned, but it didn't.

The lesson was that there was only one world to be served by the indigenous teachers and that world needed well-trained people who could cope with its secular, as well as religious, challenges more confidently. Better training could have delivered better servants to the public which the CMS mission sought to convert, but it was also significant at a personal level in the lives of teachers as children of God and pilgrims. It was necessary that they should understand well the nature of their dual citizenship – of belonging, first and foremost, to the Gogo and Kaguru societies and then to the Christian community that was created through mission Christianity. Yet, just as the catechesis failed to address the deep spiritual yearnings of the Gogo and Kaguru converts, so did the training offered for teachers in this respect.

9.2 Relevance for Mission of the Anglican Church of Tanzania

9.2.1 Toward a Revised Catechesis and Catechism

The two observations just made constitute the practical relevance of this study for the mission of the church, particularly that branch of the Anglican Church of Tanzania that replaced the CMS mission. This relevance has to be confined to the issue of catechesis. The writer makes a proposition that if the catechetical process is to address the pre-Christian social and religious needs of the converts, then the catechesis, and catechism should be thoroughly revised.

This proposition is made because this study has established a connection between nominalism and the two legacies just noted above – unfortunately bad ones – namely, the catechism's lack of relevance for the pre-baptism and post-baptism training of converts, as well as a largely irrelevant training for catechists and ordained ministers. It has shown, in several instances, that most converts and teachers maintained a significant degree of loyalty to their pre-Christian social and religious heritage even after converting to mission Christianity. The resilience of the traditional social and religious context – which shook the CMS mission and its converts almost a century ago – continues today. The church can only ignore it at its own peril.

The failure of the CMS mission to split the Gogo and Kaguru Christians into two identities was all too evident. So much so that the mission resorted to legalistic approaches to issues of discipline. But this, at worst, only created "daytime loyal Christians" and "nighttime Africans." The Anglican Church today will hardly avoid this trap if it continues to throw away the golden opportunity for revising its catechesis and offering relevant teaching during the catechetical process – teaching that is sensitive to, and conscious of, the pre-Christian social and religious context of those being catechized.

Surely, for all the good purpose it has served over the years, the age of theoretical catechesis, and irrelevant catechism as prerequisite to the administration of the rites of baptism and confirmation (the laying on of hands), is long gone. It is inadequate because it is based on the recital of the Lord's Prayer, the Ten Commandments, and the Apostles' Creed, as well as the roles of God the Father (the creator of the world), Jesus his Son, and the Holy Spirit.

The CMS mission used the formulae out of ignorance – ignorance based on the assumption that the religious needs of the Wagogo and Wakaguru were similar to those of Christians in the West. The three elements often recited during the catechesis are obviously universal and date back to the time of the early church. They have become a heritage of the world church. But they have been naively made the cornerstone of the catechesis in places where life context demands more than just a recital of historic elements of a largely Western Christian faith.

In a Tanzanian context, it might be observed that the reason they are still preferred and used today in many historic churches is that they demand less thinking and innovation on the part of those preparing candidates for baptism and confirmation. A related reason is the implicit desire of the church hierarchy to think that doing so maintains unbroken ties with the ways of the "mother" (Western) churches. Equally relevant is the pressure to reach certain numerical targets for the number of churches started each year and of baptisms performed. The frequency of confirmation visits to local congregations and parishes by senior church leaders are part of the factors that contribute to the rushing of converts through the stages of catechesis.

Yet teaching the Lord's Prayer, the Ten Commandments, and the Apostles' Creed – as well as doctrine regarding the Godhead – is one thing. Mere recital of these is quite a different thing. That is to say, there is hardly any teaching going on. The analysis of the Gogo and Kaguru social and religious life in the second chapter of this study showed that during the rites of passage, teaching was hardly theoretical. There was no room for irrelevancy. It reflected the actualities of life – the issues that the boys and girls would soon face in real life situations. They moulded behaviour, and regulated it, so that the initiates knew the rewards and the "curses" that followed conformity and nonconformity, respectively. Objections were often raised within mission circles regarding much of the content of the traditional teaching that was imparted during the rites of passage – for example, during circumcision. But the method used was acceptable even to its opponents. Indeed, those who favoured adaptation and preservation of African values hailed the traditional teaching methods.

Therefore, not only should the church address the question of the content of the catechism, but it should consider altering the method of teaching too. Is the African culture, even today, not rich in communication through stories, narratives, and real life experiences – to name a few? Aren't some aspects of life in the Biblical world (especially the earlier parts of the Old Testament and the Gospels in the New Testament) more akin to traditional African worldviews?[1]

Mention of the biblical world is not all irrelevant, for this study has quoted statements from some of the informants and former indigenous

---

1. Mbiti, "Biblical Basis," 83; Bediako, "Understanding African Theology," 17.

teachers – statements that give us some idea of the kind of biblical material that was used in the catechesis and in preaching. It centred on life to come, and one of the methods by which it was delivered was to focus not on the necessity of eternal life but on generating fear among the potential converts and converts of how they would go to hell if they didn't believe. Yet the gap could have been narrowed, for example, by exploring the concept of life after death in the traditional religion – that the dead are not altogether dead but continue to live through the living.

9.2.2 Some Modern Dangers of Post-Mission Christianity
9.2.2.1 *The potential danger of unfulfilled promises*

Apart from establishing a connection between legalism and the lack of relevant catechesis and catechism, this study has also established that there was a connection between external incentives – the leading one being the acquisition of literacy skills – and the conversion of adults and young people to mission Christianity. In the era of the CMS mission, some converts who appeared to have been converted did not necessarily abandon their allegiance to their social and religious pre-Christian heritage. CMS missionaries and some indigenous teachers were often amazed at the "inability" of the converts to grasp the Christian teaching as they presented it or to maintain a consistent Christian life. Consequently, they resorted to legalistic approaches to discipline, particularly in such issues as female circumcision, polygamy, sickness and traditional medicine, and traditional dance and beer drinking – to name a few.

Such legalistic approaches, it may be observed, did not reveal the weakness of the Gogo and Kaguru Christians as much as the frustration and helplessness of CMS missionaries and their indigenous coworkers in the face of the resilience the two societies' religions and social values. This was the case because, as Andrew Walls observes, traditional (or primal) religions are "the substratum of the religious life of the most substantial body of world's Christians."[2]

Today, in a different era, such things as mission schools and literacy training may no longer be regarded as "incentives," at least in their historic sense. Yet some converts to the Christian church in Tanzania will undoubtedly

---

2. Walls, "Africa and Christian Identity," 11.

have different reasons for becoming church members. If one's firsthand experience may be permitted as a testimony here, then it has to be said that the increasing economic difficulties, unpredictable weather conditions, and drought that often leads to famine in many parts of Tanzania (not least in Ugogo and Ukaguru) have caused the church to be a dispenser of relief. It distributes food and used clothing (acquired mainly through aid) and administers social development projects. These may give the church a similar image as that of the mission it has come to replace. In a Tanzanian (African) context, the danger is even greater. Some who have been involved in one-to-one evangelism, or house-to-house communication of the Christian message, will undoubtedly have encountered questions such as, "what will the church do to me if I become a member?" The unwise messengers (whether humble evangelists or senior church leaders), sometimes keen to attract even members of another denomination (let alone non-converts), often fall into the trap and promise one or more things – dispensary, school, or relief food – the list could grow bigger.

9.2.2.2 The potential danger of power Christianity

In addition to making promises that can hardly be fulfilled, there are some real concerns that people have in Tanzania and Africa as a whole. Sickness and misfortune, belief in witchcraft (indeed, the fear of it), childlessness – to list a few – are all staring the church in its face. Some churches, or their ministers, who realize they can't deliver material goods, resort to another dangerous yet attractive form of Christianity – "power" Christianity. It is a form of Christianity that claims to have urgent solutions to human problems such as those listed above. Any church that bases its appeal on power Christianity is likely to attract as many converts as it could possibly afford to list.

Unfortunately, converts persuaded thus (some of whom are first time hearers of the Christian message through preaching) soon find out that either the promises can't be delivered, and that life demands more realism than that, or that the Christian church they have joined is not pointing them to God for the cure of their physical and spiritual needs. They find a set of "dos" and "don'ts" – or, in a word, legalism. So ethical issues dominate sermons preached, with little else about the power of God – little else about the concerns the converts have brought with them from their previous lives in the old religion or social life.

They realize they have left one religion – the traditional religion – and have joined just another one, Christianity. The original promise, the platform upon which they were invited into the church by preachers, was that Jesus Christ, the originator of the Christian religion, delivers his promises to human beings whom he calls into relationship with him through the church. Sooner or later, converts turn elsewhere, for they do not see Jesus at work but human beings concerned with preserving a religion which, at best, they seem to misunderstand and are therefore misrepresenting.

Consequently, Christianity and traditional religion (or religions) become competitors. The one that delivers its claims fastest and does so with minimum conditions (or conditions that can be fulfilled without much struggle with one's self) acquires the upper hand in the actual control of the daily lives of people, both in church and outside the church. In most cases, it is the traditional religion that acquires the upper hand, and the reason is simple: the converts stay with what they already possess. This creates "daytime" Christians and "nighttime" Africans.

9.3 Toward a Dialogue with African Traditional Heritage

In light of what has been observed above, and in relation to the fact of the long-standing resilience of African traditional heritage, this writer makes another proposition. He proposes that perhaps one way of dealing with the problem of the creation of "daytime" Christians and "nighttime" Africans is to allow the boundaries that separate the functions of Christianity and those of the traditional religion to shrink. By this he means the need for Christian churches in Africa to unconditionally admit people into the church through baptism, and once it has done so, to begin a long process of catechesis and "negotiation."

This negotiation should focus on socioeconomic and socioreligious issues that have dominated the pre-Christian past of those who join the church (similar to the ones that became a source of continuous conflict between the CMS mission and converts in Ugogo and Ukaguru). Through catechesis, converts should be helped, step-by-step, to comprehend their dual citizenship as their knowledge of their relationship with God increases. Nothing should be forcefully driven out of them as if one was performing "exorcism" because such an act would risk forcing the converts to resort to secret practices.

The purpose of all this long process would be to allow a genuine conversion to take place, and the pre-Christian world of the converts to be dealt with properly. This, in the view of this writer, is a more responsible way of making disciples – baptising people unconditionally and then carrying out a sustained teaching after baptism. This proposition is not so radical as it might seem because, after all, some churches at present, not least the Anglican Church of Tanzania, tend to baptize "converts" soon simply on the basis of ability to recite the Lord's Prayer, the Ten Commandments, and the Apostles' Creed. Again, whether someone was baptized as a child or as an adult, the confirmation time becomes a time for more recitals and recitals! But how long can these newly baptized people, or the newly confirmed, remember what they recite? Indeed, are they different from "the established" Christians in their inability to recall and recite without struggling, especially the Ten Commandments and the Apostles' Creed? Hardly so, even though Sunday after Sunday these formulae are recited in church! There could be nothing worse than calling people out of one religion – in this case the traditional religion (where supposedly, from a Christian point of view, there is a life of bondage) – only to place them under a greater bondage of identity crisis. It should be borne in mind that as Kwame Bediako has pointed out, the pre-Christian religious culture and heritage of a convert is also his or her "pre-Christian memory."[3] Memory is "integral to identity; and without memory, none of us knows who we are."[4] Without memory we cannot know our past, and according to Andrew Walls, "without our past we are lost."[5] Perhaps some African Christians find themselves "lost" and become "daytime" Christians and "nighttime" Africans because they see the church trying to deny them their past and the memory of that past too.

But if they are allowed to bring their past and understanding into the Christian faith, unconditionally and openly, they will discover what it means to be a converted Christian. It is a past that helps an individual to make any crucial decisions that have to be made – indeed there are crucial

---

3. Bediako, "Understanding African Theology," 18.
4. Bediako, 18.
5. Walls, "Gospel as the Prisoner," 3–15.

decisions – and to do so, step-by-step, in relation to the new faith he or she has entered.[6] It leads to what Kenneth Cragg refers to (in relation to the conversion of Muslims, but equally relevant to non-Muslim converts) as "integrity in conversion: a unity of self in which one's past is genuinely integrated into present commitment, so that the crisis of repentance and faith that makes us truly integrates what we have been in what we become."[7] The question of how the "old" and the "new" could be integrated becomes an ongoing one. Constantly the African Christian seeks "to know" not simply intellectually but through a dialogue with one's self. It is a personal spiritual quest. For as Walls states, referencing the "indigenizing principle," "the fact, then, that 'if any man is in Christ he is a new creation' does not mean that he starts or continues his life in a vacuum, or that his mind is a blank table. It has been formed by his own culture and history, and since God accepts him as he is, his Christian mind will continue to be influenced by what was in it before."[8] In Christian history, Kwame Bediako asserts, it is a quest that occupied the minds of men such as Clement of Alexandria and Justin Martyr in the Hellenistic Christian era, a quest that led them to adopt a view that Christian revelation and non-Christian tradition were not mutually exclusive.[9]

Though this study is sociohistorical in nature, and is neither biblical nor theological, the analysis done earlier showed that biblical teaching was used in the preaching and catechesis. In light of this, while the concern is not to engage in biblical exegesis, some general observations could be made with regard to the relationship of the Bible and African culture. One reason is of course the fact that mission Christianity (of which the CMS mission was a part), and historic mission churches that have come to replace the missions, use the Bible as a point of reference for the claims made against African cultures.

Therefore, the point made by Ernest Ezeogu in his article "Bible and Culture in African Christianity" may be of relevance and interest here. Having noted the role of the Bible in the phenomenal growth of Christianity in Africa

---

6. Walls, 3–15.

7. Cragg, "Conversion and Convertibility," 194.

8. Walls, *Missionary Movement*, 8. By using "he" or "his," Walls is by no means excluding women.

9. Bediako, *Theology and Identity*, 435, 436.

in the twentieth century, Ezeogu goes on to observe the existence of an unhealthy dialectic approach to the Bible in African Christianity, whereby the former is seen to be radically incompatible with African culture. Without being exhaustive, he traces the root of this to missionary theology (especially pietistic evangelical teaching similar to that adopted in the CMS mission and used by indigenous teachers in Ugogo and Ukaguru, as shown earlier) and the novelty of the written word in Africa, hence the passive (uncritical) reading of the Bible.[10] Both have tended to lead to pietistic, one-dimensional understandings of the Bible and Christianity in which Christians are "vertically oriented but have no horizontal bearing," ignore "issues of doctrine or discipline that might arise between the Bible and a given African culture," and assume a "pre-packed answer: yes to the Bible and no to African culture."[11]

A possible alternative, which Ezeogu suggests – a dialogical approach – is similar to what this writer suggests in relation to Christianity and African traditional heritage. In a dialogical approach, the Bible continues to have its authority, but since it is the word of God transmitted through human beings within particular cultures, and has a "transcending and transforming character," it has nothing to fear or to lose. It enters into a give-and-take relationship (or dialogue) with African cultures.

There might be fears, of course: first, among pietistic one-dimensional Christians, church leaders, and scholars who fear that a dialogic approach could amount to dilution of the essence of the biblical message; and second, among African traditionalists who might argue that it is the African culture that will end up compromising its roots. Yet, in a give-and-take relationship, "just as a seed that takes root in a new soil bears new fruit thus perpetuating itself, so it is with the gospel when it takes root in a new culture."[12] African traditional heritage too has some concepts and symbols that might enrich the understanding of Christianity and conversion in Africa. Peter Sarpong lists some of these: for example, the concept of the wholeness of human beings and how the material and spiritual cannot be separated or isolated; the concept of the sacredness of life and nature; the concept of immortality and how it is not just about life in another world (the world to come) but also for life

---

10. Ezeogu, "Bible and Culture," 29–30.
11. Ezeogu, 31.
12. Ezeogu, 33.

here and now; the sense of community and the importance of "belonging;" and a sense of morality that goes beyond the individual.[13] This list is neither definitive nor prescriptive. But taking these concepts seriously would mean taking the dialogue between Christianity and African traditional heritage to another level. This, Louis Luzbetak argues, is not the level of accommodation, which is essentially a form of translation, but "a contextualizing translation" in which the local community engages in dialogue with the biblical message, so that the local church becomes "of the soil, planted and not transplanted."[14]

This approach to the relationship of Christianity and African traditional heritage does require, however, a high degree of integrity. It requires upholding not only what Walls calls an "indigenizing principle" (to which reference has been made above) but also what he refers to as "the pilgrim principle." In this principle, it is emphasized that "not only does God in Christ take people as they are: He takes them in order to transform them into what he wants them to be."[15] In the words of David Bosch, in his book *Transforming Mission*, contextualization does not mean "an uncritical celebration of an infinite number of contextual and often mutually exclusive theologies."[16] If Bosch warns against extreme relativism, he also decries the danger of the "*absolutism of contextualism*"[17] that has happened in Western missionary outreach: "where theology, contextualized in the West, was in essence elevated to gospel status and exported to other continents as a package deal. Contextualism thus means universalizing one's own theological position, making it applicable to everybody and demanding that others submit to it."[18] The constant tension, which may never go away (and perhaps should not), remains between the biblical message, the local culture, and the "universal" heritage (or the Christian tradition). To Bosch's point above, Luzbetak adds: "We cannot emphasize strongly enough, however, that the most important key to contextualization will always be the soul of the local community – the local ways, values, needs and traditions. . . . And if the pastor, religious educator,

---

13. Sarpong, "Can Christianity Dialogue?"
14. Luzbetak, *Church and Cultures*, 79.
15. Walls, *Missionary Movement*, 8.
16. Bosch, *Transforming Mission*, 427.
17. Emphasis in original.
18. Bosch, 428.

consultants, or church authorities happen to share the same culture as the community in question, the advice remains largely the same [as one given to the outsider]: *Know* your own culture and seek a solution from *within* and *with* those you are guiding."[19] If this is heeded, it is possible to enter into a healthy dialogue in which the catechesis becomes an ongoing process, constantly seeking to engage constructively with the pre-Christian heritage of each convert, step-by-step, without resorting to legalism and nominalism.

It may be better, for the sake of mission in Tanzania and Africa, that recognition be made of the fact that the values of African traditional heritage may be contrary to mission Christianity, but the two are not necessarily in an irrecoverable contradiction. This makes it possible for one to be authentically Christian and African. In this context, one might cross the boundary of Anglicanism and the CMS mission and quote the famous call Pope Paul VI made in Kampala in 1969: "You may, and you must, have an African Christianity."[20]

9.4 The Study of Christianity in the Non-Western World

9.4.1 Mission Christianity and African Culture in History

Leaving aside the immediate practical relevance of this study to the mission of the church in Tanzania, and Africa as a whole, this study may also have wider academic significance for scholarship in the broader non-Western world. This is both in its assessment of the relationship of mission Christianity and African culture and worldviews and in relation to methodology for mission historiography.

On the first point, which is somehow an enlargement of the points made in relation to the mission of the church, the wider contribution of this study to world Christianity is in the way it has shown in the analysis that it was not always the case that mission Christianity – (and, by implication, the Western missionary) – managed to "destroy" non-Western cultures and values. Instead, it was mission Christianity that was in a disadvantaged position of losing its battles, not non-Western cultures and religions. The fact that it

---

19. Luzbetak, *Church and Cultures*, 81.
20. Quoted in Ezeogu, "Bible and Culture," 35.

was practical expediency, or the "external" innovations of Christianity, that some people in these societies found compelling and sought to associate with suggests that they were in control of their decisions.

This is not a denial of the impact of mission Christianity on the Gogo and Kaguru societies (as on other societies in the non-Western world). In fact, the very act of some people converting to mission Christianity was, by implication, an act of "victory" for mission Christianity over the traditional indigenous social and religious life. However, this study disagrees with the assessment of the relationship of the Wagogo and Wakaguru with mission Christianity as put forward by scholars such as T. O. Beidelman. Beidelman writes: "The C.M.S. considered Kaguru customs and beliefs the antitheses of Christianity. For them, Christianity involved a wide range of European behavior, from dress and etiquette to monogamy. . . . Ironically, much that appealed to the missionaries, supposed simplicity of rural tribal life, was what evangelism destroyed."[21] On the issue of undermining the cultural confidence of converts and causing social disruption, Beidelman's view is similar to that of E. A. Ayandele, who writes:

> When a missionary converted individuals in a community he removed units from an organic whole and thereby undermined the monolithic culture of the community. . . . In [Nigeria] a country where religion was the cement of the society, the guarantor of moral principles and the basis of secular authority, renunciation of the traditional religion implied renunciation of the moral, civil and political obligations to the community.[22]

Attempts by missions to cause the kind of disruption suggested by both Beidelman and Ayandele cannot be denied. But both Beidelman and Ayandele overlook the diversity of attitudes represented by missions and the complex interests and initiatives of Africans in embracing mission Christianity. In fact, Beidelman himself has noted some of the indigenous people's motives in

---

21. Beidelman, *Colonial Evangelism*, 133.
22. Ayandele, *Missionary Impact*, 330–331.

joining the mission,²³ though he focuses more on noting the "contradictions" in the attitudes of the CMS missionaries.²⁴

On the diversity of attitudes represented by missions, and indigenous interests, R. W. Wyllie makes a point worth noting – a point he made in response to one of Beidelman's works.²⁵ Wyllie rightly argues that:

> While it is convenient to portray colonial societies in terms of fundamental opposition between two cultures, the reality is, of course, much more complex. Neither the cultures of the colonizers nor that of the colonized can be regarded as a homogenous entity carried by an undifferentiated group, since cleavages clearly exist *within*, as well as between the two broad cultures.²⁶

Wyllie illustrates his point by referring to the work of the Wesleyan Methodist mission in Ghana. But the wider significance of his statement cannot be ignored. He continues: "If the missionaries saw clearly that evangelical success depended upon their undermining of folk religion . . . the potential converts saw, equally clearly, that here was a new religion which could be made to serve well in the pursuit of mundane, this worldly interests."²⁷ The mundane interests of Ghanaians (as of many other African societies) ranged from the quest for spiritual power and protection to opportunities for social advancement, as has been demonstrated in the case of the Wagogo and Wakaguru in central Tanzania.²⁸ The sheer persistence of traditional practices, and their functional significance, meant that, since the days of missions to the present time, traditional heritage was bound to survive not only the onslaught of mission Christianity but of other manifestations of Western values. Are manifestations of the resilience of the traditional heritage, for example issues such as female circumcision, polygamy, witchcraft beliefs and practices – to mention some – not still with us? Have they not stayed? Is it not the secular

---

23. Beidelman, *Colonial Evangelism*, 25; Beidelman, "Contradiction," 90.
24. Beidelman, *Colonial Evangelism*, 16.
25. Beidelman, "Social Theory," 235–249.
26. Wyllie, "Some Contradictions in Missionizing," 198.
27. Wyllie, 200.
28. Compare with similar experiences in the interaction of the Kikuyu of central Kenya and the CMS mission early in the twentieth century. See Karanja, *African Anglican Church*, 51–64.

state in some African nations that the church looks to in dealing with female circumcision (as has happened in Senegal) and witchcraft beliefs (as is the case in Tanzania now)?

9.4.2 Use of Archival and Oral Sources

On the second issue, of methodological contribution, two points are made here. First, this study has demonstrated that a careful search of archival mission sources (though traditionally intended to show the achievements of Western missionaries) may still reveal that Western missionaries in the non-Western world recognized and acknowledged the contributions and initiatives of indigenous agents – far more than some past users of such archives (such as the CMS archives) have so far cared to admit. Second, it demonstrates that the use of oral sources can enhance the process of reconstructing local church or mission histories. At the heart of the reconstruction process is the process of empowering Christians in the non-Western world to relive their personal life-histories, as well as those of their living and deceased relatives who contributed to the process of the growth of Christianity in specific locations.

At this point, an attempt should be made to respond to at least one objection that is commonly raised against trusting and using oral history as a historical source. It was mentioned in chapter 1, in the introduction of this entire study, that one of the objections to embracing oral history unreservedly is due to the so-called "problem" of contamination or "feedback" in oral tradition through printed material. Scholars such as David Henige (to whom reference was made in chapter 1) claim that uncontaminated oral histories exist no more in oral societies. An initial response was made in chapter 1, showing that though some informants interviewed were/are literate people, there is no evidence that they depended on printed sources for their stories or that the narratives they gave were intended to enhance a particular political ideology about their ethnic group or clan.

But even if that were the case, Henige talks about "oral societies" – a phrase that by its very nature presupposes that these are societies where word of mouth is the chief mode of communication (as opposed to "literate societies" with wider access to, and use of, printed material). Yet, he then somehow manages to accord oral societies with the indomitable ability to engage with and assimilate written material and incorporate it into their traditions. This is extraordinary. Second, Henige accords too much power to the effect of the arrival of Christianity and political colonialism to alter the landscape not only of the oral traditions that existed but also of the entire life of such communities – as if politics and political ambitions alone mattered, nothing else. But based on the analysis done in chapter 2 of this study, in the case of the Wagogo and Wakaguru (as in other African societies), life was dramatized most by leaders and commoners alike in the religious sphere rather than in the political sphere.

Two authors, Justin Willis and Janet Ewald, are worth engaging here to enhance the response just made. In his article "Feedback as a 'Problem' in Oral History: An Example from Bonde,"[29] Justin Willis has demonstrated that in some oral societies the so-called "problem" of feedback has not been a unique influence in the development of oral tradition. Oral histories are therefore a product of many influences, and the idea of being corrupted assumes the existence of a "pure" tradition. This wasn't always the case. If contamination existed, it did not begin with the arrival, and availability, of written sources, "nor does the advent of written history make contamination inevitable." Instead, without denying that some literate people in some societies – for example, the Bonde in the northeast of Tanzania, in the UMCA sphere – consulted written sources (for example, published histories of a mission, mission biographies, and magazines), Willis argues that they nonetheless have recently displayed the ability to disregard such sources when these contradict their own perspective of history.[30]

Therefore, the actual problem that leads to the theory of contamination is the belief in the "power" of written documents, and this is common both in the West and in the non-Western world. Jan Vansina points out that "the layman . . . fondly imagines that written sources reveal events of the past which can be accepted as fact, but considers that oral sources tell of things about which there is no certainty – things which may or may not have happened. He forgets that any historical synthesis comprises an interpretation of facts, and is thus founded upon probabilities."[31] Such is a statement by a scholar whose name is associated so much with oral tradition (though he is in fact a trained historian), one might claim he speaks not as a historian but as an oral

---

29. In *History in Africa* 20, 1993.
30. Willis, "Feedback as a 'Problem,'" 356, 357.
31. Vansina, *Oral Tradition*, 183.

traditionalist. Yet historians such as Edward Carr, who have not concerned themselves with oral tradition, support his case. Edward Carr notes that:

> The nineteenth-century fetishism of facts was completed and justified by fetishism of documents. The documents were the Ark of the Covenant in the temple of facts. The reverent historian approached them with bowed head and spoke of them in awed tones. *If you find it in documents, it is so.* But what, when we get down to it, do these documents – the decrees, the treaties, the rent-rolls, the blue books, the official correspondence, the private letters and diaries – tell us? No documents can tell us more than what the author of the document thought – what he thought had happened, what he thought ought to happen or would happen, or perhaps only what he wanted others to think, he thought or even only what he himself thought he thought.[32]

Carr's observation about the excessive uncritical belief in the written word in historical studies (and perhaps other fields) is what Janet Ewald refers to as "graphocentrism" – a point she makes in her article "Speaking, Writing, and Authority: Explorations in and from the Kingdom of Taqali."[33] She boldly makes a personal criticism: "My Africanist training explicitly prepared me to use oral sources, but my historical background implicitly taught me to trust documents as authoritative sources. We historians do not easily grasp how the spoken word could ever convey more authority than written sources."[34] As an example, Ewald uses the 1870–1884 kingdom of Taqali in the Nuba hills of Sudan. In her study of this kingdom, she discovered that the kings had access to literacy but few printed documents existed after they ceased to rule. She points out that the Taqali people "preferred face-to-face, oral communication because it was grounded in their cultural milieu and because it sustained dynamics of their political life."[35] Ewald agrees, as does Justin Willis and this

---

32. Carr, *What Is History?*, 16. Emphasis added.

33. In *Comparative Studies in Society and History*, Vol. 30, 1988, 204.

34. Ewald, "Speaking," 202. See also Afigbo, "Colonial Historiography," 47. Afigbo points out that the implication of the fetish of the written word for African mission and church history is that for so long in the past some scholars have thought that lack of written African records meant that Africans lacked history and civilization. Mudimbe's observation on this very issue has been noted already in chapter 1.

35. Ewald, "Speaking," 202–203.

writer, that when presented with literacy, some people adopt it and use if for their own political advantage. However, like Willis, Ewald rightly contends that "only some people revere literacy, some of the time. . . . Other people mistrust and avoid it."[36] Since the 1960s, it has been established, especially in relation to African history, that orally transmitted evidence is equally an authoritative source for the study of African history.[37] That an oral source may be cross-checked and supplemented by other sources is not objected to, but as A. E. Afigbo, another African historian, counsels, the "acceptance of oral tradition as a valid source of information on the African past is not and should not solely, or even mainly depend on the support it derives from these other [written] sources."[38] If historians of non-Western societies' historical initiatives and experiences take into account the admonitions of such scholars as Afigbo, Vansina, Justin Willis, and Janet Ewald, and free themselves from undue suspicion of orally transmitted sources, data from word of mouth will continue to play an important role in the study of mission history. It becomes a heritage that can be used in the reconstruction of local mission and church histories – a heritage that can be preserved, for example, in audio and documentary forms so that it is not easily lost.

Therefore, a methodological contribution of this study in relation to oral history is both a challenge and an encouragement: despite the difficulties and limitations of obtaining and using oral data, there is a wealth of oral tradition for those seeking to rewrite local mission histories or church histories in their own contexts.

Certainly, one of the rewards such a use of oral interviews in researching mission history has given to this writer is the discovery of the existence of indigenous missionaries and pioneers who crossed cultural frontiers to work among peoples of other ethnic groups in Ugogo, Ukaguru, and Unguu (which is mainly counted with Ukaguru in this study). This may be the case in other parts of the non-Western world.

---

36. Ewald, "Speaking," 205n18.
37. See Jewsiewicki and Mudimbe, "Africans' Memories," 3.
38. Afigbo, "Oral Tradition," *History in Africa*, 3. Afigbo challenges scepticism over oral tradition exhibited by such scholars as Horton, "Stateless Societies," 78-80, and Jones, *Trading States of Oil Rivers*, 20–28.

Through the critical use of oral sources (as well as archival sources), scholars from the non-Western world will continue to question the arbitrary use of the term *missionary* in academic writing and in church circles, both historically and – even more so – in the present time, as it often depicts, almost exclusively, the Western missionary. The detriment of this to missions in non-Western societies is in the misguided belief that, in the past, the growth of Christianity was a result of the sole work of outsiders – Western missionaries. This study has demonstrated that the reality in Ugogo and Ukaguru, in central Tanzania, was different.

APPENDIX 1

Dealing with CMS Statistics: Some Problems

Two problems may be highlighted in relation to the CMS global statistics. One is lack of distinction between adult-scholars and child-scholars. In those statistics, the column head "Native Christians" – also called "Native Christian Adherents" in 1909 and "African Christian Adherents Community" in 1914[1] – only distinguishes between the baptized and the catechumens. The column head marked "Scholars" (1900–1908) is only subdivided into two categories – "Boys" and "Girls." At different times, the title of the column head changed to "Native Seminarists and Scholars" (1909), "Native Scholars" (1910), "African Students and Scholars" (1911–1913), and "Students and Pupils" (1914–1933).

In addition to young children who were starting formal school education, statistics include adult men and women who in fact were "inquirers" – namely, those in their second stage of baptismal instruction. One possible reason for the inclusion of adults in the list of "students and pupils" was perhaps the fact that they, too, were learners – learning to read and write at literacy centres.[2]

However, as evidence suggests, both adults and children continued to be counted together, and a report on the Buigiri station school in 1905 pointed out that it was "attended by both adults as well as children, [who] learnt to read the New Testament, and the scripture teaching."[3] Though the pre-war figures were maintained from 1915 onwards (because the new ones could not be obtained), the column head marked "students and pupils" in the table of

---

1. *PCMS*, 1910, 58; *PCMS*, 1915, xxiii.
2. See Knox, *Signal on the Mountain*, 169.
3. *PCMS*, 1906, 71.

statistics is subdivided into two separate categories: "men and boys" on one side and "women and girls" on the other.

The difference between the number of adults and children baptized varied each year, and it may be difficult to generalize as to which group was larger than the other. For example, on average, nearly forty-seven adults were baptized each year in the whole mission compared with forty-nine children. After the First World War, about two hundred adults were baptized each year compared to the same number of children.

The second problem worth highlighting is the lack of distinction between male and female scholars. The first indication that female and male adults were included in the statistics is found in a footnote phrase – "including men and women" – below the table of the "Statistics of the Eastern Equatorial Africa Mission for 1900."[4] The phrase refers to figures under columns headed "Boys" and "Girls." But, from 1901 to 1917, no indication was given in the statistics that adults were counted with children as scholars. This is the same in the detailed statistics for stations under single missions, as well as in the general global statistical view of the CMS missions world-wide, which often appeared in earlier pages of each annual report.

The third problem is the manner in which the listing of stations was done. From 1876 onwards, the statistical figures for the CMS mission in Tanzania were given under the East Africa mission, which included both Kenya and Tanzania. Part of the reason was that there were no figures to be included prior to 1885, the year when the first baptisms took place in Ugogo. Statistics provided in table 3.1 in chapter 3 starts from 1892. The main reason for this is that, from then on, each station of the CMS mission in central Tanzania had its statistics listed individually. But this lasted only up to 1910. Furthermore, though the mission had by now become established, statistics for the CMS mission were at times listed under the East Africa (Kenya) mission. In such cases, it is difficult to know the figures for Tanzania alone. The listing of statistics of individual stations in Tanzania and, indeed, in other CMS missions only started again in the 1918 and 1920 reports.[5]

---

4. *PCMS*, 1901, 122.
5. See *PCMS*, 1919, xvi; and *PCMS*, 1921, xvi.

Yet another problem to be noted here is the fact that, on several occasions, CMS annual reports contained figures that did not match up with those shown in the annual statistical tables. For example, the statistical table included in the report for 1919–1920 shows that, after the First World War, there were 20,417 scholars, but the annual report has 14,000.[6] It is therefore not clear where the figure 14,000 is taken from, other than that it is probably a misquote.

These are only some of the problems one is likely to encounter when dealing with the CMS statistics; the list is by no means exhaustive. One observation to be made is that the researcher should always make additional effort to crosscheck figures in the general statistical tables, as well as those in the reports. Where stations within individual missions are listed, it is also better to compare the figures with those provided for the entire mission in the annual tables (where different missions in different countries are listed).

---

6. *PCMS*, 1920, 29.

APPENDIX 2

The CMS Mission and the Maji Maji Uprising

Several references were made in chapter 6 to the leadership of indigenous teachers during the voluntary absence of CMS missionaries from their stations – for example, when they went on holiday. As for the time of forced absence, only the First World War was analysed. Only sporadic references were made in relation to the Maji Maji uprising (1905–1907) – an uprising against German colonial rule that took its name from the war cry *maji* (Kiswahili; "water"). Some additional notes are given here, particularly because of the significance of the Maji Maji uprising in terms of indigenous contributions.

Serious fighting during the uprising lasted only until about May 1906, but the situation did not return to normal in eastern and southern Tanzania (the most affected areas) until late in 1907. It should be observed that studies on Maji Maji have often focused on its political context.[1] A few have analysed the religious dimension of Maji Maji.[2] But even these have not paid attention to the impact of Maji Maji on the indigenous contributions made in the missions, including the CMS mission. It is from this perspective that these notes deal briefly with the Maji Maji movement.

An important point to be made sooner rather than later is that Maji Maji did not affect Ugogo and Ukaguru in the CMS sphere as it did the eastern and

---

1. See Bell, "Maji Maji Rebellion," 38–57; Iliffe, "Effects of the Maji Rebellion," 557–575; Iliffe, *Tanganyika under German Rule*, 9–29; Iliffe, *Modern History of Tanganyika*, 168–202; Gwassa, "German Intervention," 87–109.

2. See Iliffe, "Organization of the Maji Maji," 495–512; Gwassa, "Kinjikitile," 202–217; Wright, "Kinjikitile," 337–338; Westerlund, *Ujamaa na Dini*; Adas, *Prophets of Rebellion*, 25–34, 102–105.

southern areas of Tanzania. There, the mission stations – for example, those belonging to the Benedictine mission – were burnt at Nyangao and Lukuledi northwest of Masasi. Their bishop (Cassian Spiss, variant Spiess), two monks, and two nuns were killed at Mikukuyumbu as they travelled to Peramiho.[3]

As for its impact in Ukaguru, the testimony of Yusufu Masingisa (whose father was a servant at Mamboya station) indicates nothing severe took place. He says:

> I was only a one-year-old child during the time of Maji Maji. I was one year old. My father was one of the doctors, here. There was a doctor known as Dr Baxter. He was staying at the hill. My father had not become a teacher at the time. He was a domestic servant of that doctor. I don't know much about the strike. My father told me that the Germans issued an order that they [CMS missionaries] should go to Mpwapwa for protection because the barbarians were causing disturbances. I was crying a lot. Everyday, I was crying a lot. Therefore my father told the Europeans, "Sirs, I can't accompany you because my wife is having hard time with our child." They told him to find someone to replace him, but where could he find a replacement? Then Tadayo was found. . . . When he [Tadayo] went there with the Europeans [to Mpwapwa], everything was safe during that Maji Maji war. They fought each other but the Maji Maji soldiers were defeated. They caused trouble elsewhere but there was no trouble here.[4]

Like Ukaguru, Ugogo, too, did not experience disturbances. When the uprising started, Lazaro Ndajilo was five years of age. He recalls that Maji Maji fighters were defeated and, as a result of war in the south, some of the Wahehe refugees fled to Mvumi.[5]

However, by the end of 1905, the fighting had reached Kilosa (some sixty miles south of Mamboya), and no one could predict how far the war would

---

3. See Bell, "Maji Maji Rebellion," 48; Frederic V. Evans to Travers, 18/10/1905 OPDZ; Basil S. Cave to the Marquees of Landsdowne, 20/9/1905, OPDZ, RHL; Anderson, *Church in East Africa*, 59.

4. Yusufu Masingisa, oral interviews, 16 and 17 September 1997.

5. Lazaro Ndajilo, oral interviews, 14 and 16 June 1997.

spread further north. Earlier in the crisis, the CMS missionaries considered leaving the country and going to Kenya until the situation became normal, but the German colonial authorities could not guarantee complete security along the Kondoa route.[6] The total number of CMS missionaries gathered was sixteen – fourteen adults and two children. The German authorities advised against that option lest the ethnic groups in the north, including the Wachaga, become aware of the events in the south and join the fighting. Instead, they ordered CMS missionaries to leave all the stations, both in Ugogo and Ukaguru, and take refuge at Kiboariani sanatorium (owned by the mission) near Kongwa. This was close to the Mpwapwa fort, and from there CMS missionaries could be offered armed protection if the need arose.[7]

CMS missionaries were at the Kiboriani sanatorium from November 1905 to May 1906[8]. The executive committee held a meeting at the beginning of their stay at Kiboriani and appointed senior African teachers to become quasi-pastors and put them in charge of the districts for an indefinite period, pending the cessation of the hostilities. It was at this time when (as mentioned in chapter 6) some senior teachers were appointed to take charge of the districts. Andrea Mwaka was put in charge of Chunyu-Mlale, and Yohana Malecela looked after the Buigiri district. In Ukaguru, Yeremia Senyagwa was put in charge of the two districts of Mamboya and Berega, and possibly Itumba and Nyangala too. No mention is made of Mvumi, but probably Yohana Malecela was responsible for this district too.[9]

When asked whether the war caused disruption of mission work, Lazaro Ndajilo was emphatic in his reply: "Mission work was not disrupted."[10] Indeed, in the same 1906 report, the authors acknowledge that African members of mission staff were carrying on the work.[11] Statistics show that in 1905 there were 501 baptized Christians (excluding fifty-eight catechumens) and 2,414 scholars in the mission. Baptisms for that year stood at eighty-six.[12] In

---

6. See Special meeting of all CMS missionaries, Kiboriani, 15/11/1905, G3 A8/0/1905/16, BUL.

7. RUUM, 1906, G3 A8/0/1907/23, BUL.

8. Minutes, EC, 15/11/1905, G3 A8/O/1905/16, BUL.

9. Minutes, EC, 15/11/1905, G3 A8/0/1905/16, BUL.

10. Lazaro Ndajilo, oral interviews, 14 and 16 June 1997.

11. RUUM, 1906, G3 A8/0/1907/23, BUL.

12. See statistical table, *PCMS*, 1906, 71.

1906, when the CMS missionaries had been absent for nearly half a year, the number went up. There were 543 baptized Christians (exclusive of sixty-two catechumens), 2,688 scholars, and ninety-two adults and children were baptized that year.[13]

It is misleading, therefore, that in their 1906 annual progress report, the authors, John Briggs and Ernest Doulton, should say that the Maji Maji uprising had seriously hindered work in all districts.[14] For, as the statistical data shows, during the Maji Maji the indigenous leaders were able to discharge their leadership gifts and maintain the work and, as on other occasions, performed even better in the absence of CMS missionaries.

---

13. *PCMS*, 1907, 78.
14. RUUM, 1906, G3 A8/0/1907/23, BUL.

APPENDIX 3

Photographs of Some Indigenous Agents

Photograph 1: The First Students of Kongwa College, 1914[1]

Back Row: Paulo Chidinda, Yusufu Mgwele, Thomas Westgate (Principal), Haruni Mbega, Musa Fungo, Nuhu Sagatwa. *Front Row:* Yohana Malecela, Joshua Mkwama, Andrea Lungwa, Rubeni Chidahe, Luka Chiluwa, Andrea Mwaka, Elieza Balisidya. *Note:* Thirteen teachers attended the opening course. One student, Lazaro Hembokamu, is therefore missing from this group photograph.

---

1. Photograph supplied by Hon John S. Malecela, former Prime Minister, Tanzania. Used by permission.

Photograph 2: Andrea Mwakamubi Makanyaga, c. 1907 – First Pastor of Ugogo[2]

The Origin of the Name "Mwakamubi"

Detailed biographical notes of Andrea Mwaka were given in chapter 6. It was mentioned that his kinship name is "Mwakamubi." More details on this may now be given. Mwakamubi (Kigogo; "tragic year") refers to an event in the late nineteenth century (the date of which, unfortunately, Mwaka's son, Cleopa, couldn't remember) during which Andrea Mwaka's father, Chief Mugube Makanyaga of Kongwa and Ibwaga, lost a battle against the Wabera (a neighbouring ethnic group). The battle ensued from a dispute over elephant tusks which Makanyaga took from a dying elephant in the forest that the Wabera hunters claimed they had shot earlier (only for it to escape and die later). The elders on both sides decided, as was customary, that the dispute be settled by a hand-to-hand fight in the open on neutral ground. Only spears and shields were to be used.

But the Wabera fighters split into groups. One remained in the open, another hid in the bush along the path to the fighting ground. While the procession to the fields went on, the Wabera men who hid ambushed Makanyaga's

---

2. Photograph from St Philip's College, Kongwa.

men and shot at least two fighters. The remaining fighters and Makanyaga, their chief, both fled towards their own village. By then news had reached the council of elders that Makanyaga had lost the fight and run away. The village council of elders refused their chief entry into his palace and cursed him. He went into exile, and when initially approached by delegates from the elders to beseech him to return home, he refused, partly because he feared for his life, but also due to anger at the way his own people had treated him. He stayed in exile at a village called Nyamuhero for seven years, after which he agreed to return and assume his chieftaincy. When he returned, he renamed all his children. Unfortunately, Cleopa couldn't remember the original names of Mugube's children because the story of the event was told to him several decades ago. But the man who was later baptized "Andrea" was renamed "Mwakamubi."

Andrea Mwaka: Not a Slave

It has been noted already in chapter 6 that contrary to what some have suggested, Andrea Mwaka was not a slave. The following account gives details of how the confusion and inaccuracy over Andrea's status might have originated. Andrea was kidnapped on his way back from Mpwapwa when he got separated from his father who took another route back home. It shows that Andrea must have been an ambitious teenager, yet one who was also still prone to the deception of a local slave dealer. Some Chamuhawi villagers intervened and took Andrea to Chief Dikunguwale Madimilo, the local chief of Chamuhawi. The chief fed him but refused to let him go home and enrolled him in Cole's instruction class under his own surname as if he was one of his children. This concealed Andrea's true identity. The custom of chiefs taking slaves they owned to mission schools instead of their own sons was common in the nineteenth and early twentieth centuries.

Chief Mugube Makanyaga began the search for his son, learning that Chief Madimilo Dikunguwale had refused him permission to go home and that he demanded a ransom which, in those days, was a normal custom regarding "lost" humans, animals, or property. But given the circumstances, Makanyaga considered this to be unfair and organized his army to fight and rescue his son. Henry Cole, who lived at Chamuhawi at the time, heard the war cry and intervened. He agreed to pay the ransom to Madimilo – a large piece of garment, *mgolole*. He then asked Mugube Makanyaga to allow his son Andrea to remain at Chamuhawi mission station and continue his education there.

It is apparently this incident that some CMS missionaries misinterpreted, thinking Andrea had been enslaved in the conventional usage of the word. It is this misinterpretation that appears in archival and printed CMS sources.[3] Writers such as Keith Cole and Carl-Erik Sahlberg have followed the same misinterpretation and suggested that Andrea was a slave.[4] Andrea Mwaka's family and other people deny this and state that he was merely kidnapped and handed over to the chief of Chamuhawi, who behaved rather mischievously towards his fellow chief, Mugube Makanyaga, the father of Andrea Mwaka.[5] The only difference of opinion between Elimerik Mlahagwa of Chamuhawi and Cleopa Mwaka (Andrea's son) is that the former thought that Makanyaga went to Mpwapwa to attend a court case at the German fort, not to fetch food.

But this is less accurate because, if Mwaka was fifteen years old in 1886 at his baptism (after staying with Henry Cole for some time), his kidnapping must have taken place a couple of years or so back, around 1884. Evidence suggests that at this time the fort had not been built at Mpwapwa. Carl Peters completed his treaties with chiefs in Ukaguru and the northeast in 1886, after which he concentrated his commercial and political interests there. CMS missionaries at Mpwapwa or Chamuhawi do not mention the presence of the Germans at Mpwapwa even in their letters written in November 1888. But they mention the German presence in connection with the Arab coastal uprising in their letters written in March 1889. This suggests that the Mpwapwa fort was established at the beginning of 1889 and was commanded by Lt Giese who was in charge when Bushiri attacked it in June and July 1889.[6]

---

3. See, for instance, *PCMS*, 1904, 98: "The Christians at Kisokwe were fortunate in having Andreya, a freed slave, as their quasi-pastor."

4. Cole, *History of CMS*, 66. Sahlberg writes, "In his youth he was a slave. . . ." Sahlberg, *Krapf to Rugambwa*, 130.

5. See Cleopa Mwaka, oral interview, 4 July 1997; Elimerik Mlahagwa, oral interview, 28 June 1997.

6. See *CMI* 14 (July 1889): 433; *CMI* 14 (December 1889): 433, 739–743; *PCMS*, 1890, 54.

Photograph 3: Mama Damari Sagatwa, c. 1960 – Bible Woman and Missionary[7]

Missionary to the Wahangaza and Waha

Extended biographical notes on Mama Damari Sagatwa and her contribution to the growth of the Christianity in Ugogo and Ukaguru were given in the

---

7. Photograph from *Upanga wa Roho* 8, no. 3 (March 1961).

main text (chapter 6). What follows here relates mainly to Damari's involvement in western and northwestern Tanzania. This is beyond the period under review in this study, which is the reason for it being appended. In 1934, the focus of missionary activity in the Diocese of Central Tanganyika in the CMS sphere shifted to western and northwestern Tanzania. Mama Damari offered herself for missionary service in the western parts of Tanzania – over six hundred miles from Mpwapwa. This is significant and demonstrates her missionary zeal. Both oral and printed sources show that the majority of teachers who offered themselves for the evangelization of the Wahangaza and Waha were men, mainly from Ukaguru and Unguu (for example, Yohana Omari, Ephraim Madimilo, Simeoni Muya, Hadoram Yoshua, Stefano Msele, Naftali Goda, Eliabi Yeremia, and Azam Mkamilo). The majority of women who went to western and northwestern Tanzania were wives of those teachers. Certainly no other single or widowed Gogo or Kaguru woman known to this writer went to western Tanzania as an indigenous pioneer missionary in her own right at the time, except mama Damari Sagatwa.

Damari's offer for missionary service was discussed and approved by the Conference of Missionaries of the Western Mission of the DCT in 1936. From 1936 onwards, St Paul's Church, Ealing, London, supported her to serve as a pioneer missionary to Ngara among the Wahangaza until 1939. Ngara (Bugufi), northwestern Tanzania, had been a mission station only since 1932 – and was undoubtedly still a raw field for missionary labour that needed dedicated women such as Mama Damari. Being a *Bible woman*woman, she taught Bible classes and literacy for women and student-nurses at Murgwanza.

From October 1939, she had a transfer and went to Uha (further south) and continued her service. In addition to that, she taught baptism and post-baptism classes for catechumens and baptized Christian Kibondo in Uha, now part of the Diocese of Western Tanganyika. In 1942, she was transferred again, this time to Gihwahuru, Kasulu, another part of Uha, western Tanzania. In 1950, Damari was recalled back to Mpwapwa as she began to suffer illnesses due to old age. As indicated in chapter 6, she died 22 August 1960.[8]

---

8. Sources used for these additional notes included the following: Minutes, First Conference of Missionaries of the Western Mission (CMWM), Diocese of Central Tanganyika, 6–11/1/1936, MH; *CTDL*, no. 33 (July 1936); Viktoria Mathiya Sagatwa, oral interview, 29 June 1997; and Melea Hango, oral interview, 27 June 1997.

Photograph 4: Mama Mariamu Malogo, c. 1909 – One of the First Bible Women in Ugogo[9]

Reference to Mariamu's ministry has been made already in the main text (see chapter 6). It was stated that she was originally from Itumba, Ukaguru, where she served as a Bible woman at Kishambo from around 1903, but she moved

---

9. Photograph from St Philip's College, Kongwa.

to Ugogo as a missionary in 1906 and settled at Chamuhawi. Unfortunately, neither archival nor oral sources could yield more information about her other than what has been given already.

Photograph 5: Danieli Mbogo, c. 1909 – Musician and Reliable Companion[10]"

Biographical notes on Danieli Mbogo may be found in chapter 6.

---

10. Photograph from St Philip's College, Kongwa.

Photographs of Some Indigenous Agents 367

Photograph 6: Madari Mulutu, c. 1910 – Bible Translator[11]

Little is known about Madari Mulutu other than that he was originally from Chamuhawi and served as a teacher at Kongwa and Kiboriani from 1904 onwards. Perhaps his significant contribution, which is mentioned only very briefly in archival sources, is that of translating the Bible and other materials in Kigogo. For example, in 1904, he and Henry Cole (an Australian missionary working for the CMS mission) compiled the translation for a Kigogo-English dictionary. With Thomas Westgate, Madari Mulutu also translated Leviticus, 1 and 2 Samuel, 1 Kings, most of 2 Kings, and the fifth book of Psalms before the First World War. They started work on the translation of other Old Testament books and a prayer book and hymn book in the Kigogo language shortly before the First World War, but this work was disrupted by the war. Indeed, all manuscripts and copies of the completed translations were destroyed at Kongwa and Buigiri by the German army. Though his name is not mentioned in connection with other Kigogo translations, it is possible that he took part in the translation of other books of the Bible which were

---

11. Photograph from St Philip's College, Kongwa.

mentioned in chapter 1 – namely, Luke (1887), Matthew (1891), Epistles (1899), Ruth (1893), and John (1904).[12]

Photograph 7: Paulo Chidinda, c. 1911 – Quasi-pastor at Handali[13]

Paulo Chidinda was originally from Mima village, southwest of Mvumi. He was appointed quasi-pastor at Handali, at the start of the competition between the CMS mission and the Roman Catholic Benedictine mission. Handali was begun in 1902, along with Mwitikila, as out-stations of Mvumi.[14] At this

---

12. See section 1.2.3, including footnotes. These biographical notes on Mulutu are based on information obtained from Yohana Muhimili, oral interview, 2 July 1997; *PCMS*, 1904–1905, 90; Westgate, *In the Grip*, 12–13.

13. Photograph from St Philip's College, Kongwa.

14. *PCMS*, 1903, 104.

time, there was fear among the CMS missionaries that it could "fall" into the hands of the "enemy," so Chidinda was posted there "to fend off" the Roman Catholics. On the whole, it was the CMS missionaries who chose the indigenous staff and recommended them to the executive committee. However, some senior indigenous teachers, such as Chidinda, did the same. At Handali, Chidinda was involved in the supervision of his fellow indigenous staff who were located at smaller churches. Indeed, he was able to appoint junior teachers working under him and arrange their transfers. The teachers working under him before the First World War included Daniel Chalo Chilomo, Zakaria Mazengo Mbishai, Eliya Malugu Chisavilo, Musa Kongola Munyangwila, Nathaniel Fundi Magawa, and Yohana Mulowezi Lukuna.[15]

In 1909, Yosia, Benyamini Lungwa and Nataneli Chidosa – the teachers at Mvumi (of which Handali was an out-station) – resigned their jobs. The reasons given for the resignation was that two of the teachers were "blinded by Satan" – perhaps a reference to moral lapse – and the third, possibly Nataneli Chidosa, had ill health.[16] While lamenting these resignations, Elizabeth Forsythe expressed the encouragement she and her colleagues received from Paulo Chidinda. "To compensate us for this disappointment," Forsythe wrote, "we have been much cheered by the faithfulness of the others and especially our head teacher Pawulo Chidiuda [Paulo Chidinda] who has proved most trustworthy during our long absence at Kiboriani."[17] "Absence at Kiboriani" refers to the time when the CMS missionaries took refuge at a sanatorium on the Kiboriani hill, near Kongwa, from September 1905 to May 1906, owing to the Maji Maji uprising.

Unfortunately, despite such a praiseworthy service, several years later, Paulo Chidinda's ministry ended rather sadly around 1936 or 1937. His wife Rebeka became mentally ill, and he left her. He then married his brother's wife, for which he was excommunicated. One oral source suggests that he possibly made a public confession, was restored, and then posted to Chibogolo towards Iringa.[18] Another suggests that after the excommunication, Chidinda

---

15. Ernest Musa Kongola, oral interviews, 20 and 24 June 1997; Stephano Malecela, oral interview, 24 June 1997; Mbogoni, oral interview, 11 June 1997.
16. Minutes, EC, 9 & 10/11/1910, G3 A8/0/1910/76, BUL.
17. Elizabeth Forsythe to Baylis, annual letter 28/11/1910, G3 A8/0/1910/92, BUL.
18. Ernest Musa Kongola, oral interviews, 20 and 24 June 1997.

never rejoined the mission service but went to live at Kibogolo and became a cattle farmer.[19] Only further interviews (not possible during the field research for this study), particularly with members of his family, could help towards resolving the discrepancy. However, the two oral sources consulted agree on two things: first, that some action was taken against Chidinda for his offence; and, second, that when he retired, he went to live at Kipogolo. Despite an unhappy ending for Chidinda, his role as a supervisor of his fellow African workers shows that he was a trusted worker at Handali. He played a rare role among the indigenous teachers, and records show only Andrea Mwaka and Yohana Malecela doing the same at Chamuhawi and Ihumwa, respectively.[20]

Photograph 8: The First Indigenous Clergy – In Ugogo and Ukaguru[21]

Top: The Rev Daudi Muhando, deacon 1929, priest 1932.

Bottom Left: The Rev Andrea Mwaka, deacon 1921, priest 1924.

Bottom Right: The Rev Haruni Mbega, deacon 1921, priest 1924.

---

19. Cleopa Mwaka, oral interview, 4 July 1997.
20. Doulton to Baylis, 21/11/1910, G3 A8/0/1910/83, BUL.
21. Photograph from Chambers, *Tanganyika's New Day*.

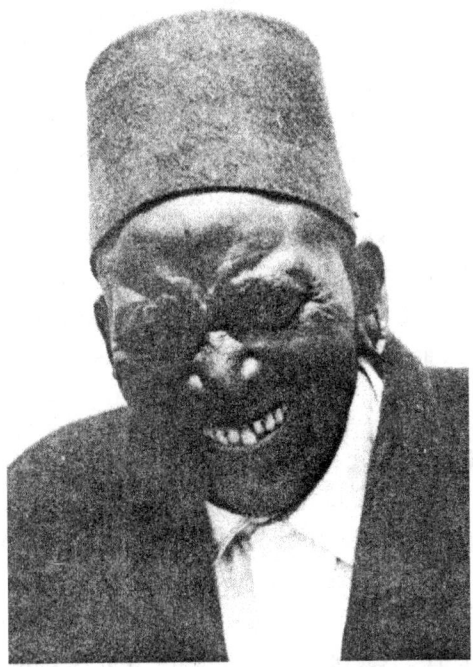

Photograph 9: Chief Mazengo Chalula – Paramount Chief of UgogoUgogo[22]

Mazengo: Profile of a Chief

Mazengo's contribution to mission work in the CMS mission has been noted already in chapter 4. These notes are therefore only additional and focus especially on his life as chief of Ugogo. The account that follows is based on oral data supplied by Lazaro Ndajilo of Mvumi Makulu (the seat of the Mvumi chiefdom). He is an authority on Mazengo and the political life of the Mvumi chiefdom. He served as Mazengo's chief palace official and administrator from 1944 to 1967. Part of the notes used are extracts from an oral interview between this writer and Ndajilo.

Date of birth

Mazengo's date of birth is not known. A biographical note about him in *Makers of Modern Africa* (the source of the above photo) gives 1852 as Mazengo's

---

22. Photograph from Uwechue, *Makers of Modern Africa*, 1991.

date of birth.²³ But this is too early. Knox suggests that Mazengo was a "child" when John Price (one of the earliest CMS missionaries at Mpwapwa) first visited what was then described as "Ugogo proper" – the "country" west of Mpwapwa – in 1888.²⁴ Perhaps not a child but a young man. Had Mazengo been a mature adult, he could have assumed the throne when his father died in the late nineteenth century. Lazaro Ndajilo suggests that Mazengo died at the age of 107. This puts his date of birth at 1860. Even so, the strange thing is that CMS archival sources do not mention him in connection with the opening of the Mvumi station in 1900 – a time when, apparently, Mazengo was forty and had assumed power from his uncle, Msonjela. Nor do they mention Msonjela.

Succession to the throne

Chief Chalula, the Chief Daudi Mazengo Chalula's father, died of smallpox sometime in the late nineteenth century. Mazengo was young, and therefore Msonjela, Chalula's younger brother, became regent. During Msonjela's regency, the chiefdom was divided. The Idifu and Chamwali people formed a new chiefdom. The rest of the chiefdom – that is, Chihembe, Mission, Ndebwe, and all the rest – remained under Mvumi. This place was called "Mvumi Makulu Itumbi." Other parts of Mvumi were called Mvumi Chelema, Mvumi Mzula, Mvumi Ndaladya, Mvumi Kikuyu, Mvumi Magudugudu, Mvumi Chandwi, and Mvumi Nhundulu, but all of it was still part of the Mvumi chiefdom.

Reference was made earlier (chapter 2) to the fact that soon after the establishment of their rule in the interior, the Germans started to stop the unlawful killing of those who were suspected to be rain-killers (*wakoma-mvula*) in Ugogo. Ndajilo gives details of how Mazengo ascended to the throne.

When Mazengo came in, he did not rule according to the old tradition. He ruled in the presence of the Germans. . . . But both his father Chalula's and uncle Msonjela's chieftainship were not under foreign rule. They had ultimate authority and power. That is why if someone was accused of witchcraft, they simply said, "Bring him here, and slaughter him." Or if they heard that someone was doing something wrong in the chiefdom, they simply said,

---

23. Uwechue, 463–464.
24. Knox, *Signal on the Mountain*, 96; *CMI* 14 (March 1889): 168

"Bring him here, and get him slaughtered." More still, if they heard news of war aggression, they simply told their people, "Get ready, we shall go to war," and so forth. . . . Killing one another was something that was happening long time ago when Msonjela was chief, before the arrival of the Germans.

> When the Germans arrived they prevented chiefs from doing such things. They questioned them saying, "You used to beat your fellows and kill them for allegedly preventing rain, you accused your fellows of witchcraft and killed them. If anyone suggested that someone was a witch, then you killed that person. If you were told that "this man prevents rain," you killed him. You must be imprisoned for years." . . . Msonjela was imprisoned for two years. And when he was freed he said, "No more of this. Being a ruler and then be under the rule of others is something I can't bear." He said, "Now my elder brother's son is old enough. I cannot work with these Europeans." Then Mazengo succeeded him."[25] It seems that Mazengo was in power when Maji Maji war broke out in 1905. In 1909, Bertha Briggs – CMS missionary at Mvumi (six miles from Mazengo"s main palace at Mvumi Makulu) described Mazengo as "the big chief of this country."[26]

It seems that Mazengo was in power when the Maji Maji war broke out in 1905. In 1909, Bertha Briggs – a CMS missionary at Mvumi (six miles from Mazengo's main palace at Mvumi Makulu) described Mazengo as "the big chief of this country."[27]

Paramount chief of Ugogo

On Mazengo's election as paramount chief of Ugogo, Ndajilo gives the following details.

> *Lazaro Ndajilo*: When the British arrived, they realized that there were too many chiefs. [They] began to re-group them. The subordinate chiefs were appointed for Handali, Idifu, Chita, Chamwali, Fufu, Loje, Ng'hong'hona, Msamalo. All these were

---

25. Lazaro Ndajilo, oral interviews, 14 and 16 June 1997.
26. Bertha Briggs to Baylis, 3/3/1909, G3 A8/O/1909/28, BUL.
27. Bertha Briggs to Baylis.

under Mazengo. Other neighbouring chiefdoms were as follows: Matumbulu, Mwitikila. Nondwa, Chinyambwa (Unyambwa), Bahi, Makutupora, Zoona, Itiso, Buigiri, and Dodoma.... The *mpembamoto* (the village headman) at Handali, at Igandu, Chamwali, Iringa Mvumi, Idifu, Chita, Ngh'ongh'ona, Msamalo, all of them ... chose Mazengo to be the paramount chief.... The mission people were in favour of his election.

Mwita Akiri: Was is not that Mazengo inherited his position as Paramount Chief, and was not elected?

Lazaro Ndajilo: No. He was chosen.... He was just chosen. Even Mr Briggs [CMS missionary at Mvumi] was in favour of seeing him chosen. The DC [district commissioner] and Mr Birinje (the chief of Dodoma), too, stood by him. The PC [provincial commissioner], DC, ... the *wapembamoto* (the village headman) – *all* of them, and the whole of Dodoma region wanted Mazengo. Birinje came second. They said, "Let him this man [Birinje] be the senior chief, because he is closer to the *boma* [Kiswahili; "fort"]. But the public refused. They said, "Even though Mazengo lives far away [some 50 km], he is the one who must become [paramount chief]."

Mwita Akiri: Does that mean that he was very much loved by many people?

Lazaro Ndajilo: They loved him. But people hesitated a little during the [Second World] War, because Chief Haule was picking people as conscripts for the British army. Mazengo did the same.... Therefore, some people with negative views on him started to ask, "*Mazengo nondomague.*" [Kigogo; "what has become of Mazengo?"]" But he responded, "Yes, Hitler must not come here. He is a German. We are used to the British. We will be better off if we continue under his rule." Truly, when Hitler had been pushed back, the British made great effort to build schools for us. Schools for standard four up to twelve. We got them.[28]

Protector of his people

Mazengo's had good relationships with the colonial governments, particularly the British, whom he supported during the Second World War. But his support had its limits. His chief official gives the story of an encounter Mazengo had with the authorities, though he does not give a date:

> *Lazaro Ndajilo*: He was gentle, kind, he didn't like corruption. He would not tolerate an order from the DC that might have resulted in cruelty to the people. He would raise it with him. He would call me and say, "Lazaro, that man [the DC] is saying we should do this or that. What do you say?" I would then tell the chief that "according to our tradition and customs, if this is done, it would result in this or that way. So let us resolve it this way. That is the best way of leading the people."
>
> *Mwita Akiri*: What kind of orders or directives from the DC would have been offensive?
>
> *Lazaro Ndajilo*: For example, if he said that people should work as slaves in order to bring development to the country. Also, about people contributing cattle towards the war costs. We responded and said that "Mr [DC], some people have five cows for feeding their children. Others have ten cows, but they also have more children. Some have ten but have no children. So let us plan well. Those who have more, fifty, from a hundred to two hundred are the ones who should make a contribution. For those who have no cows, we shall assign them to build roads that can be used by the army convoys related to the ongoing war."
>
> *Mwita Akiri*: And the DC would accept that?
>
> *Lazaro Ndajilo*: He would agree.
>
> *Mwita Akiri*: Can you name any one such a DC whom you wrestled with in that way? Do you remember any?

---

28. Lazaro Ndajilo, oral interviews, 14 and 16 June 1997.

> *Lazaro Ndajilo*: Let me try to remember. There was one whom we opposed to the extent that the minister had to intervene to resolve the case.... I think it was before the war. The PC resolved the matter between us. He said, "They are right. There are some who are poor. He may have ten children. Five cows. What will they feed on?"[29]

Polygamist and holder of chieftaincy stones

Many Wagogo chiefs (like those of Ukaguru) refused baptism for two main reasons: they were polygamists and ritual leaders of their people. Mazengo was no exception.

> *Lazaro Ndajilo*: [Mazengo] became a catechumen since the days of the German rule. But he remained in that position for a long time. The reason was that he had the stones. So Mr Briggs advised him and said, "People would be offended and hate you if you are baptized because they like the tradition of keeping the stones.... Postpone it for the moment. Because you are leader of the Wagogo." Every year whenever there was drought they washed them and used then to offer sacrifice for it to rain. He said to him, "Make a choice. Appoint a successor to be chief. If you want to be a Christian, then give yourself to Jesus."
>
> *Mwita Akiri*: What did Mazengo choose?
>
> *Lazaro Ndajilo*: He chose to continue to be chief.... He decided to continue as an inquirer. This continued until the time of independence [of Tanzania in 1961] when he stepped down as chief and was baptised later [probably in 1964].[30]

Besides being the keeper of the rain stones, Mazengo's baptism was also probably delayed by the fact that he was a polygamist. His senior wife was called Mariamu (Nyinamwaluko). The second wife was Hagulwa. Both were Christians. Mamvula (Nyinailamba) was the third. The fourth wife ran away. The bridewealth was given back because, as Ndajilo puts it, "they never

---

29. Lazaro Ndajilo, oral interviews, 14 and 16 June 1997.
30. Lazaro Ndajilo, oral interviews, 14 and 16 June 1997.

cultivated a farm together, nor did they stay together for a year.... We don't count her as being his wife." Mazengo's eldest son is called Paulo Mwaluko. Others are Mapoto, Kubota, and Mbega. Daughters were Changato, Dabwa, and Makanda. Those are his children by senior wife, Mariamu. Children by his second wife, Hagulwa were Mbeche, Welusi, Mbuchila, Mary, Msechelela (Sechelela), and Julia. By Mamvula, Mazengo had Chalula, Kenneth, Mary, and Eunike. But Ndajilo adds, "There are also children whom he fathered by making women pregnant outside marriage, an act which the Wagogo call *kutumla*. This was more so in the other villages where he had semi-official residences."

A social modernizer

Mazengo is also remembered for his promotion of health initiatives especially in the way he encouraged the Wagogo women to use modern maternity services at Mvumi hospital. In the early 1930s, he issued an order that no woman should give birth at home. Ndajilo gives the reason Mazengo gave the order: "They did not keep the new-born baby's navel hygienically, the general nursing for infants was poor. There were many infant deaths. So everyone should go to mission [hospital]. 1932 up to 1940.... It was Mazengo who first exhorted people to do that. Nowadays, people are used to this, for their own benefit.... Since he [Mazengo] was a Christian, he urged all people to take heed of education and offer voluntary help."[31] Mazengo is also remembered as one of the chiefs who supported and promoted education in his chiefdom beyond the colonial period. A government high school near Dodoma town is named after him as a tribute to him for this role.

A friend of the CMS mission

Ndajilo and his fellow palace officials used to advise Chief Mazengo about supporting the mission. Ndajilo narrates how Mazengo contributed to mission work.

> Let me say this. As Christians, we did like the mission to make progress. The mission itself had no powers to compel people to work for it. So we had to use that *method* in collaboration with the chief. First, we had to make a request to the chief, that the

---

31. Lazaro Ndajilo, oral interviews, 14 and 16 June 1997.

people living within the mission station should do the mission work instead of government work. That was the first thing we agreed on. After we had agreed on that, we summoned the *wazengamatumbi* (junior headman) responsible for the mission area. We went there and spoke to people, and said, "This church will bear fruit. If this school is built, the people of Chambi, Nhundulu, Mzula – the whole of Mvumi – will come here to learn. Isn't that beneficial to you?" They said, "Yes."

"We must therefore assist in the construction of this building," we told them. "You have heard that the people in the Birinje's chiefdom are building a church and their children are learning. What about yours?," we told them. We persuaded them using a good method. We said to the people of Chambi and Chelema that they must help the mission and told them things that were beneficial to them. For those within the mission station we said, "We can see that you are doing the Lord's work. You who have other responsibilities should fetch water, mould the clay, and make the bricks." The mission's responsibility was to hire the builder, I mean the mason who would build the wall. They also hired the roofer. That was what we did with the mission.

He also encouraged people from Nhundulu, Makulu, Chelema and so forth to send twenty volunteers each to participate in erecting a church building at Mvumi Makulu. He then instructed the *wazengematumbi* to ensure that each day there were new volunteers to ease the burden on those who were helping to build the "holy house of God". . . . That was his contribution, to make people volunteer to work without pay. Not by receiving a salary.[32]

---

32. Lazaro Ndajilo, oral interviews, 14 and 16 June 1997.

His last days as chief

Despite such contributions, like all mortals, old age defied Mazengo. Ndajilo is one of the few Wagogo who know about Mazengo's last days as a person and as chief, and watched his health disintegrate, rendering him inactive.

> He was 107 years old. He used to have multiple complaints. Sometimes pain in the eye, in the leg, and so forth, then he became blind. He couldn't see. He continued to be chief. But it was me who performed all the duties. Yes. But I would say the chief has done it. He could not write, his hands were shaking. Therefore I used to write. . . . I sent letters and said the chief had written them, but in fact it was me who composed them. . . . For things which came under my direct responsibility as a s civil servant, I signed the letters in my name, "Lazaro Ndajilo, the servant." But for matters that needed the chief's approval I had to use his official stamp . . . even if the letter was written by me. It would be regarded as the chief's order. . . . I would do the same at the store. . . . I distributed food and said the chief did it. . . . And everything was being done properly. . . . We used to sit and talk as I am doing now with you, at the palace sitting room. Only the two of us. That was what we used to do.[33]

Death and a semi-state and Christian funeral for Mazengo, 1967

Though Ndajilo performed such duties, Mazengo could not survive old age and attack by numerous illnesses. He died in 1967 and was given both a Christian and semi-state funeral to honour his contributions to the social development of Ugogo. This, according to Ndajilo, was

> because even the British loved him, and was in favour of him being the paramount chief. He was the one who enthroned President Nyerere. He rubbed flour [cereal powder] on him. That is why he used to address him as "father." That is why he [President Nyerere] sent Job Lusinde, a government minister, to represent [him]. . . . It was me and Job Lusinde who supervized Chief Mazengo's funeral. Nyerere instructed Job Lusinde. He

---

33. Lazaro Ndajilo, oral interviews, 14 and 16 June 1997.

came at the time when he was minister for Local and Regional Governments. [But] it was Job Lusinde's father [Rev Canon Petro Lusinde Malecela] who lifted Mazengo's body.... And Mbeho, and Mabichi.... We lifted the coffin from the house, and were the ones who lowered it in the grave.

Mwita Akiri: Did you perform any traditional rite of burial for the chief?

Lazaro Ndajilo: No at all. He was already a Christian. He was *Daudi*, a Christian. Bishop Stanway led the funeral. So we were chosen to supervise the burial ceremony, I mean four of us, and the purpose was to prevent the introduction of the traditional ways in the ceremony. It is not that we were against everything that was traditional. No. It was only those things which were incompatible with Christianity.

That is how the life of Daudi Mazengo Chalula ended. He was one of the greatest chiefs in central Tanzania, and arguably in Tanzania as a whole. Like most chiefs, he served both his country and the local church with dedication.

APPENDIX 4
Maps

Map 1: Location of Tanzania in Africa[1]

---

1. Source: *Africa Fact Sheet*, no. 3, published by National Council of Churches of Christ in the United States of America.

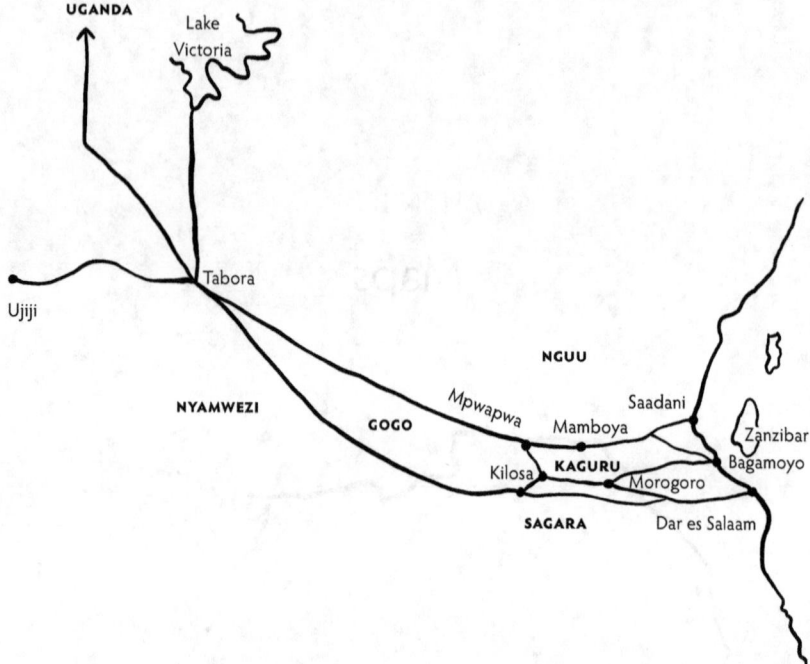

Map 2: Caravan Routes Passing Through Central Tanzania (19th Century)[2]

---

2. Source: Adapted from Beidelman, "History of Ukaguru."

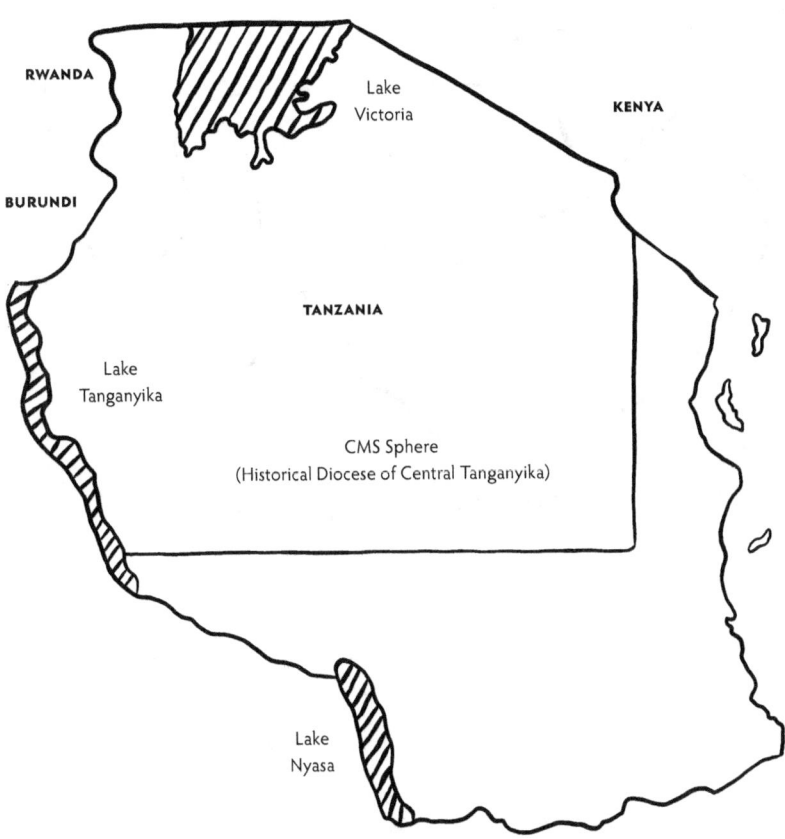

Map 3: CMS Mission Sphere[3]

---

3. Source: Adapted from *Checkpoint* (Magazine of CMS Australia), 1985.

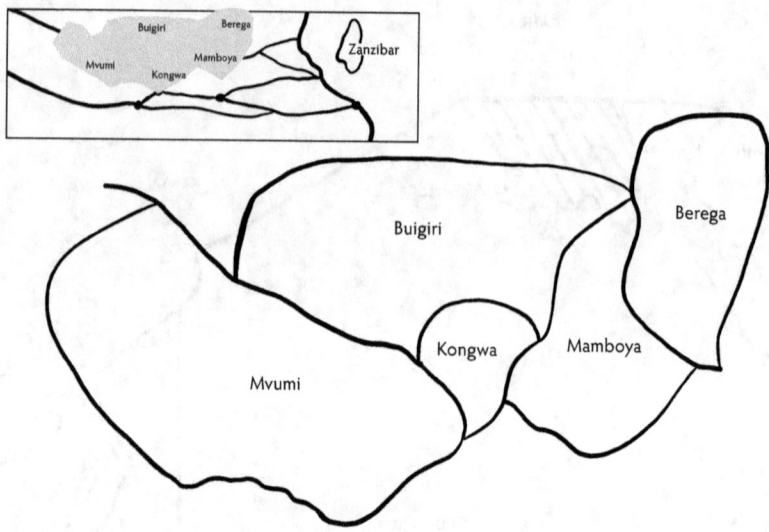

Map 4: Districts of the CMS Mission in Ugogo and Ukaguru (1913)[4]

---

4. Source: Adapted from *CMR* 65 (September 1914).

Map 5: Dioceses of the Anglican Church of Tanzania (1999) – Former CMS and UMCA Spheres[5]

---

5. Source: Provincial Office, Dodoma, Tanzania.

CMS Glossary

district: Unless so stated, this refers to a church/mission district, not a secular government administrative area.

station: A place that became the base of operations in a single district. Until 1914, the CMS often defined a station as "a place at which a clerical or lay missionary, or a native clergyman is stationed." In 1915, it modified the definition, slightly, as follows: "A STATION is a place where at least one foreign missionary *resides regularly*, or an ordained native with a similar status and responsibility." Two slight variations were that, in 1920, different points of occupation in a city were considered as one station, and by June 1933, in some places, a place where a catechist was resident was also regarded as a mission station.

out-station: A place, other than a station, with or without a resident indigenous worker.

out-school: A school other than the one at the station, whether at an out-station or not. Such a school, whether with or without a building was also called a "bush school."

CMS GLOSSARY

Bibliography

Primary Sources

Archival Sources

1. Birmingham University Library (BUL), Birmingham, England
CMS archives
Papers of the Tanganyika Mission Under Africa Group 3 (G3 A8/0) including original papers [incoming], 1900–1934 (3 boxes) containing letters, minutes, reports, manuscripts and typescripts.

2. Rhodes House Library (RHL), Oxford, England
UMCA archives
Letters from Africans, correspondence on "German East Africa," and Official Papers, Diocese of Zanzibar, 1864–1963.

3. Lambeth Palace Library (LPL), London, England
Miscellaneous Papers (Manuscript 1468) and Reports to the Missionary Council (Manuscript 3121 and 3122).

4. National Library of Scotland (NLS), Edinburgh, Scotland
Parliamentary Papers (Command Papers)
Advisory Committee on Native Education in the British Tropical African Dependencies, *Education Policy in British Tropical Africa* (Command Paper 2374), HMSO, London: 1925.
Reports from Commissioners, Inspectors and Others, *Report of the East African Commission* (Command Paper 2387), Vol. 9, HMSO, London: 1925.
Report on Tanganyika Territory, covering the period from the conclusion of the Armistice to the end of *1920*, (Command Paper 1428) HMSO, London: 1921.

Reports on the Treatment by the Germans of British Prisoners and Natives in German East Africa (Command Paper 8689), Miscellaneous No. 13, 1917, HMSO, London: 1917.

Colonial Office Papers

Advisory Committee on Education in the Colonies, *Memorandum on Education of African Communities,* Colonial No. 103, HMSO, London: 1935.

Advisory Committee on Education in the Colonies, *Mass Education in African Society,* Colonial No. 186, distributed by British Information Services, New York, 1941.

British Tropical Africa: the Place of the Vernacular in Native Education, African No. 1110, memorandum by the Advisory Committee on Native Education, Colonial Office, London: May 1927. 289.

Education Policy in Africa: A Memorandum Submitted [to the Colonial Office on behalf of the Conference of Missionary Societies in Great Britain and Ireland], London: 1923.

Foreign Office Handbooks

"Tanganyika (German East Africa)," in *Handbooks* [prepared under the direction of the historical section of the Foreign Office], No. 113, HMSO, London, 1920.

"Treatment of Natives in the German Colonies," in *Handbooks* [prepared under the direction of the historical section of the Foreign Office], No. 114, HMSO, London, 1920.

5. London University (School of Oriental and African Studies) Library.

IMC files.

IMC/CBMS files.

6. Colonial Office Library, London.

Miscellaneous Pamphlets Volume 1 & 2.

7. Diocese of Central Tanganyika (DCT), at Mackay House, Dodoma, Tanzania

Mackay House archives (MH)

(i) Logbooks

Mission station logbooks and service registers for Buigiri, Kongwa, Chamuhawi, Mamboya, Berega, Itumba, and Nyangala.

(ii) Minutes of Meetings

Minute Book of the Central Church Council of the Tanganyika Mission, 1922–1935, comprising Minutes of the Native Church Council (1930, 1931).

Minutes of the General Assembly of Clergy and Laity of the Diocese of Central
Tanganyika (1933).
Minutes of the Meetings of the Diocesan Council, 1933-1950.
Minutes of the First Conference of Missionaries of Western Mission, 1936.
Minutes of the African Advisory Council, 1942.
Minutes of the Meetings of the Synod, Diocese of Central Tanganyika, 1936-1953.
Record of Christians, Catechumens and Inquirers, CMS Muhalala, Kilimatinde
District, 1921-1952.

Records at pastors' houses or parish offices
District Baptism Register, Pastors House, Mvumi.
Mamboya Baptism Register, Pastors House, Mamboya.
Berega District Baptism Register, Parish Office, Berega.
Mamboya Village School Register, 1926 onwards, Mamboya Primary School.

Mission Periodicals
1. Diocese of Central Tanganyika periodicals
Upanga wa Roho 1953-1963.
The Central Tanganyika Diocesan Letter 1929-1945.

2. CMS reports and periodicals
The Church Missionary Intelligencer and Record, (CMIR) 1876-1889.
The Church Missionary Intelligence (CMI), 1900-1906
Church Missionary Review, 1910-1917.
The Proceedings of the Church Missionary Society for Africa and the East 1876-
1937.

Published Sources

Adas, Michael. *Prophets of Rebellion: Millenarian Protest Movements against the
European Colonial Order.* Cambridge: Cambridge University Press, 1987.
Advisory Committee on Education in the Colonies. *Mass Education in African
Society.* Colonial No. 186. Memorandum distributed by British Information
Services. New York: 1941.
———. *Memorandum on Educational Grants-in-Aid.* Colonial No. 84. London:
HMSO, 1933.
———. *Memorandum on Education of African Communities.* Colonial No. 103.
HMSO, London: 1935.
Advisory Committee on Native Education. *British Tropical Africa: The Place of the
Vernacular in Native Education.* African No. 1110. Colonial Office, London:
May 1927.

Advisory Committee on Native Education in the British Tropical African Dependencies. *Education Policy in British Tropical Africa*. Command Paper 2374. HMSO, London: 1925.

Afigbo, A. E. "Colonial Historiography." In *African Historiography: Essays in Honour of Jacob Ade Ajayi*, edited by Toyin Falola, 39-51. Harlow: Longmans, 1993.

———. "Oral Tradition in Segmentary Societies." In *History in Africa*, Vol 12, 1-10, 1985.

Ajayi, J. F. *Christian Missions in Nigeria 1841-1891: The Making of a New Élite*. London: Longmans, 1965.

Ajayi, J. F. Ade, and E. A. Ayandele. "Writing African Church History." In *The Church Crossing Frontiers: Essays on the Nature of Mission in Honour of Bengt Sundkler*, edited by Peter Beyerhaus and Carl Hallencreutz, 90-108. Lund: Gleerup, 1969

Allen, Roland. *Le Zoute: A Critical Review of "The Christian Mission in Africa."* London: World Dominion Press, 1927.

Ampofo, Rose. "The Contribution of Women to Church Growth and Development in Africa: The Case of the Presbyterian Church of Ghana." *International Review of Missions* 86, no. 345 (April 1998): 233-239.

Anderson, W. B. *The Church in East Africa 1840-1974*. Dodoma: Central Tanganyika Press, 1977.

Anderson-Morshead, A. E. M. *The History of the Universities' Mission to Central Africa 1859-1896*. London: UMCA, 1897.

———. *The History of the Universities' Mission to Central Africa 1859-1896*, revised edition. London: UMCA, 1955.

Austen, Ralph A. *Northwest Tanzania under German and British Rule: Colonial Policy and Tribal Politics, 1889-1939*. New Haven: Yale University Press, 1968.

Ayandele, A. E. *African Historical Studies*. London: Frank Cass, 1979.

———. *The Missionary Impact on Modern Nigeria, 1842-1914: A Political and Social Analysis*. London: Longmans, 1966.

Barrett, David, ed. *African Initiatives in Religion*. Nairobi: East African Publishing House, 1971.

———. *Schism and Renewal: An Analysis of Six Thousand Religious Movements*. Nairobi: Oxford University Press, 1968.

Bebbington, David. *Patterns in History: A Christian Perspective in Historical Thought*. 2nd ed. Leicester: Appolos, 1990.

Becker, C. H. "Material for the Understanding of Islam in German East Africa." Edited and translated by B. C. Martin. *Tanzania Notes and Records* 68 (February 1968): 31-61.

Bediako, Kwame. "Understanding African Theology in the Twentieth Century." *Themelios* 20, no. 1 (October 1994): 14-19.

Beidelman, T. O. "Chiefship in Ukaguru: The Invention of Ethnicity and Tradition in Kaguru Colonial History." *International Journal of African Historical Studies* 11, no. 2 (1978): 227–246.

———. *Colonial Evangelism: A Socio-Historical Study of an East African Mission at the Grassroots*. Bloomington: Indiana University Press, 1982.

———. "Contradiction between the Sacred and the Secular Life: The Church Missionary Society in Ukaguru, Tanzania, East Africa, 1876–1914." *Comparative Studies in Society and History* 23 (1981): 73–95.

———. "A History of Ukaguru: 1857–1916." In *Tanganyika Notes and Records*, no. 58/59 (March and September 1962): 11–39.

———. *The Matrilineal Peoples of Eastern Tanzania*. London: International African Institute, 1967.

———. *Moral Imagination in Kaguru Modes of Thought*. Washington, DC: Smithsonian Institution Press, 1993.

———. "Social Theory and the Study of Christian Missions in Africa." *Africa* 44, no. 3 (1974): 235–249.

———. "Some Notes on the Kamba in Kilosa District." *Tanganyika Notes and Records*, no. 57 (September 1961): 181–194.

Bell, R. M. "The Maji Maji Rebellion in the Liwale District." *Tanganyika Notes and Records*, no. 28 (January 1950): 38–57.

Bennett, Norman R. *Studies in East African History*. Boston: Boston University Press, 1963.

Blakemore, Priscilla. "Assimilation and Association in French Educational Policy: Senegal 1903–1939." In *Essays in the History of African Education*, edited by Vincent M. Battle and Charles H. Lyons, 38–57. New York: Teachers College Press, 1970.

Blood, A. G. *The History of the Universities' Mission to Central Africa*. Vol. 2, *1907–1932*. London: UMCA, 1936.

———. *The History of the Universities' Mission to Central Africa*. Vol. 3, *1933–1957*. London: UMCA, 1962.

Bradley, James E., and Muller Richard A. *Church History: An Introduction to Research, Reference Works, and Methods*. Grand Rapids: Eerdmans, 1995.

Brown, G. Gordon. "Bride-Wealth among the Hehe." *Africa* 5, no. 2 (April 1932): 145–157.

Buell, Raymond Leslie. *The Native Problem in Africa*. 2 vols. New York: Macmillan, 1928.

Burton, Richard. *First Footsteps in East Africa or An Explanation of Harar*. London: Longman, Brown Green and Longmans, 1856. Reprinted. London: J. M. Dent, 1924.

Cameron, Donald. "Native Administration Memoranda No. 1–8." In *Native Authority Ordinance 1926*. Dar es Salaam: Government House, 1926.

———. *My Tanganyika Service and Some Nigeria*. London: George Allen and Unwin, 1939.

Cameron, J, and W. A. Wood. *Society, Schools and Progress in Tanzania*. Oxford: Pergamon Press, 1970.

Carnell, W. J. "Sympathetic Magic among the Gogo of Mpwapwa District." *Tanganyika, Notes and Records*, no. 39 (June 1955): 25–38.

Carnoy, Martin. *Education as Cultural Imperialism*. New York: David McKay, 1974.

Carr, Edward. *What Is History?* London: Macmillan, 1961.

Chambers, George A. *Tanganyika's New Day*. London: CMS, 1931.

Chitemo, Gresford. "Historia Fupi ya Kanisa Anglikana Kuingia Ukaguru na Unguu 1879–1979," typed notes. Morogoro: September 1980.

Christopher, A. J. *Colonial Africa*. London: Croom Helm, 1984.

Cole, Edmund Keith. *A History of the Church Missionary Society of Australia*. Melbourne: Church Missionary Historical Publications, 1971.

Cole, Henry. "Notes on the Wagogo of German East Africa." *Journal of Anthropological Institute* 32 (1902): 305–338.

Cole, Keith. *A History of the Church Missionary Society of Australia*. Melbourne: Church Missionary Publications, 1971.

Coupland, Reginald. *East Africa and Its Invaders: From the Earliest Times to the Death of Seyyid Said in 1856*. Oxford: Clarendon Press, 1938.

Cox, James L. "Ritual, Rites of Passage and the Interaction between Christian and Traditional Religions." In *Rites of Passage in Contemporary Africa: Interaction between Christian and African Traditional Religions*, edited by James L. Cox, viii–xx. Cardiff: Cardiff Academic Press, 1998.

Curtin, Philip, D. "Field Techniques for Collecting and Processing Oral Data." *Journal of African History* 9, no. 3 (1968): 367–385.

Curtis, S. J. *History of Education in Great Britain*. 5th ed. London: Universal Tutorial Press, 1963.

Daily Nation on the Web. "Kisii Women on Warpath over Circumcision." 12 January 1999.

Davidson, Basil. *The Africans: An Entry to Cultural History*. Harmondsworth: Penguin, 1973.

———. *African History: Themes and Outlines*. St Albans: Paladin, 1974.

———. *Africa in Modern History: The Search for a New Society*. London: Allen Lane, 1978.

———. *Old Africa Rediscovered*. London: Longmans, 1970.

Davis, Jackson. "The Jeanes Visiting Teachers in the Southern States." In *Report of the Inte-Territorial Jeanes Conference 1935*, 14–25. Salisbury, Southern Rhodesia, 27 May to 6 June 1935. Lovedale: Lovedale Press, 1936.

Donovan, Vincent. *Christianity Rediscovered: An Epistle from the Masai*. London: SCM, 1982.

Dougall, James W. C. "The Development of the Education of the African in Relation to Western Contact." *Africa* 11, no. 3 (July 1938): 312–324.

———. "School Education and Native Life." *Africa* 3, no. 1 (January 1930): 49–58.

Ekechi, Felix. "Studies on Missions in Africa." In *African Historiography: Essays in Honour of Jacob Ade Ajayi*, edited by Toyin Falola, 145–165. Harlow: Longmans, 1993.

Evans, I. L. *The British in Tropical Africa: An Historical Outline*. Cambridge: Cambridge University Press, 1929.

Ewald, Janet. "Speaking, Writing, and Authority: Explorations in and from the Kingdom of Taqali." *Comparative Studies in Society and History* 30 (1988): 199–224.

Forde, Daryll, ed. *Select Annotated Bibliography of Tropical Africa*. New York: International African Institute, 1956.

Fortes, Meyer. "Some Reflections on Ancestor Worship in Africa." In *African Systems of Thought*, edited by M. Fortes and G. Dieterlen, 123–144. London: Oxford University Press, 1965.

Fraser, Donald. *The Future of Africa*. London: Young People's Missionary Movement, 1911.

Furley, O. W., and T. Watson. "Education in Tanganyika between the Wars: An Attempt to Blend Two Cultures." Reprint No 9 from *The South Atlantic Quarterly* 65, no. 4 (Autumn 1966): 471–490.

———. *A History of Education in East Africa*. New York: NOK Publishers, 1978.

Gann, L. H., and Peter Duignan. *The Rulers of British Africa, 1870–1914*. London: Croom Helm, 1978.

Geary, Christraud M. "Photographs as Materials for African History: Some Methodological Considerations." *History in Africa* 13 (1986): 89–116.

George, Poikal John. "Racist Assumptions of the 19th Century Missionary Movement." *International Review of Missions* 59, no. 235 (July 1970): 271–284.

Gifford, Prosser, and Roger Louis, eds. *Britain and Germany in Africa: Imperial Rivalry and Colonial Rule*. New Haven: Yale University Press, 1967.

Gray, Richard. *Black Christians and White Missionaries*. New Haven: Yale University Press, 1990.

Grant, James. *A Walk Across Africa; or, Domestic Scenes from my Nile Journal*. Edinburgh: W. Blackwood, 1864.

Green, Donald. "Religion and Morality in the African Traditional Setting." *Journal of Religion in Africa* 14, no. 1 (1983): 1–23.

Groves, C. P. *The Planting of Christianity in Africa*. Vol. 3, *1878–1914*. London: Lutterworth Press, 1955.

———. *The Planting of Christianity in Africa*. Vol. 4, *1914–1954*. London: Lutterworth Press, 1958.

Gwassa, G. C. K. "The German Intervention and African Resistance in Tanzania." In *A History of Tanzania*, edited by I. N. Kimambo and A. J. Temu, 85–122. Nairobi: East African Publishing House, 1969.

———. "Kinjikitile and the Ideology of Maji Maji." In *The Historical Study of African Religion with Special Reference to East and Central Africa*, edited by T. O. Ranger and Isaria Kimambo, 202–217. London: Heinemann, 1972.

Hastings, Adrian. *The Church in Africa 1450–1950*. Oxford: Clarendon Press, 1994.

———. "Were Women a Special Case?" In *Women and Missions: Anthropological and Historical Perceptions*, edited by Fiona Bowie, Deborah Kirkwood, and Shirley Ardener, 109–125. Providence; Oxford: Berg, 1993.

Hawley, Caroline. "Circumcision Trial Opens in France." *BBC Online Network*, 2 February 1999. http://news.bbc.co.uk/hi/English/world/Europe/newsid_270000/270603.stm.

Henige, David. *The Chronology of Oral Tradition: A Quest for a Chimera*. Oxford: Clarendon Press, 1974.

———. *Oral Historiography*. London: Longman, 1982.

———. "The Problem of Feedback in Oral Tradition." *Journal of African History* 14, no. 2 (1973): 223–235.

Hellberg, Carl-J. *Missions on a Colonial Frontier West of Lake Victoria: Evangelical Missions in North-West Tanganyika to 1932*. Uppsala: Gleerups, 1965.

Hewitt, Gordon. *The Problems of Success: A History of the Church Missionary Society 1910–1942*. Vol. 1, *In Tropical Africa, the Middle East, and at Home*. London: SCM, 1971.

Heyman, Richard. "The Initial Years of the Jeans School in Kenya, 1924–1931." In *Essays in the History of African Education*, edited by Vincent M. Battle and Charles H. Lyons, 105–123. New York: Teachers College Press, 1970.

Hinga, T. M. "Christianity and Female Puberty Rites in Africa: the Agikuyu Case." In *Rites of Passage in Contemporary Africa: Interaction between Christian and African Traditional Religions*, edited by James L. Cox, 168–179. Cardiff: Cardiff Academic Press, 1998.

Hodge, Alison. "The Training of the Missionaries for Africa: The Church Missionary Society's Training College at Islington, 1900–1915." *Journal of Religion in Africa* 4, no. 2 (1971): 81–96.

Hoernlé, A. W. "An Outline of The Native Conception of Education in Africa." *Africa* 4, no. 2 (April 1931): 145–163.

Hoernlé, Alfred R. F. "Education in Africa at Cross-Roads in South Africa." *Africa* 11, no. 4 (October 1938): 390–411.

Holmes, Brian, ed. *Educational Policy and the Mission Schools: Case Studies from the British Empire*. London: Routledge and Kegan Paul, 1967.

Holway, James D. "CMS Contact with Islam in East Africa before 1914." *Journal of Religion in Africa* 4 (1972): 200–212.

Hoornaert, Eduardo. *The Memory of the Christian People.* Turnbridge Wells, Kent: Burns and Oates, 1989.

Hornsby, George. "German Educational Achievement in East Africa." *Tanganyika Notes and Records* 62 (1964): 83–90.

Horton, Robin. "African Conversion." *Africa* 41, no. 2 (April 1971): 85–108.

———. "Stateless Societies in the History of West Africa." In *History of West Africa*, edited by J. F. A. Ajayi and Crowder Michael, 87–119. Vol. 1. Harlow: Longman, 1971.

Hutchinson, Edward. *The Victoria Nyanza: A Field for Missionary Enterprise.* 3rd ed. London: John Murray, 1876.

Iliffe, John. *A Modern History of Tanganyika.* Cambridge: Cambridge University Press, 1979.

———. "The Effects of the Maji Rebellion of 1905–1906 on German Occupation Policy in East Africa." In *Britain and Germany in Africa: Imperial Rivalry and Colonial Rule*, edited by Prosser Gifford and Roger Louis, 557–575. New Haven: Yale University Press, 1967.

———. "The Organization of the Maji Maji Rebellion." *Journal of African History* 8, no. 3 (1967): 495–512.

———. *Tanganyika Under German Rule 1905–1912.* Cambridge: Cambridge University Press, 1969.

Isichei, Elizabeth, *A History of Christianity in Africa: From Antiquity to the Present*, Grand Rapids, MI: Eerdmans; Lawrenceville, NJ: Africa World Press, 1995.

Jenkins, Paul. "The Roots of African Church History: Some Polemical Thoughts." *International Bulletin of Missionary Research* 10, no. 2 (April 1986): 67–71.

Jewsiewicki, B., and V. Y. Mudimbe. "Africans' Memories and Contemporary History of Africa." In *History Making in Africa*, edited by V. Y. Mudimbe and B. Jewsiewicki, 1–11. Middletown, CT: Wesleyan University Press, 1993.

Joelson, F. S. *Tanganyika Territory: Characteristics and Potentialities.* London: T. Fisher Unwin, 1920.

Jones G. I. *The Trading States of Oil Rivers.* Oxford: University Press, 1963.

Jones, Thomas Jesse. *Educational Adaptations. Report of Ten Years' Work of the Phelps Stokes Fund, 1910–1920.* New York: Phelps Stokes Fund, ca. 1920.

Jones. *Education in Africa: A Study of West, South, and Equatorial Africa by the African Education Commission, under the Auspices of the Phelps Stokes Fund and Foreign Mission Societies of North America and Europe.* New York: Phelps Stokes Fund, 1922.

———. *Education in East Africa: A Study of East, Central and South Africa by the Second African Education Commission under the Auspices of the Phelps Stokes Fund, in Co-operation with the International Board.* New York: Phelps Stokes Fund, 1925.

Kalu, Ogbu. "African Church Historiography." In *African Historiography: Essays in Honour of Jacob Ade Ajayi*, edited by Toyin Falola, 166–179. Harlow: Longmans, 1993.

———. "Church Presence in Africa: A Historical Analysis of the Evangelization Process." In *African Theology en Route*, edited by Kofi Appiah-Kubi and Sergio Torres, 13–22. Maryknoll, NY: Orbis Books, 1979.

Kanyoro, Musimbi. "Thinking Mission in Africa." *International Review of Missions* 86, no. 345 (April 1998): 221–226.

Kaplan, Steven. "The Africanization of Missionary Christianity: History and Typology." *Journal of African Religion* 16, no. 3 (1986): 166–186.

Karanja, John. "The Growth of the African Anglican Church in Central Kenya, 1900–1945." PhD thesis, University of Cambridge, 1993.

Kawawa, Zamaradi. "It Is Business as Usual as Female Circumcision Period Draws Nigh." *The Daily Mail* online, 24 November 1998. http://www.ippmedia.com/dailymail/1998/11/24/dailymail5.asp.

Kenyatta, Jomo. *Facing Mount Kenya: The Traditional Life of the Gikuyu*. London: Secker and Warburg, 1938.

King, Kenneth J. *Pan-Africanism and Education: A Study of Race Philanthropy and Education in the Southern States of America and East Africa*. Oxford: Clarendon Press, 1971.

Knox, Elizabeth. *Signal on the Mountain: The Gospel in Africa's Uplands before the First World War*. Canberra: Acorn Press, 1991.

Kongola, Ernest Musa. "Wevunjiliza – Mbukwa Muhindi wa Cimambi." Kitabu cha Tatu. Unpblished typescript, December 1990.

Kopytoff, Igor. "Ancestors as Elders." *Africa* 41 (April 1971): 129–142.

Latham, G. C. "Indirect Rule and Education in East Africa." *Africa* 7, no. 4 (October 1934): 423–430.

Latourette, Kenneth. *A History of the Expansion of Christianity*. 7 vols. London: Eyre & Spottiswoode, 1937–1945.

Lema, Anza A. "Chaga Religion and Mission Christianity on Kilimanjaro: The Initial Phase, 1893–1916." In *East African Expressions of Christianity*, edited by Thomas Spear and Isaria Kimambo, 39–62. Oxford: James Currey, 1999.

Leys, Norman. "Missions and Government: Objects of Education." *The Scots Observer* 1, no. 9 (27 November 1926): 287–290.

Listowell, Judith. *The Making of Tanganyika*. London: Chatto and Winds, 1965.

Little, Jane. "Senegal Bans Female Circumcision." *BBC Online Network*, 23 December 1998. http://news.bbc.co.uk/2/hi/africa/241230.stm.

Livingstone, David. *Missionary Travels and Researches in South Africa: Including a Sketch of Sixteen Years' Residence in the Interior of Africa*. London: Ward, Lock & Co., 1857.

Lucas, Vincent. "The Educational Value of Initiatory Rites." *International Review of Missions* 16 (1927): 192–198.

Lusinde, Naftali. "Maisha Yake Yohana Malecela." Typescript. N.d.

Luzbetak, Louis J. *The Church and Cultures: New Perspectives in Missiological Anthropology*. Maryknoll, NY: Orbis Books, 1988.

Makawia, Cathlex. "More Than 100m Girls Subjected to Genital Mutilation Annually." *The Guardian* online, 27 July 1999. http://www.ipppmedia.com/guardian/1999/07/27/ guardian4.asp.

Mayhew, Arthur. "A Comparative Survey of Educational Aims and Methods in British India and British Tropical Africa." *Africa* 6, no. 2 (April 1933): 172–186.

Mbilinyi, Marjorie J. "African Education in British Colonial Period (1919–1961)." In *Essays on Education*. Papers presented at History Teachers' Conference, Morogoro, June 1974. Dar es Salaam: Dar es Salaam University, 1979.

Mbiti, John S. *Bible and Theology in African Christianity*. Nairobi: Oxford University Press, 1986.

———. "Biblical Basis for Trends in African Theology." In *African Theology en Route*, edited by Kofi Appiah-Kubi and Sergio Torres, 83–94. Maryknoll, NY: Orbis Books, 1979.

———. *Introduction to African Religion*. 2nd rev. ed. Nairobi: African Educational Publishers, 1991.

Mirindo Oscar. "Wanawake wanatahiriwa bila ridhaa yao." *Nipashe Jumapili*, 3 January 1999. http://www.ippmedia.com/nipashe/1999/01/03/jumapili3.asp.

Moore, Donald, and Richard Roberts. "Listening for Silences." *History in Africa* 17 (1990): 319–325.

Mombo, Esther Moraa. "A Historical and Cultural Analysis of the Position of Abaluyia Women in Kenyan Quaker Christianity 1902–1979." PhD thesis, University of Edinburgh, 1998.

Moreau, R. E. "Joking Relationship in Tanganyika." *Africa* 14, no. 3 (July 1944): 386–400.

Mudimbe, V. Y., and B. Jewsiewicki, eds. *History Making in Africa*. Middelton, CT: Wesleyan University Press, 1993.

Muhando, Daudi. *Hadithi za Kiafrika Zimekuwa za Kikristo*. London: SPCK, 1962.

Mumford, W. Bryant. "Comparative Studies of Native Education in Various Dependencies." In *The Year Book of Education 1935*. London: Evans Brothers (in association with the University of London Institute of Education), 1935.

———. "Education and the Social Adjustment of the Primitive Peoples of Africa to European Culture." *Africa* 2, no. 1 (April 1929): 138–159.

———. "Malangali School: A First Year's Work in the Development of a School from Native Custom and Looking towards Adjustment to European Culture." *Africa* 3, no. 3 (July 1930): 265–291.

Mumford, W. Bryant, and R. Jackson. "The Problem of Mass Education in Africa." *Africa* 11, no. 2 (April 1938): 187–207.

Murray, A. Victor. *The School in the Bush: A Critical Study in the History and Nature of Native Education in Africa*. 2nd ed. London: Franc Cass, 1967. First published 1929 by Longmans (London) and revised in 1938.

Murray, Jocelyn. "A Bibliography of the East African Revival Movement." *Journal of Religion in Africa* 8, no. 2 (1976), 144–147

———. "The Church Missionary Society and the 'Female Circumcision' Issue in Kenya 1929–1932." *Journal of Religion in Africa* 8, no. 2 (1976): 92–104.

———. *Proclaim the Good News: A Short History of CMS*. London: Hodder & Stoughton, 1985.

Mwainyekule, Leah. "Kariakoo Bazaar Becomes Battlefield as Fanatics Fight Police." *The Guardian* online, 31 July 1999. http://www.ippmedia.com/guardian/1999/07/31/ guardian1.asp.

Nasmiyu-Wasike, Anne. "Polygamy: A Feminist Critique." In *The Will to Rise: Women, Tradition, and the Church in Africa*, edited by Mercy Amba Oduyoye and Musimbi Kanyoro, 101–118. Maryknoll, NY: Orbis Books.

Neill, Stephen. *A History of Christian Missions*. London: Penguin, 1964.

Ngũgĩ, wa Thiong'o. *Moving the Centre: The Struggle for Cultural Freedoms*. London: James Currey, 1993.

Oduyoye, Mercy Amba. "Christianity and African Culture." *International Review of Missions* 84, no. 332/333 (January/April 1995): 77–90.

Okorocha, C. C., *The Meaning of Religious Conversion in Africa: The Case of the Igbo of Nigeria*. Aldershot: Averbury Gower, 1987.

Okumu, Fred. "Circumcising Girls for Cosmetic Purposes." *The Daily Mail* online (Dar es Salaam), 13 August 1999. http://www.ippmedia.com/dailymail/1999/08/13/daily mail2.asp.

Oldham, J. H. "The Educational Work of Missionary Societies." *Africa* 7, no. 1 (January 1934): 47–59.

———. *Education Policy in Africa: A Memorandum Submitted on Behalf of the Education Committee of the Conference of Missionary Societies in Great Britain and Ireland*. London: 1923.

Oldham, J. H., and B. D. Gibson. *The Remaking of Man in Africa*. London: Oxford University Press, 1931.

Oliver, Roland, ed. *The Cambridge History of Africa*. Vol. 3. Cambridge: Cambridge University Press, 1977.

———. *The Missionary Factor in East Africa*. 2nd ed. London: Longmans, 1965. First published 1952.

Oliver, Roland, and J. D. Fage. *A Short History of Africa*. 5th ed. Harmondsworth: Penguin, 1975.

Ormsby-Gore, W. "Education in the British Dependencies in Tropical Africa." In *The Year Book of Education 1932*, 748–766. London: Evans Brothers, 1932.

Orr, Rodney Hugh. "African American Missionaries to East Africa 1900–1926: A Study in the Ethnic Reconnection of the Gospel." PhD thesis, University of Edinburgh, 1998.

Pakenham, Thomas. *The Scramble for Africa*. London: Abacus, 1991.

Papstein, Robert. "Creating and Using Photographs as Historical Evidence." *History in Africa* 17 (1990): 248–268.

Pearson, J. D. *A Guide to Manuscripts and Documents in the British Isles Relating to Africa*. 2 vols. London: Mansell, 1993–1994.

Perham, M. F. "A Re-statement of Indirect Rule." *Africa* 7, no. 3 (July 1934): 321–334.

———. "The System of Native Administration in Tanganyika." *Africa* 4, no. 3 (July 1931): 302–313.

Pirouet, Louise. *Black Evangelists: The Spread of Christianity in Uganda 1891–1914*. London: Rex Collings, 1978.

———. "East African Christians and World War I." *Journal of African History* 19, no. 1 (1978): 117–130.

———. Review of *Colonial Evangelism: A Social Historical Study of an East African Mission at the Grassroots*, by T. O. Beidelman. *The International Journal African Historical Studies* 16, no. 1 (1983).

Radcliffe-Brown, A. R. "On Joking Relationships." *Africa* 13, no. 3 (July 1940): 195–210.

Ranger, T. O. "Future Religious Research in Africa: Conclusions of Disciplinary Groups." Workshop in Religious Research, 1968. In *African Initiatives in Religion*, edited by David B. Barrett, 279–280. Nairobi: East African Publishing House, 1971.

———. "Missionary Adaptation of African Religious Institutions: The Masasi Case." In *The Historical Study of African Religion with Special Reference to East and Central Africa*, edited by T. O. Ranger and I. N. Kimambo, 221–251. London: Heinemann, 1972.

———. "New Approaches to the Mission Christianity." In *African Historiography: Essays in Honour of Jacob Ade Ajayi*, edited by Toyin Falola, 180–194. Harlow: Longmans, 1993.

Raum, J. "Christianity and African Puberty Rites." *International Review of Missions* 17 (1927): 581–591.

———. "Educational Problems in Tanganyika." *International Review of Missions* 29 (1930): 563–575.

Raum, O. F. "German East Africa: Changes in African Tribal Life under German Administration, 1892–1914." In *History of East Africa*, edited by Vincent Harlow and E. M. Chilver, 163–207. Oxford: Clarendon Press, 1965.

Reaves, Malik Stan. "Alternative Rite to Female Circumcision Spreading in Kenya." *Africa News Online*, 12 April 1998. http://www.africanews.org/specials/19971119_fgm.html.
Report of the Inte-Territorial Jeans Conference 1935. Salisbury, Southern Rhodesia, 27 May to 6 June 1935. Lovedale: Lovedale Press, 1936.
Report of the Proceedings. Education Conference between Government and Missions, 5–12 October 1925. Dar es Salaam: Government Press, 1925.
Report on Tanganyika Territory, Covering the Period from the Conclusion of the Armistice to the End of 1920. Commad Paper 1428. Presented to Parliament July 1921. HMSO, London: 1921.
Reports from Commissioners, Inspectors and Others. *Report of the East African Commission.* Command Paper 2387. Vol. 9. HMSO, London: 1925.
Reports on the Treatment by the Germans of British Prisoners and Natives in German East Africa. Command Paper 8689. Miscellaneous No. 13, 1917, HMSO, London: 1917.
Rigby, Peter. *Cattle and Kinship among the Gogo: A Semi-pastoral Society of Central Tanzania.* Ithaca: Cornell University Press, 1969.
———. "Dual Symbolic Classification among the Gogo of Central Tanzania." *Africa* 36, no. 1 (January 1966): 1–17.
———. "Joking Relationships, Kin Categories, and Clanship among the Gogo." *Africa* 38, no. 2 (April 1968): 133–155.
———. "Sociological Factors in the Contact of the Gogo of Central Tanzania with Islam." In *Islam in Tropical Africa*, edited by I. M. Lewis, 268–295. Oxford University Press, 1966
———. "The Structural Context of Girls' Puberty Rites." *Man* (N.S.) 2, no. 3 (September 1967): 434–444.
Richter, Julius. *Tanganyika and Its Future.* London: World Dominion Press, 1934.
Robert, Dana L. *American Women in Mission: A Social History of Their Thought and Practice.* Macon, GA: Mercer University Press, 1996.
Roberts, Andrew D. "A Bibliography of Primary Sources for Tanzania 1799–1899." *Tanzania Notes and Records*, no. 73 (July 1974): 65–92.
Roberts, Richard. "Reversible Social Processes, Historical Memory, and the Production of History." *History in Africa* 17 (1990): 341–349.
Robinson, Charles. *History of Christian Missions.* Edinburgh: T & T Clark, 1915.
Roscoe, John. *Twenty-Five Years in East Africa.* Cambridge: Cambridge University Press, 1921.
Sahlberg, Carl Erik. *From Krapf to Rugambwa – A Church History of Tanzania.* Nairobi: Evangel Publishing House, 1986.
Sanneh, Lamin. "Gospel and Culture: Ramifying Effects of Scriptural Translation." In *Bible Translation and the Spread of the Church: The Last 200 Years*, edited by Philip C. Stine, 1–23. Leiden: E. J. Brill, 1990.

———. "The Horizontal and the Vertical in Mission: An African Perspective." *International Bulletin of Missionary Research* 7, no. 4 (October 1983): 165–171.

———. *Translating the Message: The Missionary Impact on Culture*. Maryknoll, NY: Orbis Books, 1992.

Sarpong, Peter K. "Can Christianity Dialogue with African Traditional Religion?" 10 July 1998. http://www.afrikaworld.net/afrel/sarpong.html.

Scanlon, David G., ed. *Traditions of African Education*. New York: Bureau of Publications, 1964.

Schmidt, P. W. "The Use of the Vernacular in Education in Africa." *Africa* 3, no. 2 (April 1930): 137–145.

Scott, H. S. "The Development of the Education of the African in Relation to Western Contact." In *The Year Book of Education 1938*, 693–739. London: Evans Brothers, 1938.

———. "Educational Policy in the British Colonial Empire." In *The Year Book of Education 1937*, 411–438. London: Evans Brothers, 1937.

Shorter, Aylward, and Eugene Kataza, eds. *Missionaries to Yourselves: African Catechists Today*. London: Geoffrey Chapman, 1972.

Sibtain, Nancy de S. P. *Dare to Look Up: A Memoir of Bishop George Alexander Chambers*. Sydney: Angus and Robertson, 1968.

Smalley, William A. *Translation as Mission: Bible Translation in the Modern Missionary Movement*. Macon, GA: Mercer University Press, 1991.

Smith, Anthony. "The Missionary Contribution to Education (Tanganyika) to 1914." *Tanganyika Notes and Records*, no. 60 (1963): 91–109.

Smith, Edwin. *Aggrey of Africa: A Study in Black and White*. London: Student Christian Movement, 1929.

———. *The Christian Mission in Africa: A Study Based on the Work of the International Conference at Le Zoute, Belgium, September 14th to 21st, 1926*. London: Edinburgh House, 1926.

———. *The Golden Stool: Some Aspects of the Conflict of Cultures in Africa*. London: Edinburgh House Press, 1927.

Speke, John. *Journal of the Discovery of the Source of the Nile*. Edinburgh: W. Blackwood, 1863.

Standard English-Swahili Dictionary. 1st ed. Nairobi: Oxford University Press, 1939.

Standard Swahili-English Dictionary. Nairobi: Oxford University Press, 1994.

Stanley, Brian. "Some Problems in Writing a Missionary Society History Today: The Example of the Baptist Missionary Society." In *Missionary Encounters: Sources and Issues*, edited by Robert Bickers and Rosemary Seton, 38–50. Richmond: Curzon Press, 1996.

Stanley, Henry M. *How I Found Livingstone: Travels, Adventures, and Discoveries in Central Africa*. London: Sampson Low, 1895.

Stock, Eugene. *The History of the Church Missionary Society: Its Environment, Its Men and Its Work*. 4 vols. London: CMS, 1899–1916.

Strayer, Robert. *The Making of Mission Communities in East Africa*. London: Heinemann, 1978.

Tagart, E. S. B. "The African Chief Under European Rule." *Africa* 4, no. 1 (January 1931): 63–75.

"Tanganyika (German East Africa)." In *Handbooks*. Prepared under the direction of the historical section of the Foreign Office. No. 113. HMSO, London, 1920.

"The Tanganyika Mandate." *Official Journal of the League of Nations* 3 (1922).

Temu, A. J. *British Protestant Missions*. London: Longmans, 1972.

Thompson, A. R. "Historical Survey of the Role of the Churches in Education from Pre-colonial Days to Post-independence." In *Church and Education in Tanzania*, edited by Allan J. Gottneid, 3–130. Nairobi: East Africa Publishing House, 1976.

Thompson, A. R., and G. Hornsby. "Iss-Feres Tanz. Project." Unpublished manuscript. East Africana Collection, University of Dar es Salaam, Tanzania.

Thompson, T. Jack. *Christianity in Northern Malawi: Donald Fraser's Missionary Methods and Ngoni Culture*. Leiden: E. J. Brill, 1995.

"Treatment of Natives in the German Colonies." In *Handbooks*. Prepared under the direction of the historical section of the Foreign Office. No. 114. HMSO, London, 1920.

Tuma, Tom, Building a Ugandan Church: African Participation in Church Growth i Busoga 1891 – 1940. Nairobi: Kenya Literature Bureau, 1980.

Turnbridge, Louise. "Alternative Rite Ends Mutilation." *The Sunday Telegraph* (London), 3 January 1999.

Uledi, Michael. "Wanawake 600,000 waathirika kwa tohara Dodoma." *Taifa Letu* online, 6 December 1998. http://www.ippmedia.com/taifaletu/1998/12/06/taifa.asp.

Uwechue, Ralph, ed. *Makers of Modern Africa: Profiles in History*. 2nd. ed. London: Africa Books, 1991.

Van Pelt, P. *Bantu Customs in Mainland Tanzania*. Tabora: TMP, 1971.

Waller, Richard. "They Do the Dictating and We Must Submit: The Africa Inland Mission in Maasailand." In *East African Expressions of Christianity*, edited by Thomas Spear and Isaria Kimambo, 83–126. Oxford: James Currey, 1999.

Walls, Andrew. "Africa and Christian Identity." *Mission Focus* 6, no. 7 (November 1978): 11–13.

———. "Culture and Coherence in Christian History." *Evangelical Review of Theology* 9, no. 3 (1985): 214–225.

———. "The Gospel as the Prisoner and the Liberator of Culture." *Missionalia*, 10, no. 3 (1982): 93–105.

———. *The Missionary Movement in Christian History: Studies in the Transmission of Faith*. Maryknoll, NY: Orbis Books, 1996.

———. "Structural Problems in Mission Studies." *International Bulletin of Missionary Research* 15, no. 4 (October 1991): 146–152.

Welbourn, F. W. *East African Christian*. Ibadan: Oxford University Press, 1965.

Westerlund, David. Review of *Colonial Evangelism: A Social Historical Study of an East African Mission at the Grassroots* by T. O. Beidelman, Indiana University Press, Bloomington: 1982, in *Journal of Religion in Africa* 14, no. 2, 1983: 161–163.

———. *Ujamaa na Dini: A Study of Some Aspects of Society and Religion in Tanzania 1961–1977*. Stockholm: Almqvist & Wiksell International, 1980.

Westgate, T. B. R. *In the Grip of the German*. Belfast: n.p., 1918.

Williams, C. Peter. *The Ideal of the Self-Governing Church: A Study in Victorian Missionary Strategy*. New York: E. J. Brill, 1990.

———. "The Necessity of a Native Clergy: The Failure of Victorian Missions to Develop Indigenous Leadership." *Vox Evangelica* 21 (1991): 33–52.

Willis, Justin. "Feedback as a 'Problem' in Oral History: An Example from Bonde." *History in Africa* 20 (1993): 353–360.

Wilson, G. H. *The History of the Universities' Mission to Central Africa*. London: UMCA, 1936.

Wilson, Godfrey. "An African Morality." *Africa* 9, no. 1 (January 1936): 75–99.

Wilson, Monica. "An African Christian Morality." *Africa* 10, no. 3 (July 1937): 265–291.

Wondji, Christophe. "Toward a Responsible African Presence." In *African Historiographies: What History for Which Africa?*, edited Bogumil Jewsiewicki and David Newbury, 269–278. London: Sage Publications, 1986.

World Missionary Conference. *Education in Relation to the Christianisation of National Life*. Report of Commission 3. Edinburgh: Oliphant, Anderson and Ferrier, 1910.

World Missionary Conference. *The Missionary Message in Relation to Non-Christian Religions*. Report of Commission 4. Edinburgh: Oliphant, Anderson & Ferrier, 1910.

Wright, Marcia. *German Missions in Tanganyika 1891–1941: Lutherans and Moravians in the Southern Highlands*. Oxford: Clarendon Press, 1971.

———. "Kinjikitile." In *The Encyclopedia of Religion*, edited by Mircea Eliade, 336–338. Vol. 8. New York: Macmillan & Free Press, 1987.

Oral (Personal) Interviews

Interviewees in Ugogo (by surname, in alphabetical order)

Boma, Orpa. Born 1903 at Chamuhawi. Daughter of Mabruki Chibhanila (a former slave) who first lived at Chamuhawi mission settlement before moving to Mlanga. Interviewed 1 July 1997 at Mlanga village, Kongwa.

Chali, Esta. Single woman. Born to Zakayo Chali (formerly a church teacher at Kimagai and Mpwapwa). Brought up at Vingh'awe Mpwapwa. Worked as a domestic assistant for a female missionary at Mpwapwa. Joined Buigiri Girls' School as one of the first pupils in 1928. Left school in 1930. Interviewed 26 June 1997 at Vingh'awe, Mpwapwa town.

Chibanhila, Jackson. Born 1929 at Chamuhawi. Jackson is the grandson of Mabruki Chibanhila, a former Luguru slave who was rescued by Henry Cole, and brought to Chamuhawi mission settlement where he grew up and became Cole's domestic assistant and later a church teacher. Interviewed 28 June 1997 at Chamuhawi village.

Chidosa, Philemon. Born 1918 at Mvumi (mission). Son of Natanaeli Chidosa (one of the early local teachers at Mvumi). Retired priest (canon), Diocese of Central Tanganyika. Interviewed twice, 12 and 13 June 1997 at Mvumi (mission).

Chidosa, Yudith. Wife of Philemon Chidosa. Born 1918 at Mvumi (mission). Retired school teacher. Co-interviewed with husband 12 June 1997, then alone 13 June 1997 at Mvumi (mission).

Hango, Melea Yusufu. Born c. 1914 at Mpwapwa. Daughter of Ephraim Chalo (a colleague of Ibrahimu Mbogo, a famous builder of mission buildings), the father of Danieli Mbogo. Interviewed 27 June 1997 at Vingh'awe, Mpwapwa town.

Kongola, Ernest Musa. Born 1922 at Handali. Son of Musa and Manduga Kongola. Attended Handali school where his father was teacher. Became school teacher, and senior education and culture officer, Dodoma province. Interviewed 20 and 24 June 1997 at Mji Mpya, Dodoma town.

Lungwa, Javan. Born 1914 at Ibwaga (near Kongwa). Retired geological surveyor. Interviewed 10 June 1997 at Maili Mbili, Dodoma town.

Makanyaga, Onesimo Timotheo. Born 1922 at Chamuhawi. Distant relative of Chief Makanyaga Mugube, the father of Andrea Mwaka. Interviewed 28 June 1997 at Chamuhawi village.

Malecela, Naftali Lusinde. Born 1921 at Kikombo. Served as church teacher, and then as priest. Retired priest (canon), Diocese of Central Tanganyika. Became a Kigogo Bible translator upon retirement. Interviewed 24 June 1997 at Kilimani, Dodoma town.

Malecela, Stephano. Born 1922 at Ihumwa. Son of Daudi Malecela and grandson of Yohana Malecela Served as a catechist. Retired priest (canon), Diocese of Diocese of Central Tanganyika. Interviewed 24 June 1997 at John Malecela's home, at Kilimani, Dodoma town.

Malongo, Samson. Born 1910 at Mlanga village, Kongwa. Retired church teacher. Interviewed 1 July 1997 at Mlanga village, Kongwa.

Mapuga, Patrick. Born 1943 at Mpwapwa. Grandson of Chief Lukole (Chipanjilo) Lusito of Mpwapwa who welcomed the earliest CMS missionaries. Interviewed 27 June 1997 at Vingh'awe, Mpwapwa town.

Mbogo, Yakobo Danieli. Born 1924 at Buigiri. Son of Danieli and Loi Mbogo. Retired local government accountant and executive officer. Now a non-stipendary priest. Interviewed 30 June 1997 at Kongwa town.

Mbogoni, Dan Yona. Born 1913 at Mvumi (mission). Served as church teacher and then priest. Retired priest (canon), Diocese of Central Tanganyika. Lives at Hogolo. Interviewed 11 June 1997 at Mvumi (mission).

Mfunde, Martha Edward Madimilo. Date of birth not known. Group interview with Zakayo Sume Mfune. 28 June 1997 at Chamuhawi village.

Mfune, Zakayo Sume. Born 1922 at Idilo, near Chamuhawi; Group interview with Martha Edward Madimilo Mfune. 28 June 1997 at Chamuhawi village.

Mlahagwa, Elimerik. Born 1929. Son of Zefania Thomas Mlahagwa. Retired church teacher and evangelist, Chamuhawi (formerly Kisokwe). Parents lived first at Kikombo and Ibwaga but migrated to Chamuhawi in early 1930s. Interviewed 28 June 1997 at Chamuhawi village.

Muhimili, Yohana. Born 1912 at Mlanga. First wife (deceased) was the daughter of Musa Fungo (one of the first catechists at Mlanga, Kongwa). Interviewed 2 July 1997 at Mlanga village, Kongwa.

Mwaka, Cleopa Andrea. Born 1916 at Chamuhawi. Son of Marita and Andrea Mwaka. Attended Buigiri village school and then Handali central school from 1926. Joined Kikuyu central school in May 1928, graduated 1931. Attended Kongwa college 1933. Taught at various village schools until 1957. Gave valuable information about his father, Andrea Mwaka, and insights into mission schools. Interviewed 4 July 1997 at Kisima cha Ndege village, northwest of Dodoma.

Mwaka, Gideon Ayubu. Born 1924 at Buigiri. Former government teacher and magistrate (retired 1979). One of the grandsons of Andrea Mwaka. Interviewed 9 June 1997 at Bahi Road, Dodoma town.

Ndajilo, Lazaro. Born c. 1900 at Mvumi (Makulu). Served as church teacher and evangelist. Taught at Mvumi mission village school, joined Kongwa college 1931-1933; taught at Mwitikila, then at Mpalanga, and Mvumi Makulu. Retrenched in 1944. Became chief palace official for Chief Mazengo Chalula, paramount chief of Ugogo, from 1944-1965. Ndajilo is an authority on chiefdoms, relations of colonial governments with Mazengo, and of the CMS mission and Chief Mazengo. Interviewed twice, 14 & 16 June 1997 at Mvumi (Makulu) village.

Nyembela, Esta John. Married to John Nyembela. Born 1914 at Buigiri. Daughter of Joshua Mate, former warden of Buigiri girls' boarding school, 1928. Served as teacher in both mission and government schools. Retired 1979. Interviewed 10 June 1997 at Makole, Dodoma town.

Sagatwa, Viktoria Mathiya. Born 1924 at Mpwapwa. Daughter-in-law of Damari Sagatwa. Interviewed 29 June 1997 at Vingh'awe, Mpwapwa town.

Simule, Ayubu. Born c. 1900 at Kimagai. Taught by Zakayo Chali (the father of Esta Chali) at Kimagai. Interviewed 26 June 1997 at Vingh'awe, Mpwapwa town.

Uguzi, Nehemia Enoshi. Born 1915 at Buigiri. Son of Enoshi Uguzi Madeje (one of early local teachers at Buigiri). Former church and school teacher. Retired priest (canon), Diocese of Central Tanganyika. Interviewed twice, 18 and 19 June 1997 at Buigiri village.

Interviewees in Ukaguru
(by surname, in alphabetical order)

Chiduo, Mary Lawrence. Born 3 June 1934, and Joyce Maiko Mweli, daughters of the late Bishop Yohana Omari Boto (first African bishop in the Anglican Church of Tanzania, second African bishop in Tanzania). Group interview, 9 September 1997 at Kiwanja cha Ndege, Morogoro town.

Chitemo, Semgomba. Born c. 1900 at Nguyami. A traditional medicine practitioner. Attended a baptism class as an inquirer at Nguyami. Classes interrupted by First World War. Never attempted to join church again ever since. Interviewed 15 September 1997, Berega (Mbuyuni).

Mahimbo, Loi. Born 19 December 1919 at Berega (mission). Daughter of Yonathan Mahimbo (former church teacher). Served as a hospital evangelist at Berega. Interviewed 15 September 1997 at Berega (mission).

Makau, Phanuel. Born January 1928 at Kibedya, Gairo, Kilosa District. Son of a church teacher. Served as catechist. Retired priest (canon), Diocese of Morogoro. Interviewed 12 September 1997 at Dumila.

Makau, Rhoda. Wife of Phanuel Makau. Born 1928. Daughter of Ephraim and Nelia Madimilo. Father was one of Kaguru missionaries to western Tanzania who later became a priest. Interviewed 12 September 1997 at Dumila.

Masingisa, Yusufu. Born at Mamboya, 1904. Retired teacher and medical practitioner. He is an authority on early Mamboya secular and mission history. Interviewed twice, 16 and 17 September 1997.

Mlahagwa, Isaka. Born 1918 at Berega. Retired doctor; a serving church elder at Berega (Mbuyuni) Anglican Church, Diocese of Morogoro. Interviewed 14 September 1997.

Mngh'umbi, Eunike Fredrick. Widow. Born 1912. Interviewed at Berega (Mbuyuni) 15 September 1997.

Muhando, Loi. Born 1914 at Ngwiyami. Daughter of Daudi Muhando. Interviewed 15 September 1997 at Berega (mission).

Mukuchu, Philemon. Born October 1923 at Itumba (Uponela). Served as school teacher and catechist. Retired priest (canon), Diocese of Morogoro. Interviewed 11 September 1997 at Kilosa (retirement home).

Mwinyuma, Asdadi Musa. Born at Mbwewe, near Berega. Didn't want to reveal date of birth. Not a Christian. Interviewed at Berega, 13 September 1997.

Uledi, Dorka. Born 1919 at Mamboya. Daughter of Nataneli Chinyogoli (former church teacher). Interviewed 15 September 1997 at Berega (mission).

Langham Literature, with its publishing work, is a ministry of Langham Partnership.

Langham Partnership is a global fellowship working in pursuit of the vision God entrusted to its founder John Stott –

> *to facilitate the growth of the church in maturity and Christ-likeness through raising the standards of biblical preaching and teaching.*

Our vision is to see churches in the majority world equipped for mission and growing to maturity in Christ through the ministry of pastors and leaders who believe, teach and live by the Word of God.

Our mission is to strengthen the ministry of the Word of God through:
- nurturing national movements for biblical preaching
- fostering the creation and distribution of evangelical literature
- enhancing evangelical theological education

especially in countries where churches are under-resourced.

Our ministry

Langham Preaching partners with national leaders to nurture indigenous biblical preaching movements for pastors and lay preachers all around the world. With the support of a team of trainers from many countries, a multi-level programme of seminars provides practical training, and is followed by a programme for training local facilitators. Local preachers' groups and national and regional networks ensure continuity and ongoing development, seeking to build vigorous movements committed to Bible exposition.

Langham Literature provides majority world preachers, scholars and seminary libraries with evangelical books and electronic resources through publishing and distribution, grants and discounts. The programme also fosters the creation of indigenous evangelical books in many languages, through writer's grants, strengthening local evangelical publishing houses, and investment in major regional literature projects, such as one volume Bible commentaries like the *Africa Bible Commentary* and the *South Asia Bible Commentary*.

Langham Scholars provides financial support for evangelical doctoral students from the majority world so that, when they return home, they may train pastors and other Christian leaders with sound, biblical and theological teaching. This programme equips those who equip others. Langham Scholars also works in partnership with majority world seminaries in strengthening evangelical theological education. A growing number of Langham Scholars study in high quality doctoral programmes in the majority world itself. As well as teaching the next generation of pastors, graduated Langham Scholars exercise significant influence through their writing and leadership.

To learn more about Langham Partnership and the work we do visit **langham.org**

www.ingramcontent.com/pod-product-compliance
Lightning Source LLC
Chambersburg PA
CBHW061703300426
44115CB00014B/2542